CANCUN
HANDBOOK

AND MEXICO'S CARIBBEAN COAST

CANCUN
HANDBOOK

AND MEXICO'S CARIBBEAN COAST

CHICKI MALLAN
PHOTOS BY
OZ MALLAN

PUBLICATIONS, INC.

CANCUN HANDBOOK AND MEXICO'S CARIBBEAN COAST

Please send all comments, corrections, additions, amendments and critiques to:

**CHICKI MALLAN
C/O MOON PUBLICATIONS, INC.**

**722 WALL STREET
CHICO, CALIFORNIA 95928, USA**

Printing History
1st edition — March 1990
Reprinted —October 1990
2nd edition—June 1991
Reprinted —January 1992

Published by
Moon Publications, Inc.
722 Wall Street
Chico, California 95928, USA
tel (916) 345-5473

Printed by
Colorcraft Ltd.

© **Chicki Mallan 1990**

Library of Congress Cataloging in Publications Data
Mallan, Chicki, 1933
    Cancun Handbook and Mexico's Caribbean Coast / Chicki Mallan. — 2nd ed.
        p.   cm.
    Includes bibliographical references.
    ISBN 0–918373–73–5
    1. Yucatán Peninsula—Description and travel—1981- —Guide-books.
2. Cancún (Mexico)—Description—Guide-books.   I. Title.
II. Title: Cancun handbook.
F1376.M26   1990
917.2'67—dc20   89-29901
                                       CIP

Front cover photo of the Cancun coastline by Oz Mallan.

To Barbara and Bruce.

ACKNOWLEDGEMENTS

Cancun Handbook has been a joy to create. Thanks to the friendly folk of Mexico's Caribbean state Quintana Roo, the work went quickly and (mostly) enjoyably. Time spent with Pablo Bush discussing the early days and his role in the growth of the area was a real pleasure. A vote of praise for Javier Rivas in Mexico City, Hill Knowlton in New York and Los Angeles, Mexicana Airlines, Ogilvy & Mather in San Francisco, and in Cancun the Camino Real Hotel, Hyatt Regency, and Hyatt Caribe.

As usual, the Moon staff did their "stuff." Where would an author be without fine editors like Taran March and Christa Jorgensen, or the superb layout-master Dave Hurst who put the book together, handling the Mac like a fine-tuned instrument. Thanks Louise Foote and Bob Race for excellent maps and illustrations, along with Todd Clark for two fine drawings. How nice to have access to Asha Johnson, resident computer genius available for "50 Questions" at almost any ridiculous hour. My photographer husband Oz Mallan's photos are really extraordinary, as usual! A big thanks for the enthusiasm of sales directors/promoters Donna Galassi and Virginia Michaels. And I cannot forget official keepers of the records Cindy Fahey, Bette Wells, Rick Johnson, and the voice on the phone, Lucinda. In my office much appreciation goes to Michelle Bonzey and Beth Rhudy for inputting text and laying out charts. In my kitchen, a word of praise for my two kids Patti and Bryant Lange. And none of this would be possible if it weren't for something my mom and dad, Barbara and Tony, did too many years past. And no, I won't ever forget what a good Moon-friend did for me a long time ago —thanks, Bill!

On this visit to the Yucatan Peninsula I accidentally slipped while exploring and managed to break both ankles. I only allude to this because it would be unfair not to mention the marvelous Mexican people who came forward with concern and care, doing what they could to help the situation. Many thanks to the attentive Bush family at Akumal, Laura, Myrna, Paul, and the waiters, maids, and bellhops where I holed up for four days with feet in the air. Thanks to Karen Wirth at Puerto Aventuras, who tried so hard to find us a plane to take my broken bones home. Thanks also to Yolanda Bernardac at the Hyatt Caribe, to Manolo from Faces Hotel, and Hotel Trinidad in Merida. I consider myself fortunate to have such fine friends so far away from home.

PHOTO AND ILLUSTRATION CREDITS

Photos: All photographs by Oz Mallan. **Illustrations:** Diana Lasich Harper: pages 6, 15, 18, 20, and 21. Louise Foote: pages 14, 43, 72, 134, 195, 206, 209, and 215. Bob Race: pages 48, 59, 66, 212. Kathy Escovedo-Sanders: pages 49, 54, 90, 161. Frederick Catherwood (courtesey Dover Publications): page 139.

CONTENTS

LIST OF MAPS

KEY TO MAPS

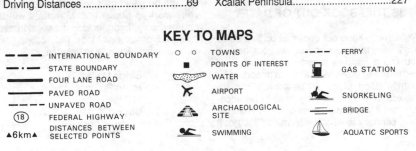

INTERNATIONAL BOUNDARY

STATE BOUNDARY

FOUR LANE ROAD

PAVED ROAD

UNPAVED ROAD

(18) FEDERAL HIGHWAY

▲6km▲ DISTANCES BETWEEN SELECTED POINTS

o o TOWNS

■ POINTS OF INTEREST

WATER

✈ AIRPORT

▲ ARCHAEOLOGICAL SITE

🏊 SWIMMING

- - - - FERRY

⛽ GAS STATION

🏊 SNORKELING

BRIDGE

⛵ AQUATIC SPORTS

All maps are oriented with North at the top unless otherwise noted.

FROM THE AUTHOR

Most people who enjoy Mexico are aware that many changes are taking place, mostly with the fluctuating peso. Even while producing this book, we were aware that prices would be out of date before the book was published. Prices will mostly be listed in US dollars—which change more slowly than pesos. Please use the prices in this book as a *general guide only*—we have tried to supply addresses where you can check for the most current prices available. As we go to press, (Dec. 1989) the dollar value is 2400 pesos.

IS THIS BOOK OUT OF DATE?

We strive to keep our books as up to date as possible and would appreciate your help. If you find a hot new resort or attraction, or if we have neglected to include an important bit of information, please let us know. Our mapmakers take extraordinary care to be accurate, but if you find an error or if you find anything contrary to what we have told you, jot it down in the margin of the book. When you return home, let us know and we'll pass the information along.

We're especially interested in hearing from female travelers, backpackers, RVers, outdoor enthusiasts, expatriates, and local residents. We're also interested in any comments from the Mexican tourist industry, including hotel owners and individuals who specialize in accommodating visitors to their country.

If you have outstanding photos or artwork that you feel could be used in an upcoming edition, send us duplicate slides or drawings. You will be given full credit and a free book if your work is published. Materials will be returned only if you include a self-addressed stamped envelope. Moon Publications will own all rights. Address your letters to:

Chicki Mallan
Moon Publications, Inc.
722 Wall St.
Chico, CA 95928, USA

INTRODUCTION

THE LAND AND SEA

Cancun is located on the east coast of Mexico's Yucatan Peninsula in the state of Quintana Roo which is bordered by the state of Yucatan to the northwest Campeche to the west, and the country of Belize to the south. Quintana Roo occupies 50,350 square km and has a population of almost 200,000. Mostly flat, this long isolated state is covered with tropical forest and boasts the most beautiful white-sand beaches on the Peninsula. Several islands lie offshore, and a magnificent 250-km-long reef runs parallel to the Quintana Roo coast from the tip of Isla Mujeres to the Bay of Honduras, whose undersea life provides a world-class attraction. Chetumal, capital of the state, borders Belize, formerly known as British Honduras.

Geologically this flat shelf of limestone and coral composition is like a stone sponge: rain is absorbed into the ground and delivered to natural stone-lined sinks and underground rivers. The abundant limestone provided the early Maya with sturdy material close at hand to create the mammoth structures that have survived hundreds of years. It was readily cut with hand-hewn stonecutting implements, but created a problem for the Maya as they searched for a primary necessity of life—water. In the northern region of Quintana Roo there are few rivers and lakes. Only in the extreme south is there a river, the Rio Hondo, which cuts a natural boundary between Belize and Quintana Roo at the city of Chetumal. Four lakes at Coba are scattered among the ancient ruins.

Climate
Quintana Roo has a tropical climate and during the summer months becomes hot and humid; the farther south, the more humidity is

QUINTANA ROO

U.S.A.

GULF OF MEXICO

MEXICO

QUINTANA ROO

AREA DESCRIBED IN TEXT

0   500 km

PACIFIC OCEAN

felt. The major portion of rain falls between May and Oct.; cooling trade winds, which blow most of the time, make it pleasant during the dry season, but also contribute to higher rainfall than the northern part of the Peninsula. Annual rainfall in the south averages 1,553 mm (61 inches). The northern part of the Peninsula gets less; north Peninsula landscape is arid with vegetation described as cacti-thorn scrub forest or subdeciduous. The Peninsula's flat plain gradually gets greener as it spreads into the south end, where moisture is abundant and rainforest conditions are the norm.

Cenotes (Natural Wells)

Limestone and coral create eerie shorelines, caves, and (fortunately) water holes. When flying over the Peninsula you can see circular ground patterns caused by the hidden movement of underground rivers and lakes. The water level rises and falls with the cycle of rain and drought. This constant ebb and flow erodes the underlying limestone, creating steep-walled caverns; the surface crust eventually caves in exposing and allowing access to the water. Around these sources of water Maya villages grew. Some of the wells are shallow, seven meters below the jungle floor; some are treacherously deep, with the surface of the water as much as 70-90 meters deep. In times of drought, the Maya carved stairs into slick limestone walls or hung long ladders into abysmal hollows leading to under-ground lakes. John Stephens' book, Incidents of Travel in the Yucatan, covers the 1841 expedition of Frederick Catherwood and Stephens. Catherwood's realistic art accurately depicts how the Indians survived in the northern part of the Peninsula from year to year with little or no rainfall by burrowing far into the earth to retrieve water. The two American explorers observed long lines of naked Indian men carrying the precious liquid from deep holes back to the surface in calabash containers.

The Quintana Roo Coast

The Quintana Roo Coast is composed of many lagoons, sandbars, and mangrove swamps and is edged with coral reefs; several islands lie offshore—Cozumel, Isla Mujeres, and Contoy. The fifth largest reef in the world, the Belizean Reef, extends from the tip of Isla Mujeres 250 km south to the Bay of Honduras. Many varieties of coral—including rare black coral found at great depths—grow in the hills and valleys of fathoms-deep reef that protects Quintana Roo, the east coast of Mexico's Caribbean. In many places along the reef it is illegal to dive for the coral, and where it is permitted it's a dangerous (but moneymaking) occupation. Since tourists are willing to buy it, the local divers continue to retrieve it from the crags and crevices of underwater canyons. The coral ridges of the reef attract curious divers from all over the world.

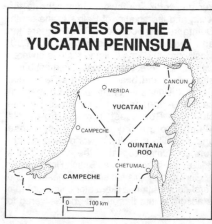

STATES OF THE YUCATAN PENINSULA

CANCUN

MERIDA

YUCATAN

CAMPECHE

QUINTANA ROO

CHETUMAL

CAMPECHE

0   100 km

AGRICULTURE

The land in the northernmost part of the Yucatan was described by Diego de Landa, an early Spanish priest, as "a country with the least earth ever seen, since all of it is one living rock." Surprisingly, the thin layer of soil supports agriculture. This monotonous stony plain is dotted with a multitude of sword-shaped plants called henequen. The Spanish settlers on the Peninsula made vast fortunes growing and selling henequen (used for rope making) at the turn of the century. However, it was the Maya that showed the Spanish its value; it was used in many ways, but especially for building their (*palapa*) houses. Without nails or tools, the house was "tied together" with henequen strands twisted by hand into sturdy twine. Wherever *palapa*-style structures are built today by the Indians the same nail-free method is used.

Food Crops

With careful nurturing of the soil, the early Indians managed to support a large population of people on the land. Though rainfall is spotty and unreliable, the land is surprisingly fertile and each year produces corn and other vegetables on small farms. Toward the northwest of the Peninsula where tradewinds bring more rain, the land is greener. As you travel south the desert gradually becomes green until you find yourself in a jungle plain in southern Quintana Roo fringed by the turquoise Caribbean. Along the coast of Quintana Roo remnants of large coconut plantations, now broken up into small tracts and humble *ranchitos* are being developed by farmers with modest government assistance. Before the "yellowing" disease which attacked and killed many coconut palms, it was commonplace to see copra lining the roadsides, drying in the sun. The copra farmers in most sections of Quintana Roo have lost major portions of their coco plantations.

Different parts of the Peninsula produce different crops. In most areas juicy oranges grow, which you find for sale everywhere; in the marketplace and along the road, oranges are often sold with the green peel removed, the sweet fruit ready to eat. Cacao beans grow in different parts of the Yucatan Peninsula. A drink made of cacao was developed by the Maya and presented to the Spanish. Today chocolate is manufactured and shipped all over the world from Mexico. Bananas of many kinds, from finger-sized to 15-inch red plantains, are grown in thick groves, especially along the Gulf of Mexico coast. Tabasco bananas are recognized worldwide as among the finest.

REEFS ALONG THE QUINTANA ROO COAST

The sea is a magical world unto itself. Man is just beginning to learn of the wonders that take place within its depths. Some dreamers predict that a time is coming when oceans of the world will provide all the nutrients humans need and that people will live comfortably side-by-side with the fish in the sea. For now, men and women are content just to look at what's there.

Coral

Coral is a unique limestone formation that grows in innumerable shapes: delicate lace, trees with reaching branches, pleated mushrooms, stove pipes, petaled flowers, fans, domes, cabbage heads, and stalks of broccoli. Corals are formed by millions of tiny carnivorous polyps that feed on minute organisms and live in large colonies of flamboyantly colored individual species. These small creatures can be less than a cm long or as big as 15 cm in diameter. Related to the jellyfish and sea anemone, polyps need sunlight and clear saltwater not colder than 20 degrees C to survive. Coral polyps have cylinder-shaped bodies. One end is attached to a hard surface (the bottom of the ocean, rim of a submerged volcano, or the reef itself) and the other—mouth end—is circled with tiny tentacles that capture its minute prey with a deadly sting.

Colonies are formed when polyps attach themselves to each other. Stony coral, for example, makes the connection with a flat sheet of tissue between the middle of both bodies. They develop their limestone skeletons by extracting calcium out of the seawater and depositing calcium carbonate around the lower half of their bodies. They reproduce from buds or eggs. Occasionally, small buds appear on the adult polyp; when mature they separate from the adult and add to the growth of existing colonies. Eggs, on the other hand, grow into tiny forms that swim away and settle on the ocean floor. When developed, the egg begins a new colony.

A Reef Grows

As these small creatures continue to reproduce and die, their sturdy skeletons accumulate. One small piece of coral represents millions of polyps and many years of construction. Over eons broken bits of coral, animal waste, and granules of soil all contribute to the strong foundation for a reef, which slowly rises toward the surface. A reef must grow from a base no more than 25 meters below the water's surface; in a healthy environment it can grow four to five cm a year.

Reefs are divided into three types: atoll, fringing, and barrier. An atoll can be formed around the crater of a submerged volcano. The polyps begin building their colonies on the round edge of the crater, forming a circular coral island with a lagoon in the center. Thousands of atolls occupy tropical waters throughout the world. A fringing reef is coral living on a shallow shelf that extends outward from shore into the sea. A barrier reef runs

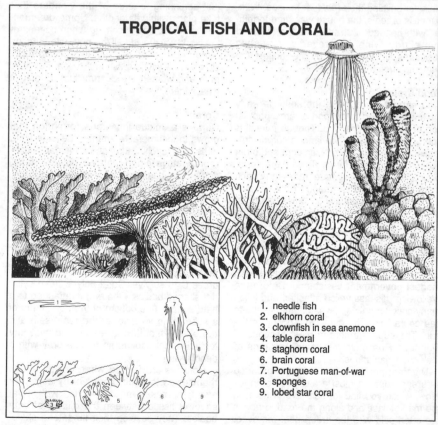

TROPICAL FISH AND CORAL

1. needle fish
2. elkhorn coral
3. clownfish in sea anemone
4. table coral
5. staghorn coral
6. brain coral
7. Portuguese man-of-war
8. sponges
9. lobed star coral

FORMATION OF A LAGOON

LONGEST REEFS IN THE WORLD

Great Barrier Reef, Australia	1,600 km
S.W. Barrier Reef, New Caledonia	600 km
N.E. Barrier Reef, New Caledonia	540 km
Great Sea Reef, Fiji Islands	260 km
Belizean Reef	250 km
S.Louisiade Archipelago Reef, PNG	200 km

parallel to the coast, and water separates it from the land. A reef of this type can be a series of reefs with channels of water in between, as is the case with some of the largest barrier reefs in the Pacific and Indian Oceans.

The Yucatan Peninsula has a barrier reef extending from the tip of Isla Mujeres to Sapodilla Cay in the Gulf of Honduras. This reef, known by various names (Belizean Reef is the most common), is 250 km long, fifth longest in the world. The Belizean Reef's unspoiled beauty attracts divers and snorkelers from all parts of the world.

The Meaning Of Color

Most people interested in reefs already know they're in for a brilliant display of colored fish. But in the fish world, color isn't only for exterior decoration. Fish change hues for a number of reasons, including anger, protection, and sexual attraction. Fish coloration is still not completely understood. For example, because of their many colors, marine biologists are uncertain how many species of groupers there are—different species or different moods? A male damsel fish clearly imparts his aggression—and his desire for love—by turning vivid blue. Some fish have as many as 12 different recognizable color patterns they can change within seconds.

These color changes, along with other body signals, combine to make communication simple between species. Scientists have discovered that a layer of color-bearing cells lies just beneath a fish's transparent scales. These cells contain orange, yellow, red, or black pigments; others combine to make yellow or green. A crystalline tissue adds white, silver, or iridescence. Color changes occur when the pigmented cells are revealed, combined, or masked.

Fish communicate in many surprising ways including electrical impulses and flashing bioluminescence (cold light). If fish communication intrigues you, read Robert Burgess' *Secret Languages of the Sea* (Dodd, Mead and Co.).

Conservation

The Mexican government has strict laws governing the reef, to which most divers are more than willing to comply in order to preserve this natural phenomenon and its inhabitants. It takes hundreds of years to form large coral colonies, so please don't break off pieces of coral for souvenirs. After a very short time out of water the polyps lose their color and you have only a piece of chalky white coral—just like the pieces you can pick up beachcombing. Strict fines await those who remove anything from the reef. Spear fishing is allowed in some areas along the Yucatan coast, but not on the reef itself. The spear must be totally unmechanical and used freehand or with a rubber band only (no spear guns). If you plan on fishing, write to Oficina de Pesca, 1010 2nd Ave., Suite 1605, San Diego, CA 92101, tel. (619) 233-6956, for more details; a fishing license is required.

Hurricane Gilbert

On Sept. 13, 1988, a hurricane of extreme force hit the Yucatan Peninsula. Strong winds and high waves blasted onto shore, uprooting trees, destroying buildings, and tearing away roadways and coastline. In hit and miss fashion, the revolving fingers of the whorl caused damage in some locations, leaving areas 20 feet away unscathed. Cancun probably lost more glass than anything, though large areas of sandy beaches were swallowed by the sea; other areas had sand dumped as though by the truckload, creating high dunes where not needed. The eye of the hurricane passed between Playa del Carmen and Puerto Morelos. While a few buildings were totally washed away, others were destroyed on the inside (in one case two stories were gutted) with the outside walls left intact. Because so little time has passed, wounds are fresh and stories abound. One woman in Puerto Morelos told of taking refuge in a friend's house near the jungle after evacuating from her beachfront home. While walking through a dark hall one night (the electricity was off for 15 days along this section of the Coast) she stepped on and was struck by two tropical snakes obviously trying to escape their water-

SPECIES OF FISH IN THE CARIBBEAN

blue chromis	stoplight parrotfish	sand tilefish
toadfish	French grunt	triggerfish
porkfish	spotted drum	sergeant major
trunkfish	angel fish	big eye
queen angelfish	barred cardinal	bluestriped grunt
grouper	trumpetfish	butterfly

SHELLS YOU MIGHT FIND ON THE BEACH

horse conch	queen conch	West Indian fighting
cowrie	olive	conch
prickly cockel	cut-ribbed ark	West Indian top

SPONGES TO LOOK FOR

tube	encrusting	basket
vase	rope	barrel

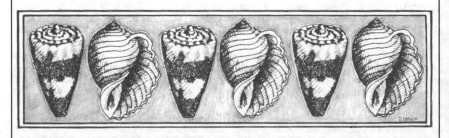

logged jungle environment. After treatment (in a Merida Hospital) she returned to find the house and everything in it gone. However, like most of the Yucatecans she has built a small bungalow for herself, as well as three others to rent.

Another man told of the birth of his son at the height of the storm. He, his wife, and their two children gathered a bag of supplies containing candles, water, matches, canned food, can opener, blankets, and clothes including necessities for the expected infant. After his wife announced the birth was imminent he carefully boiled a new pair of shoelaces (to tie the umbilical cord), sterilized a kitchen knife (to cut the cord), and began reading directions in the LaMaze training book under emergency deliveries. As the hurricane pounded Cancun and the wind constantly shifted directions, the small family moved from one room to the next, fearing the rattling glass would burst even though taped. The windows didn't shatter, and he and his two children assisted his wife in the delivery of a baby boy. No, they didn't name him Gilbert!

The people of the Yucatan Peninsula always felt the reef that protects their coastline from a strong surge would keep hurricane tides away. Now they know the strength of a hurricane as well as their own. Cancun has been rebuilt in record time, and it's better than ever. Even the beaches that were destroyed are slowly being replaced by the sea. The small villages along the coast have

These tractors worked around the clock trying to retrieve sand washed out to sea by Hurricane Gilbert.

for the most part put their lives and homes back on track. The Caribbean Sea, as beautiful as ever, continues to welcome visitors.

FAUNA

Many exotic animals are found in the thick jungles and flatlands of Quintana Roo, many that aren't found elsewhere in Mexico. With patience it's possible to observe animals not normally seen in the wild. If you're serious about this venture, bring a small folding stool (unless you prefer to sit in a tree), a pair of binoculars, possibly a camera, and plenty of bug repellent! The distribution of animal and plant life is a direct result of the climatic zones, which are in turn affected by their different altitudes and proximity to the sea.

REPTILES

Reptiles thrive in Yucatan's warm sunny environment—man is their worst enemy. Though against the laws of most countries today, in the past some species were greatly reduced in number because they were hunted for their unusual skin. Snake and crocodile skin when tanned makes sturdy, attractive, waterproof leather, previously used in luggage, shoes, and ladies' handbags. A few black marketeers still take their toll on the species.

Iguana

This species—American lizards of the family *Iguanidae*—includes various large planteaters typically dark in color. Seen frequently in Quintana Roo, they come in many sizes with slight variations in color. The young iguana is bright emerald green. This common lizard grows to one meter long, has a blunt head and long flat tail. Bands of black and gray circle its body, and a serrated column traces down the middle of its back almost to the tail.

Very large and shy, the lizard's forelimbs hold the front half of its body up off the ground while the two back limbs are kept relaxed and splayed alongside its hind-quarters. However, when the iguana is frightened, its hind legs

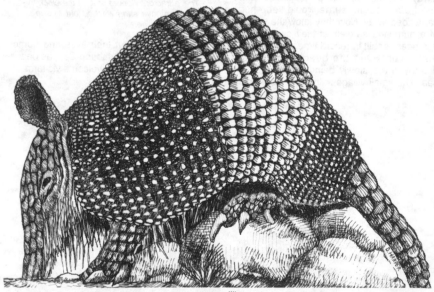

armadillo

iguana

do everything they're supposed to, and the iguana crashes quickly (though clumsily) into the brush searching for its burrow and safety. Though not aggressive, if cornered it will bite and use its tail in self-defense. It mostly enjoys basking in the bright sunshine along the Caribbean. Though they are herbivores, the young also eat insects and larvae. Certain varieties in some areas of the Peninsula are almost hunted out—for example, the spiny-tailed iguana in the central valley of Chiapas. A moderate number are still found in the rocky foothill slopes and thorn-scrub woodlands. In Quintana Roo it is not unusual to see locals along dirt paths carrying sturdy specimens by the tail to put in the cookpot.

From centuries past recorded references attest to the medicinal value of this lizard, which partly explains the active trade of live iguana in the marketplace of some parts of the Peninsula. Iguana stew is believed to cure or relieve various human ailments such as impotence. Another reason for their popularity at the market is their delicate white flesh that tastes much like chicken but is much more expensive.

Other Lizards
You'll see a great variety of lizards, from a skinny two-inch miniature gecko to a chameleon-like black anole that changes colors to match the environment either when danger is imminent or as subterfuge to fool the insects that it preys on. At mating time, the male anole's bright red throat-fan is puffed out to make sure that all female lizards will see it. Some are brightly striped in various shades of green and yellow; others are earth colors that blend with the gray and beige limestone which dots the landscape. Skinny as whisps of thread running on hind legs or chunky and waddling with armor-like skin, the range is endless—and fascinating!

Coral Snakes
Seen from the southern part of the Yucatan Peninsula to Panama, these coral snakes grow much larger (1-1¹/₂ motoro) than tho ones in the southern U.S. The body is slender, with no pronounced distinction between head and neck. In North and South America are several genera of true coral snakes, which are close relatives of cobras. Many false coral snakes with similar coloring are around though harmless. Nocturnal, they spend the day in mossy clumps under rocks or logs.

Note: The two North American coral snakes have prominent rings round their bodies in the same sequence of black, yellow or white, and red. They don't look for trouble and seldom strike, but they will bite if stepped on; their short fangs, however, can be stopped by shoes or clothing. Even though the Mexicans call this the "20-minute snake" (meaning if you are bitten and don't get antivenin within

20 minutes, you die), it's actually more like a 24-hour period. According to Mexico's Instituto Nacional de Higiene, an average of 135 deaths per year (mostly children) are reported for the country, the number declining as more villages receive antivenin.

Chances of the average tourist being bitten by a coral (or any other snake) are slim. However, if you plan on extensive jungle exploration, check with your doctor before you leave home. Antivenin is available in Mexico, and it's wise to be prepared for an allergic reaction to the antivenin by bringing antihistimine and adrenalin. The most important thing to remember if bitten: *don't panic and don't run*. Physical exertion and panic cause the venom to travel through your body much faster. Lay down and stay calm; have someone carry you to a doctor.

Tropical Rattlesnakes

Called *cascabel* in Mexico and Mesoamerica, this species is the deadliest and most treacherous of all rattlers. It differs slightly from other species by having vividly contrasting neck bands. Contrary to public myth, this serpent doesn't always rattle a warning of its impending strike. It grows 2-2½ meters long and is found mainly in higher, drier areas of the tropics.

Caymans

The cayman is part of the crocodilian order; crocodiles' and alligators' habits and appearance are very similar. The main difference is the underskin. The cayman's skin is reinforced with bony plates on the belly, making them useless for the leather market (lucky them!); alligators and crocodiles, with smooth belly skin and sides, in some parts of the globe have been hunted almost to extinction. There are laws that now protect the crocodilia, though certain governments allow farming the animal for leather production.

Of the five species of cayman, several frequent the brackish inlet waters near the estuaries on the north edge of the Yucatan Peninsula along the Rio Lagartos (loosely translated to mean "River of Lizards"). They are broad-snouted and often look as though they sport a pair of spectacles. A large cayman can be 2½ meters long, very dark gray-green with eyelids that look swollen and wrinkled. Some species have eyelids that look like a pair of blunt horns. They are quicker than alligators and have longer, sharper teeth. Their disposition is vicious and treacherous; don't be fooled by the old myth that on land they're cumbersome and slow moving. When cornered they move swiftly and are known for not liking people. The best advice one can heed is to give the cayman a wide berth when spotted.

Sea Turtles

At one time many species of giant turtles meandered the coastal regions of Quintana Roo, laying their eggs in the warm Caribbean sands. Though many didn't survive birds, crabs, and sharks, thousands of hatchlings managed to return each year to their birthplace. The Sea Turtle Rescue Organization claims that in 1947, during one day, over 40,000 sea turtles (Kemp's ridley) nested on the one Mexican beach instinct returns them to each year. In 1984 less than 500 Kemp's ridleys nested during the entire season.

In spite of concentrated efforts by the Mexican government, the number of turtles is still decreasing. They were a valuable source of food for the Maya Indians for centuries. But only in recent years has the wholesale theft of turtle eggs, coupled with the senseless slaughter of the lovely hawksbill (for its beautiful shell), begun to deplete the species. Refrigeration and freezer holds enable large fishing boats to capture thousands of turtles at one time, and smuggle meat by the ton into various countries to be canned as soup or frozen for the unwary consumer: processors often claim the turtle meat in their product is from the legal freshwater variety.

Another problem is the belief that turtle eggs cure impotence. Despite huge fines for anyone possessing turtle eggs, every summer nesting grounds along the Yucatan Peninsula are raided. There is *no* hunting season for these threatened creatures, and the meat is illegal on menus throughout the state. Though some restaurants ignore the law and verbally offer turtle meat, it never happens with the eggs! They are forbidden fruit.

hitching a ride on a giant turtle

toward the sea, hopefully imprinting a sense of belonging there so that they will then return to their place of "birth." Afterward, the hatchlings are scooped up and placed in tanks, and allowed to grow larger before being released into the open sea to increase their chances of survival. All of these efforts are in the experimental stage; the results will not be known for years. For more information write to the Sea Turtle Rescue Fund, 624 9th St. N.W., Washington, D.C. 20001.

ENDENTATA FAMILY

Nine-banded Armadillos
This strange creature looks like a miniature prehistoric monster. The size of a small house dog, its most unusual feature is the tough coat of plate armor which encases it. Even the tail has its own armor! Flexibility comes from nine bands (or external "joints") that circle the midsection. Living on a diet of insects, the armadillo's extremely keen sense of smell can locate grubs 15 cm underground. The front paws are sharp, enabling it to dig easily into the earth and build underground burrows. After digging the hole, the animal carries up to a bushel of grass down to make its nest. Here it bears and rears its young and sleeps during the day. Unlike some armadillos that roll up into a tight ball when threatened, this species will race for the burrow instead, stiffly arch its back, and wedge in so that it cannot be pulled out. The tip of the Yucatan Peninsula is a favored habitat due to its scant rainfall and warm temperatures; too much rain floods the burrow and can drown young armadillos.

Giant Anteaters
This extraordinary cousin of the armadillo measures two meters long from the tip of its tubular snout to the end of its bushy tail. Its body is colored shades of brown-gray; the hindquarters become darker in tone, while a contrasting wedge-shaped pattern of black outlined with white decorates the throat and shoulder. This creature walks on the knuckles of its paws, keeping the foreclaws razor sharp. If threatened, anteaters can be deadly;

Ecological organizations are trying hard to save the dwindling turtle population. Turtle eggs are kept in captivity; when the hatchlings break through their shells, they are brought to a beach and allowed to rush

more importantly, they are capable of ripping open the leathery mud walls of termite or white ant nests, the contents of which are a main food source. After opening the nest, the anteater begins flicking its viscuous tongue. Ants don't have a chance; they stick to the long tongue that quickly transfers them into a toothless, elongated mouth.

Tapirs

South American tapirs are found from the southern part of Mexico to southern Brazil. A stout-bodied animal, it has short legs and tail, small eyes, and rounded ears. The nose and upper lip extend into a short but very mobile proboscis. Totally herbivorous, tapirs usually live near streams or rivers in the forest. They bathe daily and also use the water as an escape when hunted either by man or by its prime predator, the jaguar. Shy, unaggressive animals, they are nocturnal with a definite home range, wearing a path between the jungle and their feeding area. If attacked, they lower their head and blindly crash off through the forest; they've been known to collide with trees and knock themselves out in their chaotic attempt to flee!

Peccaries

Next to deer, peccaries are the most widely hunted game on the Yucatan. Other names for this pig-like creature are musk hog and javelina. Some compare peccaries to the wild pigs found in Europe, though, in fact, they're part of an entirely different family.

Two species found on the Peninsula are the collared and the white-lipped peccary. The feisty collared peccary stands 50 cm at the shoulder and can be one meter long, weighing as much as 30 kg. It is black and white with a narrow semi-circular collar of white hair on the shoulders.

In Spanish *javelina* means "spear," descriptive of the two spear-like tusks that protrude from its mouth. This more familiar peccary is found in desert, woodland, and rainforests, and travels in groups of five to 15. Also with tusks, the white-lipped peccary is reddish-brown to black and has an area of white around the mouth. This larger animal, which can grow to 105 cm long, is found deep in tropical rainforests and lives in herds of 100-plus.

CATS

Seven species of cats are found in North America, four tropically distributed. The jaguar is heavy chested with sturdy, muscled forelegs. It has small rounded ears and its tail is relatively short. Color ranges from tan on top to white on the underside or pure black. The male can weigh 65-115 kg, females 45-85 kg. Largest of the cats on the Peninsula, the jaguar is about the same size as a leopard. Other cats found in Quintana Roo are the ocelot and puma. In tropical forests the large cats are the only predators capable of controlling hoofed game such as deer, peccaries, and tapirs. If hunting is poor and times are tough, the jaguar *(el tigre)* will go into the rivers and scoop fish with its large paws. The river is also a favorite spot for the jaguar to hunt the large tapir when it comes to drink.

The giant anteater's forelimbs have undergone anatomical changes making them effective shovels.

MANATEE

Probably the most unusual mammal, the manatee is an elephantine creature of immense proportions with gentle manners and the curiosity of a kitten. Though today seldom seen, this enormous animal, often referred to as the sea cow, at one time roamed the shallow inlets, bays, and estuaries of the Caribbean in large numbers. The manatee is said to be the basis of myths and old seamen's references to mermaids. In South America this particular mammal is revered by certain Indian tribes. The manatee image is frequently seen in the art of the ancient Maya, who hunted it for its flesh. In modern times, the population has been reduced by the encroachment of large numbers of people in the manatees' habitats along the riverways

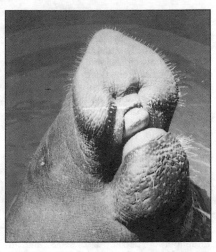

a close-up of the truncated snout and prehensile lips of the manatee, which surprisingly is a distant relative of the elephant

and shorelines. Ever-growing numbers of boats with motors inflict often deadly gashes on the nosy creature.

The manatee weighs 30-35 kg at birth and is gray with a pinkish cast; it can grow to three to four meters long and weigh over a ton. Shaped like an Idaho potato, it has a spatulate tail, two forelimbs with toenails, pebbled coarse skin, tiny sunken eyes, numerous fine-bristled hairs scattered sparsely over its body, and a permanent Mona Lisa smile. The head of the mammal seems small for its gargantuan body, and its preproboscidean lineage includes dugongs (in Australia), hydrax, and elephants. The manatee's truncated snout and prehensile lips help to push food into its mouth. The only aquatic mammal that exists on vegetation, the manatee grazes on bottom-growing grasses and other aquatic plant life. It ingests as much as 225 kg per day, cleaning rivers of oxygen-choking growth. It is unique amongst mammals in that it constantly grows new teeth—worn teeth fall out and are replaced. Posing no threat to any other living thing, it has been hunted for its oil, skin, and flesh, which is said to be tasty.

This baby tigre from a neighboring jungle needed to be hand fed after its mother was killed.

The mammal thrives in shallow warm water; in Quintana Roo and coves of Belize the manatee has been reported in shallow bays between Playa del Carmen and Punta Allen but very infrequently anymore. One spring evening recently in a small bay in Belize near the Chetumal border, a curious manatee spent about an hour lazily swimming the cove, lifting its truncated snout out of the water about every four minutes, often its entire head. The few people standing on a small dock in the bay were thrilled to be seeing the shy animal.

In neighboring Guatemala, the government is sponsoring a manatee reserve in Lago de Izabal. In the U.S. the mammal is found mostly in the inshore and estuarine areas of Florida. It is protected under the Federal U.S. Marine Mammal Protection Act of 1972, the Endangered Species Act of 1973, and the Florida Manatee Sanctuary Act of 1978. It is estimated their population numbers about 2,000.

BIRDS OF QUINTANA ROO

Since a major part of the Yucatan Peninsula is still undeveloped and covered with trees and brush, it isn't surprising to find exotic, rarely seen birds all across the landscape. The Mexican government is beginning to realize the great value in this (almost) undiscovered treasure-trove of nature (attracting both scientists and laymen) and is making initial efforts to protect nesting grounds. The birds of the Yucatan have until recent years been free of pest sprays, smog, and human beings' encroachment. If you're a serious birdwatcher, you know all about Quintana Roo. Undoubtedly, however, change is coming as more people intrude into the rangeland of the birds, exploring these still undeveloped tracts on the Yucatan Peninsula. Hopefully, stringent regulations will take hold before many of these lovely birds are chased away or destroyed.

Quintana Roo is one of the better ornithological sites. Coba, with its marshy-rimmed lakes, nearby cornfields, and relatively tall,

humid forest, is worth a couple of days to the ornithologist. One of the more impressive birds to look for is the keel-billed toucan, often seen perched high on a bare limb in the early hours of the morning. Others include *chachalacas* (held in reverence by the Maya cult), screeching parrots, and occasionally, the ocellated turkey. For an excellent bird book that deals with the Yucatan Peninsula, check out *100 Common Birds of the Yucatan Peninsula* written by Barbara MacKinnon. Barbara, a well-known birdwatcher has lived in the Cancun area for many years, is donating all of the profits of her book to the Sian Ka'an Reserve. Available through Amigos de Sian Ka'an, Apto Postal 770, Cancun, Quintana Roo, Mexico 77500.

Sooty Terns

In Cancun on a coral island just offshore from the Camino Real Hotel, a breeding colony of sooty terns has been discovered. The sooty tern is not the only seabird which lacks waterproof feathers, but it is the only one that will not land and rest on a passing ship or drifting debris. The bird feeds on tiny fish and squid that swim close to the surface of the sea. While hovering close to the water they snatch the unsuspecting prey. The birds nest from April till Sept., and Barbara MacKinnon tells us that if left undisturbed, the colony should raise about 150-200 chicks this summer (1989). The Camino Real Hotel is being urged to warn guests to stay away from the rocky island. Man is the sooty tern's only predator. If frightened the parent-birds panic, leave the eggs exposed to the hot tropical sun, or knock the young into the sea where they drown immediately.

Flamingos

In the far north of the Peninsula at Rio Lagartos, thousands of long-necked, long-legged flamingos are seen during the nesting season. They begin arriving around the end of May, when the rains begin. This homecoming is a breathtaking sight: a profusion of pink/salmon colors clustered together on the white sand or sailing across a blue sky, long curved necks straight in flight, the flapping move-

BIRDS OF THE YUCATAN

Marsh Birds
white ibis
white-faced ibis
roseate spoonbill

Wading Birds
American flamingo

Water Birds
fulvous tree-duck
black-bellied tree-duck
trumpeter swan
whistling swan
white-fronted goose

Lowland Birds
rufous-tailed hummingbird
violaceous trogon
blue-crowned motmot
collared toucan
keel-billed toucan
golden-olive woodpecker
barred antshrike
masked tityra
boat-billed flycatcher
social flycatcher
kisadee flycatcher
olivaceous flycatcher
white-tipped brown jay
barred wren
spotted-breasted wren
clay-colored robin
singing blackbird
yellow-throated euphonia
blue tanager
song tanager
crimson-collared tanager
black-headed saltator

Birds In The Dense Forest
little tinamou
spotted wood-quail
short-billed pigeon
white-fronted dove
ruddy quail dove
white-bellied emerald
collared trogon
violaceous trogon
keel-billed toucan
golden-olive woodpecker
lineated woodpecker
brown woodpecker

flint-billed woodpecker
olivaceous creeper
sulphur-bellied flycatcher
green jay
spotted-breasted wren
lowland wood-wren
white-throated robin
gray-headed vireo
blue honeycreeper
golden-crowned warbler
red-crowned tanager
jungle tanager
black-faced grosbeak

Birds At Beaches, Bays, And Adjacent Ocean
brown pelican
magnificent frigatebird
black vulture
spotted sandpiper
laughing gull
black tern
least tern
royal tern

Birds Seen At Lagoons, Tidal Flats, Shallow Estuaries, And Mangrove Swamps
olivaceous cormorant
magnificent frigatebird
great blue heron
little blue heron
reddish egret
common egret
snowy egret
Louisiana heron
yellow-crowned night heron
American widgeon
black vulture
American coot
jacana
killdeer
spotted sandpiper
laughing gull
royal tern
mangrove swallow
mangrove warbler
boat-tailed grackle

Birds Seen In Villages And Overgrown Fields
black vulture

common ground-dove
ruddy ground-dove
groove-billed ani
Vaux's swift
tropical house wren
tropical mockingbird
clay-colored robin
boat-tailed grackle
singing blackbird
gray saltator

Birds Seen At Partially Cleared Archaeological Sites, Woodland Edge, Or Scrubby, Deciduous Woodland
plain chachalaca
Yucatan bobwhite
white-winged dove
common ground-dove
ruddy ground-dove
white-fronted dove
Aztec parakeet
groove-billed ani
ferruginous pygmy owl
lesser nighthawk
pauraque
turquoise-browed motmot
golden-fronted woodpecker
laughing creeper
rose-throated coptinga
masked tityra
tropical kingbird
boat-billed flycatcher
social flycatcher
olivaceous flycatcher
yellow-billed elaenia
cave swallow
Yucatan jay
white-browed wren
spotted-breasted wren
white-bellied wren
blue-gray gnatcatcher
white-lored gnatcatcher
peppershrike
mangrove vireo
red-eyed cowbird
altamira oriole
hooded oriole
black-headed saltator
gray saltator
blue-black grassquit

ment exposing contrasting black and pink on the undersides of their wings. The estimated flamingo population on the Yucatan Peninsula is 30,000. Many of these "greater" flamingos winter in Celestun, a small fishing village on the northwest coast a few km north of the Campeche-Yucatan state border. Celestun lies between the Gulf of Mexico and a long tidal estuary known as La Cienega. If you're visiting Merida and want to see flamingos, it's a closer drive to Celestun (about one hour) than to Rio Lagartos (about three hours). Don't forget your camera and color film!

Estuary Havens

Estuaries play host to hundreds of bird species. A boat ride into one of them will give you an opportunity to see a variety of ducks; this is a wintering spot for many flocks of North American species. Among others, you'll see the blue-winged teal, northern shoveler, and lesser scaup along with a variety of wading birds feeding in the shallow waters, including numerous types of heron, snowy egret, and (in the summer) white ibis. Seven species of birds are endemic to the Yucatan Peninsula: ocellated turkey, Yucatan whippoorwill, Yucatan flycatcher, orange oriole, black catbird, yellow-lored parrot, and the quetzal.

Quetzals

Though the ancient Maya made abundant use of the dazzling quetzal feathers for ceremonial costume and headdress, they hunted other fowl in much larger quantities for food; nonetheless, the quetzal is the only known bird from the pre-Columbian era that is almost extinct. Close by, the Guatemala government has established a quetzal sanctuary not too far from the city of Coban. The beautifully designed reserve is open to hikers, with several km of good trails leading up into the cloud forest. For the birder this could be a worthwhile detour to search out the gorgeous quetzal. The tourist office, INGUAT, in Coban hands out an informative leaflet with a map and description of the quetzal sanctuary.

INSECTS

Any tropical locale has literally tens of thousands of insects. Some are annoying (mosquitos and gnats), some are dangerous (black widows, bird spiders, and scorpions), and others can cause pain when they bite (red ants), but many are beautiful (butterflies and moths), and *all* are fascinating studies in evolved socialization and specialization.

Butterflies And Moths

The Yucatan has an abundance of beautiful moths and butterflies. Of the 90,000 types of butterflies in the world, a large percentage are seen in Quintana Roo. You'll see, among others, the magnificent blue morpho, orange-barred sulphur, copperhead, cloudless sulphur, malachite, admiral, calico, ruddy dagger-wing, tropical buckeye, and emperor. The famous monarch is also a visitor during its annual migration from the Florida Peninsula. They usually make a stopover on the east coast of Quintana Roo, including Cancun and

---

DIFFERENCES BETWEEN MOTHS AND BUTTERFLIES

1. Butterflies fly during the day; moths fly at dusk and during the night as well.

2. Butterflies rest with their wings folded straight up over their bodies; most moths rest with their wings spread flat open.

3. All butterflies have bare knobs at the ends of both antennae (feelers); moths' antennae are either plumy or hairlike and end in a point.

4. Butterflies have slender bodies; moths are plump. Both insects are of the order *lepidoptera*. So *lepidopterists* bring your nets! For you are in butterfly heaven in the jungles of Quintana Roo.

Cozumel, on their way south to the Central American mountains and Mexican highlands where they spend the winter. Trying to photo-graph a butterfly (live) is a testy business. Just when you have it in your cross hairs, the comely critter flutters off to another spot!

FLORA

Flora of the Yucatan Peninsula varies widely from north to south, and even east to west. The Yucatan is subject to tropical storms and occasional hurricanes. Although these tremen-dous winds seldom reach the interior, they are a factor in periodically damaging vegeta-tion in their paths. They also pick up and dis-perse seeds from the Caribbean basin (where the storms originate), spreading plants and flowers across political boundaries.

The Forests

Among the plant life of Quintana Roo are mangroves, bamboo, and swamp cypresses, plus ferns, vines, and flowers creeping from tree to tree and creating a dense growth. On topmost limbs, orchids and air ferns reach for the sun. In the southern part of the Yucatan Peninsula with its classic tropical rainforest are the tall mahoganies, *campeche, sapote,* and *kapok,* also covered with wild jungle vines.

Palms

A wide variety of palm trees and their rela-tives grow on the Peninsula—tall, short, fruit-ed, even oil producers. Though similar, vari-ous palms have distinct characteristics. Royal palms are tall with smooth trunks. Queen palms are often used for landscaping and bear a sweet fruit. Thatch palms are called *chit* by the Indians; the frond of this tree is used extensively on the Peninsula for roof thatch. Coconut palms serve the Yucatecan well. One of the 10 most useful trees in the world, it produces oil, food, drink, and shelter. The tree matures in six to seven years and then for five to seven years bears coconuts, a nutritious food that is also used for copra and valued as a money crop by the locals. Pre-sently, this source of income has all but dis-appeared in a good part of the Quintana Roo coast due to the "yellowing" disease that's attacked the Caribbean coast from Florida to Central America. Henequen is a cousin to the palm tree; from the fiber comes twine, rope, matting, and other products. New uses are constantly being sought since this plant is common and abundant.

From Fruit To Flowers

Quintana Roo grows delicious sweet and sour oranges, limes, and grapefruit. Avocado is abundant, and the papaya tree is practical-ly a weed. The mammey tree grows tall (15-20 meters) and full, providing not only wel-come shade but also an avocado-shaped fruit, brown on the outside with a vivid salmon-pink flesh that makes a sweet snack (the flavor similar to a sweet yam). Another unusual fruit tree is the *guaya* (part of the litchi nut family). This rangy evergreen thrives on sea air and is commonly seen along the coast and through-out the Yucatan Peninsula. Its small green leathery pods grow in clumps like grapes and contain a sweet, yellowish, jelly-like flesh—tasty! The calabash tree, a friend to the Indian for many years, provides a gourd used for containers.

The tall ceiba is a very special tree to those close to the Maya religious cult. Con-sidered the tree of life, even today it remains undisturbed whether it has sprouted in the middle of a fertile *milpa* (cornfield) or any-where else. At first glance when visiting in the summer, it would seem that all of the state favors the beautiful *flamboyanes* (royal poin-ciana). As its name implies, when in bloom it is the most flamboyant tree around, with wide-spreading branches covered in clusters

of brilliant orange-red flowers. These trees line sidewalks and plazas and when clustered together present a dazzling show.

Orchids

While traveling through remote areas of Quintana Roo one of the more exotic blooms, the orchid, is often found on the highest limbs of tall trees. Of the 71 species reported on the Yucatan Peninsula, 20% are terrestrial and 80% are epiphytic, attached to a host plant (in this case trees) and deriving its moisture and nutrients from the air and rain. Both species grow in many sizes and shapes: tiny buttons, spanning the length of a long branch, large-petaled blossoms with ruffled edges, or intense, tiger-striped miniatures. The lovely flowers come in a wide variety of colors, some subtle, some brilliant.

Nature's Hothouse

In spring, flowering trees are a beautiful sight—and sound, attracting hundreds of singing birds throughout the mating season. While wandering through jungle landscapes, you'll see thriving in the wild a complete gamut of plants that we so carefully nurture and coax to survive in a pot on a windowsill at home. Here in its natural environment, the croton exhibits wild colors, the pothos grows 30-cm leaves, and the philodendron splits every leaf in gargantuan glory.

White and red ginger are among the more exotic herbs that grow on the Peninsula. Plumeria (in the South Pacific called frangipani) has a wonderful fragrance and is seen in many colors. Hibiscus and bougainvillea bloom in an array of bright hues. A walk through the jungle will introduce you to many delicate strangers in the world of tropical flowers. But you'll find old friends too, such as the common morning glory creeping and climbing for miles over bushes and trees. You'll notice thick viny coils that thicken daily. Keeping jungle growth away from the roads, utility poles, and wires is a constant job because humid warm air and ample rainfall encourage a lush green wonderland.

SIAN KA'AN

With the growing number of visitors to Quintana Roo and the continual development of its natural wonders, there's a real danger of decimating the wildlife and destroying the ancient culture of its people. These are *the* two reasons that most travelers come to Quintana Roo—how foolhardy to kill the goose that laid the golden you-know-what. Because of that possibility, authorities and scientists first put their heads together in 1981 and the seeds of an idea began to grow.

In 1986 the culmination of this group effort, the **Sian Ka'an Biosphere Reserve,** came to fruition. It takes into account land titles, logging, hunting, agriculture, cattle ranching, and tourist development. The local people feel comfortable with it, and in Oct. 1986 Sian Ka'an was officially incorporated into the World Network of Biosphere Reserves of UNESCO.

Several important issues were addressed. Deforestation is becoming commonplace in Quintana Roo as the growing population clears more land for farms and ranches. Even in traditional fishing villages growth is affecting the environment. In Punta Allen, to supplement their income fishermen were turning to the ancient method of slash-and-burn agriculture which for centuries had worked fine for the small groups of people that inhabited the Quintana Roo region. But with the continued systematic destruction of the forest to create new growing fields the entire rainforest along the Caribbean could be destroyed in just a few years.

However, the people need an alternative to support their families. The Amigos de Sian Ka'an and reserve administrators along with the local population have been working in the field (thanks to support from the World Wildlife Fund U.S.) and have come up with an experimental farm (called "el Ramona") which consists of one acre of land transformed by crop rotation and interplanting of various fruit and vegetables. It is an ecologically sound procedure using biodegradable pesticides and a minimum of fertilizers; this allows for constant production of diverse crops. The fishermen at Punta Allen were able to observe an operating prototype and have seen that this "new" method works. The cost of the farm, including a drip irrigation system, construction of a well plus the purchase of a gas pump and plastic tubing was US$2000, within the means of the Punta Allen fishermen. This compromise provides the fishermen with produce, slows deforestation, and creates a self-supporting farm.

Other problems are being dealt with as well. The palm is an important part of the cultural and practical lifestyle of the indigenous people of Quintana Roo. The Maya have for years used two particular types of palm (*Thrinax radiata* and *Coccothrinax readdi*) as thatch for the roofs of their houses, and in the past 10 years fishermen have been selectively cutting *thrinax* to construct lobster traps. It is becoming more difficult to find populations of this palm in the Reserve today. Amigos de Sian Ka'an with World Wildlife Funds, are studying the palms' growth patterns and rates, anticipating a management plan that will encourage future growth. Other problems being faced include limiting commercial fishing, relocating an entire fishing village to a more suitable location which will better support the families, putting up a red light for tourist development where it will endanger the ecology, and a study of the lobster industry and its future. Many more worthwhile projects are waiting in line. Like most ambitious projects, these take a lot of money. If you're

WHAT IS A BIOSPHERE RESERVE?

The biosphere is the thin mantle of the earth in which we live. It consists of parts of the lithosphere, hydrosphere, and atmosphere. The biosphere maintains our life and that of all organisms. We need to protect it and keep it liveable.

The program *Man and Biosphere* was created by UNESCO in 1971, and it deals with the interactions of man with his environment. The program contains various projects, among which the concept of biosphere reserve has gained popularity and has become very important worldwide.

The idea of a biosphere reserve is new in conservation. It promotes the protection of different natural ecosystems of the world, and at the same time allows the presence of human activities through the rational use and development of natural resources on an ecological basis.

A biosphere reserve has a nucleus which is for conservation and limited scientific investigation only. A buffer zone would surround this nucleus in which people may live and use the resources on a regulated, ecological basis. Conservation in a biosphere reserve is the challenge of good use rather than prohibiting use. This concept sets it apart from the national parks in which people are only observers. Biosphere reserves are especially appropriate in Mexico where the conservation and ecomomic development are equally important.

—From the bulletin of the Amigos de Sian Ka'an

interested in helping out, join the booster club. Your donation will really be doing a good job, and you'll get a bulletin/newsletter with fascinating facts about the area and the people as well as updates on current projects. For more detailed information write to: Amigos de Sian Ka'an, Apto Postal 770, Cancun, Quintana Roo, Mexico 77500.

For birders or any visitor intrigued with wildlife and interested in helping the ecological preservation of the Yucatan Peninsula, a brand new bird book, *100 Common Birds Of The Yucatan Peninsula,* by Barbara MacKinnon is available through the Amigos de Sian

Ka'an. All proceeds from the book go to benefit the Quintana Roo Biosphere Reserve. For more information and price write to Amigos de Sian Ka'an, Apto Postal 770, Cancun, Quintana Roo, Mexico 77500.

Another publication, *The Rainforest News*, keeps the world in touch with facts concerning the rainforests of Mesoamerica and a yearly subscription is available with donations of over US$4 per year. For more information, donations, and subscriptions, contact The Rainforest Fund, P.O. Box 140681, Coral Gables, FL 33114. To contact the Mesoamerica Foundation, write to A.P. 1575, Ad. 1, Merida, Yucatan, Mexico.

HISTORY

THE ANCIENTS

Earliest Man
During the Pleistocene Epoch (50,000 B.C.) when the level of the sea fell, men and animals crossed the Bering land bridge from Asia to the American continent. For nearly 50,000 years, man made an epic trek southward until approximately 1000 B.C., when it is believed that the first Indians reached Tierra del Fuego, located at the tip of South America.

As early as 10,000 B.C., Ice Age Man hunted woolly mammoth and other large animals roaming the cool moist landscape of central Mexico. Between 7000 and 2000 B.C., society evolved gradually from hunting and gathering to truly agricultural. Such crops as corn, squash, and beans were independently domesticated in widely separated areas of Mexico after about 6000 B.C. The remains of clay figurines from the Preclassic period, presumed to be fertility symbols, announced the rise of religion in Mesoamerica, beginning around 2000 B.C.

Around 1000 B.C. the Olmec Indian culture spread and the first large-scale ceremonial centers grew along Gulf Coast lands. Much of Mesoamerica was touched and influenced by the spread of these Olmecs' often sinister religion of strange jaguar-like gods, the New World's first calendar, and a beginning system of writing.

Classic Period
The arrival of the Classic Period, about A.D. 300, began what would be hailed as the peak of cultural development among the Maya Indians as well as cultures in other parts of Mexico. Until A.D. 900, phenomenal progress was made in the development of artistic, architectural, and astronomical skills. The most impressive buildings were constructed during this period, and the codices (folded bark books) were written and filled with hieroglyphic symbols that detailed complicated mathematical calculations of time: days, months, and years. Only the priests and privileged held this knowledge, continuing to learn and develop, until for some still unexplained reason (see p. 38 for speculation) there was a sudden halt to this growth.

Postclassic
After A.D. 900, the Toltec influence took hold. This marked the end of the most artistic era; a new militaristic society arose built around a blend of ceremonialism, civic and social organization, and conquest. The Toltecs were achieving their highest expression as Cortes' fleet appeared on the horizon of the Yucatan Peninsula.

COLONIAL HISTORY

Hernan Cortes
Following Columbus' arrival in the New World, other adventurers traveling the same seas quickly found the Yucatan Peninsula. In 1519, 34-year-old Hernan Cortes in an insubordinate act sailed from Cuba without the authority of the Spanish governor, taking 11 ships, 120 sailors, and 550 soldiers searching for slaves. His attack began on the Yucatan coast, encompassed most of Mexico, and continued through years of bloodshed and

Hernan Cortes

death for many of his men. (It didn't *really* end on the Peninsula until the Chan Santa Cruz Indians finally signed a peace treaty with the Mexican Federal Government in 1935, over 400 years later.) Eventually the destruction and elimination of most Indian cultures that had existed throughout Mexico for thousands of years was accomplished. By the time Cortes died in 1547 (while exiled in Spain), the Spanish military and Franciscan friars were well entrenched in the Yucatan.

Diego De Landa

The Franciscan priests were shocked at what they believed to be influences of the devil, such as body mutilation and human sacrifice, in the name of the Maya religion. The Franciscans felt it their duty to God to eliminate these ceremonies and all traces of the Maya cult, and gather the Indians into the fold of Christianity. Friar Diego de Landa, who later became a bishop, was instrumental in destroying thousands of their idols. He oversaw the burning of 27 codices filled with characters and symbols that he could not understand but believed to contain nothing but superstitions and evil lies of the devil. Since then, only three others have been found and studied but remain largely undeciphered. While Landa was directly responsible for destroying the history of these ancient people, he did in fact redeem himself before his death by writing the most complete and detailed account of the life of the Maya in his book *Relaciones de las Cosas de Yucatan.* Landa's book describes daily living in great detail, including growing and preparing food, the structure of society, the priesthood, and sciences. Although he was aware of their sophisticated "count of ages," he didn't understand it. Fortunately, he left a one-line formula which, used as a mathematical and chronological key, opened up the science of Maya calculations and their great knowledge of astronomy.

Landa was called back to Spain in 1563 after complaints from colonial civil and religious leaders accusing him of "despotic mismanagement." He spent a year in prison, and while his guilt or innocence was being decided, he wrote his book in defense of the charges. During his absence, his replacement, Bishop Toral, acted with great compassion toward the Indians. Landa was ultimately cleared and allowed to return to the New World in 1573, where he took up the duties of bishop and quickly resumed his previous methods of proselityzing. He lived in Yucatan until his death in 1579.

PRE-COLUMBIAN?

The word "pre-Columbian" establishes the time before Columbus discovered the New World. His arrival on the scene was the catalyst that would bring to an end the cultures of the period that were then thriving. Some of the ancient cultures had died out many years before the Spanish arrived; but some of them continued beyond 1492, as in the case of the Aztec culture which continued until about 1521. The Maya culture endured (though in much smaller numbers) until well toward the end of the 16th century.

Franciscan Power

Bishop Toral was cut from a different cloth. A humanitarian, he was appalled by the unjust treatment of Indians. Though Toral, after Landa's imprisonment, tried to impose sweeping changes and sent his suggestions to Europe, he was unable to make inroads into the power held by the Franciscans in the Yucatan. Defeated, he ultimately retired to Mexico; it wasn't until a short time before his death (1571) that his reforms were implemented with the "Royal Cedula," which prohibited friars from shaving heads, flogging the Maya, and having prison cells in monasteries; it also called for the immediate release of all Indians held prisoner.

Catholicism

Over the years, the majority of Indians were indeed baptized and made part of the Catholic faith. In fairness, most priests did their best to educate the people, teach them to read and write, and protect them from the growing number of Spanish settlers who used them as slaves. The Indians, then and now, practice Catholicism in their own manner, a combination of their ancient cult beliefs handed down through centuries and Christian doctrine. These mystic yet Christian ceremonies occur in baptism, marriage, courtship, illness, farming, housebuilding, and fiestas.

Further Subjugation

While all of Mexico dealt with the problems of economic colonialism, the Yucatan Peninsula had an additional one: harrassment by vicious pirates who made life on the Gulf coast tenuous. Around 1600, when production of silver began to flag, Spain's economic power faltered. In the following years, haciendas (self-supporting estates or small feudal systems) began to thrive. Before these haciendas, *ejidos* (pre-Columbian Indian villages jointly owning the land and living in a communal society) defined the living situation. But between 1700 and 1810 as Mexico endured the backlash of several government upheavals in Europe, Spanish settlers on the Peninsula began exploiting the native Maya in earnest. The passive Indians were ground down, their lands taken away, and their numbers greatly reduced by the white man's epidemics and mistreatment.

Caste War

The Spaniards grabbed the Maya land and relentlessly planted it with tobacco and sugar cane year after year until the soil was worn out. Coupled with the other abuses it was inevitable that the Indians would ultimately explode in a furious attack. This bloody uprising in the 1840s was called the Caste War. Though the Maya were farmers, not soldiers,

Franciscan church

this savage war saw them taking revenge on every white man, woman, and child by means of rape and violent murder. European survivors made their way to the last Spanish strongholds of Merida and Campeche. The governments of these two cities appealed for help to Spain, France, and the United States. No one answered the call, and it was soon apparent that the remaining two cities would be wiped out. But the fates would not have it that way; just as the governor of Merida was about to begin evacuating the city, the Maya picked up their primitive weapons and walked away.

Sacred Corn

Attuned to the signals of the land, the Maya knew that the appearance of the flying ant was the first sign of rain. Corn was their sustenance, a gift from the gods without which they would not survive. When the rains came, the corn must be in the soil otherwise the gods would be insulted. When, on the brink of destroying the enemy, the winged ant made an unusually early appearance, the Indians turned their backs on certain victory and returned to their villages to plant corn.

This was just the breather the Spanish settlers needed. Help came from Cuba, Mexico City, and 1,000 U.S. mercenary troops. Vengeance was merciless. Most Maya, no matter what their beliefs, were killed. Some were taken prisoner and sold to Cuba as slaves; others left their villages and hid in the jungles, in some cases for decades. Between 1846-1850 the population of the Yucatan Peninsula was reduced from 500,000 to 300,000. Guerilla war ensued, the escaped Maya making sneak attacks upon the whites. Quintana Roo along the Caribbean coast was considered a dangerous no man's land for almost another hundred years. (In 1936, President Lazaro Cardenas declared Quintana Roo a territory under the jurisdiction of the Mexican government; in 1974, with the promise of the birth of tourism, the Territory was admitted to the Federation of States of Mexico.)

Growing Maya Power

In this coastal area of Quintana Roo, the Chan Santa Cruz Indians revived the cult of the "talking cross," a pre-Columbian oracle representing gods of the four cardinal directions. This was a religious/political marriage, with a priest, a master spy, and a ventriloquist in charge, all wise leaders who knew their people's desperate need for divine leadership. As a result of the words from the talking cross, shattered Indians came together in large numbers and began to organize. The community guarded the cross's location, and advice from it continued to strengthen the Maya.

The community, located close to the British Honduras border (present-day Belize), did a thriving business with the British selling timber and buying arms. With these arms in 1857 the Indians took advantage of the internal strife that weakened relations between Spanish Campeche and Merida and would end with Campeche seceding from the state of Yucatan in 1857. The Indians seized the Fort at Bacalar, which put them in control of the entire Caribbean coast from Cabo Catouche to the border of British Honduras, and in three years destroyed numerous towns, slaughtering or capturing thousands of whites.

The Indians of the coastal community of Chan Santa Cruz became known as Cruzobs. For years they murdered their captives, but starting in 1858 they took lessons from the colonials and began to keep whites for slave labor in the fields and forest; women were put to work doing household chores and some were concubines. For the next 40 years, the Chan Santa Cruz Indians kept the east coast of the Yucatan for themselves; a shaky truce with the Mexican government endured. The Indians were financially independent, self-governing, and with no roads in, totally isolated from technological advancements beginning to take place in other parts of the Peninsula. They were not at war so long as everyone left them alone and stayed away.

The Last Stand

It was only when President Porfirio Diaz took power in 1877 that the Mexican federal government began to think about the Yucatan Peninsula. It rankled Diaz that a handful of Indians had been able to keep the Mexican federal army at bay for so long. In 1901 under the command of army General Ignacio Bravo the feds made a new assault on the Indians. The general captured a village, laid railroad tracks, and built a walled fort. Supplies got through the jungle to the fort by way of the railroad, but General Bravo also suffered at the hands of the clever Indians; the garrison was besieged for a year until reinforcements arrived from the capital and the upstarts were finally put down. Brutal Mexican occupation continued from 1901 till 1915, but the scattered Indians didn't give up. They persisted with guerilla raids from the rainforest until the Mexicans pulled out and returned Quintana Roo to the Maya. From 1917 till 1920 hundreds of thousands of Indians died from influenza and smallpox epidemics (introduced by the Spanish). An Indian leader, General May, took stock of his troops, and it was apparent that the old soldiers were fading. They put up a long tough battle to hold onto their land and culture. In 1920, the chicle boom began bringing chicleros to work the trees—it was then that General May demanded (and received) a negotiated settlement. In 1935 the Chan Santa Cruz Indians signed a peace treaty with the Mexican Federals. Now came a time of new beginnings, new growth, and another era of government.

MODERN TIMES

Meanwhile, in the northern part of the Peninsula, prosperity settled upon Merida, capital of the state of Yucatan. In 1875, the henequen boom began. Twine and rope made from the sword-shaped leaves of this variety of agave plant were in demand all over the world. Merida became the jewel of the Peninsula. Spanish haciendas with their Indian slaves cultivated the easily grown plant, and for miles the outlying areas were planted with the henequen which required little rainfall and thrived in the Peninsula's thin rocky soil. Beautiful mansions were built by entrepreneurs who led the gracious life, sending their children to Europe to be educated, taking their wives by ship to New Orleans, looking for new luxuries and entertainment. Port towns were developed on the Gulf coast, and a two-km-long wharf named Progreso was built to accommodate the large ships that came for sisal (hemp from the henequen plant). The only thing that didn't change was the lifestyle of the *peone.* The Indian peasants' life was still (reluctantly) lacking in human rights; they labored long hard hours to keep henequen production up. Living in constant debt to the company store, where their meager peso wage was spent before it was received, the Indians were caught up in a cycle of bondage that existed for many years in Merida. During this time the lovely *huipil* (Indian dress) was mandated to be worn by all mestizos (those of mixed blood) on the Peninsula.

Hacienda Wealth

The outside world was becoming aware of the Peninsula, its newly found economic activity, and its rich *patrones.* In 1908, an American journalist, John Kenneth Turner, stirred things up when he documented how difficult for the Indians and how prosperous for the owners life was on a henequen plantation. From this time forward, change was inevitable. In 1915, wealthy hacienda owners were compelled to pay an enormous tax to then President Venustiano Carranza. This tax was extracted under duress and the watchful eye of General Alvarado and 7,000 armed soldiers, who needed the money to put down revolutionists Emiliano Zapata and Pancho Villa in the northern sections of Mexico. Millions of pesos changed hands.

The next thorn in the side of the hacienda owners was upstart Felipe Carrillo Puerto, the first Socialist governor of Merida. Under his tutelage the Indians set up a labor union, educational center, and political clubs— "leagues of resistance." These leagues gave the *peones* the first secular hope ever held out to them. Through the leagues, workers wielded a power wealthy Yucatecans were forced to acknowledge. Carrillo pushed on, making agrarian reforms at every turn. He decreed that abandoned haciendas were up for appropriation. He was very successful, so much so that his opponents began to worry seriously about the power he was amassing. With his followers growing conservatives knew he must be stopped and saw only one

henequen

way out. In 1923 Felipe Carrillo Puerto was assassinated—but not his cause.

The Revolution

A continual fight against wealthy landowners and the power-elite followed Carrillo's murder. In the south, Emiliano Zapata was demanding land reform; shortly thereafter, the revolution put an end to the uneven control of wealth in the country. The new constitution (1917) was instrumental in dividing the large haciendas, giving the country back to the people, and making sweeping political changes. The education of all children was decreed, and schools were built to implement it. Power of the church was curtailed and land redistributed. In this war of ideals, communal groups were broken up and turmoil continued; it wasn't until recent years that the Indians have benefited from this land division, when President Lazaro Cardenas (1934-40) gave half the usable land in Quintana Roo to the poor.

Mexican Unity

Between 1934-40, the Mexican government nationalized most of the foreign companies that were taking more out of the country than they were putting in. Mexico passed through a series of economic setbacks but gained a unity and a national self-confidence that enthusiastically heralded the economic strides to come. Like a crawling child trying to walk, the country took many falls. But progress continued, the people of the country saw more jobs, fairer wages, and more products on the market—until the 1970s.

During the '70s, inflation began to grow, and by 1976 it was totally out of hand. Mexico was pricing itself out of the market, both for tourists and capital investors. Ultimately, a change in the money policy let the peso float and find its own value against the dollar. This legislation brought back tourists and investors. The condition of the peso is a boon for visitors, but a burden for the people. The belief is that enough foreigners coming and spending their money will create more jobs so that in time the economic condition will remedy itself. Based on this belief, smart Mexican businesspeople began developing the natural beauty of the Caribbean coast, and indeed visitors are coming from all over the world.

ECONOMY

Mexico is trying valiantly to pull itself out of the realm of a developing country and continues to make rapid strides in economic growth. The average yearly wage per person has grown to the equivalent of US$2000, but inflation defeats the gains that have been made. However, the country has many natural resources to work with and if it can begin to control inflation it will be able to make use of them and provide jobs to keep up with the rapid population growth.

World's Largest City
Mexico is suffering from a population explosion. Mexico City, with 20 million people, is the largest city in the world. Each year 800,000 people enter the city's job market; only 400,000 jobs are available. Roughly 65% of the national population resides in cities, partly due to continuing migration from rural areas. In addition, a certain number of young Mexican adults, many accompanied by their families, try to make their way across the U.S. border, where there's more hope of getting jobs; about six million Mexicans presently live in the U.S. Because of this leave-the-land movement, the country's agriculture has suffered. Mexico imports corn, cereals, and sugar, among other products, and exports coffee, cotton, sisal, honey, bananas, and beef cattle.

Industries
Mexico's chief industries are oil, mining, and tourism. After the oil industry was nationalized in 1938, a time of transition slowed down production. Pemex, the state oil corporation, does not belong to the Organization of Petroleum Exporting Countries (OPEC), but keeps its prices in line with it. Most of the oil produced in Mexico is shipped to the U.S. (its number-one customer), Canada, Israel, France, and Japan. Rich in natural gas, the country sends the U.S. 10% of its total output. Two-thirds of Mexico's export revenue comes from fossil fuels.

Mexico is still the world's largest producer of silver and fluorspar. It also processes large quantities of barite, antimony, bismuth, copper, and sulphur. Other minerals mined are gold, tin, manganese, zinc, coal, and iron. Although mining has always been important to the economy of Mexico, growth of the industry is slow, about a 2% increase per year. Around 60% of the country's industrial plants are concentrated around Mexico City though

Many shops do a good business selling souvenirs.

the government is developing petrochemical processing industries along the U.S. border.

The Yucatan
Without question the leading moneymaker on the Peninsula is the oil business. Along the Gulf coast from Campeche south into the state of Tabasco, the oil industry is booming. Yucatan cities are beginning to show the signs of good financial health. Yucatecan fisheries are abundant along the Gulf coast. At one time fishing was not much more than a "ma-and-pa" business here, but today fleets of large purse seiners with their adjacent processing plants can be seen just south of the city of Campeche and on Isla del Carmen. With this renewed interest in preserving fishing grounds for the future, the industry could continue to thrive for many years.

Products from the U.S. such as dresses and leather goods are begun in the States, then sent to Mexico to be completed by the cheaper labor force. These *maquiladoras* plants are enthusiastically being developed. Tourism is developing into the number-two contributor to the economy. Going with a good thing, the government has set up a national trust to finance a program of developing beautiful areas of the country to attract visitors.

Cancun
Until recently the economy of the lost territory of Quintana Roo amounted to very little. For a few years the chicle boom brought a flurry of activity centered around the harbor of Isla Cozumel. Native and hardwood trees have always been in demand; coconuts and fishing were the only other natural resources that added to the economy—but none on a large scale. Today the face of Quintana Roo is changing. Tourism is its number-one attraction with the development of an offshore sandbar, Cancun, into a million-dollar resort. Building and construction is continuing south along the coast with new roads giving access

developing Cancun

to until-now unknown beaches and often unseen Maya structures. Cancun is one successful result. This overgrown sandbar is one of Mexico's most modern and popular resorts. Other naturally attractive sites are earmarked for future development. Extra attention is also being given to archaeological zones ignored for hundreds of years: building restrooms, ticket offices, and fences to keep out vandals.

Travel in Mexico gets better every day. For the Mexican people, the deflated peso is a sock in the eye. For the traveler in Mexico, the dollar is worth more than ever and is attracting visitors in large numbers which in turn helps Mexico's economy. Now is definitely the time to take a vacation in Quintana Roo.

THE PEOPLE

For hundreds of years, scholars of the world have asked, "What happened to the Maya people?" Their magnificent structures, built with such advanced skill, still stand. Many carvings, unique statuary, and even a few colored frescoes remain. All of this art depicts a world of intelligent human beings living in a well-organized, complex society. It's apparent their trade and agricultural methods supported a large population. Scholars agree the Maya was the most advanced of all ancient Mesoamerica cultures. Yet all signs point to an abrupt work stoppage. After around A.D. 900, no buildings were constructed, and no stelae, carefully detailing names and dates to inform future generations of their roots, were erected. So what happened? Where did the people go?

Traveling through the Peninsula, it becomes apparent that *the people* didn't go far! In every village you are greeted with the same faces and profiles that are frozen in carved panels displayed on elegant structures throughout Mayaland. Anthropologists and historians do know that thousands, perhaps as many as 500,000, were decimated by such diseases as smallpox after the arrival of the Spaniards. But no one really knows for sure what halted the progress of the Maya culture.

A Society Collapses

Priests and noblemen, the guardians of religion, science, and the arts, conducted their ritual ceremonies and studies in the large stone pyramids and platforms today found in ruins throughout the jungle. More specific questions arise: what happened to the priests and noblemen? Why were the centers abandoned? What happened to the knowledge of the intelligentsia who studied the skies, wrote the books, and designed the pyramids? Theories abound. Some speculate about a revolution of the people or decentralization with the arrival of outside influences. Others suggest the Indians tired of subservience and

were no longer willing to farm the land to provide food, clothing, and support for the priests and nobles. Whatever happened, it's clear that the special knowledge concerning astronomy, hieroglyphics, and architecture was apparently not passed on to Maya descendants. Sociologists who have lived with Indians in isolated villages are convinced that this privileged information is no longer known by today's Maya. Why did the masses disperse, leaving once-sacred stone cities unused and ignored? It's possible that lengthy periods of drought, famine, and epidemic caused the people to leave their once-glorious sacred centers. No longer important in day-to-day life, these structures were ignored for a thousand years and faced the whimsy of nature and its corroding elements.

The Maya question may never be answered with authority. One non-conforming theory suggests that these stone cities were built by people from outer space. Another considers the possibility that the descendants of the Maya today are no relation to the people who built the structures, made near-perfect astronomical observations, and discovered infinity a thousand years ago—instead a society long gone.

Modern Times

However, there's hope in today's technology. Astronauts, for example, have seen many wonders from outer space. Spotting within the thick uninhabited jungle of the Yucatan many untouched structures, large treasures of knowledge just waiting to be rediscovered. As new finds are made, the history of the Maya develops new depth and breadth. Archaeologists, ethnologists, art historians, and linguists continue to unravel the ongoing mystery with constant new discoveries of temples and artifacts, each with a story to tell. Native writings such as the *Chalam Balam* follow the history and traditions of the period just before the Spanish came, and a few books written soon after the Spanish conquest provide vivid first-hand accounts of Maya life in its last days of cultural purity, especially Diego de Landa's complete description of Maya life, *Relaciones de las Cosas de Yucatan*.

PHYSICAL CHARACTERISTICS

Maya men and women average 1.62 and 1.50 meters tall respectively. Muscular bodied, they have straight black hair, round heads, broad faces with pronounced cheekbones, aquiline noses, almond-shaped dark eyes, and eyelids with the epicanthic or Mongolian fold (a prolongation of a fold of the upper eyelid over the inner angle or both angles of the eye). Some of the highland groups, such as the Tzeltals and Tzotzils, have elongated heads—perhaps as a result of their centuries-long geographic and genetic isolation.

contraption used to flatten the heads of the newborn

Stylized Beauty

Bishop Diego de Landa writes in his *Relaciones* that when the Spanish arrived, the Maya still practiced the ancient method of flattening a newborn's head with a press made of boards. By pressing the infant's forehead, the fronto-nasal portion of the face was pushed forward, as can be seen in carvings and other human depictions from the pre-Columbian period; this was considered a very important sign of beauty. Further, they dangled a bead in front of a baby's eyes to encourage cross-eyedness, another Maya beauty mark. Dental mutilation was practiced by filing the teeth to give them different shapes or by making slight perforations and inlaying pyrite, jade, or turquoise. Tattooing and scarification were accomplished by lightly cutting a design into the skin and purposely infecting it, creating a scar of beauty. Adult noblemen often wore a phony nosepiece to give the illusion of an even longer nose sweeping back into the long flat forehead.

The Maya Bloodline

In the past, few outsiders ever stayed long in the Yucatan. Wherever the Spanish had a stronghold, the purity of Spanish blood precluded contact with the Indian slaves. Mixed marriages were not permitted. Even as recently as the turn of this century, cities boasted about their pure line of Spanish blood, particularly the towns of Izamal and Merida. Similarly, isolation of the Indian people kept the Maya pure. Their resemblance to the people of a thousand years ago is thus understandable, but still amazing!

Today, 75-80% of the entire population of Mexico is estimated to be mestizo (mixed blood, mostly Indian and Spanish), with 10-15% pure Indian. (For comparison, as recently as 1870, pure-blooded Indians made up over 50% of the population.) While no statistics are available, it's believed most of the 15% who are pure Indian live on the Peninsula.

ANCIENT CULTURE OF THE
YUCATAN PENINSULA

RELIGION AND SOCIETY

The Earth

The Maya saw the world as a layered flat square. At the four corners (each representing a cardinal direction) stood four bearded gods called Becabs that held up the skies. In the underworld, four gods called Pahuatuns steadied the earth. The layered skies and underworld were divided with a determined number of steps up and down. The gods and each direction were associated with colors: black for west, white for north, yellow for south, and most important, red for east. In the center of the earth stood the Tree of Life, *la ceiba*. Its powerful roots reached the underworld, and its lofty foliage swept the heavens, connecting the two. The *ceiba* was associated with the color blue-green (*yax*) along with all important things—water, jade, and new corn.

The Indians were terrorized by the underworld and what it represented: odious rivers of rotting flesh and blood and evil gods such as Jaguar, god of the night, whose spotty hide was symbolized by the starry sky. Only the priests could communicate with and control the gods. For this reason, the populace was content to pay tribute to and care for all the needs of the priests.

Ceremonies

Ceremony appears to have been a vital part of the daily lives of the Maya. Important rituals took place on specific dates of their accurate calendar; everyone took part. These often bizarre activities were performed in the plazas, on the platforms, and around the broad grounds of the temple-cities. Sweat baths are commonly found at the centers and were incorporated into the religion. Some rituals were secret and only priests took part within the inner sanctums of the temple.

Other ceremonies included fasts, abstinences, purification, dancing, prayers, and simple sacrifices of food, animals, or possessions (jewelry, beads, and ceramics) amid clouds of smoky incense. The later Maya took part in self-mutilation. Frequently, carvings found depict an Indian pulling a string of thorns through a hole in his tongue or penis and the blood that ensued. The most brutal were sacrifices including death by a variety of causes. Sacrificial victims were thrown into a sacred well; if they didn't drown within a certain length of time (often overnight), they were rescued and then expected to relate the conversation of the spirits that lived in the bottom of the well. Other methods of sacrifice were spearing, beheading, or removing the heart of the victim with a knife and offering it still beating to the spirits.

Sacrifices were made to gain the approval of the gods. Although old myths and stories say young female virgins were most often sacrificed in the sacred *cenotes,* anthropological dredging and diving in the muddy water in various Peninsula ruins has turned up evidence proving most of the victims were young children, both male and female.

Time

The priests of the Classic Period represented time as a parade of gods who were really numbers moving through Maya eternity in careful mathematical order. They were shown carrying heavy loads with tumplines around their heads. The combination of the gods and their burdens reflected the exact number of days gone by since the beginning of the Maya calendar count. Each god has particular characteristics; number nine, an attractive young man with the spots of a serpent on his chin, sits leaning forward, jade necklace dangling on one knee, right hand reaching up to adjust his tumpline. His load is the screech owl of the *baktun* (the 144,000-day period). Together, the two represent nine times 144,000, or 1,296,000 days—the number of days elapsed since the beginning of the Maya day count and the day the glyph was carved, maybe 1,275 years ago. Archaeologists call this a Long Count date. Simpler methods also were used, including combina-

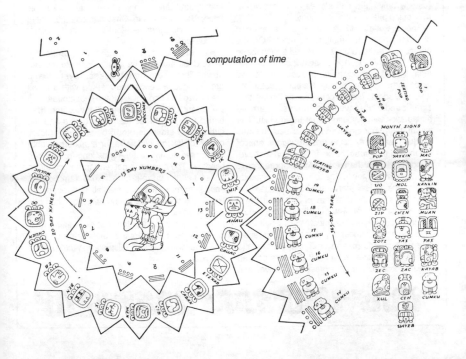

computation of time

A CEREMONY FOR CHAC

Maya rituals are still practiced for many occasions, but usually within the confines of the village or the home—seldom when outsiders are around. These rituals are a fascinating marriage of Catholic and Maya mysticism. At a *Chachaac* rite, a Maya priest and the people beseech the rain god Chac for help. The altar (often set up in a clearing in a jungle) is made of poles and branches that would be at home in a Catholic church. With four distinct corners (with a tall candle at each), the altar has been dedicated to the four cardinal points—sacred in the Maya cult. In the center is a crucifix with a figure of Christ dressed, not in a loincloth, but in a white skirt embroidered with bright red flowers like a *huipil*.

The priest is a reverred village elder and is brought offerings of cigarettes, soda pop, sometimes food, maybe a raw chicken. Onlookers (usually only men) find stones and sit down in front of the priest for the ceremony.

The cigarette offerings are placed on one end of the altar next to small gourd bowls. On the ground nearby lies a plastic-covered trough made from a hollowed log. At the beginning of the ceremony (dusk), the priest lifts a plastic sheet and drops something into the log. He pours water into a bucket, adding ground corn and mixing it with a small bundle of leaves and kneels on an old burlap sack with a young helper beside him. The two of them pray quietly in Maya dialect to Chac for quite awhile. At some unseen signal, one of the men in the group throws incense on a shovel of hot coals; as the exotic aroma spreads the priest begins praying in Spanish. Everyone stands up and chants Hail Marys and Our Fathers. The priest dips his sheaf of leaves in a gourd and scatters consecrated water in all directions—now the ceremony begins in earnest.

Young boys sit under the altar and make repetitive frog sounds (a sign of coming rain) while gourds of the sacred corn drink *zaca* are passed to each person. Christian prayers continue, and more *zaca* is passed around. The ceremony continues for many hours with occasional rests in between. Bubbling liquid sounds come from the log trough. It's a mixture of honey, water, and bark from a *balche* tree.

As the evening passes the priest takes intermittent naps between rounds of prayers. The men occasionally stop and drink beer, or smoke a cigarette from the altar. The young acolyte gently nudges the napping priest and the praying starts again. Each round of prayers lasts about 45 minutes, and nine rounds continue throughout the night. No one leaves, and the fervor of the prayers never diminishes.

At dawn, after a lengthier than usual round of prayers, the priest spreads out polished sacred divination stones on a burlap sack and studies them for some time. Everyone watches him intently and after a long silence, he shakes his head. The verdict is in, Chac has communicated that there will be no rain for the village this planting season.

The sun comes up and the men prepare a feast. Chac must not be insulted despite the bad news. Thick corn dough cakes, layered with ground squash seeds and marked with a cross are placed in a large pit lined with hot stones. The cakes are covered with palm leaves and then buried with dirt. While the bread bakes and the gift-chicken stews in broth, blood, and spices, gourds of *balche*, coca cola, or a mixture of both are passed around to all—for as long as they can handle it. The mixture is not fermented enough to be as hallucinogenic as it is proclaimed, but enough to make a strong man ill. The rest of the morning is spent feasting and drinking. Chac has spoken, so be it.

The priest accurately forecast the weather that night; no rain fell the rest of that spring or summer. The villagers didn't raise corn in their *milpas* that year.

tions of dots and bars (ones and fives, respectively, with special signs for zero). Most Mayanists agree that the date of the beginning of the Long Count was August 10, 3114 B.C.

Status

If the Maya's sophisticated calendar sounds complicated to you, so will the complex, stratified society that made up the Maya civilization. Their society of many classes was headed by the elite, who controlled matters of warfare, religion, government, and commerce. Also in this group were architects who designed the magnificent temples and pyramids. Skilled masons belonged to a class that included servants of royalty. Priests directed the people in the many rites and festivals required of a realm governed by a pantheon of gods who demanded constant homage and penance.

Farmers were instrumental in maintaining the social order. They battled a hostile environment, constantly fighting the jungle and frequent droughts. Creativity enabled them to win out most of the time. They slashed fields from rainforest, constructed raised plots in swampy depressions, and built irrigation canals. In some areas farmers terraced the land to conserve soil and water. The results of working by hand and using stone and wood tools were sufficient to feed a population that ultimately grew to large numbers. All aspects of Maya life maintained a close relationship to Maya religion.

THE ARTS

Pottery

The Maya were outstanding potters. Some of the earliest Maya pottery art is dated to 36 B.C. and found at Izapan. Evidence of artistic advancement is apparent with the variety of new forms, techniques, and artistic motifs that developed during the Classic Period. Growth has been traced from simple monochrome ceramics of early periods to bichrome and later to rich polychrome; polychrome drawings on pottery work has been found with recognizable color still visible.

Though the Maya did not use the wheel in day-to-day life, they built this small toy animal with wheels.

Three-legged plates with a basal edge and small conical supports, as well as covered and uncovered vessels, were prevalent. A jar with a screw-on lid was found recently in Rio Azul, a Maya site in an isolated corner of Guatemala; an amazing find!

Figurines, especially those found in graves on the island of Jaina, were faithful reproductions of the people and their times. Many decorated pottery vessels used for everyday purposes tell us something about these people who enjoyed a touch of class along with the mundane. Decorative motifs ranged from simple geometric designs to highly stylized natural figures to simple true-to-life reproductions. We have learned much from Maya artists' realistic representations of their bodies (even of those that were pathologically deformed) and garments and adornments that were typical of their time. Through this precise method we get a glimpse into the lives of people of all social classes: common men and women, noblemen and priests, musicians, craftsmen, merchants, warriors, ballplayers, even animals. Many of these clay figurines were used as flutes, whistles, ocarinas, rattles, or incense holders. Noteworthy are the quantity of female figurines that represent the fertility goddess Ixchell.

Sculpture

The Maya used their great talent for sculpture almost exclusively to decorate temples and sanctuaries. They employed a variety of techniques depending on the areas and what natural resources were available. They excelled in free-standing stone carving, such as the stelae and altars. In areas, such as Palenque, where stone wasn't as available, stucco art is outstanding. The Indians added rubber to the plaster-and-water mixture, creating an extremely durable surface that would polish to a fine luster. In Palenque you'll see marvelous

examples of stucco bas-reliefs adorning pyramids, pillars, stairways, walls, friezes, masks, and heads. Sculpting was done not only in stone but also in precious materials such as gold and silver. Some of the Mayas' finest work was done in jade, a substance they held in great reverence.

Painting

Paints were of mineral and vegetable origin in hues of red, yellow, brown, blue, green, black, and white. Mural painting reached a high degree of expression by the Maya. Murals found in several ancient sites depict everyday life, ceremonies, and battle scenes in brilliant colors. Bright color was also applied to the carved stone structures, pyramids and stelae. Today all color has disappeared from the outside of these buildings along with most of the finishing plaster that was used as a smooth coating over large building stones. When Cortes' men first viewed the coast of Tulum, it must have been quite a sight to behold: brilliantly colored buildings in the midst of lush green jungle overlooking a clear turquoise sea.

SCIENCE

Maya inscriptions relate to calculations of time, mathematics, and the gods. Astronomy was also a highly developed science integrated within the cult. The Maya shared their calendar system and concept of zero with other Mesoamerican groups. But they went on to perfect and develop their sophisticated calendar, more exact to a ten-thousandth of a day than the Gregorian Calendar in use today.

Hieroglyphics

The hieroglyphics the Maya used in scientific calculations and descriptions are seen everywhere on the Yucatan Peninsula, in carved temple panels, on pyramid steps, and in stelae commonly installed in front of the great structures, carrying pertinent data about the building and people of that era. The most important examples of the system are the three codices that were not destroyed with the coming of the conquistadores. In the codices, symbols were put carefully on pounded fig bark with brushes and various dyes developed from plants and trees. As with all fine Maya art, it was the upper class and priests who learned, developed, and became highly skilled in hieroglyphics. When they suddenly and inexplicably stopped functioning around A.D. 900, long before the Spanish arrived on the Peninsula, science and artwork gradually ceased.

MAYA "BASKETBALL"

Ballparks were prevalent in the ceremonial centers located throughout the Yucatan Peninsula. Though today's Maya are peaceful, at one time bloody games were part of the ancient cult as seen from the remaining artwork (for example the panel in Chichen Itza's Temple of the Bearded Man). The carvings graphically show that either the losing (or as a few far-out scientists have suggested) the winning team was awarded a bloody death. The players were heavily padded with leather, and the object of the game was to hit a hard rubber ball into a cement ring attached to a wall eight meters off the ground. Legend says the game went on for hours and the winners (or losers) were awarded clothes and jewelry from the spectators.

HOUSING

Thanks to remaining stone carvings, we know how the ancient Maya lived. We know that their houses were almost identical to the *palapa* huts that many people still live in today. Huts were built with tall thin sapling trees placed close together forming the walls, then topped with a *palapa* roof. This type of house provided circulation through the walls, and the thick *palapa* roof allowed the rain to run off easily, keeping the inside snug and dry. In the early years there were no real doors and few furnishings. Then as now, families slept in hammocks, the coolest way to sleep. For the rare times that it turned cold, tiny fires were built on the floor below the hammocks to keep the family warm. Most of the cooking was done either outdoors or in another hut. Often a small group of people (extended family) built their huts together on one plot and lived almost a communal lifestyle. If one member of the group brought home a deer, everyone shared in this trophy. Though changing, this is still commonplace throughout the rural areas of the Peninsula.

little boy and typical hut

SPANISH CULTURE

Cortes' arrival was greeted by a peasant culture. According to Bishop de Landa, the people still practiced the ancient cult, but the huge stone monoliths were already being overtaken by the jungle. It was inevitable that the Spanish culture would ultimately supplant the Indians'. Maya books were destroyed and the Indians themselves overpowered by the

Yucatan hammocks have a reputation for being the best in the world. Many local people sleep in them and love it. *Hamacas* are cool, easy to store, make wonderful cribs that babies cannot fall out of (at least not easily), and come in a variety of sizes.

It's important to know the size you want when shopping. The Yucatecans make a matrimonial which is supposed to be big enough for two persons to sleep comfortably; for even more comfort, ask for the familiar, weavers say the whole family fits! A good hammock stretches out to approximately five meters long (one-third of which is the woven section), and the width three to five meters pulled out (gently, don't stretch!). Check the end strings, called *brazos;* there should be at least 100 to 150 triple loops for a *matrimonial.*

A variety of materials is used: synthetics, henequen, cotton, and linen. It's a toss-up whether the best is pure cotton or linen. The finer the thread the more comfortable; the tighter the weave the more resilient. Experts say it takes eight km of thread for a *matrimonial.*

Spanish belief that Maya ways were evil. Ultimately, the old beliefs and Catholic orthodoxy were mixed in a strange rendition of Christianity. Surprisingly, the Catholic priests accept this marriage of religions, and it can be seen today in many functions and holiday celebrations. In small rural pockets that have had little contact with the modern world, certain customs and ceremonies still take place, but in secret. The Maya learned their lessons the hard way, and some anthropologists believe that they still maintain an underground pipeline of the ancient culture. However, as more tourists and travelers come into the area, this culture is becoming diluted with modern ways.

TODAY'S CULTURAL CHARACTERISTICS

Language

The farther away you go from a city, the less Spanish is spoken—only Maya or a dialect of Maya is heard. The government estimates that of the ten million Mexican Indians in the country, about 25% speak only an Indian dialect. Of the original 125 native languages, 70 are still spoken. Of this number, 20 are different Maya languages, including Tzeltal, Tzotzil, Chol, and Yucatec Mayan. (Though mandatory education in Mexico was initiated in 1917, like most laws, this one didn't reach the Yucatan Peninsula till quite recently.) Despite efforts to integrate the Indian into Mexican society, many remain content with the status quo. Schools throughout the Peninsula use Spanish-language books, even though many of these children speak only some form of Maya. In some of the smaller schools in rural areas (such as in Akumal), bilingual teachers (Spanish and local dialects) are recruited to help children make the transition.

Higher Education

For years, Peninsula students wanting an education had to travel to the university at Merida. The number of students going on to college grows with each generation and universities are slowly being built. The state of

teacher and students along the Caribbean coast

Quintana Roo still does not have a university, but college is available in Campeche and Tabasco; and a second one has been built in Merida.

Today's Housing

The major difference in today's rural housing is the growth of the *ranchito*. Only one hut sits on a family farm where corn and sometimes a few pigs and turkeys, maybe even a few head of cattle, are raised. The Indians have become slightly more comfortable than their ancestors, with a table and chairs, lamp, and maybe a metal bathtub as the only furnishings in their homes. In the southern Quintana Roo huts are often built of planks with tin roofs. In the north more are constructed with stucco walls. The only modern touch to the house design is the frequently seen electric meter and wires poking through even the sapling walls. Many huts have electric lighting and often radios; some even have refrigerators.

Family

Small children in Mexico are treated with great love and care. Until recently families always had many children. A man validated his masculinity with a large family, the more children, the more respect. The labor around the family plot was happily doled out to each as they came along. Today's young couples encounter the same problem that plague parents everywhere: the expense of raising children is increasing. Just providing the basics—food, clothing, housing—is creating havoc for the poorer families. Though education is free, many rural parents need their children to help with work on the *ranchito*. That and the cost of books still prevent many Yucatecan children from getting a higher education. Gradually this is changing, and the government is trying to impress upon the people the importance of education by providing school in all areas.

FIESTAS AND CELEBRATIONS

Mexico knows how to give a party! Everyone who visits the Yucatan should take advantage of any holidays falling during the visit. Workers are given a day off on legal holidays. See chart, p. 52 for dates of the biggest fiestas.

As well as the public festivities listed, a birthday, baptism, saint's day, wedding, leaving, returning, good crop, and many more reasons than we'd ever think of are good excuses to celebrate with a fiesta. One of the simplest but most charming celebrations is Mother's Day in Playa del Carmen. Children both young and old serenade mothers (often with a live band) with beautiful music outside their windows on the evening of the holiday. If invited to a fiesta, join in and have fun. Even the most humble family manages to scrape together money for a great party on these occasions.

tacos, *refrescos* (soft drinks), *churros* (fried dough dusted with sugar), *carne asada* (barbecued meat), and plenty of beer chilling in any convenient ice-filled container.

Beware "The Egg"

You'll find innocent-looking little old ladies selling the "dreaded eggshell" filled with confetti, ready to be smashed on an unsuspecting head. So be prepared if you're the only gringo around! Your head or any convenient body part will be pummeled with the colorful bombs by anyone tall enough. This is followed by a quick getaway and lots of giggles from onlookers. The more you respond good naturedly, the more you will continue to be the target—and what the heck, whether the headache is from too much beer or too many eggs doesn't matter. (Besides, it might be time for you to plunk out a few pesos for your own bombs!

Village Festivities

More money means fancier fireworks. Half the fun is watching preparations which generally take all day and involve everyone. Both big and little kids get goose bumps watching the *especialista* wrapping and tying bamboo poles together with mysterious packets of paper-wrapped explosives. At some point this often tall *castillo* (structure holding the fireworks) will be tilted up and admired by all. Well after dark, at the height of the celebration, the colorful explosives are set off with a spray of light and sound and appreciative cheers of delight.

Village fiestas are a wonderful time of dancing, music, noise, colorful costumes, good food, and usually lots of drinking. A public fiesta is generally held in the central plaza surrounded by temporary stalls where you can get Mexican fast food: tamales (both sweet and meat), *bunuelos* (sweet rolls),

A Marriage Of Cultures

Many festivals in Mexico are in honor of religious feast days. You'll see a unique combination of religious fervor and ancient cult mixed with plain old good times. In the church plaza, dances that have been passed down from family to family since before Cortes introduced Christianity to the New World continue for hours. Dancers dress in symbolic costumes of bright colors, feathers, and bells, reminding crowds of onlookers about their Maya past. Inside the church is a constant stream of candlecarrying devout, some traveling long distances to *perigrinate* (make a devout journey), sometimes even traveling several km entirely on their knees to the church, repaying a promise made to a deity months before in thanks for a personal favor, a healing, job found, or who knows what.

continued on page 51

BULLFIGHTING

The bullfight is not for everyone. Many foreigners feel it's inhumane treatment of a helpless animal. There *is* bloodletting. If you can't tolerate this sort of thing, you'd probably be happier not attending a bullfight. Bullfighting is big business in Mexico, Spain, Portugal, and South America. The *corrida de toros* (running of the bulls) is made up of a troupe of (now) well-paid men all playing an important part in the drama. In the country's largest arena (in Mexico City), 50,000 people fill it for each performance on Sundays and holidays. The afternoon starts off (promptly at 1600) with music and a colorful parade of solemn pomp with *matadores* and *picadores* on horseback and *banderilleros,* plus drag mules and many ring attendants. The *matadores* ceremoniously circle the crowded arena to the roar of the crowd. The afternoon has begun!

Traditional customs of the ring have not changed in centuries. The *matador* is the star of the event. This ceremony is a test of man and his courage. He's in the arena for one purpose, to kill the bull—but bravely and with classic moves. First the preliminary *quites* and then a series of graceful *veronicas* heightens the excitement brushing

the treacherous horns with each move. The *matador* wills the animal to come closer with each movement of the *muleta*. He is outstanding if he performs his ballet as close to the bull's horns as possible (oh, how the crowd cheers!). He must elude the huge beast with only a subtle turn of his body (now they love him!). To add to the excitement, he does much of this on his knees. At *the hour of truth,* the crowd gives its permission for the *matador* to dedicate the bull to a special person in the crowd. He throws his *montera* (hat) to the honored person and will now show his stuff.

At just the right moment he slips the *estoque* into the bull's neck. If he's an artist, he will sever the aorta and the huge animal immediately slumps to the ground and dies instantly. If the *matador* displays extraordinary grace, skill, and bravery, the crowd awards him the ears and the tail, and their uncontrollable respect.

Bullfighting has long been one of the most popular events in Mexico. *Aficionados* of this Spanish artform thrill to the excitement of the crowd, the stirring music, the grace and courage of a noble *matador*, and the bravery of a good bull. A student of Mexican culture will want to take part in

continued

continued from previous page
the *corrida,* to learn more about this powerful art. *Art* is the key word. A bullfight is not a fight, it is an artistic scene of pageantry and ceremony handed down from the middle ages that was celebrated all over Europe.

Records of the first primitive bullfight come to us from the island of Crete, 2,000 years before the time of Christ. At the same time in Spain savage wild bulls roamed the Iberian peninsula. When faced with killing one of these vicious animals, young men, not to be outdown by the Cretons, would "dance" as closely as possible to the brute to show their bravery before finally killing the animal with an axe.

The Romans began importing Spanish wild bulls for Colosseum spectacles and the Arabs in Spain stimulated *tauromachia* (bullfighting). In 1090, El Cid (Rodrigo Diaz de Vivar), the hero of Valencia and subject of romantic legend, is believed to have fought in the first *organized* bull festival. He lanced and killed a wild bull from the back of his horse showing great skill. In this era, only noblemen were allowed to use a lance, and the *corrida* soon became the sport of kings. Even Julius Caesar is said to have gotten in the ring with a wild bull. Bullfighting quickly became popular, and it was *the* daring event for the rich. Spain's ancient Roman colosseums (such as in Merida) were used. A feast day celebration wasn't complete without a *corrida de toros.* The number of noblemen killed while participating in this wild event began to grow.

To try to stop the *corrida,* Pope Pius V issued a papal ban threatening to excommunicate from the church anyone who was killed while bullfighting. This didn't dull the enthusiasm of the Spanish; the ban was withdrawn, the danger and the fight continued. Queen Isabella and then finally King Philip ordered these encounters halted, and the fight ceased. Whether it was out of respect for their monarch or a new brave twist given the *corrida* by the common man (now facing the bull on foot), will never be known.

Since the lance was forbidden, commoners intrigued with the excitement of the event began fighting the bull on foot using a cape (*muleta*) to hide the sword (*estoque*) and confuse the bull. This was the beginning of the *corrida* as we know it today.

The *corrida* has changed little in the past 200 years. The beautiful clothes originally designed by the famous artist Goya, are still used. Richly embroidered silk capes add a gala touch draped over the railing of the arena. Even in the smallest Yucatecan village *corrida* the costume design persists. Though made of simple cotton (rather than rich satin and gold-trimmed silk) and delicately embroidered with typical designs of the Yucatan, the *torero* is impressively dressed.

Gone are the wild bulls; the animals are bred on large Mexican ranches (all of Spanish ancestry) just for the bullring. Only the finest: those showing superior strength, cunning, and bravery are sent to the ring. *El toro* is trained for one shining day in the arena.

The season begins in December and lasts for three months. The rest of the year it's the *novilleros* (neophyte *matadors)* that are seen in the plazas across the country. They must prove themselves in the arena before they are acknowledged as respected (high paying) *matadores.* Bullfighting is as dangerous now as when the Pope tried to have it banned in the 16th century. Almost half of the most renowned *matadores* in the past 250 years have died in the ring.

Outside of special events, bullfights take place on Sunday afternoons and the best seats are on the shady side of the arena (*la sombra*)—and are more costly. Ask at your hotel or local travel agency for ticket information. But remember, the *corrida* is not for everyone.

continued from page 48
Some villages offer a *corrida* (bull fight) as part of the festivities. Even a small town will have a simple bullring; in the Yucatan these rings are frequently built of bamboo. In Maya fashion, no nails are used—only twine (made from henequen) to hold together a two-tiered bullring! The country *corrida* has a special charm. If celebrating a religious holiday, a procession carrying the image of the honored deity might lead off the proceedings. The bull has it good here; there are no bloodletting ceremonies and the animal is allowed to live and carry on his reproductive activities in the pasture. Only a tight rope around its middle provokes sufficient anger for the fight. Local young men perform in the arena with as much heart and grace as professionals in Mexico City. And the crowd shows its admiration with shouts, cheers, and of course, *musica!*—even if the band is composed only of a drum, a trumpet, and a guitar. Good fun for everyone, even those who don't understand the art of the *corrida*.

Religious Feast Days

Christmas and Easter are wonderful holidays. The *posada* (procession) of Christmas begins nine days before the holiday, when families and friends take part in processions which portray Mary and Joseph and their search for lodging before the birth of Christ. The streets are alive with people, bright lights, and colorful nativity scenes. Families provide swinging piñatas (pottery pots covered with papier maché in the shape of a popular animal or perky character and filled with candy and small surprises). Children and adults alike enjoy watching the blindfolded small fry swing away with a heavy board or baseball bat while an adult moves and sways the piñata with a rope, making the fun last, giving everyone a chance. Eventually, someone gets lucky, smashes the piñata with a hard blow (it takes strength to break it) and kids skitter around the floor retrieving the loot. Piñatas are common, not only for Christmas and Easter but also for birthdays and other special occasions in the Mexican home.

The Fiesta And Visitors

A few practical things to remember about fiesta times. Cities will probably be crowded. If you know in advance that you'll be in town, make hotel and car reservations as soon as possible. Easter and Christmas at any of the beach hotels will be crowded, and you may need to make reservations as far as six months in advance. Some of the best fiestas are in more isolated parts of the Yucatan and neighboring states. Respect the privacy of people; the Indians have definite feelings and religious beliefs about having their pictures taken, so ask first and abide by their wishes.

FIESTAS AND CELEBRATIONS

Jan. 1: **New Year's Day.** Legal holiday.

Jan. 6: **Dia De Los Reyes Magos.** Day of the Three Kings. On this day Christmas gifts are exchanged.

Feb. 2: **Candelaria.** Candlemas. Many villages celebrate with candlelight processions.

Feb. 5: **Flag Day.** Legal holiday.

Feb./March: **Carnival.** The week before Ash Wed., the beginning of Lent. Some of the best determined festivals of the year are held this week. In Merida, Isla Mujeres, Cozumel, Campeche: Easter parades with colorful floats, costume balls, and sporting events. Chetumal: a parade with floats, music, and folk dances from all over Mesoamerica.

March 21: **Birthday Of Benito Juarez** (1806). Legal holiday.
Chichen Itza. Vernal equinox, a phenomenon of light and shadow displaying the pattern of a serpent slithering down the steps of the Pyramid of Kulkucan.

May 1: **Labor Day.** Legal holiday.

May 3: **Day Of The Holy Cross.** Dance of the Pig's Head performed during fiestas at Celestun, Felipe Carrillo Puerto, and Hopelchen.

May 5: **Battle Of Puebla,** also known as **Cinco De Mayo.** In remembrance of the 1862 defeat of the French. Legal holiday.

May 12-18: **Chankah Veracruz** (near Felipe Carrillo Puerto), honoring the Virgin of the Immaculate Conception. Maya music, bull fights, and religious procession.

May 15: **San Isidro Labrador.** Festivals held at Panaba (near Valladolid) and Calkini (southwest of Merida).

May 20-30: **Becal.** Jipi Fiesta in honor of the plant *jipijapa,* used in making Panama hats, the big money-maker for most of the population.

June 29: **Day Of San Pedro.** All towns with the name of San Pedro. Fiestas held in Sanah-cat and Cacalchen (near Merida), Tekom, and Panaba (near Valladolid).

Early July: **Ticul** (near Uxmal). Week-long fiesta celebrating the establishment of Ticul. Music, athletic events, dancing, and fireworks.

Sept. 15: **Independence Day.** Legal holiday.

Sept. 27-Oct.14: **El Señor De Las Ampollas** in Merida. Religious holiday. Big fiesta with fireworks, religious services, music, and dancing.

Oct. 4: **Feast Day Of San Francisco De Asisi.** Usually a week-long fiesta precedes this day in Uman, Hocaba, Conkal, and Telchac Pueblo (each near Merida).

Oct. 12: **Columbus Day.** Legal holiday.

Oct. 18-28: **Izamal.** Fiesta honoring el Cristo de Sitilpech. A procession carries an image of Christ from Sitilpech to the church in Izamal. Religious services, fireworks, music, and dancing. Biggest celebration on the 25th.

Oct. 31: **Eve Of All Souls' Day.** Celebrated all through the Yucatan. Flowers and candles placed on graves, the beginning of an eight-day observance.

Nov. 1-2: **All Souls' Day And Day Of The Dead.** Graveside and church ceremonies. A party like atmosphere in all the cemeteries. Food and drink vendors do a lively business, as well as candy makers with their sugar skulls and skeletons. A symbolic family meal is eaten at the gravesite.

Nov. 8: **Conclusion Of El Dia De Muerte.** Day of the Dead.

Nov. 20: **Dia De La Revolucion.** Revolution Day of 1910. Legal holiday.

Dec. 8: **Feast Of The Immaculate Conception.** Fiestas at Izamal, Celestun (including a boat procession), and Chompoton (boat procession carrying a statue of Mary, water-skiing show, other aquatic events, dancing, fair).

Dec. 12: **Our Lady Of Guadalupe.**

Dec. 25: **Christmas.** Legal holiday.

ACCOMMODATIONS

Quintana Roo offers a wide variety of accommodations. There's a myriad of hotels to choose from in Cancun, the offshore islands, and most of the coastal areas—in all price ranges. If you like the idea of light housekeeping, including your own food preparation, condos are available in many locales. If your lifestyle is suited to outdoor living, beach camping is wonderful along the Caribbean, and small bungalows for tourists are growing rapidly.

If traveling in an RV, a vehicle permit must be obtained when entering the country (see p. 86). Camping with a vehicle allows you to become a "luxury camper," bringing all the equipment you'll need (and more!). A van or small camper truck will fit on almost any road you'll run into. With an RV you can "street camp" in the city. The parking lot of a large hotel (check with the manager) or a side street near downtown activities are generally safe and offer easy entertainment possibilities.

Vehicle Supplies
A few reminders and some common-sense planning make a difference when traveling and camping with a vehicle. Near the Caribbean coast are many swampy areas so check for marshy ground before pulling off the road. When beach camping park above the high-tide line. Remember that gas stations are not as frequently found in Quintana Roo as in most parts of Mexico. If you plan on traveling for any length of time, especially in out-of-the-way places, carry extra gas, and fill up whenever the opportunity arises. Along with your food supply always carry enough water for both the car and passengers. Be practical and come prepared with a few necessities (see box).

Sleeping Outdoors
Sleeping under a jeweled sky in a warm clime can be either a wonderful or excrutiating experience. (Two factors that will make or break it are the temperature in conjunction

with your personal body thermostat, and the mosquito population in the immediate vicinity.) Some campers sleep in tents to get away from biting critters, which helps but is no guarantee; also, heat hangs heavy inside a closed tent. Sleeping bags cushion the ground but tend to be much too warm. If you have a bag that zips across the bottom, it's cooling to let your feet hang out (well marinated in bug repellent or wearing a pair of socks, a dark color the mosquitos might not notice). An air mattress softens the ground (bring along a patch kit). Mexican campers often just roll up in a lightweight blanket, covering all skin, head to toe to defy possible bug attacks.

The most comfortable option (according to Yucatecans and backpackers) is to sling a hammock between two palm trees, protecting yourself with a swath of mosquito netting and bug repellent. Some put a lightweight blanket between themselves and the hammock strings. For a very small fee, many homey resorts provide *palapa* hammock-huts that usually include water (for washing only); these places are great if you want to meet other backpackers. Though they are fast giving way to bungalow construction, a few hammock-huts are still found along the Caribbean coast.

HOTELS

In Cancun modern hotels are springing up faster than any guidebook can keep track of. All are trying to outdo themselves with luxury, service, amenities, and beauty. As a result, when construction is completed in 1995, Cancun will probably offer the greatest concentration of world-class hotels than most resorts in the world. Today there are 13,000 rooms available in the hotel zone, and by 1995 there will be 25,000

Reservations

Traveling during the peak season (15 Nov.-15 April) requires a little planning if you wish to stay at the popular hotels. Make reservations in advance. Many hotels can be contacted through an 800 number, travel agency, or auto club. Many well-known American chains are represented in the larger resorts (Cancun, Playa del Carmen) and their international desks can make reservations for you. Many now have fax numbers, much quicker than regular mail. If not, write to them direct and enclose a deposit check for one night (if you don't know how much, guess). Ask (and allow plenty of time) for a return confirmation. If traveling in May-June or Sept.-Oct., rooms are generally available. Many parts of the coast are quiet in the summer. However, beginning in July Cancun is the destination for many Mexican families vacationing, so reservations are suggested.

Luxury Accommodations

Some of the familiar hotel names found in Quintana Roo are the Presidente Stouffer, Camino Real, Hyatt, Sheraton, Omni, Holiday Inn Crowne Plaza, and Hilton. They offer endless luxuries, including lovely bathrooms—some with hair dryers, marble fixtures, separate showers, and thick fluffy towels—in-room

---

VEHICLE SUPPLIES

- ✔ Couple of extra fan belts
- ✔ Long towing rope or chain
- ✔ Bottle of Windex
- ✔ Set of spark plugs
- ✔ Points and condenser
- ✔ Emery boards
- ✔ Feeler gauge (to set the points)
- ✔ Oil and gas filter
- ✔ Gas can
- ✔ Oil
- ✔ Fuses
- ✔ Extra tire, patch kit
- ✔ Air supply
- ✔ Good-sized machete to hack your way through vines and plants
- ✔ Shovel
- ✔ Flares
- ✔ Flashlight
- ✔ A few basic tools
- ✔ Paper towels

Cancun hotel

safes, cable television, mini-bars, a/c, good beds, suites, jr. suites, balconies, terraces, gorgeous ocean views, green garden areas, pools (one a km long) with swim-up bars, nightclubs and fabulous restaurants, entertainment, travel agents, car rentals, gift shops, and delicatessens, almost all accept credit cards.

Condominiums

Cancun has hundreds of condos lining the beach and many under construction. Isla Mujeres and Cozumel have a few condominiums and others are sprouting up along the southern coastal beaches as well. If vacationing with family or a group, condo living can be a real money-saver while still enjoying the fine services of a luxury hotel. Fully equipped kitchens make cooking a snap. In many cases the price includes daily maid service. Some condos (like the Condumel on Isla Cozumel) welcome you with a refrigerator stocked with food basics; you pay only for the foods and beverages that you use each day. Details are given in the appropriate travel sections.

Traveler Beware!

Condomania is putting down roots. One of the biggest complaints from travelers to Cancun and Cozumel in the last couple of years concerns the salespeople who pester visitors to buy condos and timeshare accommodations. Their come-on is an offer for a free breakfast and often a free day's rental of a motorbike. After breakfast they give a sales presentation, a tour of the facilities, and then each guest gets a hard pitch from a very experienced salesman. These people have learned American sales methods down to the nitty gritty. If you succumb to the offer of free breakfast and aren't interested in buying, better practice saying **no.**

Moderate Hotels

In downtown Cancun and a few scattered locations within the hotel zone, moderate hotels are available. They aren't nearly as glitzy, probably don't have telephones, or multiple restaurants and bars, maybe not even a swimming pool, and they are not on the beach. However, the better ones provide transportation or are close to a bus stop. Prices can be one-third the cost of the hotel zone.

Budget Inns

Travelers looking to spend nights cheaply can find a *few* overnight accommodations in Cancun (the downtown area), more in Cozumel, Isla Mujeres, Playa del Carmen, and many along the Caribbean coast. During the peak season in Cancun it takes a little (sometimes a lot of) nosing around (starting out early in the day helps) but this type of hostelry is available, and searching for one offers a good way to see the city and meet friendly locals as well.

For the adventurer in small rural villages, ask at the local cantina, cafe, or city hall for a hotel or boardinghouse-type accommodation. These hotels are *usually* clean, and more than likely you'll share a toilet and (maybe) a shower. Sometimes you'll share the room itself, a large area with enough hammock hooks scattered around the walls to handle several travelers. The informed budget traveler carries his hammock (buy it on the Yucatan Peninsula if you don't already have one—they're the best made) when wandering around the Caribbean. When staying in the cheaper hotels in out-of-the-way places, come prepared with toilet paper, a towel, soap, and bug repellent, and expect to buy bottled drinking water. Most of the villages have a small cantina that serves a *comida corrida* (set lunch) or ask your host; credit cards are *not* the norm. However, the price will be right and the family that runs it will offer a cultural experience that you won't forget.

Youth hostels, though few and far between, are good bargains on the Peninsula, especially in Cancun.

YOUTH HOSTELS ON OR NEAR THE YUCATAN PENINSULA

CREA Cancun
km 3, 200 Boulevard Kukulcan
Zona Hotelera
Cancun, Quintana Roo, Mexico

CREA Campeche
Ave. Agustin Melgar S/N, col. Buenavista
Campeche, Campeche, Mexico

CREA Chetumal
Alvaro Obregon y General Anaya S/N
Chetumal, Quintana Roo, Mexico

CREA Tuxtla Gutierrez
Calz. Angel Albino Corzo No. 1800
Tuxtla Gutierrez, Chiapas, Mexico

For more information write to:
CREA, Agencia Nacional de Juvenil Gloriet
  Metro Insurgentes
Local CC-11 col. Juarez
C.P. 06600 Mexico, D.F.
Tel. 525–25–48/525–29–74

FOOD

Many of the crops now produced by American farmers were introduced by the Maya and Aztecs, including corn, sweet potatoes, tomatoes, peppers, squash, pumpkin, and avocados. Many other products favored by Americans are native to the Yucatan Peninsula: papaya, cotton, tobacco, rubber, vanilla, and turkey.

EARLY AGRICULTURE

Enriching The Soil

Scientists believe Maya priests studied celestial movements. A prime function performed in the elaborate temples (built to strict astronomical guidelines) may have been charting the changing seasons and deciding when to begin the planting cycle. Farmers used the slash-and-burn method of caring for their soil (and still do today). When the time was propitious (before the rains began in the spring), Indians cut the trees on their land, leaving stumps about half a meter above ground. Downed trees were spread evenly across the landscape in order to burn uniformly; residual ash was left to nourish the soil. At the proper time, holes were made with a pointed stick, and precious maize kernels were dropped into the earth, one by one. At each corner (the cardinal points) of the cornfield, offerings of *pozole* (maize stew) were left to encourage the gods to give forth great rains. With abundant moisture, crops were bountiful and rich enough to provide food even into the following year.

The Maya knew the value of allowing the land to lay fallow after two seasons of growth, and each family's *milpa* (cornfield) was moved from place to place around the villages scattered through the jungle. Often, squash and tomatoes were planted in the shade of towering corn stalks to make double use of the land. Today, you see windmills across the countryside (many stamped "Chicago, Inc."); with the coming of electricity to the outlying areas, pumps are being used to bring water from underground rivers and lakes to irrigate crops. Outside of irrigation methods, the Maya follow the same ancient pattern of farming as that of their ancestors.

Maize

Corn was the heart of Maya nutrition, eaten at each meal of the day. From it the Indians made tortillas, stew, and beverages both alcoholic and nonalcoholic. Because growing corn was such a vital part of Maya life, it is represented in drawings and carvings along with other social and religious symbols. Corn tortillas are still a main staple of the Mexican people. Native women in small towns can be seen early in the morning carrying bowls of corn kernels on their heads to the tortilla shop for grinding into tortilla dough. This was done

tortilla maker at the Sheraton Tower

ladies with bowls of corn

Seafood

You won't travel far before realizing that one of Yucatan's specialties is fresh fish. All along the Caribbean and Gulf coasts are opportunities to indulge in piscine delicacies: lobster, shrimp, red snapper, sea bass, halibut, barracuda, and lots more. Even the tiniest cafe will prepare sweet fresh fish "a la Veracruz" using ripe tomatoes, green peppers, and onions. Or if you prefer, ask for the fish *con ajo,* sautéed in garlic and butter—scrumptious! Most menus offer an opportunity to order *al gusto* (cooked to your pleasure).

Try the unusual Conch (*kawnk*), which has been a staple in the diet of the Maya along the Caribbean coast for centuries (see p. 178). It's often used in *ceviche.* Some consider this raw fish; actually, it's marinated in a vinegar or lime dressing with onions, peppers, and a host of spices—no longer raw and very tasty! Often conch is pounded, dipped in egg and cracker crumbs, and sautéed quickly (like abalone steak in California), with a squirt of fresh lime. Caution: if it's cooked too long it becomes tough and rubbery.

If you happen to be on a boat trip where the crew prepares a meal of fresh fish on the beach, more than likely you'll be served *tik n' chik.* The whole fish (catch of the day) is placed in a wire rack and seasoned with onions, peppers, and *achiote,* a fragrant red

by hand for centuries (and still is in isolated places). With the advent of electricity to the Peninsula it's much quicker to pay a peso or two and zap—tortilla dough! Others pay a few more pesos (price is controlled by the government) and buy their tortillas by the kilo hot off the griddle. It's amazing that the Maya came up with the combination of corn and beans without a dietician telling them it was a complete protein; they did not raise cattle, sheep, or pigs before Spanish times.

GASTRONOMICAL ADVENTURE

Taste as many different dishes as possible! You'll be introduced to spices that add a new dimension to your diet. Naturally, you won't be wild about everything—it takes a while to become accustomed to squid served in its own black ink, for instance! A hamburger might not taste like one from your favorite fast foodery back home. It should also not come as a shock to find your favorite down-home Tex-Mex enchiladas and tacos are nothing like those you order in Mexican restaurants. Be prepared to come into contact with new and different tastes—you're in *Mexico,* after all!

SALT AND THE MAYA

Salt was a valuable trade item in the economy of the Maya Indian. It was farmed from low marshy areas near the sea in several locations on the Yucatan Peninsula.

The Indians dammed up the mouth of a low-lying area trapping seawater that flooded the land at high tide. As the water evaporated in the sun, a thick salt crust was formed. This was ground into powder form and used for trade.

The salt flats on the northern tip of the Peninsula at Las Coloradas have been in operation for hundreds of years, still worked by the descendants of the Maya Indians. Other salt flats on the Peninsula stretch along the Gulf of Mexico coastline.

CHAC, THE MAYA RAIN GOD

Families today still maintain a small *milpa,* or cornfield. It is handled in much the same manner as in their ancestors' days, even down to a Chac ritual. Performed at the end of each April, the ceremony arouses Chacs from their seasonal sleep. Bowls of corn porridge are left at the four corners of a family's *milpa* for the Chacs—age-old deities who are still treated with great respect. To anger the Chacs could bring a drought and without the yearly rains the corn crop fails. Today, corn is not the critical staple that it was before the days of stores and supermarkets; though many poor villages still rely only on what the people raise in their fields to survive.

Corn, the sustenance of Maya life, was more than food. Legendary beliefs of man's beginnings were intertwined with the magic of corn. This is seen in many of the remaining carvings and drawings (such as a fresco at the ruins of Tulum showing man's feet as

corn). The crop was so significant to the Maya that everything else would stop when the signs implied it was time to plant the fields. In ancient times, it was Maya priests who calculated when it was the perfect time to fire the fields before the rains. This was done by relating the ritual calendar to the solar year, as at Chichen Itza during the vernal equinox. Today the farmer observes nature's phenomena such as the swarming of flying ants and the rhythm and frequency of croaking frogs—a Maya version of a Farmer's Almanac. However, many Maya still refer to the calendar keeper of the village.

Corn is still planted in the centuries-old method of the Maya. First trees and grasses are cut and left in the field to dry before being set aflame. The fire is allowed to burn until all is reduced to ash. A stick is used to poke a hole in the ash-covered earth where seeds are then dropped one by one.

This mural, "The Creation of Maya Man" by Raul Anguiano, was inspired by the myth of creation as read in Popul Vuh. It can be seen in Maya Hall at the Anthropological Museum in Mexico City.

spice grown on the Peninsula since the time of the early Maya. Bishop Diego de Landa identified *achiote* in his *Relaciones* written in the 1500s.

Wild Game

The Yucatecans are hunters, and if you explore the countryside very much, you'll commonly see men and boys on bicycles, motorscooters or horses, with rifles slung over their shoulders and full game bags tied behind them. Game found in the jungle varies. *Pato* (wild duck) is served during certain times of the year and is prepared in several ways that must be tried.

Restaurants

Most small cafes that cater to Mexican families are open all day and late into the night. The Mexican custom is to eat the heavier meal of the day between 1300-1600. In most of these family cafes a generous *comida corrida* (set lunch) is served at this time. If you're hungry and want an economical (but filling) meal, that's what to ask for; though you don't know exactly what's coming, you get a table full of many delights. Always expect a large stack of tortillas, and five or six small bowls filled with the familiar and the unfamiliar: it could be black beans, a cold plate of tomatoes and the delicious Yucatan avocado, *pollo pibyl* (chicken in banana leaves), fish, and whatever. Cafes in the larger hotels that cater to tourists don't serve this set meal. Late in the evening a light supper is served from 2100-2300. Hotels with foreign tourists offer dinner earlier to cater to British and American tastes. Some restaurants add a service charge onto the bill. If so, the check will say *incluido propina*. It's still gracious to leave a few coins for the waiter. If the tip isn't added to the bill, leaving 10-15% is customary.

Strolling musicians are common in Mexican cafes. If you enjoy the music, P100-200 is a considerate gift.

In certain cities, it's common at cafes that cater to Mexicans to serve free snacks in the afternoon with a beer or cocktail. The Cafe Prosperidad (Calle 56 No. 456-A) in downtown Merida is very generous with their *antojitos* (snacks). The place is always packed with locals ordering the *comida corrida*, com-

---

TORTILLAS

One of the fascinating operations in the public market is watching the tortilla machine. Always the busiest shop, housewives line up to buy two, four, or six kg of tortillas every day. Still the staple of the Mexican diet, many women continue to make them by hand at home, but a large percentage buy them for a reasonable price saving hours of work on the *metate* and the griddle. One traveler tells of spending 20 minutes in fascinated concentration observing the 50-lb. plastic sacks of shucked corn kernels stacked in a corner of the stall, the machinery that grinds it, the pale yellow dough, the unsophisticated conveyor belt that carries it across the live-flame cooking surface, the patrons that patiently line up for the fresh results, and the baker who hands the traveler several tortillas hot off the fire along with a friendly smile that says thanks for being interested.

---

plete with live entertainment and waitresses wearing a long version of the *huipil*. Here you'll get the real essence of the city, and you may be the only gringo present. Remember, we didn't say the cafe is spotless!

Yucatan has its own version of junk food. You'll find hole-in-the-wall *torta* (sandwich) stands, and the same goes for tacos, tamales, *liquidos* (fruit drinks), as well as corner vendors selling mangos on a stick, slices of pineapple, peeled oranges, candies of all descriptions, cotton candy, and barbecued meat. The public markets have foods of every description, usually very cheap. In other words, there's a huge variety to choose from, so have fun.

A ploy used by many seasoned adventurers when they're tired of eating cold food from their backpacks: in a village where there isn't a cafe of any kind, go to the local cantina (or grocery store, church, or city hall) and ask if there's a housewife in town who (for a fee) would be willing to include you at her dinner table. Almost always you'll find someone, usually at a fair price (determine price when you make your deal). With any luck you'll find a woman renowned for not only her *tortillas por manos* but also for the tastiest *poc chuc* this side of Tikal. You gain a lot more than food in this arrangement; the culture swap is priceless.

Food Safety

When preparing your own food in the back country, a few possible sources of bacteria are fresh fruit and vegetables, especially those with a thin skin that don't get peeled, like lettuce or tomatoes. When washing these foods in local water (and they should definitely be washed thoroughly before consuming), add either bleach or iodine (eight to ten drops per quart) to the wash water. Soaking vegetables all together in a container or plastic bag for about 20 minutes is easy; Ziploc bags are essential to carry. If at the beach and short of water, substitute sea water (for everything but drinking). Remember not to rinse the bleached food with contaminated water, just pat dry, and if they have a distasteful lingering flavor, a squirt of lime juice tastes great and is very healthy. Some foods nature has packaged hygienically; a banana has its own protective seal so is considered safe (luckily, since they're so abundant on the Peninsula). Foods that are cooked and eaten immediately are also considered safe.

ACTIVITIES

UNDERWATER SPORTS

Not everyone who travels to the Yucatan Peninsula is a diver or even a snorkeler—at first! One peek through the "looking glass"—a diving mask—changes that situation. The Caribbean is one of the most notoriously seductive bodies of water in the world. Turquoise-blue and crystal clear with perfect tepid temperature, the protected Yucatan coast (thanks to off-shore reefs) is ideal for a languid float during hot humid days.

DIVING

You'll find that the sea is where you'll want to spend a good part of your trip. So even if you never considered underwater sports in the past, you'll be willing—no, eager!—to learn. It's easy for the neophyte to learn how to snorkel. Once you master breathing through a tube, then it's simply a matter of relax and float. Time disappears once you are introduced, through a four-inch glass window, to a world of fish in rainbow colors of garish yellow, electric blue, crimson, and a hundred shades of purple. The longer you look, the more you'll discover: underwater caverns, tall pillars of coral, giant tubular sponges, shy fish hiding on the sandy bottom, and delicate wisps of fine grass.

Diving Wonderland

For the diver, there's even more adventure. Reefs, caves, and rugged coastline harbor the unknown. Ships wrecked hundreds of years ago hide secrets as yet undiscovered. Swimming among the curious and brazen fish puts you literally into another world. This is raw excitement!

Expect to see an astounding variety of fish, crustaceans, and corals. Even close to shore, these amazing little animals create exotic displays of shape and form, dense or delicate depending on species, depth, light, and current. Most need light to survive; in deeper, low-light areas, some species of coral take the form of a large plate, thereby performing the duties of a solar collector. Sponge is another curious underwater creature and it comes in all sizes, shapes, and colors, from common brown to vivid red.

Be Selective

Diving lessons are offered at nearly all the dive shops on the Peninsula. Before you make a commitment, ask about the instructor and check his accident record, then talk to the harbormaster, or if you're in a small village, ask at the local cantina. Most of these divers (many are American) are conscientious, but a few are not, and the locals know whom to trust.

Bringing your own equipment to Mexico might save you a little money, depending on he length of your trip and means of transportation. But if you plan on staying just a couple of weeks and want to join a group onboard a dive boat by the day, it's generally not much more for tank rental, which will save you the hassle of carrying your own.

Choose your boat carefully. Look it over first. Some aren't much more than fishing boats with little to make the diver comfortable. Ask questions; most of the dive masters who take divers on their boats speak English. Does it have a platform to get in and out of the water? How many tanks of air may be used per trip? How many dives? Exactly where are you going? How fast does the boat go and how long will it take to get there? Remember some of the best dive spots might be farther out at sea. A more modern boat (though costing a little more) might get you extra diving time.

Detailed information is available for divers and snorkelers who wish to know about the dive sites they plan to visit. Once on the Yucatan Peninsula, pamphlets and books are available in dive shops. Look for Ric Hajovsky's detailed pamphlet on reefs, depths, and especially currents. Wherever diving is good, you'll almost always find a dive shop. There are a few high-adventure dives where diving with an experienced guide is recommended (see "Diving" in "Cozumel").

DIVING HAZARDS

Underwater
A word here about some of the less-inviting aspects of marine society. Anemones and sea urchins are everywhere. Some can be dangerous if touched or stepped on. The long-spined, black sea urchin can inflict great pain and its poison can cause an uncomfortable infection. Don't think that you're safe in a wetsuit and booties *or even if wearing gloves!* The spines easily slip through the rubber. In certain areas, such as around the island of Cozumel, the urchin is encountered at all depths and is very abundant close to shore where you'll probably be wading in and out of shallow water; keep your eyes open. If

diving at night, use your flashlight. If you should run into one of the spines, remove it quickly and carefully, disinfect the wound and apply antibiotic cream. If you have difficulty removing the spine, or if it breaks, see a doctor—pronto!

First Aid
Cuts from coral, even if only just a scratch, will often cause an infection. Antibiotic cream or powder will usually take care of it. If you should get a deep cut, or if minute bits of coral are left in the wound, a serious and long-lived infection can ensue. See a doctor.

If you should get a scrape on red, or fire coral you'll feel a burning sensation for a few minutes to five days. On some, it causes an allergic reaction and will raise large red welts. Cortisone cream will reduce inflammation and discomfort. While it wouldn't be fair to condemn all red things, you'll notice in the

Local fishermen know the best dive spots.

next few paragraphs that the creatures to avoid are all red!

Fire worms (also known as bristle worms) if touched will deposit tiny cactus-like bristles in your skin. They can cause the same reaction as fire coral. *Carefully* scraping the skin with the edge of a sharp knife (as you would to remove a bee stinger) might remove the bristles. Any leftover bristles will ultimately work their way out, but you can be very uncomfortable in the meantime. Cortisone cream helps to relieve this inflammation, too.

Several species of sponges have fine sharp spicules (hard, minute, pointed calcareous or siliceous bodies that support the tissue) that should not be touched with the bare hand. The attractive red fire sponge can cause great pain; a mild solution of vinegar or ammonia (or urine if there's nothing else) will help. The burning lasts a couple of days, and cortisone cream soothes. Don't be fooled by dull-colored sponges. Many have the same sharp spicules, and touching them with a bare hand is risky at best.

Protect Your Hands And Feet

Some divers feel the need to touch the fish they swim with. A few beginners want an underwater picture taken of them feeding the fish—bad news! When you offer fish a tasty morsel from your hand (whether gloved or not), you could start an underwater riot. Fish are always hungry and always ready for a free meal. Some of those denizens of the deep may not be so big, but in the frenzy to be first in line, their very efficient teeth have been known to miss the target. Another way to save your hands from unexpected danger is by keeping them out of cracks and crevices. Moray eels live in just those kinds of places in a reef. A moray will usually leave you alone if you do likewise, but their many needle-sharp teeth can cause a painful wound that's apt to infect.

A few sea-going critters resent being stepped on and they can retaliate with a dangerous wound. The scorpion fish, hardly recognizable with its natural camouflage, lies hidden most of the time on a reef shelf or the bottom of the sea. If you should step on or touch it you can expect a painful, dangerous

sting. If this happens, see a doctor immediately.

Another sinister fellow is the ray. There are several varieties in the Caribbean, including the yellow and southern sting rays. If you leave them alone they're generally peaceful but if they get stepped on they will zap you with a tail that carries a poisonous sting which can cause anaphylactic shock. Symptoms include respiratory difficulties, fainting, and severe itching. Go quickly to the doctor and tell him what caused the sting. One diver suggests a shuffling, dragging-of-the-feet gait when walking on the bottom of the ocean. If bumped, the ray will quickly escape, but if stepped on it feels trapped and uses its tail for protection. Jellyfish can also inflict a miserable sting. Avoid particularly the long streamers of the Portuguese man-of-war though some of the smaller jellyfish are just as hazardous.

Don't let these what-ifs discourage you from an underwater adventure, though. Thousands of people dive in the Caribbean every day of the year and only a small percentage of accidents occur.

SAFETY REFERENCES

Check with your divemaster about emergency procedures before your boat heads out to sea. A safety recompression chamber is located on the Island of Cozumel, tel. 2-01-40. Here are some other useful numbers:

La Costera (Coast Guard)
Radio: channel 16
(canal numero diez y seis)

Divers Alert Network (DAN)
(919) 684–8111
Dial this number for information about Cozumel's recompression chamber or for assistance in locating a chamber in the U.S.A.

Air–Evac International
(619) 278–3822
located in San Diego, CA.

Life Flight
(713) 797–4357
(800) 854–2567
air ambulance service located in
Houston, TX.

OTHER WATER SPORTS

With so many fine beaches, bays, and coves
along the Caribbean, all water sports are
available. Because so many beaches are
protected by the reef that runs parallel to
Quintana Roo's east coast, calm **swimming
beaches** are easy to find and many hotels
have pools. **Water-skiing** is good on Nichupte
Bay in Cancun, and **parasailing** is popular
there also. **Windsurfing** lessons are given,
and rental boards are available at most of the
resort areas: Cozumel, Cancun, Akumal, and
Playa del Carmen.

FISHING AND HUNTING

Fishing
A fishing license is required for all persons 16
years or older, good for three days, one month,
or a year, available for a small fee at most
fresh- and saltwater fishing areas from the
local delegate of the Fishing Secretariat. Ask
in the small cafes at the more isolated beaches. Check with the closest Mexican consulate
where you can get a permit for your sport-
fishing craft; you can also get current information there on fishing seasons and regulations which vary from area to area. Fishing
gear may be brought into Mexico without customs tax; however, the customs officials at
the border crossing from Brownsville, Texas,
into Mexico are notorious for expecting to
have their palms greased before allowing the
RVer or boater to cross the border. If you find
yourself in this position start with $1 bills
(have lots of them with you); there are several people that need to be soothed before you
can cross. If you choose not to pay the bribe,
they can keep you hanging around for hours,
even days, before they will allow you to
cross. Sadly, it's a no-win situation. For more

crane

fishing information write to: General de Pesca,
Av Alvaro Obregon 269, Mexico 7, D.F.

Hunting
A seasonal license for small-game (including
birds) must be purchased from the state
where the hunting is intended. Any Mexican
consulate or tourist office will provide information on obtaining a firearms permit as well
as current hunting season dates and regulations, which vary yearly. Big-game hunting
requires a special one-time permit (expensive)
from the Mexican Department of Wildlife. Start
making your preparations well in advance of
your hunting date. For more hunting information write: Direccion General de Caza, Ser-
dan 27, Mexico, D.F. After obtaining Mexican
information, write to the Dept. of Wildlife in
Washington, D.C., or go to the nearest customs office and ask for the booklet, "Pets and
Wildlife." This lays out the U.S. government
rules and regulations on importing game.

The safest and least confusing way to go
hunting is to either travel from the states with

an American guide who makes the trek each year (check with your travel agent or hunting club), or to make arrangements in advance with a hunting lodge in Mexico. Another source of hunting lodge information is the back ad sections of *Field And Stream* and *Hunter* magazines. By mail they will walk you through the whole planning procedure, but allow *plenty* of time!

OTHER ACTIVITIES

Birdwatching is wonderful throughout the Yucatan. From north to south the variety of birds is broad and changes with the geography and the weather. Bring binoculars and wear boots and lightweight trousers if you plan on *watching* in jungle areas. Studying **tropical flora** is also a popular activity. For this you most certainly will be in the back country—don't forget bug repellent and be prepared for an occasional rain shower, even in the dry season. For most orchids and bromeliads look up in the trees. However, Yucatan does have ground orchids to look for. Remember, don't take anything away with you except pictures.

Photography
There's a world of beauty to photograph here, what with the sea, the people, and the natural landscape of the Peninsula. If you plan on **videotaping,** check with your local Mexican Tourist Office for information on what you can bring into the country. Most archaeological zones prohibit tripods. For the photographer who wants to film *everything,* small planes are available for charter in the larger cities and resorts. In Cancun, for instance, you can take pictures from a plane that tours for about 15 minutes over Cancun and the surrounding coast. Per person price is US$30-40. (For further photography info see p. 84-86.)

OTHER SPORTS

Tennis courts are scattered about Quintana Roo; the large hotels at Cancun, Akumal, Cozumel, and Puerto Aventuras have courts. Bring your own rackets. **Golf courses** are few, but you can plan on playing in Cancun and Puerto Aventuras.

GETTING THERE AND AROUND

For centuries, getting to the Yucatan Peninsula required a major sea voyage to one of the few ports on the Gulf of Mexico followed by harrowing and uncertain land treks limited to mule trains and narrow paths through the tangled jungle. Today the Peninsula is accessible from anywhere in the solar system! Arrive via modern airports, a network of new (good) highways, a reasonably frequent train schedule (very limited), or an excellent bus service that reaches most cities and small villages. **Note**: Sanborn's Mexican Insurance Co. offers a computerized **TripShare Service** for those who don't wish to travel alone, tel. (512) 682-1354.

BY CAR

An international driver's license is not required to drive or rent a car in Mexico. However, if you feel safer with it, get one from an auto club. At AAA in California you will need two passport pictures and $5 along with a current driver's license from your home state. The international license is another good form of identification if you should have an accident or other driving problem.

When you cross the border from the U.S. into Mexico, your car insurance is no longer valid. You can buy insurance from AAA or an auto club before you leave home. Numerous insurance agencies at most border cities sell Mexican insurance: Sanborn's is one of the largest. Ask Sanborn's for their excellent free road maps of the areas you plan to visit. For more information write: Sanborn's Mexican Insurance Service, P.O. Box 310, McAllen, TX 78501, tel. (512) 686-0711.

In the last 15 years highway construction has been priority work on the Peninsula. A growing number of well-engineered roads throughout the area provide access to cities and towns. However, before taking your car into the country, consider the condition of the car and the manufacturer. Will parts be available in the event of a breakdown? Volkswagen, Renault, Ford, General Motors, and Chrysler have Mexican branches and parts should be available. If you drive an expensive foreign sports car or a large luxury model, you might be better off making other arrangements. Repairs might be unavailable and you could be stranded in an unlikely place for days waiting for a part. It's always wise to make sure you and the mechanic understand the cost of repairs before he begins—just like at home! **Note:** Selling your car in Mexico is highly illegal.

Highways To Yucatan

In California, main highways cross the Mexican border from San Diego to Tijuana and from Calexico to Mexicali. From Arizona go through Tucson to Nogales. From Texas, El Paso leads to Juarez, Eagle Pass to Piedras Negras, Laredo to Nuevo Laredo, and Brownsville to Matamoros. From each of these gateways, good highways bring you to the capital of the country, Mexico City.

From the capital the easiest and most direct route to Merida and other Peninsula cities is on Mex. 190D, a toll road to Puebla. At Puebla there's an interchange with Mex. 150D, another tollway that parallels the older free road (Mex. 150). On 150D you cross the plateau climbing to 2,385 meters at the summit of the Cumbres de Maltrata, after which a 22.5 km curving road drops you down quickly. Though this road is often foggy, it beats the alternative on 150, which hairpins through the Cumbres de Acultzingo, a narrow, heart-thumping drop of 610 meters in only 11 km. Mexico 150D eliminates going through Mt. Orizaba; the old road (150) takes it in. In Cordoba 150 ends and the two roads meet; continue on 150 to the humid coastal plain. At Paso del Toro turn southeast onto 180, which leads to Veracruz. Following 180 takes you through Coatzacoalcos to Villahermosa. From here you can continue on 186 which loops southeast, close to Palenque, and then north through Escarcega where the road meets 261. Stay on 186, travel due east across the Peninsula to Chetumal on the Caribbean coast. At Chetumal 307 follows the coast northeast to Cancun. From Cancun take 180 southwest to Merida.

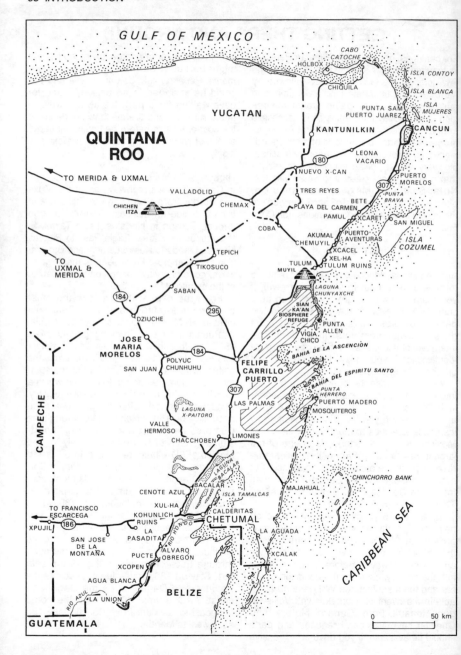

Another option from Villahermosa is to take 180 following the Gulf coast. This route includes several ferry boats (that have frequently interrupted schedules due to rough seas), takes you through Isla del Carmen, Champoton, Campeche, and then on to Merida. With *no* delays figure the trip from Villahermosa and Champoton to take about 8½ hours.

Just past Villahermosa, 186 provides the fastest route to Champoton. Take 186 to Escarcega, turn onto 261 and follow it for 85 km to Champoton. Though longer, this is a much faster and less complicated route and avoids several ferries.

Driving Tips

In Quintana Roo, it's recommended you don't drive outside the cities at night unless it's a necessity. The highways have no streetlights—it's hard to see a black cow on a black road in the black night. Also, pedestrians have no other place to walk; shoulders are nonexistent on the roads. Public phones are few and far between, and gas stations close when the sun goes down. If you should have a problem while driving during daylight hours on a *main* road, it's advisable to stay with your car. The Green Angels, a government-sponsored tow truck service, cruise the roads several times a day on the lookout for drivers

DRIVING DISTANCES

DISTANCES IN KM

GULF OF MEXICO

RIO LAGARTOS
PROGRESO
33
63 MERIDA
CELESTUN
CANCUN
68
48
TIZIMIN
52 159
160
PLAYA
DEL CARMEN
VALLADOLID 37
AKUMAL
194 233 26
TULUM
FELIPE 98
CARRILLO
CAMPECHE PUERTO

134

CUIDAD
DEL CARMEN
FRONTERA 151 154
93 213 ESCARCEGA 110
XPUJIL
75 206 CHETUMAL

159
(99 mi)

VILLA HERMOSA
115
278 27
PALENQUE
BELIZE CITY CARIBBEAN
SEA
207
BELIZE

GUATEMALA

83 SAN CRISTOBAL
DE LAS CASAS
TUXTLA
GUTIERREZ

0   100 km

THE ANTHROPOLOGICAL MUSEUM OF MEXICO

Passing through Mexico City? Take at least one day to thoroughly explore the Anthropological Museum in Chapultapec Park. The park covers four square km, with a children's playground, a lake with boating activities, water birds including lovely white and black swans, a botanical garden, zoo, Chapultapec Castle, and two important museums: Anthropological and Modern Art. The park is the scene of concerts, theater, children's programs, picnics—and much more. People of the city come to enjoy cultural offerings plus grass, trees, and a feeling of being in the country.

Many flights to the Yucatan Peninsula from the U.S. stop in Mexico City for a change of planes. Though it would take days to really tour the Capital city properly, while on your way to Mayaland a highly informative adjunct to your trip would be three days in Chapultapec Park. Devote much of that time to the Anthropological Museum, take in the Museum of Modern Art, and by all means spend half a day at the castle made famous by Maximillian and Carlotta, short-term king and queen from France.

The Anthropological Museum complex was built in 1963-4, beautifully designed by Pedro Ramirez Vasquez. The museum presents a surprisingly harmonious example of contemporary architecture. Incorporated in the roof is an enormous stone umbrella supported on a column 12 meters high with a curtain of water dropping into a basin below.

As you enter the museum the shop on the left is well stocked with a great selection of catalogs, brochures, and informative books (in several languages) on many subjects including the Indian cultures of ancient Mexico, and an excellent museum guidebook. Some of the finer reproductions of Maya art are available here at reasonable prices. Unfortunately, the store doesn't ship to the states, so you must either lug your purchases around with you on the rest of your trip or take the time to wrap and ship them yourself.

If time is limited, there are well-informed guides who speak English. For a moderate fee you can join a small group that will give you concentrated information either on the entire museum or the salons you're interested in. Each culture is represented in its own well-laid-out salon. Tickets (small fee) to the museum are sold in the vestibule at the main entrance of the two-story building.

In the Salon of the Maya you'll see some of the finest treasures found on the Yucatan Peninsula. The terra cotta figures from the Island of Jaina are remarkable images of people portraying various lifestyles. Reproductions of the colored frescoes found in Bonampak are outstanding, as are the delicate carvings from Chichen Itza.

A theft during the Christmas season of 1985 saw the tragic loss of some spectacular remnants of Maya history. The fabled jade mask of Pacal found in a tomb in the depths of the Temple of the Inscriptions at Palenque was among the valued pieces stolen.

After visiting the museum and seeing the artifacts you will have gained a greater understanding of the people who created the mysterious structures you visit on the Yucatan Peninsula.

If you plan on staying for awhile, the Presidente Hotel in Chapultapec park is within walking distance of all the park attractions and a colorful Mexican hotel. The Nikko Hotel is next door, a new Japanese-style hostel, very modern, and very large. Mexico City has a plethora of hotels to fit every pocketbook and if you're looking for a luxurious splurge, this is where you'll find sophisticated, beautiful, world-class inns that compete with any in the world.

Budget travelers can find a good selection of hotels all over the large city plus three youth hostels:

SETEJ, Cozumel 57, tel. 286-91-53, four blocks south of Metro Sevilla station (Line 1), which is on Av. Chapultapec, between Zona Rosa and Chapultapec Park.

CREA Hostel (IYHF), tel. 286-91-53, one block south of Villa Olimpica, on Insurgentes Sur.

International Mexicano Norteamericano de Relaciones Culturales, Hamburgo 115, between Genova and Amberes, in Zona Rosa (no phone).

in trouble. They carry gas and small parts, and are prepared to fix tires. Each car is equipped with a CB radio and the driver is trained to give first aid, or will call a doctor. If you foolishly decide to travel an isolated road after dark and break down, your best bet is to lock yourself in and stick it out for the night; go for help in the morning. The Mexican people are friendly, especially when they see someone in trouble; sometimes you have more help than you want.

BY PLANE

Today, planes fly to two international airports in the state of Quintana Roo. The newest and most modern is at Cancun, Yucatan's most sophisticated resort. Jets arrive daily, with connections from most countries in the world. It's also possible to fly internationally to the small island of Cozumel. In Quintana Roo there are several small landing strips for private planes and small commuter airlines.

AIR ROUTES TO CANCUN

BY TRAIN

For many years Mexico has had a fairly efficient railway service. Traveling by train is relaxing and the scenery is outstanding. You can make an entire trip from the States to Merida by rail (a 45-minute flight to Cancun). From several stateside cities along the border, buses or trains drop off passengers at Mexican train connections. For example, you can catch a Golden State Bus at the Los Angeles main terminal which crosses the border to Mexicali. Here you board a 1st-class train to Guadalajara (US$60) which does not have a sleeping car. The price includes four meals in the dining car. (This train is three years old.) From Guadalajara take (all-sleeper-car) a train to Mexico City (about 12 hours); two people can travel in a private compartment with two beds and a bathroom. The

AIRLINES SERVING THE YUCATAN PENINSULA

Airline	To	From
American	Cancun, Cozumel	Dallas, Fort Worth
Aeromexico	Cozumel, Mexico, Merida, Chetumal, Monterey, Cancun	Houston, Los Angeles
Continental	Cancun, Cozumel	Los Angeles, Houston, Denver, San Francisco
Eastern	Cancun	New Orleans
LACSA	Cancun	Guatemala, Costa Rica, New Orleans
Mexicana	Cancun, Cozumel	Miami, Dallas, Philadelphia
United	Cancun	Chicago

train also offers a dining car, a/c, and daily departures. From Mexico City to Merida a 36-hour sleeper car trip is US$30; a 1st-class train ticket is US$52. Reservations are necessary especially during holiday seasons. In the Los Angeles area call Orozco Travel, (213) 626-2291.

It's possible to travel by rail from Merida to most cities in Mexico. The prices are cheap, and for a little more you can get a sleeping car. For 1st-class you need reservations; even if there's no dining car (ask), you can bring a lunch or depend on the (frequent) stops at stations along the way, where vendors sell everything, including Mexican fast food, tamales, and the like. For information on other departure points along the border plus schedules and prices deal directly with the railway companies; schedules and prices change frequently. Some travel agents have train information, but not all. Government tourist offices can give you schedules and prices for a specific trip. For further information write: Mexican National Railways, 489 Fifth Ave., Suite 2601, New York, NY 10017.

BY BUS

Bus service to Quintana Roo is very efficient. Fares will fit the most meager budget, scheduling is frequent, and even the smallest village is accessible from most cities in northern Mexico. From the U.S. it's smart to make reservations with Greyhound or Trailways to your final destination on the Peninsula. The bus driver will take you to the border and then help you make the transfer (including your luggage) to a Mexican bus line. This service saves you a lot of time and confusion when in a strange bus station. When making return reservations, make them straight through across the border, even if only to the first town on the U.S. side; again you will have an easier time crossing the border and making the connection.

Class Choice

You have a choice of super-deluxe, deluxe, 1st-, 2nd-, and 3rd-class. Third-class passengers can bring their animals (and often do); buses are older models usually, with no toilets or a/c. Third-class bus tickets can be as cheap as a Mexican dinner at Taco Bell in the U.S. First-class and above buses have assigned seats, are more comfortable, and still very moderately priced. Make reservations in advance. Your ticket will say *asiento* (seat) with a number. Some 1st-class buses sell food and drinks on board. If you're traveling a long distance, buy 1st-class; the difference in price is worth the small added expense. Second- and 3rd-class buses stop for anyone who flags them, and at every small village along the way. First-class operates almost exclusively between terminals. This cuts a lot of time off a long journey.

Luggage

If it fits in the overhead rack almost anything can be carried on board. Usual allowance is 25 kg, but unless you're ridiculously overloaded, no one ever objects to what you bring aboard. If a driver should refuse your load, usually you can come to an amicable (monetary) agreement. Larger luggage is carried in the cargo hold under the bus where breakables have a short lifespan. Purses and cameras are best kept between your feet on the floor, rather than in the overhead rack—just in case. Luggage should always be labeled, inside and out, with your name.

Seat Comfort

Seats in the middle of the bus are a good choice. When choosing a seat, if you can, pick the shady side of the bus during the day: going south sit on the left side and going north sit on the right. At night sit on the right, which eliminates the glare of oncoming headlights. Steer clear of seats near the bathroom, usually the last few rows. They can be

---

LUGGAGE TIP

Both in large and small terminals, look for a sign that says GUARDA EQUIPAJE if you wish to leave your luggage for a few hours or even overnight. Your ticket may be all you need, others charge a small fee. Ask if there's a time limit.

smelly and the aisle traffic and constant door activity can keep you awake. Bring a book and ignore the bus driver and his abilities; in other words, just relax.

OTHER TRANSPORTATION

By Ship

Cruise ships stopover at several ports on Mexico's Caribbean coast. Some lines will take you one way and drop you off at Cozumel, or Playa del Carmen. Check with Princess Lines and Carnival Cruises; your travel agent can give you the name of others that stop along the Yucatan coast. New cruise ships are continually adding the Mexican Caribbean to their list of ports of call. Cruise passengers are offered the opportunity to make shore excursions from the Caribbean coast ports to Chichen Itza, Tulum, Coba, and Xelha. Shopping and beach time is also included. For less adventurous travelers, this may be the best way to visit Maya archaeological sites.

Group Travel

If you prefer to go with a group, travel agents have many choices of escorted tours. You pay a little extra, but all arrangements and reservations are made for you to tour by plane, train, ship, or RV caravan. Also, special-interest groups with a guest expert are another attraction. For instance, archaeology buffs can usually find a group through a university that includes a knowledgeable professor to guide them through chosen Maya ruins. Evenings are spent together reviewing the day's investigation and discussing the next day's itinerary. Archaeology laymen will find many opportunities, including trips offered through Earthwatch, Box 403, Watertown, MA 02172, an institute of volunteers where participants can physically work on a dig under the supervision of professionals; destinations change regularly. The Intercare Organization, FACHCA Director, Box 8561, Moscow, Idaho 83843, of interest to nursing home administrators and people in related fields, travels to cities around the globe, visiting nursing homes, comparing and learning about facilities similar to their own, and scheduling lectures and seminars. *Transitions Abroad*, 18 Hulst Rd., Box 344, Amherst, MA 01004, is a magazine that offers information about study and teaching opportunities around the world. Travel agencies, student publications, and professional organizations can give you more information. It's a good way to mix business with pleasure, and in certain instances the trip is tax-deductible.

For those who travel *light*, but don't want to carry a backpack, here's a great softsided bag that opens flat because of extra long zippers, allowing efficient packing in separate zippered compartments. It has a shoulder strap, fits under the seat on an airplane, and holds clothes and shoes to sustain the careful traveler for three weeks. Dimensions are 20 x 13 x 10 inches, made of durable puncture-resistant ballistic nylon. This is the way to go. Called Bayley's 147 3-zip Carryon, it is available at Easy Going Travel Shop, 1400 Shattuck, Berkeley, CA 94709, tel. (415) 843-3533, and 167 Locust, Walnut Creek, CA 94596, tel. (415) 947-6660. For *super efficiency*, either of

CAR RENTAL TIPS

Renting a car in Mexico is usually a simple matter but can be much more costly than in the U.S.—and always subject to Murphy's Law. If you know exactly when you want the car and where, it's helpful to make reservations in the States in advance. Renting a car once in Mexico, you pay the going rate, which can add up to about $60 per day for a small car; most offices give little or no weekly discount. This is not to say that you can't take part in the favorite Mexican pastime, bargaining. You might get lucky. If it's just before closing time, and if someone cancelled a reservation, and if it's off-season on the Peninsula, it's possible to get a car for a good rate. However, that's a lot of ifs to count on when you want and need a car as soon as you arrive. Also, it's often difficult to get a car without reservations; you may have to wait around for one to be returned.

Affordable Mexico

Representatives of Hertz, Avis, and Budget can be found in many parts of Mexico. These are separate franchises. Though not run by the mother companies, U.S. corporate offices will honor a contract price made in the States previous to your arrival in Mexico. If you should run into a problem and you still want the car, pay the higher price and write a brief protest on the contract right then.

Hertz runs a special deal a good part of the year called "Affordable Mexico." In March 1991, the rate for a VW Bug or a Renault was US$280 per week, including 2,000 km free, plus 15% Mexican tax and US$ collision insurance. You can only get this rate by making the deal in the U.S. in advance. If you belong to AAA automobile club, many offices will give you another 10-20% discount when returning the car and making the final calculation (have your membership card). This is the cheapest fee for car rentals in Mexico, and unless you plan to use a car for only one or two days, the price is definitely right. Hertz, Avis, and Budget list toll-free 800 phone numbers in the yellow pages of all U.S. cities. You need a major credit card to make phone reservations.

Insurance

Mexican insurance from the rental car agencies runs about US$6 per day and covers only 80 percent of damages (which many travelers are unaware of). However, it's dangerous to skip insurance; in most cases in Mexico, when there's an accident the police take action first and ask questions later. With an insurance policy, most of the problems are eased over. Rental agencies also offer medical insurance for US$4 per day. Your private medical insurance should cover this (check). If not, many travelers-cheque packages come with some sort of medical insurance for a small extra fee (see "Health").

Getting The Car

Another advantage to making reservations in advance is the verification receipt you receive. Hang onto it; it's like money in the bank. When you arrive at the airport and show your verification receipt (be sure you get it back), a car will almost always be waiting for you. Once in awhile you'll even get an upgrade for the same fee if your reserved car is not available. On the other side of the coin, be sure that you go over the car *carefully* before you take it far. Drive it around the block and check out the following:

TOPE

When you see a sign that says "TOPE," slow down; you'll soon learn that it means a traffic bump is imminent. They are often very high, sometimes with spikes sticking up. If you hit them fast they can cause severe damage to your car as well as your head. *Tope* signs precede almost every town and school on the Yucatan peninsula.

✓ Spare tire and working jack.

✓ All door locks.

✓ Make sure the seats move forward, have no sprung backs, etc.

✓ All windows should lock, unlock, roll up and down properly.

✓ Trunk should lock and unlock.

✓ Proper legal papers for the car, with address and phone numbers of associate car rental agencies in cities you plan to visit in case of an unexpected car problem.

✓ Horn, emergency brake, and foot brakes should work properly.

✓ Clutch, gear shift, all gears (don't forget reverse).

✓ Directions to the nearest gas station; the gas tank may be empty. If it's full it's wise to return it full, since you'll be charged top dollar per liter of gas. Ask to have any damage, even a small dent, missing door knob, etc., noted on your contract, if it hasn't been already.

✓ Note the hour you picked up the car and try to return it before that time: a few minutes over will get you another *full* day's rental fee.

Payoff Time

When you pick up your rental car, the company makes an imprint of your credit card on a blank bill, one copy of which is attached to the papers you give the agent when you return the car. Keep in mind that if you're driving for a long period, three to four weeks, the car agency has a limit of how much you can charge on one card at one time (ask the maximum when you pick up the car). If you go over the limit be prepared to pay the balance in cash or with another credit card. If you pick up a car in one city and return it to another there's a hefty drop-off fee (per km). Most agents will figure up in advance exactly how much it will be so there aren't any surprises when you return the car.

In 99 cases out of 100, all will go smoothly. However, if you run into a problem or are overcharged, don't panic. You might be at an office that never heard of Affordable Mexico, even though it is specified on your verification. Go ahead and pay (with plastic money), save all your paper work, and when you return to the States, make copies of everything, call the company, and chances are very good that you'll get a refund.

WHAT TO TAKE

Whatever time of year you travel to Mexico's Caribbean coast you can expect warm weather, which means you can pack less in your suitcase. If you're planning on a one-destination trip to a self-contained resort hotel and want a change of clothes each day, most airlines allow you to check two suitcases, and you can bring another carry-on bag that fits either under your seat or in the overhead rack. But if you plan on moving around a lot, keep it light.

Experienced women travelers pack a small foldable purse into their compartmented carry-on which then gives them only one thing to carry while en route. And be sure to include a few overnight necessities in your carry-on in the event your luggage doesn't arrive when you do. Valuables are safest in your carry-on stowed under the seat in front of you or between your feet whether you're on a plane, train, or bus.

Security

It's smart to keep passports, travelers cheques, money, and important papers on your person at all times. The do-it-yourselfer can sew inside pockets into clothes; buy extra long pants that can be turned up, and sewn three-fourths of the way around, the last section closed with a piece of Velcro. Separate shoulder-holster pockets, money belts, and pockets around the neck inside clothing—all made of cotton—are available commercially. If you're going to be backpacking and sloshing in jungle streams etc. put everything in Ziploc plastic bags before placing them in pockets. Waterproof plastic tubes are for sale that will hold a limited number of items around your neck while swimming. It's always a good idea to write down document numbers (such as passports); keep them separated in your luggage and leave a copy with a friend back home. This expedites replacement in case of loss.

Clothing

A swimsuit is a must, and if you're not staying at one of the larger hotels, bring a beach towel. In today's Mexico, *almost* any clothing is acceptable. If traveling the winter months of Nov., Dec., and Jan. bring along a light wrap because it can cool off in the evening. The rest of the year you'll probably carry the wrap in your suitcase. For women, a wraparound skirt is a useful item that can quickly cover up shorts when traveling through the villages and some cities (many small-village residents really gawk at women wearing shorts; whatever you do, don't enter a church wearing them). The wraparound skirt also makes a good shawl when it cools off. Cotton underwear is the coolest in the tropics, but nylon is less bulky and dries overnight, cutting down on the number needed. Be sure that you bring broken-in, comfortable walking shoes; blisters can wreck a vacation almost as much as a sunburn.

Necessities

Anyone planning an extended trip in Mexico should bring an extra pair of glasses or carry the lens prescription; the same goes for medication (make sure it's written in general terms) though many Mexican pharmacies sell prescription drugs over the counter.

Reading Material

Avid readers in any language besides Spanish should bring a supply of books; English-language reading materials are available in limited quantities, mostly in big hotel gift shops and only a few bookstores. Most travelers are delighted to trade books.

Backpackers

If you plan on hitchhiking or using public transportation, don't use a large external-frame pack; it won't fit in most small cars or public lockers. Smaller packs with zippered compartments that will accommodate mini-padlocks are most practical. A strong bike cable and lock secures the pack to a YH bed or a bus or train rack. None of the above will deter the real criminal, but might make it just difficult enough to discourage everyone else.

Experienced backpackers travel light with a pack, an additional canvas bag, small water- and mosquito-proof tent, hammock and mosquito netting. What camping supplies to bring depends on your style of traveling.

HEALTH CARE

TOURISTA

Some travelers to Mexico worry about getting sick the moment they cross the border. But with a few simple precautions, it's not a foregone conclusion that you'll come down with something in Mexico. The most common illness to strike visitors is *tourista,* Montezuma's Revenge, the trots, or in plain Latin—diarrhea. No fun, it can cause uncomfortable cramping, fever, dehydration, and the need to stay close to a toilet for the duration. It's caused, among other things, by various strains of bacteria managing to find your innards, so it's important to be very careful of what goes into your mouth.

Possible Causes
Statistics show that the majority of tourists get sick on the third day of their visit. Interested doctors note that this traveler's illness is common in every country. They say that in addition to bacteria a change in diet is equally to blame and suggest that the visitor slip slowly into the eating habits of Mexico. In other words, don't blast your tummy with the *habanera* or *jalapeno* pepper right off the bat. Work into the fried food, drinks, local specialties, and new spices gradually; take your time changing over to foods that you may never eat while at home, including the large quantities of wonderful tropical fruits that you'll want to eat every morning. Blame is also shared by mixing alcohol with longer than usual periods of time in the tropical sun.

It's The Water
While these theories are valid for the rest of Mexico, in Quintana Roo water is probably the worst culprit. Many parts of the Yucatan Peninsula have modern sewage systems, but the small villages and more isolated areas still have little or none. So all waste is redeposited in the earth and can contaminate the natural water supply. While in these places you should take special precautions.

In the backcountry, carry your own water, boil it, or purify it with chemicals, whether the source is out of the tap or a crystal clear *cenote.* That goes for brushing your teeth as well. If you have nothing else, a bottle of beer will make a safe (though maybe not sane) mouth rinse. If using ice, ask where it was made and if it's pure. Think about the water you're swimming in; some small local pools might be better avoided.

The easiest way to purify the water is with purification tablets; Hidroclonozone and Halazone are two, but many brands are available at drugstores in all countries—and in Mexico ask at the *farmacia.* Another common method is to carry a small plastic bottle of liquid bleach (eight to ten drops per quart of water) or iodine (called *yodo,* five to seven drops per quart). Whichever you use, let the water stand for 20 minutes to improve the flavor. If you're not prepared with any of the above, boiling the water for 20-30 minutes will purify it. Even though it takes a heck of a lot of fuel that you'll probably be carrying on your back, don't get lazy in this department. One can get very sick drinking contaminated water and you can't tell by looking at it—unless you travel with a microscope!

When camping on the beach where fresh water is scarce, use seawater to wash dishes and even yourself. Liquid Ivory or Joy detergents both suds well in saltwater. It only takes a small squirt of the detergent to do a good

f soap on the bottom of pots and ᴇ setting them over an open fire easy cleaning after cooking.)

In ᴛᴎᴇ larger cities purified water is generally provided in bottles in each room, or if the hotel is large enough it maintains its own purification plant on the premises. In Cozumel, for example, the Sol Caribe Hotel has a modern purification plant behind glass walls for all to see, and they're proud to show it off and explain how it works. If the tap water is pure, a sign over the spigot will specify this—except in Cancun which, with its modern infrastructure, brags that they're the only Mexican city in which every tap gives purified water. If you're not sure about the water, ask the desk clerk; he'll let you know the status—they prefer healthy guests that will return.

Other Sources Of Bacteria

Handling money can be a source of germs. Wash your hands frequently, don't put your fingers in your mouth, and carry individual foil packets of disinfectant cleaners, like Wash Up, that are handy and refreshing in the tropic heat. Hepatitis is another bug that can be contracted easily if you're around it.

When in backcountry cafes, remember that fruits and vegetables, especially those with a thin edible skin (like tomatoes), are a possible source of bacteria. If you like to eat food purchased from street vendors (and some should not be missed), use common sense. If you see the food being cooked (killing all the grubby little bacteria) before your eyes, have at it. If it's hanging there already cooked and nibbled on by small flying creatures, pass it by. It may have been there all day, and what was once a nice sterile morsel could easily have gone bad in the heat, or been contaminated by flies. When buying food at the marketplace to cook yourself, use the hints given in "Food."

Treatment

Remember, it's not just the visiting gringo who gets sick because of bacteria. Many Mexicans die each year from the same germs, and the Mexican government is working hard to remedy their sanitation problems.

Tremendous improvements have taken place that ultimately will be accomplished all over Mexico, but it's a slow process. In the meantime, many careful visitors come and go each year with nary a touch of *tourista*. If after all your precautions you still come down with traveler's illness, many medications are available for relief. Most can be bought over the counter in Mexico, but in the States you'll need a prescription from your doctor. Lomotil is common, and it certainly turns off the faucet after a few hours of dosing; however, it has the side effect of becoming a plug. It does not cure the problem, only the symptoms; if you quit taking it too soon your symptoms reappear and you're back to square one. In its favor, Lomotil probably works faster than any of the other drugs, and if you're about to embark on a 12-hour train ride across the Yucatan Peninsula you might consider Lomotil a lifesaver. A few other over-the-counter remedies are Kaopectate in the U.S., Immodium and Donamycin in Mexico. If you're concerned, check with your doctor before leaving home. Also ask him about some new formulas called Septra and Bactrim. Don't forget the common Pepto Bismol—some swear by it; be aware that it can turn the tongue a dark brownish color—nothing to be alarmed about.

For those who prefer natural remedies, lime juice and garlic are both considered good when taken as preventatives. They need to be taken in large quantities. Douse everything with the readily available lime juice (it's delicious on salads, fresh fruit, and in drinks). You'll have to figure your own ways of using garlic (some believers carry garlic capsules, available in most health food stores in the U.S.). *Pero te* (dog tea) is used by the Mexicans, as well as fresh coconut juice (don't eat the oily flesh, it makes your problem worse!). Plain boiled white rice soothes the tummy. While letting the ailment run its course stay away from spicy and oily foods and fresh fruits. Don't be surprised if you have chills, nausea, vomiting, stomach cramps, and run a fever. This could go on for about three days. But if the problem persists, see a doctor.

SUNBURN

Sunburn can spoil a vacation quicker than anything else, so approach the sun cautiously. Expose yourself for short periods the first few days; wear a hat and sunglasses. Use a good sunscreen, and apply it to all exposed areas of the body (don't forget your feet, hands, nose, back of the knees, and top of forehead—especially if you have a receding hairline). Remember that after every time you go into the water for a swim, sunscreen lotion must be reapplied. Even after a few days of desensitizing the skin, when spending a day snorkeling, wear a T-shirt in the water to protect your exposed back, and thoroughly douse the back of your neck with sunscreen lotion. PABA (para amino benzoic acid) solutions offer good protection and condition the skin. It's found in many brand names and strengths and is much cheaper in the U.S. than in Mexico. The higher the number on sunscreen bottles, the more protection.

If, despite precautions, you still get a painful sunburn, do not return to the sun. Cover up with clothes if it's impossible to find protective deep shade (like in the depths of a dark, thick forest). Keep in mind that even in partial shade (such as under a beach umbrella), the reflection of the sun off the sand or water will burn your skin. Reburning the skin can result in painful blisters that easily become infected. Soothing suntan lotions, coconut oil, vinegar, cool tea, and preparations like Solarcaine will help relieve the pain. Mostly a cure takes just a couple of days out of the sun. Drink plenty of liquids (especially water) and take tepid showers.

HEALING

Most small cities in Quintana Roo have a resident doctor. He may or may not speak English, but will usually make a house call. When staying in a hotel, get a doctor quickly by asking the hotel manager; in the larger resorts, an English-speaking doctor is on call 24 hours a day. If you need to ask someone to get you a doctor, say *necessito doctor, por favor!* Emergency clinics are found in all but the smallest villages, and a taxi driver can be your quickest way to get there when you're a stranger in town. In small rural villages, if you have a serious problem and no doctor is around, you can usually find a *curandero*. These healers deal with the old natural methods (and maybe just a few chants thrown in for good measure). This person could be a help in a desperate situation away from modern technology.

Self Help

The smart traveler carries a first-aid kit of some kind with him. If backpacking, at least carry the following:

> Alcohol
> Adhesive tape
> Aspirin
> Baking soda
> Band-Aids
> Cornstarch
> Gauze
> Hydrogen peroxide
> Iodine
> Insect repellent
> Lomotil
> Needle
> Pain pills
> Antibiotic ointment
> Pain killer
> Sunscreen
> Tweezers
> Water purification tablets

Many of these products are available in Mexico, but certain items, like aspirin and Band-Aids, are sold individually in small shops and are much cheaper bought in your hometown. Even if not out in the wilderness you should carry at least a few Band-Aids, aspirin, and an antibiotic ointment or powder or both. Travelers should be aware that in the tropics, with its heavy humidity, a simple scrape can become infected more easily than in a dry climate. So keep cuts and scratches as clean and as dry as possible.

Another great addition to your first-aid kit is

David Werner's book, *Where There Is No Doctor.* Also published in Spanish, it can be ordered from Hesperian Foundation, Box 1692, Palo Alto, CA 94302. David Werner drew on his experience living in Mexico's backcountry to create this informative book.

Shots
Check on your tetanus shot before you leave home, especially if you're backpacking in isolated regions.

SIMPLE FIRST-AID GUIDE

Acute Allergic Reaction
This, the most serious complication of insect bites, can be fatal. Common symptoms are hives, rash, pallor, nausea, tightness in chest or throat, trouble in speaking or breathing. Be alert for symptoms. If they appear, get prompt medical help. Start CPR if needed and continue until medical help is available.

Animal Bites
Bites, especially on face and neck, need immediate medical attention. If possible, catch and hold animal for observation taking care not to be bitten. Wash wound with soap and water (hold under running water for two to three minutes unless bleeding is heavy). *Do not* use iodine or other antiseptic. Bandage. This also applies to bites by human beings. In case of human bites the danger of infection is high.

Bee Stings
Apply cold compresses quickly. If possible, remove stinger by gentle scraping with clean fingernail and continue cold applications till pain is gone. Be alert for symptoms of acute allergic reaction or infection requiring medical aid.

Bleeding
For severe bleeding apply direct pressure to the wound with bandage or the heel of the hand. Do not remove cloths when blood-soaked, just add others on top and continue pressure till bleeding stops. Elevate bleeding part above heart level. If bleeding continues, apply pressure bandage to arterial points. *Do not* put on tourniquet unless advised by a physician. *Do not* use iodine or other disinfectant. Get medical aid.

Blister On Heel
It is better not to open a blister if you can rest the foot. If you can't, wash foot with soap and water; make a small hole at the base of the blister with a needle sterilized in 70% alcohol or by holding the needle in the flame of a match; drain fluid and cover with strip bandage or moleskin. If a blister breaks on its own, wash with soap and water, bandage, and be alert for signs of infection (redness, festering) that call for medical attention.

Burns
Minor burns (redness, swelling, pain): apply cold water or immerse burned part in cold water immediately. Use burn medication if necessary. **Deeper burns** (blisters develop). immerse in cold water (not ice water) or apply cold compresses for one to two hours. Blot dry and protect with sterile bandage. *Do not* use antiseptic, ointment, or home remedies. Consult a doctor. **Deep burns** (skin layers destroyed, skin may be charred): cover with sterile cloth; be alert for breathing difficulties and treat for shock if necessary. *Do not* remove clothing stuck to burn. *Do not* apply ice. *Do not* use burn remedies. Get medical help quickly.

Cuts

For small cuts wash with clean water and soap. Hold wound under running water. Bandage. Use hydrogen peroxide or other antiseptic. For large wounds see "Bleeding." If a finger or toe has been cut off, treat severed end to control bleeding. Put severed part in clean cloth for the doctor (it may be possible to reattach it by surgery). Treat for shock if necessary. Get medical help at once.

Diving Accident

There may be injury to the cervical spine (such as a broken neck). Call for medical help. (See "Drowning.")

Drowning

Clear airway and start CPR even before trying to get water out of lungs. Continue CPR till medical help arrives. In case of vomiting, turn victim's head to one side to prevent inhaling vomitus.

Food Poisoning

Symptoms appear a varying number of hours after eating and are generally like those of the flu—headache, diarrhea, vomiting, abdominal cramps, fever, a general sick feeling. See a doctor. A rare form, botulism, has a high fatality rate. Symptoms are double vision, inability to swallow, difficulty in speaking, respiratory paralysis. Get to emergency facility at once.

Fractures

Until medical help arrives, *do not* move the victim unless absolutely necessary. Suspected victims of back, neck, or hip injuries should not be moved. Suspected breaks of arms or legs should be splinted to avoid further damage before victim is moved, if moving is necessary.

Heat Exhaustion

Symptoms are cool moist skin, profuse sweating, headache, fatigue, drowsiness with essentially normal body temperature. Remove victim to cool surroundings, raise feet and legs, loosen clothing and apply cool cloths. Give sips of salt water—one teaspoon of salt to a glass of water—for rehydration. If victim vomits, stop fluids, take the victim to emergency facility as soon as possible.

Heat Stroke

Rush victim to hospital. Heat stroke can be fatal. Victim may be unconscious or severely confused. Skin feels hot, is red and dry, with no perspiration. Body temperature is high. Pulse is rapid. Remove victim to cool area, sponge with cool water or rubbing alcohol: use fans or a/c and wrap in wet sheets, but do not over chill. Massage arms and legs to increase circulation. *Do not* give large amount of liquids. *Do not* give liquids if victim is unconscious.

Insect Bites

Be alert for acute allergic reaction that requires quick medical aid. Otherwise, apply cold compresses, soothing lotions.

Jellyfish Stings

Symptom is acute pain and may include feeling of paralysis. Immerse in ice water from five to ten minutes or apply aromatic spirits of ammonia to remove venom from skin. Be alert for symptoms of acute allergic reaction and/or shock. If this happens, get victim to hospital as soon as possible.

Mosquito Bites

Apply cold compresses and a mild lotion to relieve itching. If bites are scratched and infection starts (fever, swelling, redness), see a doctor.

Motion Sickness

Get a prescription from your doctor if boat traveling is anticipated and this illness is a problem. Many over-the-counter remedies are sold in the U.S.: Bonine and Dramamine are two and if you prefer not to take
continued on next page

continued from previous page
chemicals or get drowsy something new, the Sea Band, is a cloth band that you place around the pressure point of the wrists. For more information write:

Sea Band
1645 Palm Beach Lake Blvd.
Suite 220
W. Palm Beach, FL 33401
(305) 684-4508

Medication is also available by prescription from your doctor that's administered in adhesive patches behind the ear.

Muscle Cramps
Usually a result of unaccustomed exertion. "Working" the muscle or kneading with hand relieves cramp. If in water head for shore (you can swim even with a muscle cramp), or knead muscle with hand. Call for help if needed. *Do not* panic.

Mushroom Poisoning
Even a small ingestion may be serious. Induce vomiting immediately if there is any question of mushroom poisoning. Symptoms—vomiting, diarrhea, difficult breathing — may begin in one to two hours or up to 24 hours. Convulsions and delirium may develop. Go to a doctor or emergency facility at once.

Nosebleed
Press bleeding nostril closed or pinch nostrils together or pack with sterile cotton or gauze. Apply cold to nose and face. Victim should sit up, leaning forward, or lie down with head and shoulders raised. If bleeding does not stop in 10 minutes get medical help.

Obstructed Airway
Find out if victim can talk by asking "Can you talk?" If he can talk, encourage victim to try to cough obstruction out. If he can't speak, a trained person must apply the Heimlich method. If you are alone and choking, try to forcefully cough object out. Or press your fist into your upper abdomen with a quick upward thrust, or lean forward and quickly press your upper abdomen over any firm object with rounded edge (back of chair, edge of sink, porch railing). Keep trying till the object comes out.

Ivy, Oak, Or Sumac
After contact, wash affected area with alkali-base laundry soap, lathering well. Have a poison-ivy remedy available in case itching and blisters develop.

Plant Poisoning
Many plants are poisonous if eaten or chewed. Induce vomiting immediately. Take victim to emergency facility for treatment. If the leaves of the diffenbachia (common in the Yucatan jungle) are chewed, one of the first symptoms is swelling of the throat.

Puncture Wounds
Usually caused by stepping on a tack or a nail. They often do not bleed, so try to squeeze out some blood. Wash thoroughly with soap and water and apply a sterile bandage. Check with doctor about tetanus. If pain, heat, throbbing, or redness develop, get medical attention at once.

Rabies
Bites from bats, raccoons, rats, or other wild animals are the most common threat of rabies today. Try to capture the animal, avoiding getting bitten, so it can be observed; do not kill the animal unless necessary and try not to injure the head so the brain can be examined. If the animal can't be found, see a doctor who may decide to use anti-rabies immunization. In any case, flush bite with water and apply a dry dressing; keep victim quiet and see a doctor as soon as possible.

Scrapes

Sponge with soap and water; dry. Apply antibiotic ointment or powder and cover with a non-stick dressing (or tape on a piece of cellophane). When healing starts, stop ointment and use antiseptic powder to help scab form. Ask doctor about tetanus.

Shock

Can be a side effect in any kind of injury. Get immediate medical help. Symptoms may be pallor, clammy feeling to the skin, shallow breathing, fast pulse, weakness, or thirst. Loosen clothing, cover victim with blanket but do not apply other heat, and place him lying on his back with feet raised. If necessary, start CPR. *Do not* give water or other fluids.

Snakebite

If snake is not poisonous, toothmarks usually appear in an even row (an exception, the poisonous gila monster, shows even tooth marks). Wash the bite with soap and water and apply sterile bandage. See a doctor. If snake is poisonous, puncture marks (one to six) can usually be seen. Kill the snake for identification if possible, taking care not to be bitten. Keep the victim quiet, immobilize the bitten arm or leg, keeping it on a lower level than the heart. If possible, phone ahead to be sure antivenin is available and get medical treatment as soon as possible. *Do not* give alcohol in any form. If treatment must be delayed and snakebite kit is available, use as directed.

Spider Bites

The black widow bite may produce only a light reaction at the place of the bite, but severe pain, a general sick feeling, sweating, abdominal cramps, and breathing and speaking difficulty may develop. The more dangerous brown recluse spider's venom produces a severe reaction at the bite, generally in two to eight hours, plus chills, fever, joint pain, nausea, and vomiting. Apply a cold compress to the bite in either case. Get medical aid quickly.

Sprain

Treat as a fracture till injured part has been X-rayed. Raise the sprained ankle or other joint and apply cold compresses or immerse in cold water. If swelling is pronounced, try not to use the injured part till it has been X-rayed. Get prompt medical help.

Sunburn

For skin that is moderately red and slightly swollen, apply wet dressings of gauze dipped in a solution of one tablespoon baking soda and one tablespoon cornstarch to two quarts of cool water. Or take a cool bath with a cup of baking soda to a tub of water. Sunburn remedies are helpful in relieving pain. See a doctor if burn is severe.

Sunstroke

This is a severe emergency. See "Heat Stroke." Skin is hot and dry; body temperature is high. The victim may be delirious or unconscious. Get medical help immediately.

Ticks

Cover ticks with mineral oil or kerosene to exclude air from ticks and they will usually drop off or can be lifted off with tweezers in 30 minutes. To avoid infection, take care to remove whole tick. Wash area with soap and water. Check with doctor or health department to see if deadly ticks are in the area.

Wasp Sting

Apply cold compresses to the sting and watch for acute allergic reaction. If such symptoms develop, get victim to medical facility immediately.

CAMERAS AND PICTURE TAKING

Bring a camera to Cancun! Nature and Maya combine to provide unforgettable panoramas, well worth taking home with you on film to savor again at your leisure. Many people find simple cameras such as Instamatics or disc-types easy to carry and uncomplicated. Others prefer 35mm, which offer higher-quality pictures, are easier than ever to use, and available in any price range. They can come equipped with built-in light meter, automatic exposure, self-focus, and self-advancing—with little more to do than aim and click.

Film

Two reasons to bring film with you are that it's cheaper and more readily available in the States. Two reasons *not* to bring lots of film are that space may be a problem, and heat can affect film quality, both before and after exposure. If you're traveling for more than two weeks in a car or bus a good part of the time, protect the finished product by carrying film in an insulated case. You can buy a soft-sided insulated bag in most camera shops or order one out of a professional photography magazine. For the average vacation, if your

film is kept in an air-conditioned room there should be no problem. Most varieties of Kodak film are found in camera shops and hotel gift shops in Cancun, Cozumel, and Isla Mujeres. In the smaller towns along the Caribbean coast you may not be able to find slide film.

X-ray Protection

If you bring your film from home remember to take precautions when traveling by plane. Each time film is passed through the security X-ray machine, a little damage is done. It's cumulative, and perhaps one time won't make much difference, but most photographers won't take the chance. Request hand inspection. With today's tight security at airports, some guards insist on passing your film and camera through the X-ray machine. It's wise to keep it in protective lead bags if packed in your checked luggage. Lead-lined bags are available at camera shops in two sizes: the larger size holds up to 22 rolls of 35mm film, the smaller holds eight rolls. If you use fast film, ASA 400 or higher, buy the double lead-lined bag designed to protect more sensitive film. Carry an extra lead-lined bag for your film-loaded camera if you want to drop it into a piece of carry-on luggage. (And for non-photographers, these bags protect medications from X-ray damage.)

If you decide to request hand examination (rarely if ever refused at a Mexican airport), make it simple for the security guard. Have the film out of boxes, placed together in one clear Ziploc plastic bag that you can hand him for quick examination both coming and going. He'll also want to look at the camera; load it after crossing the border.

Film Processing

For processing film the traveler has several options. Most people take their film home and have it processed at a familiar lab. Again, if the trip is lengthy and you are shooting lots of film, it's impractical to carry used rolls around for a couple of months. One-hour photo labs are found in the larger cities and resort areas in Quintana Roo, but they only handle color prints; color slides must be processed at a lab in Mexico City, which usually takes a week or two. If you'll be passing through the same city on another leg of your trip, the lab is a good cool place to store your slides while you travel. Just tell the lab technician when you think you'll be picking them up. Kodak mailers are another option but most photographers won't let their film out of sight until they reach their own favorite lab.

Camera Protection

Take a few precautions with your camera while traveling. At the beach remember that a combination of wind and sand can really gum up the works and scratch the lens. On 35mm cameras keep a clear skylight filter on the lens instead of a lens cap so the camera can hang around your neck always at the ready for that spectacular shot that comes when least expected. And if something is going to get scratched, better a $15 filter rather than a $300 lens. It also helps to carry as little equipment as possible. If you want more than candids and you carry a 35mm camera, basic equipment can be simple. Padded camera cases are good and come in all sizes. A canvas bag is lighter and less conspicuous than a heavy photo bag, but isn't padded. At the nearest surplus store you can find small military bags and webbed belts with eyelet holes to hang canteen pouches and two clip holders. These are perfect size for holding one or two extra lenses (safely tucked into a canteen pouch) and film. They're comfortable hanging on the hips and free the hands while climbing pyramids or on long hikes.

Safety Tips

Keep your camera dry; carrying a couple of big Ziploc bags affords instant protection. If you plan to be in small boats that put you close to the water, keep the cameras in the zipped bags when not in use. Don't *store* cameras in plastic bags for any length of time because the moisture that builds up in the bag can damage a camera as much as leaving it in the rain. It's always wise to keep the cameras out of sight in a car or when camping out. Put your name and address on the camera. Chances are if it gets left behind or stolen it won't matter whether your name is there or not, and don't expect to see it again; however, miracles do happen. (You *can* put a rider on most homeowner's insurance policies for a nominal sum that will cover the cost if a camera is lost or stolen.) It's a nuisance to carry cameras every second when traveling for a long period. During an evening out, you can leave your cameras and equipment (out of sight) in the hotel room—unless it makes you crazy all evening worrying about it!

Cameras can be a help and a hindrance when trying to get to know the people. Traveling in the backcountry you'll run into folks frightened of having their pictures taken. Keep your camera put away until the right moment. The main thing to remember is to ask permission first and then if someone doesn't want his/her picture taken, accept the refusal with a gracious smile and move on.

Videos

Would you like a visual preview of what to expect in Cozumel, or for that matter many other Mexican destinations? If so, take a look at *Travelview International's* quality videos that give an excellent profile of the island. Each cassette includes a reference guide to the services and amenities of hotels on the island. The videos are available at Blockbuster Video and Walden Book Stores, or contact Travelview International direct for a complete worldwide listing of more than 80 titles, tel. (800) 325-3108, in Texas tel. (713) 975-7077

OTHER PRACTICALITIES

ENTRY AND DEPARTURE

U.S. and Canadian citizens can obtain a free tourist card with proof of citizenship (birth certificate, passport, voter's registration, or notorized affidavit) good for 180 days. It can be obtained at any Mexican consulate or tourist office, at all border entry points, or from airport ticket offices for those traveling by plane. Hang on to your tourist card for the entire trip. If visiting Mexico for 72 hours or less, a tourist card is not needed. Ask at the Mexican consulate about extensions for longer periods. If you're a naturalized citizen, carry your naturalization papers or passport. Certificates of vaccination are not required to enter Mexico from U.S. or Canadian citizens; other nationals should check with a local Mexican consulate. Those under 18 without a parent or legal guardian must present a notorized letter from the parents or guardian granting permission to travel alone in Mexico. If a single parent is traveling with a minor, he or she should carry a notorized letter from the other parent granting permission. This is important going in both directions.

Bring A Passport
Hang onto your tourist card! You won't need it after you go through customs until it's time to leave the country. Then you must give it back. If you have a passport, bring it along even though it's not required (tuck your tourist card inside); it's the simplest ID when cashing travelers cheques, registering at hotels, and going through immigration. If you're visiting an area that has a current health problem and you have a health card with current information, keep that with the passport also. Keep all documents in a waterproof plastic case and in a safe place. Write to the U.S. Secretary of State for the most recent information about isolated areas that might be on the list for immunization. If traveling to such places, you'll need proof of vaccination to get back into the U.S. and perhaps other countries as well.

Driving Procedures
If traveling by car or RV, the tourist card serves as a vehicle permit when completed and validated at the border point of entry. Vehicle title or registration and driver's license are required. If you should happen to reach a remote border crossing at night, you may find it unmanned. *Do not* cross the border with your car until you have obtained the proper papers; if you do it will cause problems when you exit the country. Mexican vehicle insurance is available at most border towns 24 hours a day.

If traveling with a pet, a veterinarian's certificate verifying good health and a rabies inoculation within the last six months is required. This certificate will be validated by any Mexican consulate for a small fee.

Purchases
When departing by land, air, or sea, you must declare at the point of reentry into your own country all items acquired in Mexico. To facilitate this procedure, it is wise to register any foreign-made possessions with customs officials before entering Mexico and to retain the receipts for purchases made while there. Limitations on the value of imported, duty-free goods vary from country to country and should be checked before traveling. U.S. citizens are allowed to carry through customs $400 of purchases per person duty free and up to $1000 for 10% tax. However, about 2,700 items are exempt from this limit, most of which are handcrafted or manufactured in Mexico. Consular offices or embassies in Mexico City can supply additional information

on exempt items. Plants and certain foods are not allowed into the U.S. Authentic archaeological finds, colonial art, and other original artifacts cannot be exported from Mexico. And of course trying to bring pot or any other narcotic out of Mexico and into the U.S. is foolhardy. Jail is one place in Mexico a visitor can miss.

Bargaining
This is how a visitor really gets to know the people. Although the influx of many outsiders who don't appreciate the delicate art of bargaining has deteriorated this traditional verbal exchange it's still a way of life between locals, and it can still build a bridge between the gringo and the Mexican. Some Americans accustomed to shopping with plastic money either find bargaining distasteful or go overboard and insult the merchant by offering far too little. It would not be insulting to begin the bargaining at 50% below the asking price; expect to earn about a 20% discount (and new respect) after a lively repartee often filled with joviality between buyer and seller.

Shipping
Mailing and shipping from Mexico is easy within certain limitations. Packages of less than $25 in value can be sent to the U.S. The package must be marked "Unsolicited Gift— Under $50" and addressed to someone other than the traveler. Only one package per day may be sent to the same addressee. Major stores will handle shipping arrangements on larger items and duty must be paid; this is in addition to the $400 carried in person across the border.

COMMUNICATIONS

Telephone
Large cities in Mexico have direct dialing to the U.S., with international operators available to assist whenever necessary. Many cities in Quintana Roo still have a less-efficient system, and often a long-distance call can take several hours to place. **Note**: All calls to Cozumel from the U.S. should begin with 011-52-987-your number.

Telegraph And Postal
Even the smallest village has a telegraph office. Wires can often be sent direct from the larger hotels. Almost every town in Quintana Roo has a post office. If you can't find it by looking, ask—it may be located in someone's front parlor. Airmail postage is recommended for the best delivery. Post offices will hold mail for travelers one week if it is marked *a/c Lista de Correos* ("care of General Delivery"). Hotels will extend the same service for mail marked "tourist mail, hold for arrival."

Radio And Television
AM and FM radio stations, in Spanish, are scattered throughout the Peninsula. Television is becoming more common as well. In

---

TELEPHONE AND EMERGENCY INFORMATION

Information (national)	01
Long-distance operator	02
Time	03
Information (local)	04
Police radio patrol	06
Bilingual emergency information	07
International operator (English)	09
Long-distance direct service:	
station to station (national)	91 plus area code and number
person to person (national)	92 plus area code and number
Long-distance direct services:	
station to station (international)	95 plus area code and number
person to person (international)	96 plus area code and number
Worldwide:	
station to station	98
person to person	99

the major cities hotel rooms have TV entertainment. The large resort hotels have one or more cable stations from the U.S., on which you can expect to see all the major baseball and football games, news, and latest movies.

MONEY

Currency Exchange

The peso, the basic medium of exchange in Mexico, has floated on the free market since 1976. The money is issued in paper bills (1,000, 5,000, 10,000, 20,000, and 50,000 denominations) and coins (up to 500 peso pieces). Curiously, coins of smaller value are measured in centavos (10, 20, and 50), but no one is really sure what to use them for since nothing sells for centavos.

Usually your best rate of exchange is the bank, but small shops frequently give a better rate. Hotels notoriously give the poorest exchange. Check to see what kind of a fee, if any, is charged. In today's Mexican economy, it's not usual to have money-changers approach you in the bank while you're waiting in line and offer you better than the posted rate. There's no harm in this—except, can you tell the difference between counterfeit pesos and the real thing? You can learn the current exchange rate daily in all banks and most hotels. Try not to run out of money over the weekend because the new rate often is not posted until noon on Monday and you will get the previous Friday rate of exchange even if the weekend newspaper may be announcing an overwhelming difference—in your favor.

Credit Cards

Major credit cards are accepted at all of the larger hotels, travel agencies, and many shops throughout Quintana Roo. But don't take it for granted, ask. In rare instances you will be asked to pay a fee on top of your charged amount. Gas stations *do not* accept credit cards.

Business Hours

Banks open from 0900-1330, Mon. to Friday. Business offices open from 0800 or 0900-1300 or 1400, then reopen at about 1530-1600, until 1800. Government offices are usually open from 0830-1500. Stores in cities in Quintana Roo are generally open from 1000-1900 or 2000, closing from 1300-1600. Government offices, banks and stores are closed on national holidays.

Tipping

If not already included, 10-20% of the bill is standard. Tips for assistance with bags should be equivalent to US$.50 per bag. Chambermaids should receive about US$1 per day. It is not necessary to tip taxi drivers unless they have performed a special service. Tour guides should receive US$1 for a half-day trip and US$3 per day for longer trips. Gas station attendants are tipped P500 or P1000 for pumping gas, cleaning the windshield, checking the oil and water, and providing other standard services. Often tips are the main part of the provider's income.

MISCELLANEOUS

Time

The state of Quintana Roo is in U.S. Central Time Zone.

Electricity

Electric current has been standardized throughout Mexico, using the same 60-cycle 110-volt AC current common in the U.S. Small travel appliances can be used everywhere; if you have a problem, it will be because there's no electricity at all. In some areas of Quintana Roo, electricity is supplied by small generators and generally turned off at 2200. The hotels will offer you gas lanterns after the lights go out.

Studying In Mexico

In addition to fulfilling the requirements for a tourist card, students must present documents to a Mexican consulate demonstrating that they have been accepted at an educational institution and that they are financially solvent. A number of courses and workshops are offered throughout Mexico lasting two to eight weeks in addition to full-time study programs. The United Nations Institute of International Education can supply information on study projects in Mexico. Many adults as well as younger folks are taking part in language programs where the student lives with a family (that speaks only Spanish to them) for a period of two to four weeks and attends language classes daily. This total immersion into the language, even for a short time, is quite successful and popular as a cultural experience.

Also write to the National Registration Center for Study Abroad (NRCSA), 823 North Second St., Milwaukee, WI 53203, or phone (414) 278-0631. Request their "Directory of Educational Programs," which describes programs in a number of cities in Mexico.

Churches And Clubs

Mexico is predominantly a Catholic country. However, you'll find a few churches of other denominations in the larger cities (if you find a synagogue, let me know!). Local telephone books and hotel clerks have these listings. Many international organizations like the Lions, Rotary, Shriners, and foreign social groups have branches.

U.S. Embassies And Consulates

If an American citizen finds himself with a problem of any kind, the nearest consul will provide advice or help. Travel advisories with up-to-the-minute information about traveling in remote areas of Mexico are available.

CANCUN

By now everyone knows the story of a wise Mexican computer that in 1967 chose a small, swampy finger of land in an isolated part of the Mexican Caribbean, and pixels flashed, "Let There Be Tourists." And so it happened—Cancun resort was born. Designing Cancun, an island shaped like a seven with a bridge at both ends connecting the mainland, began from the ground up in 1968: new infrastructure, modern electrical plants, purified tap water, paved tree-lined avenues, and buildings which fit into the landscape (reincarnated Mayas could almost mistake some of them for new pyramids). When the first hotels opened their doors in 1972, visitors began coming and haven't stopped since.

For some, the name Cancun conjures immediate images of sugar-fine sand, a palette-blue sea, and flashing dollar signs. Think again! The beaches *are* stunning, the water *is* enticing, and it *does* take lots of money to enjoy Cancun if you just drop in at one of the fabulous resorts in the hotel zone. However, with the constant additions in downtown Cancun and careful shopping for package deals from your travel agent or in the travel pages of your local newspaper there's something to fit every pocket, the best of both worlds. You just have to look a little harder for the less-expensive world.

At one end of the bridge is the "island," the hotel zone where the most elegant hotels are located; on the other end is Cancun city, where new moderately priced hotels and condos continue to be built. Hotels in the city serve up the flavor of Yucatan in the moderate US$30- to $80-a-night category and offer easy access to crowded sidewalk cafes (good for meeting people), romantic dinners, hot discos, intimate bistros, cinemas, buses, and a multitude of shops to explore—all within a few kilometers of the beach and lagoon. But if you need a shot of luxury, Hotel Row is the place to get it. Here, the most modern hostelries on Mexico's Caribbean coast provide a first-rate vacation in a sunny tropical setting. There's glamour, excitement, excellent service, great entertainment, lavish rooms, and epicurean delights—to say nothing of the surroundings, which bombard the senses with nature's simple beauty.

SIGHTS

Archaeological Zones

Cancun has little to offer the archaeology buff by comparison to the larger sites at Chichen Itza, Uxmal, and Palenque. But surprisingly, structures built on this narrow strip of land have contributed important information to our knowledge about the people that lived here hundreds of years ago. Remnants of two sites, **Del Rey** on the south end of the island (close to Club Med) and **Yamil Lu'um** "Hilly Land" next to the Sheraton Hotel, are both worth a look; Yamil Lu'um is also on the highest point of mostly flat Cancun. The two small temples (15 meters high) were probably used as watchtowers and lighthouses along this navigational route. Between 400-700 years old, they were first noted by two intrepid American explorers—John L. Stephens and Frederick Catherwood in 1841.

Museum Of Anthropology

Located in the Convention Center, the museum houses Maya artifacts found on Cancun and other parts of the Peninsula. Though small, it graphically answers some questions about the everyday life of the Maya Indian. For example, a display of misshapen skulls has an accompanying explanation of how the Maya formed the heads of infants to conform to their idea of beauty. The museum is open from 10 a.m.-2 p.m. and 5-8 p.m. daily; small entrance fee.

Scenic Spots

All of Cancun is scenic. But the most scenic beaches are on the seaward side of the island, extending 21 km and parallel to Paseo Kukulkan. If you haven't been to Cancun since before Hurricane Gilbert, you will see some rearrangements of the beaches. In some areas sand was whisked out to sea, in others the beach was widened with sand deposits. Walking along the coast is rated a five-star activity, and it's free (all beaches in Mexico are public). The panorama is capricious—the color of the sea changes subtly throughout the day from pale aqua at dawn to deep turquoise at noon to cerulean blue under the blazing afternoon sun to pink-splashed purple during the silent sunset.

Nichupte Lagoon

This large lagoon which parallels Paseo Kukulcan is a combination of sweet water fed by underground springs and saltwater that enters from two openings to the sea. In certain areas where the water is still and swampy, mangroves provide hiding places for the cayman,

Yamil Lu'um

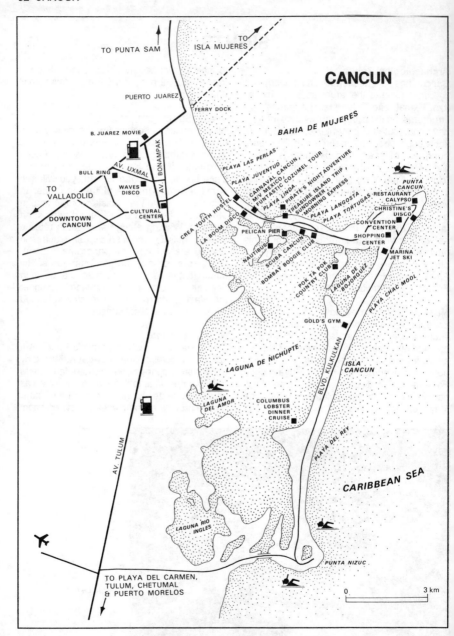

little brother of large crocodilians found on other parts of the Peninsula. Birdlife is plentiful, with a treasure trove of over 200 cataloged species including herons, egrets, ospreys, screaming parrots, and parakeets; the sooty tern returns here to nest each year. The best way to see the lagoon and its wildlife is by boat. One of the many travel agents or your hotel can arrange a boat and a guide who knows his way around. Along the north end of the lagoon the marinas bustle with activity, and the trim greens of the Pok Ta Pok golf course extend out over the water. Nichupte is a favorite for water-skiing, sailing (Sunfish and Hobie cat rentals), and sailboarding. Restaurants from exotic to generic are open all day, with a variety of shopping centers offering something for everybody. The arts and crafts center offers those who find bargaining stimulating a chance to practice the art. For the more timid who may be used to paying the marked price, there are also shops which have become very Americanized. *Almost* all businesses in Cancun accept plastic money.

DRIVING DISTANCES FROM CANCUN

Airport	20 km
Akumal	104 km
Aventuras (playa)	107 km
Bacalar	320 km
Chemuyil	109 km
Chetumal	382 km
Chichen Itza	192 km
Club Med	25 km
Coba	167 km
Kohunlich	449 km
Merida	312 km
Pamul	92 km
Playa del Carmen	65 km
Puerto Juarez	2 km
Puerto Morelos	32 km
Punta Sam	7 km
Tulum	130 km
Valladolid	152 km
Xcaret	72 km
Xelha	123 km

BEACHES

Note!
The water on the ocean side of Cancun can be hazardous. Pay particular attention to warning signs, and if in doubt, don't swim. Each year a few people drown off the beaches of Cancun because of a lack of respect for the power of this beautiful sea.

Bus To The Beach
Cancun is one big beach, or more accurately, a series of breathtaking beaches laid end to end and around corners and curves. It's simple to reach any beach by bus; the route begins in downtown Cancun, making a circuit along Paseo Kukulcan, through the hotel zone, past the Convention Center, and on to the last hotel, whichever that happens to be at the time you're visiting. Bus stops are frequent and marked with blue signs that say *Parada*. However, most drivers will stop for a waving arm almost anywhere (if there's room). Bus fare is about US$.50 to anyplace.

Beginning Snorkelers
Cancun's beaches are for relaxing and soaking up the sun. The sandy sea-floor along here doesn't provide hiding places for the kind of sealife that prefers cool caves and rocky crevices. (Don't despair; there are a number of reefs in the area with rich marine-life to explore.) But for beginners (including children), this is a great place to learn to snorkel—and sun-loving fish such as tanned beauties and burnt-back beach nappers will provide the thrill of accomplishment when viewed for the first time through the glass. Guests at the Camino Real Hotel have a lovely, calm manmade lagoon ideal for learning, with tropical fish and sea turtles from small to very large to swim with.

Lifeguards
The hotels on the island all have beaches with various activities; some provide *palapa* sun shelters, volleyball courts, aerobic classes, bars, restaurants, showers, restrooms, and towels for their guests, and most importantly, lifeguards. Everyone is free to use the

60-foot strip of sand along the sea on any part of Cancun; signs indicating this are prominently posted everywhere by Sectur, the Ministry of Tourism. Visitors staying in the city have been known to spend their entire vacations (on their own towels) under the eye of a hotel lifeguard.

Public Beaches

Don't expect lifeguards or showers; some have snack stands and good parking areas. **Playa Linda** is close to the city (ten minutes by bus) located on Paseo Kukulcan near the Nichupte bridge. Two km past Playa Linda on Paseo Kukulcan is **Playa Tortuga,** easily spotted by a sign that reads Playa Recreativa. The water is crystal clear, calm, and deep; on the beach is a *palapa*-covered snack bar. RV travelers often park here.

Around the point beyond the Convention Center is **Playa Chacmool.** This stunning beach displays the vibrant colors that make the Caribbean famous. You can walk out to sea 14 meters in shallow water before it begins to drop off. Check the tide conditions on a sign just south of the beach cafe—the water can be changeable here and at times gets rough.

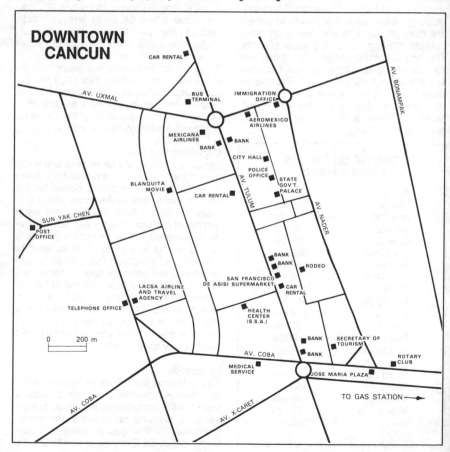

DOWNTOWN CANCUN

CAR RENTAL

AV. UXMAL

BUS TERMINAL

IMMIGRATION OFFICE

AV. BONAMPAK

AEROMEXICO AIRLINES

MEXICANA AIRLINES

BANK

BANK

CITY HALL

POLICE OFFICE

STATE GOV'T. PALACE

AV. TULUM

AV. NADER

BLANQUITA MOVIE

CAR RENTAL

SUN YAK CHEN

POST OFFICE

BANK

BANK

RODEO

SAN FRANCISCO DE ASISI SUPERMARKET

CAR RENTAL

LACSA AIRLINE AND TRAVEL AGENCY

TELEPHONE OFFICE

HEALTH CENTER (S.S.A.)

0   200 m

BANK

BANK

SECRETARY OF TOURISM

ROTARY CLUB

AV. COBA

MEDICAL SERVICE

JOSE MARIA PLAZA

AV. COBA

AV. X-CARET

TO GAS STATION →

The Surf
There isn't a beach suitable for surfing anywhere on Cancun. Where protected by the reef, the Peninsula is a placid sea ideal for swimming. After leaving the city, the first stretch of beach from the YH to Hotel Cancun Viva provides calm water and is also protected from strong currents and dangerous surf. The water at the lagoon is usually calm, but not as clear as the sea. Along the lagoonside you'll find many marinas and headquarters for water activities. On the east (the Caribbean or windward) side from Punta Cancun to Punta Nizuc the surf can be as high as three feet, and at certain times you'll encounter an undertow. If you don't see a water —condition sign, ask at the concession stand — or *don't* swim. The calmest and most protected beaches on the windward side face Bahia Mujeres on the north end of the island.

WATER SPORTS

The Reefs
One of the most popular reefs despite its shallow depths is **Chital,** located a short distance north of Hotel Stouffer Presidente on the island. The reef Is made up of two sections, both about 20 meters wide. Expect a one-knot current and clear visibility up to 33 meters. **Cuevones Reef,** about three km north of Punta Cancun, is just what its name tells us in Spanish, "small caves." Here the body of the reef is comprised of elkhorn, rock, and brain coral. The series of caves varies in size from a five-meter cavern to a two-meter hole, all at a depth of about 10 meters. With an amazing 45-meter visibility, divers find themselves surrounded by large schools of reef fish, groupers, amberjack, and the ever-lurking predators, barracudas. **Manchones Reef** is a shallow reef closer to Isla Mujeres (three km south) than to Cancun (eight km northeast). Its ten-meter depth, 60-meter visibility, lack of current, and abundant sealife make it an ideal learning reef for beginning scuba divers.

Snorkeling
The experienced snorkeler will want to observe the beauty of the reefs, which are mainly made up of a variety of uniquely shaped and textured coral. In the immediate vicinity the most popular snorkeling areas are Chital, Cuevones, and Manchones reefs. They are home to large populations of reef fish, including blue chromis and barracuda. Chital, two km north of the island, has good snorkeling with depths between two to five meters. Cuevones and Manchones reefs are between Cancun and Isla Mujeres, with depths 10-15 meters. Usually dive boats will take snorkelers along (room permitting) on scuba trips. Tour boats leaving daily for Garrafon Beach on Isla Mujeres carry snorkeling equipment. Garrafon is a logical spot for beginners and intermediates. Non-divers, bring dry bread to feed the little critters. They'll jump from the water and eat out of your hand—watch the fingers! Snorkeling equipment is available for rent at all the marinas and some of the hotels.

WATER SAFETY

The usual precautions apply. Don't swim alone in isolated places; take small children to calm surf areas, especially if there isn't a lifeguard. Common sense protection with sun-screen lotions, broad-brimmed hats, and dark glasses are suggested for anyone still walking around in winter-whites (skin). Familiar brands of American sun-screen lotions are available at all pharmacies and many hotel gift shops—but will cost much less in the States.

Familiarize yourself with the beach before splashing into the surf. Most of the beaches are posted with surf condition signs (in Spanish) which specify the condition each day with a colored flag. Red is high surf or undertow—DANGEROUS; yellow is medium high surf—USE WITH CAUTION; green is CALM. While swimming, if you feel yourself being pulled out to sea, don't panic, and don't wear yourself out trying to swim to shore. Instead, swim parallel to the beach in either direction, and usually after swimming three or four meters you'll be out of the undertow—then swim to shore.

Dive Certification

Cancun has a good selection of dive shops; check with the marinas for recommendations. Before a diver can rent equipment, it's necessary to show a certified diver's card. If not certified, resort courses (for one dive accompanied by the divemaster) and certification classes (around 40 hours) are offered. For class info call **Mundo Marina,** PADI, tel. 3-05-54; **Neptune,** NAUI, tel. 3-07-22; **Aqua Tours,** tel. 3-02-07.

Scuba Diving

For the experienced scuba diver, Cancun would be second choice; Cozumel is unquestionably *numero uno!* For dive spots, however, none of the Caribbean is dull. An abundance of rich sealife surrounds each of the reefs; though around Cancun they're somewhat shallow, the beauty and excitement of the scenery are still dramatic. At **Punta Nizuc** (next to Club Med), experienced divers can explore the starting point of the Belize barrier reef that runs south 250 km parallel to the Quintana Roo coast to the Gulf of Honduras. This reef is the fifth-longest reef in the world. From largest to smallest they are: Great Barrier Reef, Australia (1,600 km); Southwest Barrier Reef, New Caledonia (600 km); Northeast Barrier Reef, New Caledonia (540 km); Great Sea Reef, Fiji Islands (260 km); Belizean Reef (250 km); South Louisiade Archipelago Reef, Papua New Guinea (200 km).

Windsurfing

For anyone who doesn't know, a windsurfer (also known as a sailboard) is comprised of a surfboard with a sail on a mast attached to the board by a swivel joint. This is controlled by a standing passenger who manipulates the sail with a wishbone tiller. It's a great wind-powered sport; in a brisk breeze the sail billows and this surfboard-cum-sailboat takes its sailor on an exhilarating ride skimming across the waves at mind-boggling speeds. Lessons are available at most of the marinas or the International Windsurfer Sailing School at Playa Tortuga, tel. 4-20-23. Usually six hours of lessons give you a good start. Sailboards are available to rent at many of the hotels and the marinas.

Sailboats

If your idea of a ride in the wind includes a deck under foot and a tiller in hand, Hobie cat and Sunfish rentals are available at a few hotels and most of the marinas. These small boats will give you a good fast ride if the wind is up. Negotiate for the fee you prefer to pay (remember, you're in Mexico)—sometimes you can get a good daily rate, better than the hourly rate posted.

beaches of Cancun

Water-skiing
Most water-skiers prefer Nichupte Lagoon, although skiers are seen on calm days in Bahia de Mujeres north of the island. Equipment and instruction information are available from the marinas.

Jet-skiing And Parasailing
One of the new speed thrills on the lagoon is jet-skiing, obtained by means of a small motorized sled that will slowly circle around the driver should he or she fall off (rentals available at most marinas). Parasailing is popular at the busy beaches. The sailor, strapped into a colorful parachute and safety vest, is pulled high over the sand and surf by a speedboat; after about ten minutes of "flying" he is gently deposited back on land with the help of two catchers. Once in awhile the rider gets wet when he is inadvertently dropped in the bay—usually to the guffaws of the beach crowd.

Marinas
Cancun offers many marinas with a variety of services. Some provide diving equipment and boats to the best scuba grounds; others have docks for a variety of sports equipment, including a flight on an ultralight, and still other docks are pickup points for organized boat tours. (See pages 98-99 for a complete listing of Marinas.)

FISHING

Deep-sea Fishing
Fishermen come to Cancun for what is considered some of the finest game fishing in the world. Charters are available and easily arranged with a day or two advance reservation. For information on half- and whole-day trips, call the marinas or check with your hotel. On full-day trips you can cap off the afternoon with a fish barbecue on the beach (ask the captain in advance). One of the most exciting game fish, the sailfish, runs from March to mid-July, bonito and dolphin from May to early July, wahoo and kingfish from May to Sept., and barracuda, red snapper, bluefin, grouper, and mackeral are plentiful all year.

Shore Fishing
Once you find a place to fish from shore, you'll catch plenty. Try fishing in the lagoon off the Nichupte bridge. Perhaps now you're spoiled, used to seeing the crystal-clear water of the Caribbean; well, the water is not as clear, but the fish are down there. Expect needlefish or a possible barracuda, and rumor has it that an occasional shark takes a wrong turn at the bridge and finds itself in the lagoon. Contrary to universal belief, this type of shark is good eating.

ESCORTED TOURS

Organized Boat Trips
Many tour boats are available for a variety of trips, most going to nearby Isla Mujeres: glass-bottom boats slowly drift above flamboyant undersea gardens, or on a musical cruise you can dance your way over to the small island. These tours often include snorkeling, and the necessary equipment is furnished. The *Aqua-Quin* is a motorized trimaran going twice daily to Isla Mujeres for snorkeling at Garrafon Beach, a buffet lunch, open bar, music, and fun. Reservations required; check at Hotel Camino Real or Hotel Fiesta Americana marina—fare is about US$40 pp.

The B/M *Carnaval Cancun*, a large triple decker that cruises to Isla Mujeres, serves a buffet lunch on board with an open bar, stops for snorkeling, and allows time for shopping in downtown Isla Mujeres. Called the Skin Tour, the boat leaves the Playa Linda pier daily; fare is about US$32.

Another popular cruise is the *Carnaval's* "party animal's cruise," which includes a calypso cookout on the beach, with an open bar, music, limbo contest, and other games (with prizes) that can last the whole night through. Fare is about US$42. For reservations check with your hotel or travel agency. To get information on trips that explore the lagoon, visit the Del Rey ruins, or take sightseers to close-by reefs, ask at your hotel or call one of the marinas.

The *Nautibus* (referred to as a floating submarine) is a double-keeled boat with transparent panels and individual stools in

CANCUN MARINAS

NAME:	**Aqua-Quin**
ADDRESS:	Marina at hotels Camino Real and Fiesta Americana
PHONE:	3-01-00
HOURS:	8:30 a.m.-6 p.m.
SERVICES:	diving, snorkeling, windsurfing, fishing; catamaran tours to Isla Mujeres

NAME:	**Aquatours**
ADDRESS:	km 6.25 Av. Kukulcan
PHONE:	—
HOURS:	8:30 a.m.-8 p.m.
SERVICES:	boat slips, diving, fishing, water-skiing, yacht tours, market (all credit cards accepted)

NAME:	**Carlos 'n' Charlies**
ADDRESS:	km 5.5 Av. Kukulcan
PHONE:	3-08-46
HOURS:	7:30 a.m.-8:30 p.m.
SERVICES:	boat tours and sportfishing

NAME:	**Carnaval Cancun**
ADDRESS:	Playa Linda Pier
PHONE:	—
HOURS:	10 a.m.-4 p.m.
SERVICES:	*Carnaval* cruiser to Isla Mujeres, includes open bar, Continental breakfast, buffet, lunch, live music

NAME:	**Fiesta Maya**
ADDRESS:	km 8 Av. Kukulcan
PHONE:	3-03-08/3-04-18
HOURS:	10 a.m.-4 p.m.
SERVICES:	trips to Isla Mujeres via glass-bottomed *Fiesta Maya* (no credit cards accepted)

NAME:	**Krystal Divers**
ADDRESS:	Hotel Krystal
PHONE:	—
HOURS:	8 a.m.-7 p.m.
SERVICES:	dive trips—US$50 (two tanks), plus lessons—US$15; snorkel equipment rental—US$9 per day; boogie board rental—US$5 per hour

NAME:	**Lucky Hooker**
ADDRESS:	Playa Linda Pier
PHONE:	4-21-01/4-29-76
HOURS:	9 a.m.-5 p.m.
SERVICES:	Contoy Island tour, Tues.-Sat.—US$46; Lucky II fishing tour—US$40

NAME:	**Mauna Loa**
ADDRESS:	km 9 Av. Kukulcan
PHONE:	4-17-16
HOURS:	9 a.m.-5 p.m.
SERVICES:	jet-skiing, water-skiing, speedboats, kayaks, windsurfing, diving, fishing, snorkeling trips, charters available

CANCUN MARINAS

NAME:	**Mundo Marina, S.A.**
ADDRESS:	km 5.5 Av. Kukulcan
PHONE:	3-05-54
HOURS:	8 a.m.-9 p.m.
SERVICES:	big and small game fishing, dive and snorkel trips, boat tours, charters

NAME:	**Neptuno**
ADDRESS:	Hotel Verano Beat
PHONE:	—
HOURS:	8 a.m.-4 p.m.
SERVICES:	dive tours and lessons, underwater videos, snorkeling and fishing tours, tour to Isla Mujeres via trimaran

NAME:	**Pelican Pier Avioturismo**
ADDRESS:	km 5.5 Av. Kukulcan
PHONE:	—
HOURS:	7:30 a.m.-8 p.m.
SERVICES:	Cessna air taxi; fishing—US$66 pp, or four hours for US$240, six hours US$336, eight hours US$384; rides in ultralight plane—US$40. (VISA and MasterCard accepted)

NAME:	**Royal Marina**
ADDRESS:	Omni and Oasis Hotels
PHONE:	5-03-91/5-06-41
HOURS:	—
SERVICES:	diving, snorkeling trips, jet-skiing, water-skiing, windsurfing/sailing school, *Columbus* lobster-dinner cruise, Captain's Cove Restaurant, 7-11 market, and more

NAME:	**Scuba Cancun**
ADDRESS:	km 5 Av. Kukulcan
PHONE:	3-10-11/4-23-36
HOURS:	9 a.m.-6 p.m.
SERVICES:	dive trips, night dives, certification courses, Cancun's only decompression chamber, PADI and NAUI training facility, Tropical Cruiser Tours, Playa Langosta dock. For tours, all to Isla Mujeres: Morning Express 10 a.m.-5 p.m.; Treasure Island, closed Sundays. For reservations and details call 3-14-88

NAME:	**Uno Mas/Roman Lopez**
ADDRESS:	Mundo Marina
PHONE:	3-05-54
HOURS:	—
SERVICES:	light-tackle fishing tours, reservations required

NAME:	**Wild Goat**
ADDRESS:	km 5 Av. Kukulcan
PHONE:	—
HOURS:	8 a.m.-8 p.m.
SERVICES:	fishing—US$34 pp (shared boat); Contoy Island trip—US$40 pp; or charter the "Goat Boat" (maximum six persons): four hours—US$240; six hours—US$350; eight hours—US$385; full day—US$450. (VISA and MasterCard accepted)

two air-conditioned compartments. In the submerged keels passengers get the feeling of drifting among the schools of fish that live in Chital reef. Hundreds of sergeant majors rush alongside the windows, and the boat travels directly over unique coral formations.

Traveling to the reef on *Nautibus*'s top deck, you get a good view of one of the channels along the mangrove-lined Nichupte Lagoon under the Playa Linda bridge and a look at the beaches in front of many upscale hotels on the way to the reef. The entire trip takes just under two hours, with three daily departures (10 a.m., noon, and 2 p.m.) from San Marino Pier in the hotel zone. Fare is about US$20 and includes all the beer and sodas you can drink.

Self-guided Tours

If you prefer to investigate Garrafon Beach on your own, it's easy and cheap. On Av. Tulum catch the city bus marked Ruta 1-A to Puerto Juarez (runs every 15 minutes). Take the passenger boat to Isla Mujeres (about US$.50), and from here if you want to spend your day diving, take a taxi to Garrafon Beach (about US$2, one to four passengers), or it's a five-km walk. Garrafon admission is about US$1, snorkeling equipment rents for about US$5 (per day). A snack stand serves light lunch and cold drinks. If there's time before the last ferry back to Cancun, take a look at the town of Isla Mujeres.

OTHER SPORTS

The **Pok Ta Pok Club de Golf** has tennis courts and a well-kept 18-hole golf course designed by Robert Trent Jones. The golf club is a great sports center, with a pro shop, swimming pool, marina, restaurant, bar, and even its own small restored Maya ruin. Temporary club membership allows you to play golf or tennis at the club; arrangements can be made through your hotel. Green fees about US$30. Many of the hotels on the island also have tennis courts, some with night lighting for a fee.

Nautibus

ACCOMMODATIONS

DELUXE

Every hotel on the "island" or hotel zone fits into this category. All offer at least one swimming pool (sometimes more) and good beaches; an assortment of restaurants, bars, and nightlife; beach activities and gardens; travel, tour, and car agencies; laundry and room service. In fact, a few tourists find everything for a complete vacation under one roof and stay pretty close to the hotel. Rates on the island begin at about US$80 and can get as expensive as you wish.

The hotels themselves showcase brilliant architecture, using the lines that would best fit into nature's environment, with a suggestion of the ancient Maya thrown in; add extraordinary comfort, and total luxury for an overall description of the majority of the hotels in Cancun's hotel zone. If a rainy afternoon discourages beaching, take a tour of the hotels. It would take a whole book just to describe all the hotels in Cancun, so we have chosen a few that are beautiful, comfortable, and offer the ultimate in luxury. See a complete list of Cancun hotels on p.103-105.

Hyatt Regency
And The Hyatt Cancun Caribe

Both are sensational hotels. The Regency's breathtaking 18-floor-high central atrium takes in the entire lobby, where afternoon drinks are accompanied by piano music. A bubbling waterfall separates the two swimming pools, where daily games of volleyball keep the actives busy. The views are breathtaking and the services perfect. The rooms are beautifully appointed with mini-bars and cable TV, and babysitting is available. Each hotel offers their special hotels within the hotels, like the Regency Club in the Hyatt Cancun Caribe, where services include complimentary Continental breakfast and afternoon cocktails and snacks, along with luxury amenities in the rooms.

The **Hyatt Cancun Caribe** has recently been remodeled and for a little more money the Regency Club villas offer lovely sitting areas and share a private pool, jacuzzi, and comfortable clubhouse near the pool for complimentary breakfast and afternoon cocktails. For reservations and information about both hotels call Hyatt's toll-free number in the states, (800) 228-9000. And if you want to have a

Hyatt Regency

really scrumptious dinner New Orleans style, go to the **Blue Bayou** at the Hyatt Cancun Caribe. Fourth- and fifth-time returnees continue to rave about the exquisite food at the Blue Bayou. Not only will you hear great jazz, but authentic Cajun and Creole cuisine is served amidst a lush setting of waterfalls and bayou swamp—Louisiana swamps never looked like this!

Camino Real

One of the all-time favorites is the durable **Camino Real Cancun.** Spread out on lovely grounds on the tip of the island, you never feel crowded. The new **Tower** on the premises offers complimentary Continental breakfast, afternoon tea, and snacks; morning wake-up service means a hot cup of coffee served by the Tower butler at your requested time. The rooms have beautiful views with private balconies, and color cable TV. In the main building live music is played at cocktail hour and in the evening. Take your choice of several restaurants (including gourmet-lovers' **Calypso**), bars, and coffee shops. Gourmands, do try dinner at the Calypso, a few favorites are: chilled lobster gazpacho, *camarones empanizados con coco fresco* (jumbo shrimp breaded with fresh coconut), and apple tort aruba, a flaky crust with juicy apples surrounded by flowers sculpted from peaches, plums, grapes, and kiwis. The Camino Real has its own small lagoon inhabited by colorful fish and turtles. Be sure to watch the turtles being fed, scrubbed, and cared for. This is also a calm body of water on which to learn windsurfing and snorkeling.

Hyatt Caribe

CANCUN ACCOMMODATIONS

NAME	RATING	TELEPHONE	TELEFAX	NO. OF ROOMS
Antillano	★★★	—	—	48
Aquamarina Beach	★★★★★	4-4205	—	—
Aristos	★★★★	3-0011	3-0078	222
Bahia de Mujeres	★★★★	3-0415	—	—
Beach Club Cancun	★★★★★	3-1597	3-1177	78
Calinda Quality Inn	★★★★	3-1600	3-1857	280
Camino Real Cancun	GT	3-0100	3-1739	205
Cancun Clipper Club	—	3-1130	—	—
Cancun Playa	—	5-1111	5-1151	266
Cancun Plaza	★★★★★	5-0072	5-0236	190
Cancun Viva	★★★★★	—	—	210
Caribbean Club	—	4-4340	—	90
Caribbean Suites	—	3-2300	5-1593	—
Caribe Mar	★★★★	3-0811	—	—
Carisa y Palma	★★★	3-0211	—	122
Carrousel	★★★★	3-0513	—	149
Casa Maya	★★★★★	3-0555	3-0881	237
Castel Flamingo	GT	3-1544	—	—
Castel Sol y Mar	★★★★★	3-1832	4-4521	—
Club Caribe Cancun	★★★★	3-0811	3-0384	113
Club Internacional	★★★★	3-0855	—	200
Club Las Perlas	★★★	3-0869	3-1471	81
Club Mediterranee	★★★	4-2900	4-2090	410
Club Privado	★★★★★	—	—	420
Club Verano Beat	★★★★	3-0772	3-0772	77
Coconut Inn	★★★	—	—	—
Condessa Cancun	GT	5-1000	5-1800	474
Crowne Plaza Holiday Inn	GT	5-1050	5-1050	380
Dos Playas	★★★★	3-0500	—	29
El Pueblito	★★★★	5-0849	4-0422	239
Fiesta Americana Condessa	GT	5-1000	5-1800	474
Fiesta Americana Playa Cancun	GT	3-1400	3-2502	636
Fiesta Inn	★★★★	3-2200	3-2532	84
Flamingo	★★★★★	3-1544	3-1029	69
Fontain Marina Club	★★★★	—	—	94
Galerias Plaza	★★★	—	—	58
Girasol	★★★	3-0624	3-2246	110
Green 16	★★★	3-1415	—	288
Hotel Beach Cancun Club	★★★★★	3-1177	5-0439	157
Hotel Cancun Handall	★★	—	—	58
Hotel Cancun Palace	GT	5-0533	5-1593	388
Hotel Colonial	★★★	4-1535	—	—
Hotel Hacienda	—	4-1208	—	—

GT= *Gran Turismo*—better than the best

continued

CANCUN ACCOMMODATIONS (CONT.)

NAME	RATING	TELEPHONE	TELEFAX	NO. OF ROOMS
Hotel Plaza Del Sol	—	4-3888	—	—
Hyatt Cancun Caribe	★★★★	3-0044	3-1514	162
Hyatt Regency Cancun	GT	3-0966	3-1349	291
Imperial Las Perlas	★★★	3-0193	3-0106	53
Intercontinental Cancun	GT	5-0755	5-0021	239
Kokai	★★★	—	—	62
Krystal Cancun	GT	3-1133	3-1790	330
Laguna Cancun Resort	—	3-0070	—	48
Las Velas	★★★★★	3-2150	3-2118	226
Mary Tere	—	4-2473	—	42
Mauna Loa	—	3-0693	—	—
Maya Caribe	★★★★	3-2000	3-0650	40
Miramar Mision	★★★★★	3-1755	3-1136	179
Novatel	★★	429-99	—	40
Oasis Cancun	GT	5-0877	5-0131	1200
Omni Cancun	GT	5-0741	4-0689	281
Palace Hotel	GT	5-0533	—	—
Parador Hotel	—	4-1922	—	—
Paraiso Radisson	★★★★★	5-0112	5-0999	283
Park Inn Sol y Mar	—	5-0500	5-0934	257
Piramides del Rey	GT	3-1988	—	42
Playa Blanca	★★★★★	3-0028	3-0904	150
Plaza Caribe	—	4-1377	—	—
Plaza Kokai	★★★★	4-3666	—	48
Plaza Las Glorias	★★★★	3-0811	3-0901	112
Ramada Renaissance	★★★★	5-0100	5-0354	239
Royal Caribbean	★★★★★	—	—	92
Royal Mayan	—	5-0144	5-0032	200
Salvia Condominiums	★★★	3-2286	3-2568	80
San Marino	★★★	3-0815	—	42
Sheraton Resort	GT	3-1988	3-1450	745
Sierra Intercontinental	GT	—	—	261
Sina Suites	★★★	3-1017	—	—
Soberanis	★★★	4-1858	—	20
Solynar	★★★★★	—	—	156
Stouffer Presidente	★★★★	3-0200	3-2515	—
Suites Atlantis	—	4-1622	7-3362	—
Suites Brisas	★★★★★	4-1643	5-0060	25
Suites Caribbean	—	3-2300	3-2072	—
Suites Dos Playas	—	3-0500	7-3374	—
Suites Kin-Ha	—	3-2152	3-2147	85
Suites Las Gaviotas	—	3-1499	—	—
Suites Marbella	—	3-0572	—	—
Terramar Plaza Suites	★★★★	3-1588	3-1479	72
Tropical Oasis	★★★★★	5-1364	5-1363	154

CANCUN ACCOMMODATIONS (CONT.)

NAME	RATING	TELEPHONE	TEL .:FAX	No. OF ROOMS
TucanCun Beach	★★★★★	5-0058	—	39
Vacation Clubs International	★★★★★	3-0855	3-0206	200
Valma Kan	★★★★★	5-0107	5-0168	40
Villas Cerdena	★★★★	3-2055	—	26
Villas Kin-Ha	★★★★	—	—	193
Villas Marlin	★★★★	5-0532	5-0411	60
Villas Maya Cancun	—	4-1762	—	—
Villas Plaza	—	3-1022	3-2270	40
Villas Presidente	★★★★	3-0022	—	—
Villas Tacul	★★★★★	3-0000	—	23
Viva	★★★★★	3-0800	3-2087	210

Crowne Plaza Holiday Inn
When walking from the lobby to the pool area, you see an optical illusion that makes the far end of the pool fade into the horizon of the sea behind, giving the impression that the pool continues into the Caribbean and the horizon. The **Crowne Plaza Holiday Inn** hotel is truly lovely, using bright Mexican purples and blues against elegant marble in an immense airy lobby surrounded by public rooms. All 380 rooms are very comfortable, have an ocean view, security box, and balcony; guests will find several great restaurants and bars. **Alghero** specializes in Italian and Mediterranean/Arabic food; **Los Gallos** offers Mexican specialties. The sports nut has four swimming pools to choose from along with a well-equipped health club. All the doors in the hotel are fire doors with automatic locks. This hotel is a wonderful combination of high-tech American know-how from the Holiday Inns combined with the luxury touches of the Crowne Plaza—a pleasurable mix for those willing to pay the price.

Hotel Krystal Cancun
This is one of the all-time greats in Cancun, and it just continues to get better. The special dimension of the **Hotel Krystal Cancun** combines the greatest advances in worldwide hotel-keeping with the timeless charm and scenic delight that belong to Mexico's Carib-

bean coast. Comfort and service are the bywords. Each of the 330 rooms looks as though it has been decorated individually, with luxury in mind. A few suites come with private swimming pools; all rooms offer servibars, satellite TV, and room service. For those guests that concentrate on keeping their bodies fit even on vacation, the health club offers tennis and racquet ball courts, private clubroom pool and hydromassage pool. In line with the newest concept of hotel-keeping, the Krystal Club is a sophisticated private club on the top floors of the building that offers complete access to all services in the entire hotel, along with specialized service, personalized attention, private clubroom pool, and exclusive lounge with magnificent food and beverage service. Every guest in the hotel needs to know there are two restaurants at the Krystal that should be shared with that very special person. The **El Mortero** is a duplication of a 17th C. hacienda located in Durango in the north part of Mexico. When you step through the door into the outdoor patio, you leave the 20th C. behind. The ambience is colonial Mexican with old-time charm, and guests have a choice of haute Mexican cuisine or Continental food. If you're lucky, a very old, leathery-faced cook will come out into the candlelit patio and sing a romantic Latin love song accompanied by
continued on page 108

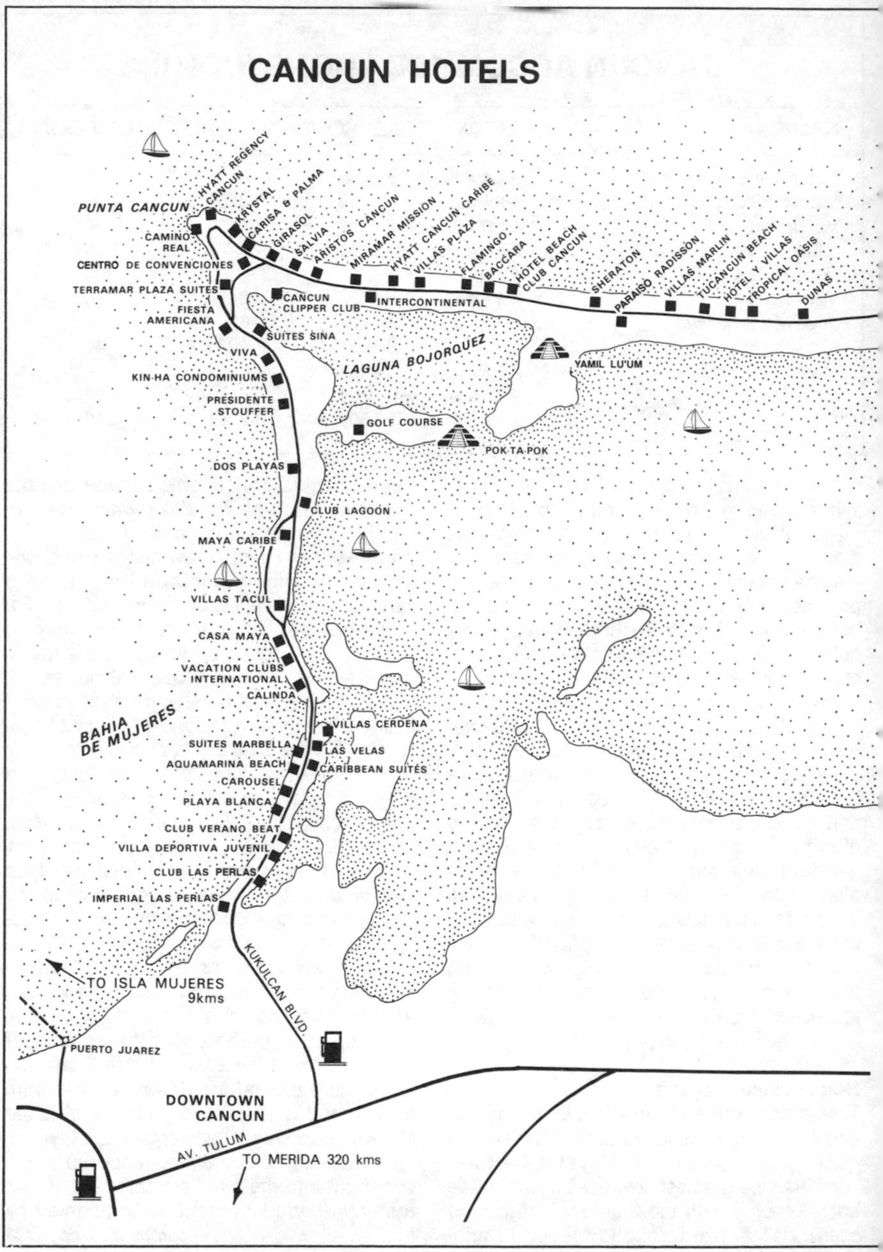

CANCUN HOTELS

PUNTA CANCUN

HYATT REGENCY
CANCUN
CRYSTAL
CARISA & PALMA
GIRASOL
BALVIA
ARISTOS CANCUN
MIRAMAR MISSION
HYATT CANCUN CARIBE
VILLAS PLAZA
FLAMINGO
BACCARA
HOTEL BEACH
CLUB CANCUN
SHERATON
PARAISO RADISSON
VILLAS MARLIN
TUCANCUN BEACH
HOTEL Y VILLAS
TROPICAL OASIS
DUNAS

CAMINO
REAL
CENTRO DE CONVENCIONES
TERRAMAR PLAZA SUITES
FIESTA
AMERICANA

CANCUN
CLIPPER CLUB
INTERCONTINENTAL

VIVA
SUITES SINA

LAGUNA BOJORQUEZ

YAMIL LU'UM

KIN-HA CONDOMINIUMS
PRESIDENTE
STOUFFER

GOLF COURSE
POK-TA-POK

DOS PLAYAS

CLUB LAGOON

MAYA CARIBE

VILLAS TACUL

CASA MAYA

VACATION CLUBS
INTERNATIONAL
CALINDA

BAHIA
DE MUJERES

VILLAS CERDENA

SUITES MARBELLA
AQUAMARINA BEACH
CAROUSEL
PLAYA BLANCA
CLUB VERANO BEAT
VILLA DEPORTIVA JUVENIL
CLUB LAS PERLAS
IMPERIAL LAS PERLAS

LAS VELAS
CARIBBEAN SUITES

TO ISLA MUJERES
9kms

PUERTO JUAREZ

KUKULCAN BLVD.

DOWNTOWN
CANCUN

AV. TULUM

TO MERIDA 320 kms

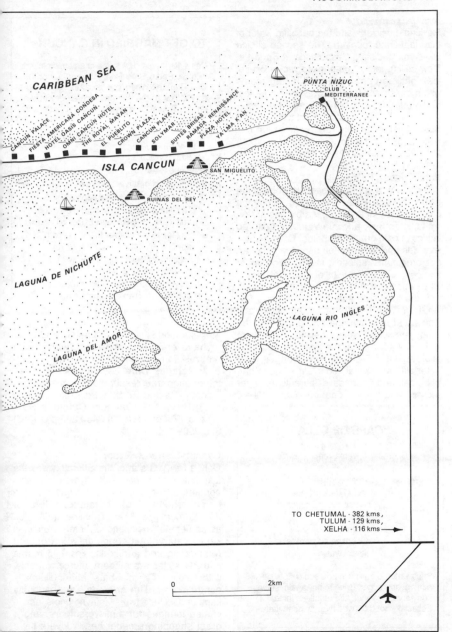

continued from page105
Mexican musicians and the bubbling water of the plant-lined fountain. The second choice takes you to distant Casablanca at **Bogart's.** Slow ceiling fans, high-backed wicker chairs, low light, and small intimate dining rooms with moorish architecture present the perfect background for a romantic dinner. For reservations and more Krystal information, contact Hotel Krystal Cancun 12625 High Bluff Dr., Suite 205, San Diego, CA 92130, tel. (800) 231-9860, fax (619) 792-1872.

Hotel Cancun Palace
When you walk into the spacious lobby of the **Hotel Cancun Palace** a tranquil elegance predominates: rich woods, marble floors, skylights, greenery, and marvelously textured fabrics in pale grays and beige. Each room is spacious and includes full bar, king beds, art and ornaments, splendid views, balconies or terraces, a/c, suites with outdoor hot tubs—all of this on a 492-foot-oceanfront beach with the turquoise sea and sand just a few feet from your hotel. For the ambitious add tennis and a health spa to the list of swimming, jet-skiing, fishing, sailing, snorkeling, and scuba diving. For the less ambitious, the pools are lined with chaise lounges near waterfalls, snack bar, pool bar, sunken bar, lobby bar, and gourmet restaurants that offer seafood and international cuisine. Excellent

---

CAFE DE OLLA
Served at the
Sheraton Towers Breakfast Buffet

Recipe: 1 small earthen pot
3 tbs. of dark roasted
coarse ground coffee
1 cinnamon stick
3 cloves
dark brown sugar to taste
1 liter of water

Bring water to boiling in pot, add coffee, cinnamon, and sugar. Bring to boil again, strain and serve. Optional: add tequila to taste. Especially good brewed over an open fire!

TO GET MARRIED IN CANCUN

Call 4-13-11, ext. 129 to make an appointment with Sr. Pedro Solis Rodriguez, official of the Civil Registry. When you go to the Civil Registry Office at the city hall located downtown on Av. Tulum have available from bride and groom:

✔ Tourist cards

✔ Birth certificates

✔ Blood tests

✔ Passports or driver's licenses

✔ Final divorce decrees if applicable

✔ The names, addresses, ages, nationalities, and tourist card numbers of four witnesses

✔ Pay fee to the cashier at the city hall, about US$35.

✔ Fill out application which you will be given by the judge.

✔ Very important: these things must be done at *least* two days before the wedding.

Mexican food is served at **Las Golandrinas,** or have breakfast and lunch with gentle breezes from the sea at the enchanting outdoor **Palapas Cafe Las Redes.** For more information and reservations contact Hotel Cancun Palace, Boulevard Kukulcan km. 14.5, Box 1730, Cancun, Quintana Roo, Mexico 77500; tel. (800) 346-8225, fax (305) 375-9508.

Cancun Sheraton Resort
Only a few years ago, the Sheraton was the last hotel on the road. Not anymore: the strip continues to grow, with somewhere in the neighborhood of 147 hotels for a total of 25,000 rooms by 1995. The Sheraton hotel, as one of the "experienced" hotels around, is kept in marvelous condition with frequent remodeling and additions. The 745 rooms and 211 suites are modern and comfortable, with satellite TV, mini-bars, and individually controlled air. The grounds are beautifully kept, and include two swimming pools, ample chaise lounges for sun worshipers, and a great shopping arcade; beach lovers have

half a mile of white-powder sand and blue sea to frolic in. Archaeology buffs will even find on the grounds a small remnant of the Maya past, **Yamil Lu'um,** one of the few remaining Maya structures in Cancun. Visitors play tennis on one of six lighted courts, visit the fitness center with sauna, steam bath, and whirlpool, or play golf on the mini course; children enjoy the playground.

The newest improvement is the Sheraton Towers, 167 rooms, each with a balcony and a spectacular view of the the turquoise sea, some suites with terraces and jacuzzis. All of these in a new separate seven-story building. The Towers is an exclusive concept which reflects elegance and class. Its goal is to pamper guests with personalized consideration such as exclusive registration, private Towers Lounge; special complimentary services include concierge, coffee or tea with your morning wake-up call, Continental breakfast in the Towers Lounge, daily newspaper, clothes pressing, hors d'oeuvre service each evening, and luxurious amenities in the rooms like hair dryers, safety boxes, alarm clocks, and a special treat from the pastry chef upon retiring.

The Sheraton offers a variety of restaurants and bars to all of its guests: **La Gaviota** offers piano music with dinner; **La Duna** has a garden and pool view; **Yalma Caan Lobby Bar** has a lively happy hour with the sea in the background; and **Daphny's Video Bar** continues late into the night with snappy entertainment in colorful surroundings. For more information and reservations in Canada and the United States, call (800) 325-3535 or call your travel agent.

Continental Plaza Villas Cancun
Located between Nichupte Lagoon and the Caribbean Sea, the **Continental Plaza Villas Cancun** is a unique mix of Colonial, Moorish, and Caribbean architecture. A cloud of pink from a distance, this complex is made up of 636 rooms and suites scattered about in 26 villas and one tower. Rooms decorated in pastel colors are cozy and comfortable, a/c, with views of either the sea or the lagoon. Four beautiful swimming pools and 500 yards of white-sand beach

encourage guests to hang around. Tennis courts, squash courts, and racquet ball are on premises along with instructors for all manner of water sports. Five restaurants and three bars cater to every taste including **Las Cupulas** with special Italian cuisine. Looking for something special? On the sixth floor of the Plaza section is the **Plaza Club.** Special service includes 24-hour concierge service, Continental breakfast, and an open bar at happy hour. For more information and reservations call (800) 223-2332.

Fiesta Americana Condessa
Scene of the Miss Universe contest in 1989, the **Fiesta Americana Condessa** is a smashing hotel. Guests enter through a 117-foot-tall *palapa* at the entrance (with escalator, thank you), the highest *palapa* roof in Mexico. The Disney people helped with the design of the hotel—and it shows. The magnificent lobby is decorated with stylized marble floors, jewel-toned fabrics, upholstered smart wicker furni-

Fiesta Americana Condessa

ture, and brilliant stained-glass awnings, which extend over the bars and here and there. The hotel is reminiscent of a small (upscale) Mexican village with greenery everywhere. Rooms are comfortable, many with spectacular views. Swimming pools are joined with arched bridges, and excellent restaurants scattered about offer a variety of ethnic foods to choose from. If you just can't drag yourself out of the pool try a game of backgammon on a floating table available for the asking. For the health buff, there are three a/c indoor tennis courts and a complete spa and gym. For more information and reservations call (800) 223-2332.

All Inclusive

More and more all-inclusive resorts are springing up. (There is comfort in knowing exactly how much you'll spend on vacation, beginning to end, including all meals, beer and wine, water sports, etc.) One of the nicest in Cancun is **Cancun Puerta Al Sol.** Beautiful rooms and ambience, great food, spacious grounds and beach, and when you stay for eight days or more, two complimentary sidetrips are thrown in (your choice of Chichen Itza, bullfights, Tulum, etc.). Per

person charge is US$140, but packages are available; call for prices and information, tel. (800) 346-8225, fax (305) 375-9508. **Club Med** is located near the tip of Punta Nizuc in Cancun's hotel zone. Probably the best snorkeling in Cancun is right here, along with all other water sports—a lively village for singles and couples; tel. (800) CLUB MED.

Condominiums

Cancun is sprouting condos everywhere you look. While one wonders when the building will end, they provide some of the best bargains in town for families or small groups. For as low as US$130 a night, a family of five can stay in lovely surroundings near the beach with a pool, cooking facilities, often two bathrooms, and daily maid service included in the price.

Rates can soar much higher or at certain times of the year can even be less. Travel agents can help you find them or you can write directly to the managers. For the daring, good buys come if you just arrive on the scene without reservations, go from condo to condo, and negotiate the price of one that isn't reserved. However, you run a certain risk of not finding what you want, especially during the winter months. The following company rents condos from the U.S.: Luxury Villas of Cancun, Box 18225, San Antonio, TX, tel. (800) 531-7211.

Moderate

Though sometimes crowded, these hotels are good bargains. The Yucatecan ambience pervades, and each has a helpful staff willing to answer questions about the city. The hotels have private baths, a/c, hot water, phone in room, swimming pool, bar, and restaurant. The rates run from about US$40 d to about US$100. Check out **Hotel Plaza Caribe,** corner of Av. Uxmal, tel. 4-13-77; **Hotel Cancun Handall,** Av. Tulum, tel. 4-19-47; **Hotel America Cancun,** Av. Tulum and Calle Brisa, tel. (800) 262-2656, 4-15-00; **Hotel Plaza del Sol,** Av. Yaxchilan, tel. 4-38-88; **Hotel Hacienda,** Av. Sunyaxchen, tel. 4-12-08; and **Novatel,** Av. Tulum and Uxmal, tel. 4-29-99.

TIPPING

Tipping is of course up to the individual, but for a guideline on the Peninsula the following seems to be average.

Porters: about US$.50 per bag. If you're staying at a hotel with no elevator and three flights of stairs and lots of luggage, you may wish to be more generous.

Hotel Maids: If staying more than one night, US$1-2 per day left at the end of your stay.

Waitresses: 10-15% is average.

Tour Guides: For an all-day trip, US$5 is appropriate, and the driver US$1.

When visiting a ruin, cave, or lighthouse you will usually be accompanied by a young boy to show you the way—US$.50 is customary.

Tipping taxi drivers is not customary.

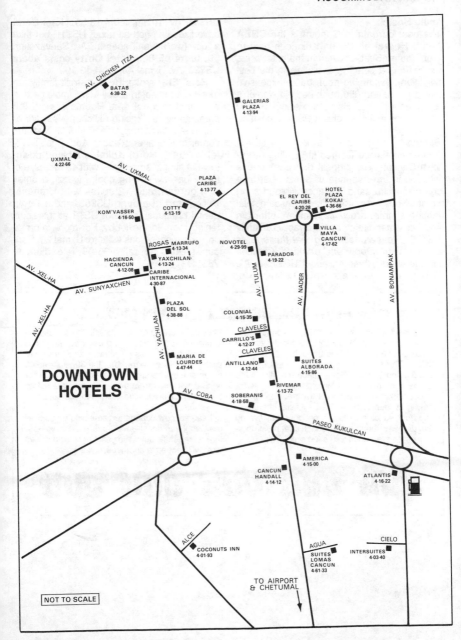

DOWNTOWN HOTELS

NOT TO SCALE

AV. CHICHEN ITZA

BATAB
4-38-22

GALERIAS
PLAZA
4-13-94

AV. UXMAL

UXMAL
4-22-66

PLAZA
CARIBE
4-13-77

EL REY DEL
CARIBE
4-20-28

HOTEL
PLAZA
KOKAI
4-36-66

KOM'VASSER
4-16-50

COTTY
4-13-19

VILLA
MAYA
CANCUN
4-17-62

ROSAS MARRUFO
4-13-34

NOVOTEL
4-29-99

AV. XEL-HA

HACIENDA
CANCUN
4-12-08

YAXCHILAN
4-13-24

PARADOR
4-19-22

AV. SUNYAXCHEN

CARIBE
INTERNACIONAL
4-30-87

AV. XEL-HA

AV. NADER

AV. BONAMPAK

PLAZA
DEL SOL
4-38-88

COLONIAL
4-15-35

CLAVELES

AV. YACHILAN

CARRILLO'S
4-12-27

CLAVELES

AV. TULUM

MARIA DE
LOURDES
4-47-44

ANTILLANO
4-12-44

SUITES
ALBORADA
4-15-86

RIVEMAR
4-13-72

AV. COBA

SOBERANIS
4-18-58

PASEO KUKULCAN

AMERICA
4-15-00

CANCUN
HANDALL
4-14-12

ATLANTIS
4-16-22

ALICE

COCONUTS INN
4-01-93

AGUA

CIELO

SUITES
LOMAS
CANCUN
4-61-33

INTERSUITES
4-03-40

TO AIRPORT
& CHETUMAL

Youth Hostel
The best bargain in Cancun is the **CREA Youth Hostel** on Paseo Kukulcan next to Club Verano Beat. Located in the hotel zone, the YH has a beach (not always in the best condition), swimming pool, bar, inexpensive dining room, and 650 bunk beds in women's and men's dorms. Rates are about US$10 pp, bedding included, plus a US$7 deposit.

Budget
Budget hotels are located in bustling downtown Cancun. The biggest drawback to this location is the absence of beach, but blue sea and white sand are accessible in short order by bus every 15 minutes. These hotels, though simple, are *usually* clean, offer a/c and hot water. Rates begin at approximately US$35. *Please understand that these rates change with supply and demand.* Choices include **Hotel Rivemar,** about US$45 d, Av. Tulum, tel. 4-17-08, and **Hotel Tulum,** about US$35, Av. Tulum, tel. 4-13-55. **Hotel Coral** advertises its price as about US$11, but take a look (we haven't seen it), Av. Sunyaxchen 50, tel. 4-05-86. **Hotel Cotty** costs about US$20, Av. Uxmal 44, tel. 4-13-19.

Hotel El Rey Caribe is a small family-run motel-like inn set in a well-kept simple garden with pool and hot spa. Rooms are old but presentable and include kitchenettes, a/c or ceiling fan; rates from US$37 to $70. Near the corner of Uxmal and Nader, Apto Postal 417, tel. 4-20-28. **Hotel Kokai** is located downtown, a simple small hotel with 48 rooms, a/c, lobby bar, swimming pool, jacuzzi, a small roof garden, and 12 suites with kitchens. Prices start at around US$50, and a Continental breakfast is about US$3 at the small dining room in the lobby. For more information and reservations write to: Uxmal 26, Cancun, Mexico, or call 4-36-66, telex Ikeame 73341.

CAN FOREIGNERS OWN LAND IN MEXICO?

As a result of legislation in 1971, it is possible for a foreigner to own land within the coastal zone of Mexico. The ownership is through a *fideicomiso* (trust). This process requires the foreigner who is purchasing to mandatorily place the title to the property in trust with a Mexican financial institution empowered to act as a trustee. The foreign owner is then conveyed a beneficial interest in the trust, which means the foreigner may live on the property, rent it, or in general treat the property as if it were owned with a fee simple title.

Should the foreigner wish to sell, the transaction occurring is the assigning of rights acquired through the *fideicomiso*. The maximum duration of such a trust is 30 years. After the 30-year period, the trust must be either renewed or the property sold at fair market value. As in any real estate transaction, it is recommended that you consult a lawyer first.

Beautiful new condos are springing up all over the Caribbean coast—some are good buys—but they were terrific buys five years ago. Who knows what will happen in another five years.

FOOD

Restaurants

If you stayed for three or four months, it might be possible to sample each of the fine restaurants in Cancun city and the island—maybe. Most budget cafes are found on Av. Tulum and Av. Yaxchilan. For more *tipico* food and ambience, walk along Av. Yaxchilan until you find a place that appeals to you. On the two main streets, Av. Tulum and Uxmal, many resort-like touristy sidewalk cafes are busy, noisy, Americanish, and fun! For the epicurean explorer, there's Swiss, French, Chinese, Italian, Mexican, Arabic, Polynesian, Texan, Yucatecan, and Continental; there's fastfood, simplefood, fancyfood, seafood, homemade, rushed, and romantic, hamburgers, hot dogs, tacos, and *tortas,* and don't forget the great Creole food at the Hyatt's Blue Bayou. This is gourmet headquarters for the state of Quintana Roo, and all you have to do is look! Most restaurants accept credit cards.

A curious food fact: Mexico is one of the leading coffee producers of the world, but in spite of this most restaurants in Mexico serve instant coffee. Cancun, however, is the exception. Almost all of its cafes serve good brewed coffee—brewed decaf is available in only a few. On some Cancun menus you can find an old traditional favorite, *cafe de olla* (coffee cooked and served in a small earthen mug). Remember, in Mexico it's considered an insult for a waiter to submit a bill before it's requested; when you're ready to pay, say, "*la cuenta, por favor*" (the bill please).

The following restaurants represent a few of Cancun's ethnic assortment. CAJUN: **Blue Bayou,** very elegant, Hyatt Cancun Caribe Villas and Resort, tel. 3-00-44, reservations recommended. CHINESE: **Mauna Loa,** Polynesian atmosphere, nice, shows 7-9 p.m. nightly, Mauna Loa Shopping Center, tel. 3-06-93, reservations required. FRENCH: **Du Mexique,** a tastefully chic restaurant, casual, Av. Coba downtown, tel. 4-10-77, reservations required. All credit cards accepted except Diners. **L'Alternative,** casual-elegant, Av. Kukulcan and Bonampak downtown. **Maxime,** sophisticated-elegance, casual, Av. Kukulcan, Pez Volador #8, oceanfront (next to the Casa Maya Hotel), tel. 307-04/304-38. GERMAN: **Karl's Keller,** German beer-garden atmosphere, casual, Plaza Caracol.

INTERNATIONAL: **El Mural,** quietly elegant, casual allowed, Carrousel Hotel, tel. 3-03-88. **El Pirata,** lively, casual, 19 Azucenas St. downtown, 4-13-38. **La Ola,** Caribbean view, casual, Hotel Suites Brisas. **Peacock Grill,** garden dining, casual, Hotel Plaza Cari-

Sheraton Towers breakfast buffet

be downtown, tel. 4-13-77. **Plaza Girasoles,** open-air patio, casual, Hotel Plaza del Sol, 31 Yaxchilan downtown, tel. 4-38-88. Reservations required. **Seagull,** ocean view, casual, Calinda Hotel, tel. 3-16-00. **Tunkul,** elegant, Hotel Oasis, tel. 5-08-67. ITALIAN: **Don Giovanni,** traditional Italian, casual, Av. Kukulcan, near Mexicana, downtown, tel. 4-50-63. **Savio's,** elegant bistro, casual-chic, Plaza Caracol II, all credit cards except Diners. **Scampi,** elegant, quiet, dressy, Hyatt Regency Hotel, tel. 3-09-66, reservations required. JAPANESE: **Tokyo Surf Club,** light, fun, casual, 3 Calle Azucenas downtown. MEDITERRANEAN: **Alghero,** intimate, Mediterranean style, dressy, Crowne Plaza Cancun tel. 5-10-50.

MEXICAN WINE

it would seem the most natural thing in the world for Mexico to produce good wines, considering the Spanish Conquistadores came from a land with a long history of growing rich flavorful grapes and were experts in the field of fermentation. Pre-Hispanics didn't have wine as the Spanish knew it, but did make fermented beverages from such things as corn. It was not long before vine cuttings were brought to the "New World" and colonists were tending vineyards. By 1524 wine was so successful that Mexican wines were soon competing with Spanish wines. Pressure from vintners at home forced King Felipe II to outlaw its production in Mexico. However, over the years church-use continued and no doubt many gallons of the forbidden drink found its way to private cellars. But for all practical purposes and development, the industry was stopped before it had the opportunity to make itself known around the world.

Not until 1939 under then-president Lazaro Cardenas did Mexican wine-making begin to make a name for itself. Experts from around the world are beginning to recognize the industry in general and several of the wines are considered world-class. Over 125,000 acres of vineyards are under cultivation in the states of Baja California Norte, Aguascalientes, Queretaro, and Zacatecas. It's the vineyards of Baja that produce almost 80% of the country's wines located within the so-called "international wine belt" (between latitudes 30 and 50). Some of the well-known wineries (and their wines) from this area are: **Domecq** (Padre Kino, Calafia, Los Reyes, and Fray Junipero); **L.A. Cetto** (Don Angel); and **Santo Tomas.**

The wineries, **Cavas de San Juan** (Hidalgo, Edelmann, Carte Blanche, etc.) and **Casa Martell** are found in Queretaro, some 2,000 miles south of Baja. This was due to the suggestion of a University of California professor of enology who came to the conclusion that the area's 6,100-foot-altitude compensated for its being outside the celebrated "wine belt." Zacatecas is the location of the relatively new and promising **Union Vinicola Zacateca** (Los Pioneros), and Aguascalientes of **La Esplendida** (Armilita) and **Valle Redondo.**

According to Walter Stender of ACA Imports, some Mexican wines are even being imported to the U.S. Please note: Mexican wines don't age well and one need not be impressed by dates. In other words, the whites are ready when released, the reds need "age" no more than 18 months.

If you want champagne, remember to ask for *vino espumoso* or "bubbly wine." A label that reads *methode champenoise* means the French system for producing sparkling wine was used. Mexico signed an agreement with the French government not to label its sparkling wines *champagne*—along with all other major wine-producing nations of the world except the U.S. Of course there are many imported wines from all over the world available in the fine restaurants of Cancun—many from California—but while in Mexico be adventurous and try the Mexican wine. A personal favorite is L.A. Cetto's white.

MEXICAN: **Careyes Restaurant,** elegant, dressy, Hotel and Villas Tropical Oasis. **El Campanario de los Armandos,** wild Mexican party, casual, 12 Av. Coba downtown, tel. 4-41-80. **El Cortijo,** Mexican party atmosphere, casual, Plaza Flamingos, **Fonda del Angel,** very "old Mexico," casual-nice, 85 Av. Coba downtown, tel. 4-33-93. **Pericos,** lively, casual, 71 Av. Yaxchilan, tel. 4-31-52. **Restaurant Mexicano,** very elegant, dressy, La Mansion-Costa Blanca Shopping Center, hotel zone, tel. 3-22-20. **The Mine Co.,** a Mexican fiesta atmosphere, casual-nice, Av. Kukulcan next to Verano Beat, tel. 3-07-72/3-06-70. **Xenia,** high-style Mexican, nice, Cancun Plaza Hotel, hotel zone, tel. 5-00-72.

SEAFOOD: **Captain's Cove,** elegant, tropical dining, casual, Av. Kukulcan across from the Royal Mayan, Omni, and Oasis hotels. **El Pescador,** a homey restaurant, casual, Tulipanes #28 downtown, tel. 4-26-73. **La Bamba,** lively Caribbean/Mexican atmosphere, ocean view, casual, Playa Langosta, hotel zone. **Mi Casa,** high-style, casual, on the beach at km. 4 of the Puerto Juarez-Punta Sam Highway. **Soberanis,** lively, singles bar, Av. Coba and Tulum, downtown, tel. 4-11-25/ 4-18-58.

SPANISH: **Olé y Olé,** traditional Spanish style, nice, Plaza Terramar, tel. 4-13-38, reservations recommended. SWISS-ITALIAN: **Casa Rolandi,** Mediterranean atmosphere, casual, Plaza Caracol, tel. 3-18-17.

For a great roast beef sandwich (under US$4), on crisp French bread, good bagels, excellent breakfast, a brownie sundae, tabouleh, or a choice selection of imported beer, try breakfast or dinner at **Cafe Amsterdam** downtown, run by a Dutch woman. The food is great, the prices reasonable. **100% Natural** on Sunyaxchen serves good vegetarian, makes great shakes. **Pollo Goyo** offers a big menu with satisfying salads, good chicken, and a "bucket of soup."

Groceries

Mercado Municipal, six blocks north of the bus station on Av. Tulum, is well supplied; come early for the best selection of fresh produce and meat. **Javier Rojo Gomez** behind the post office on Sunyaxchen is a smaller version of Mercado Municipal. **Super Carniceria Cancun,** Av. Sunyaxchen 52, sells familiar American-style cuts of meat. **San Francisco de Asisi Super Market** on Tulum is a modern well-stocked market designed for one-stop shopping (somewhat novel to much of Yucatan): butcher case, bakery counter, row upon row of groceries, liquor, electric appliances, even clothes. Another smaller supermarket down Av. Tulum just past the *glorietta* (traffic circle) is the **Glorietta Supermarket.**

Bakeries

Indulge yourself in fine Mexican pastries and crusty *bolillos* at the **Panificadora Covadonga** on Av. Tulum, a few hundred meters north of Av. Uxmal. Another smaller bakery is **Los Globos** on Tulipanes just west of Av. Tulum. The **Glorietta Market** and **Don Giovanni Bakery** have delicious baked goodies.

ENTERTAINMENT

Nightlife

Cancun offers a marvelous choice of night-time entertainment. It's easy to dance the night away at any one of a number of inviting places. Most of the hotels on the island have discos in motion until the early hours of morning. Some *cantinas* offer live bands ranging from jazz to popular marimba to reggae. Many of the touristy hotels offer Mexican "fiestas" weekly, including *tipico* dinners, traditional dances, and colorful costumes. The auditorium at the Convention Center regularly presents the **Ballet Folklorico de Naucalpan** and a tasty dinner, and often brings in other special shows. The **Lone Star Bar** in downtown's Hotel Maria de Lourdes advertises that they "speak Texan," has great down-home country-western music, and is busy at happy hour, when they serve each

dancing girl at Hyatt Regency fiesta night

patron a free margarita (8-10 p.m. Sun., Tues., and Thurs.). **The Mine Co.** disco next to the YH on Paseo Kukulcan charges a small cover.

For zany fun with wild and comedic waiters as well as exceptionally good food (try the Mexican combination plate with *carne asada*), you can't beat **Carlos N' Charlie's,** on Paseo Kukulcan (count your money while the waiter is still there; one reader recently had a problem). For more romantic live music try **La Cantina** in Cancun 7 p.m. at the Convention Center. And for a serene romantic spot to begin or end an evening, watch Cancun's sensational sunset or glittering stars in **La Palapa,** a mellow bar in a thatched-roof pavilion on the end of its own pier over the lagoon at Hotel Club Lagoon Caribe, Paseo Kukulcan. La Palapa serves snacks, exotic drinks, and has live music and dancing from 9 p.m.-1:30 a.m.

Bars And Nightclubs

Cancun has some of the most upscale, modern discos in Mexico with all the newest effects to make for the best entertainment. Check out: **Aquarius Disco,** high-tech disco, dressy, Hotel Camino Real, tel. 3-01-00; **Bombay Boogie Club,** very splendid, dressy, Av. Kukulcan next to the Bombay Bicycle Club; **Casis Lobby Bar,** contemporary elegance, nice, Hyatt Cancun Caribe Villas and Resort, tel. 3-00-44; **Christine's Disco,** superb sound and light show, dressy, next to Hotel Krystal, tel. 3-11-33; **Daphny's Video Bar,** casual and fun, Sheraton Hotel, tel. 3-19-88; **Extasis Disco,** high-tech, sophisticated, nice, km 3.5 Av. Kukulcan; **Gifry's Piano Bar,** elegant, chic bar, stylish, same entrance as L'Alternative Restaurant, Av. Coba downtown, tel. 4-12-29; **La Boom Disco,** high-tech disco, nice, km 3.5 Av. Kukulcan; **Lobby Bar, Hyatt Regency,** elegant, classy, casual-nice, Hotel Hyatt Regency, tel. 3-09-66; **Tropical Oasis Piano Bar,** casual, Hotel and Villas Tropical Oasis; **Mexican Fiesta** at Hyatt Regency, a full-on party, casual, Hyatt Regency, tel. 3-09-66, ext. 2; **Reflejos Video Bar,** upbeat and lively, casual-nice, Hyatt Regency, tel. 3-09-66.

Cancun Evening And Dining Cruises

Two favorite dinner cruises are the **Columbus "Lobster Dinner Cruise,"** featuring a superb charcoal-grilled lobster, spectacular sunsets, and casual atmosphere, Royal Marina, tel. 3-13-57 or 3-18-53, reservations required; and **Pirate's Night,** casual, tel. 3-14-88, reservations required.

Cinema

Unlike most Peninsula cities, the majority of films shown in Cancun are usually American made with Spanish subtitles. Expect the bill to change every three or four days. However, **Cines Cancun,** Av. Xcaret #112, tel. 4-16-46, and **Cine Royal,** Av. Tulum, offer Mexican films that provide a cultural experience. Some of the larger hotels have their own movie theaters and large-screen TV.

Shopping Centers

La Mansion-Costa Blanca, small, exclusive, and painted hot pink, this mall features unique boutiques, several of the city's top restaurants, a money exchange, and a bank. El Parian shops are constructed around a lovely garden off to one side of the Convention Center. A lot of variety here in terms of shops, plus a money exchange and several good restaurants. **Las Velas,** though small, includes a pizza parlor, liquor store, exotic leather shop, art gallery, fancy-dress boutique and more. **Mauna Loa,** a diminutive cluster of shops that face the lagoon just opposite the Convention Center, encompasses a bookstore/pharmacy, real estate office, convenience store, a few interesting boutiques, a marina, a pizza parlor, and two of Cancun's top restaurants. **Mayfair Gallery,** one of Cancun's newer malls, is located opposite the Fiesta Americana Hotel, and contains a wide variety of boutiques and restaurants in a lovely atrium-roofed, two-story building. **Plaza Caracol,** one of Cancun's biggest and most contemporary shopping centers, is conveniently located in the hub of the hotel zone, fully air-conditioned, and elaborately finished

with marble floors and lots of windows. This two-story mall consists of over 200 shops and boutiques, including signature stores of the world's most famous labels: Gucci, Fiorucci, Christian Dior, Benetton, and more.

Plaza Flamingo is the newest addition to Cancun's plethora of modern malls. Flamingo, a one-story center with Mayan-inspired architecture, beautiful marble floors, and high-tech lighting features over 100 shops plus several restaurants, including a **Denny's** that serves good enchiladas (true, true!), and **Golds,** a fully equipped gym. **Plaza La Fiesta** is actually a huge one-floor department store featuring all the fabulous crafts of Mexico; they offer a particularly fine selection in gold and silver jewelry.

Plaza Lagunas, located at the center of the hotel zone, features all manner of sportswear, including those of famous designers. Various small restaurants, a snack bar, and an ice cream parlor are set among the shops. **Plaza Nautilus,** a modern, two-story plaza with over 70 businesses, is a potpourri of shops and art galleries, including a bookstore, video games arcade, and two fine restaurants. **Terramar,** located opposite the Fiesta Americana Hotel, is a city block of shops, eateries, real estate offices, a pharmacy, and a small hotel.

Downtown, **Plaza America** is located on Av. Kukulcan just as you leave town. This large mall houses over 40 shops, a money-exchange house, snack bar, and a fine French restaurant among other upmarket boutiques and craft shops. **Plaza Bonita** is housed in a large hacienda-style structure replete with hand-painted Mexican tiles and a collection of many fine shops, boutiques, eateries, and imported goods.

Plaza Mexico on Av. Tulum is an air-conditioned mall which specializes in Mexican crafts, among them Maya textiles, leather goods, wood carvings, stoneware, and sportswear. **Plaza Safa,** a lovely arcade which fronts Av. Tulum houses a snack bar, series of shops, a money exchange, and a very popular cantina on the second floor. **Tropical Plaza,** an interesting new mall, has shops selling everything from jewelry to designer clothing; there's also a bank, travel agency, real estate office, and a great restaurant for beef eaters. It's next door to Plaza Mexico. **Via Benetto** is a colorful arcade lined with a wide range of shops featuring everything from silver jewelry to textiles. Access from Av. Tulum.

Craft Markets

In the hotel zone, **Coral Negro** is located next to the Convention Center. This market is a collection of approximately 50 stalls selling handicrafts from all parts of Mexico. Located downtown on Av. Tulum, **Ki Huic** is Cancun's main crafts market. Over 100 different vendors feature just about every kind of craft and souvenir you can imagine. **Plaza Garibaldi** is also downtown at the center of Av. Tulum and Uxmal South, 90 stalls of serapes, tablecloths, traditional clothing, onyx, and other handcrafted items.

Miscellaneous

Alberto's Jewelers, 21 Av. Tulum, Plaza Mexico and Plaza Tropical, downtown. **Foto Omega—Prints and Supplies,** 103 Av. Tulum and 45 Av. Uxmal, tel. 4-38-60/4-16-79. **Pama** is a modern department store featuring imported cosmetics, perfumes, and food stuffs as well as sportswear, designer clothing, and more.

SERVICES

Laundromat

A large pleasant laundromat is located downtown at 5 Av. Nader. Either you can do it yourself or pay extra to have it done for you—laundry and dry cleaning are tremendously cheaper here than at the hotels. A shady patio offers chairs for waiting.

Medical Information

Most hotels in Cancun can provide the name of a doctor who speaks English. For medical assistance in dire emergency, call 3-01-63 or the American Consular Office, tel. 4-16-38.

Post Office And Telegrams

The post office is west of Av. Tulum on Av. Sunyaxchen; open 9 a.m.-noon and 3-5 p.m., Mon. to Sat., tel. 4-14-18. Telegraph office, tel. 4-15-29.

Consulate

To reach the American consular agent, call 4-16-38.

Tourist Information

One info center is downtown on Av. Tulum next to the Ki Huic shopping mall; another is at the El Parian Convention Center in the hotel zone, tel. 4-33-40. The informed staffs are bilingual, cheery, and genuinely helpful. Ask for maps, brochures, prices, schedules, or directions. The Chamber of Commerce is also a good source of information, tel. 4-12-01.

Travel Agencies

With the advent of the tour guide's union, tours to Tulum and Chichen Itza are the same price at every agency, US$21 and $28 respectively. **Best Day** in the Kin-Ha Condominiums lobby, tel. 3-21-55/3-20-19, offers scheduled tours to Chichen Itza, Tulum, and Xel-Ha; private tours to Cozumel, Isla Mujeres, etc. can be arranged. **Buen Viaje** at Hotel America, downtown, tel. 4-54-41, open 8 a.m.-3 p.m., offers scheduled tours to Chichen Itza, Tulum, Cozumel, Isla Mujeres, and Contoy Island. **Contours Operadora** is at Av. Tulum and Claveles St. downtown, tel. 4-25-74/4-61-95, open 8:30 a.m.-1:30 p.m.; and 4:30-8 p.m.; closed Sundays. Services include: all local and Yucatan tours, all travel arrangements. **Ceiba Tours,** 146 Av. Nader, S.M. 3, downtown, tel. 4-20-62 or 4-19-62, open 7 a.m.-10 p.m., offers scheduled tours to Chichen Itza, Tulum, Merida, Isla Mujeres, Cozumel, and Contoy; ask about private tours. Additional services: national and international airline tickets. **Incentives and Vacations Inc.** at Suites Lomas, S.M. 4, downtown, tel. 4-61-33, open 8 a.m.-8 p.m., can provide tours to Chichen Itza, Tulum, and Isla Mujeres. Additional services: teen parties, destination manager services company, full support service.

Intermar Caribe, Plaza Quetzal, hotel zone, tel. 3-02-44, open 7 a.m.-8 p.m. Scheduled tours: Tulum, Chichen Itza, Coba, Isla

Mujeres, Cozumel; private and charter groups. **Mayaventuras,** 11 & 12 Av. Coba, tel. 4-22-44, open 8 a.m.-1 p.m. and 4-8 p.m. Scheduled tours: Chichen Itza, Tulum, Cozumel, Isla Mujeres, and Contoy Island, plus airline ticketing. **Mexicanos Profesionales de Viajes,** Hotel Fiesta Americana (lobby), tel. 3-14-00/3-14-26, open Mon.-Sat. 8 a.m.-8 p.m., Sun. 8 a.m.-6 p.m. Tours: Chichen Itza, Tulum, Cozumel, Isla Mujeres; horse riding at Rancho Victoria. **Turismo Aviomar,** 30 Venado, S.M. 20, downtown, tel. 4-67-42, 4-66-56, or 4-64-33, fax 4-64-35, open 8 a.m.-8 p.m. Tours and services: Chichen Itza, Tulum-Xel-Ha, Cozumel, Isla Mujeres, Uxmal, and Merida; airline ticketing. **Turismo Caleta,** Plaza Quetzal Ste. 11, hotel zone, tel. 3-16-59, 3-05-91, or 3-25-38, open 8 a.m.-8 p.m. Tours: all local services and tours; groups, conventions, and private tours.

    Viajes Cancun Holiday, S.A., Plaza Bombay, tel. 3-01-61/3-00-05. Open 8 a.m.-8 p.m. Tours: Chichen Itza; Tulum and Coba; city tours to Isla Mujeres, Cozumel, Chichen Itza, Uxmal (nightly light and sound show), and Merida; flights using the Helicar service can be arranged. VISA and MasterCard accepted. **Viajes Inolvidables,** Plaza Quetzal, tel. 3-17-82/3-10-41, open 7:30 a.m.-8 p.m. Tours: Chichen Itza, Tulum, Cozumel, Isla Mujeres, etc. Additional services: national and international packets. **Viajes Thomas Moore, S.A.,** km. 16 Av. Kukulcan across from the Royal Mayan, tel. 5-01-44, ext. 164, or 5-02-66, open 8 a.m.-7 p.m. Tours: Chichen Itza, Tulum, Isla Mujeres, Merida, Uxmal, Cozumel, Contoy, plus windsurfing lessons, jet-ski and water-ski bookings. Banamex and MasterCard accepted. **Viajes Turquesa,**

EMERGENCY NUMBERS	
Police	4-19-13
Fire	4-12-02
Air-Vac Medical Life Service, Houston Texas	(713) 961-4050

Suites Lomas, S.M. 4, downtown, tel. 4-20-75/4-35-95, open 7 a.m.-2 p.m. and 4-7 p.m. **Visusa,** 64 Av. Bonampak, downtown, tel. 4-30-95/4-28-82, open 8 a.m.-8 p.m. daily. Tours: Chichen Itza, Tulum, Isla Mujeres, Cozumel, and Uxmal. VISA is accepted. **Wagons Lits,** Calinda Hotel, Camino Real Hotel, tel. 3-08-47/3-08-24, open: 8 a.m.-8 p.m. Tours and services: Tulum, Chichen Itza, and more; airline ticketing.

Immigration

Remember that you must turn in your Mexican visitor's card when you leave the country. If you should lose it, need an extension, or have any questions, call Mexican Immigration, tel. 4-28-92 and at the airport, tel. 4-29-92.

Bookstores

Don Quixote Bookstore in downtown Cancun on Tulum (one block south of Tulipanes) carries a limited supply of English-language books, both fiction and nonfiction. Most of the island's hotel gift shops sell American magazines as well as a supply of paperback novels, Spanish-English dictionaries, and several English-language newspapers: *The News* (published in Mexico City), *Miami Herald, New York Times Weekly Review,* and *USA Today.*

GETTING THERE

Airport
Quintana Roo's busiest airport is 20 km south of Cancun. Along with everything else around this infant city, the airport is new and shiny and continues to grow and add to its facilities each season. By the time you are reading this book a new runway should be in operation. Visitors from many cities in the U.S. arrive daily on **Mexicana, Aeromexico, United, Continental,** and **Lacsa** airlines. **Aerocaribe** and **Aerocozumel** bring passengers on daily flights from Isla Cozumel. Car rentals, taxis, and yellow-and-white combis are available at the airport to bring you to town or the island (hotel zone). Remember to reconfirm your flight 24 hours in advance and be at the airport one hour before local flights or two hours before international flights.

By Bus
From Merida and Chetumal, buses make frequent trips daily, linking smaller villages to Cancun en route. The bus terminal is located in downtown Cancun on Av. Tulum. Call or go to the terminal for complete schedules—they change frequently.

Car Rentals
Car rentals are available from Mexican and American agencies at Cancun airport and many hotels. Remember there is a hefty drop-off fee in a city other than the origination point. If driving to Cancun, the 320-km, four-hour drive from Merida is on a good highway (Hwy. 180) through henequen-dotted countryside, historic villages, and aged archaeological ruins. From Chetumal (Hwy. 307) it's 343 km (four hours) along a well-maintained high-

AIRLINE DIRECTORY

Airline	Offices	Telephone	Arrivals	Departures
American	Airport	4-29-47 4-26-51	Dallas	Dallas
Aerocaribe	Av. Tulum at Uxmal	4-12-31 4-13-64	Cozumel Isla Mujeres Chichen Itza	Cozumel Isla Mujeres Chichen Itza
Aeromexico	—	4-56-40	Mexico City	Los Angeles
Continental	Airport	4-25-40	Los Angeles Houston	Los Angeles Houston Denver
Lacsa	Av. Taxchilan 5	4-12-76	Guatemala New Orleans	New Orleans San Jose
Mexicana	Av. Coba	4-12-65 4-11-54	Mexico Miami Dallas Philadelphia	Mexico Miami Dallas Philadelphia
United	Airport	4-28-58 4-25-28	Chicago	Chicago

way through thick tropical brush parallel to the Caribbean coast. Car rentals in Cancun can be found at: **Avis,** Viva Hotel, tel. 3-08-28, open 8 a.m.-2 p.m. and 4-7 p.m.; **Budget,** 15 Av. Tulum downtown, tel. 4-02-04/4-21-26, open 7:30 a.m.-1:30 p.m. and 4:30-7 p.m., all major credit cards accepted; **Cuzamil Car Rental,** Av. Kukulcan, km 9.5, hotel zone, tel. 3-00-43, open 8 a.m.-1 p.m. and 4-8 p.m.

Dollar Rent-A-Car, 235 Av. Tulum, downtown, tel. 4-22-29, open 8 a.m.-1 p.m. and 4-

7 p.m., all major credit cards except American Express; **Economovil Rent,** Cancun Airport, tel. 4-84-82, all major cards accepted; **Hertz,** 35 Reno, S.M. 20, downtown, tel. 4-13-26/4-46-92, open 7 a.m.-10 p.m., all major credit cards accepted; **Rentautos Kankun,** Plaza Caribe Hotel downtown, tel. 4-11-75, open 8 a.m.-1 p.m., and 5-8 p.m., Mon.-Sat., all major credit cards accepted; **Xel-Ha Car Rental,** 13 Av. Tulum , downtown and at the airport, tel. 4-13-38/4-41-38, open 8 a.m.-4 p.m. daily.

DAY TRIPS TO THE SURROUNDING AREA

From Cancun, Cozumel, Playa del Carmen, and Akumal many travel agencies and hotels offer day trips to outstanding pre-Columbian Maya sites nearby and some *not* so nearby. Look into the different options. In some cases a day trip just isn't enough time to really absorb what you're seeing. However, it may be just what you are looking for. If you want to explore further, a few ways to do it on your own would be renting a car (see "Car Rentals," p. 74-75), taking a local bus (check with the hotel concierge), or hiring a car and driver for two or three days (local travel agencies can recommend someone).

Chichen Itza

This is one of the finest Maya archaeological sites in the northern part of the Yucatan Peninsula. Largely restored, Chichen Itza is about a three-hour drive from Cancun and a favored destination of those fascinated with Maya culture. Chichen Itza is a mingling of two distant cultures: ancient Maya and later-arriving Toltecs. The oldest buildings are good examples of Late Classic Maya construction from the 5th C. to the 1100s, when the Toltecs invaded and then ruled Chichen Itza for 200 years. The Toltecs built new structures and added to many already in place—all bear a remarkable similarity to those in the ancient Toltec capital of Tollan (today called Tula) 1,200 km away in the state of Hidalgo.

Two centuries of mingling cultures added a new dimension to 800 years of Maya history.

The carvings found on buildings of different eras vary between the rain god Chac (early Maya) to the cult of the feathered serpent (late Mexicanized Maya). Though Chichen Itza was most likely abandoned toward the end of the 13th C., Maya were still making pilgrimages to the sacred site when Montejo the Younger, the Spaniard who played a role in ultimately subjugating the Maya, settled his troops among the ruins of Chichen Itza in 1533. However, although they placed a cannon on top of the pyramid of Kukulcan, they were unable at that time to conquer the elusive Indians and after a year left Chichen Itza for the coast. The pilgrimages continued.

Today, a different breed of pilgrim comes to Chichen Itza from all over the world to walk in the footsteps of great rulers, courageous ball players, mysterious priests, and simple peasants. Chichen Itza is considered the best restored archaeological site on the Peninsula. Restoration, begun in 1923, continued steadily for 20 years. Work is still done intermittently, and there are enough unexcavated mounds to support continued exploration for many years into the future.

Travel Tips

You can easily walk the 10-square-km grounds; as previously mentioned, taking two days is a relaxing way to do it, but it can be done in a day. Wear walking shoes for this entire expedition: climbing around in sandals can be uncomfortable and unsafe. For some, a short walk around the grounds will satisfy their

Kukulcan is also known as El Castillo.

curiosity, and they can say they've "been there." For a ruins nut, however, the best advice is to spend the night either at a hotel adjacent to the ruins where you can be up and on the grounds as soon as the ticket taker is there (usually 8 a.m.), or at the nearby town of Piste, which allows a good shot at getting to the site as early as possible. Two good reasons for arriving early are the weather (it's much cooler in the early hours) and the absence of the crowds that arrive later in tour buses. Taking two days you can study these archaeological masterpieces at your leisure, have a chance to climb at your own pace, and be there at the odd hours when the inner chambers open (only for short periods each day). This also allows time to return to your hotel for a leisurely lunch (maybe a swim), a short siesta, and an afternoon return visit (free with your ticket). The ruins are open daily from 8 a.m.-5 p.m., although some of the structures have special hours (posted on the buildings or ask at the entrance). Admission is under US$1.50 pp plus a small fee to use the parking lot. The lovely new visitor center offers clean restrooms, a cafe, a small museum, an auditorium where short informative films are shown, a bookstore, gift shop, and information center.

SIGHTS

Chichen Itza's large park-like area is easy to stroll through. Eighteen structures have been excavated, many of those restored. The uses for these buildings are not truly understood. Archaeologists can only study and guess from the few *real* facts that have been found. Near the sacred *cenote* a snack bar sells cold drinks, light snacks, postcards, and a few curios. A clean restroom is available at the back of the *palapa* building.

Temple Of The Warriors

On a three-tiered platform, the Temple of the Warriors stands next to the impressive **Group of a Thousand Columns**—reminiscent of Egypt's Karnak. Many of the square, stone columns have carvings still in excellent condition. In 1926 during restoration, a subtemple found underneath was named **Chacmool Temple.** The former color on the columns of the inner structure is still slightly visible. Close to the Thousand Columns on the east side of the plaza is a simple sweat house cleverly constructed with an oven and a channel under the floor to carry off the water thrown against the hot stones to create steam. Indian sweat houses are a combination religious and health-giving experience still used today on American Indian reservations.

The Platforms

Strolling the grounds you'll find the **Platform of Venus** and another called **Platform of Tigers and Eagles.** The flat square structures with a low stairway on each of four sides were used for ritual music and dancing and, according to Diego de Landa (infamous 16th-C. Franciscan bishop), farce and comedy were presented for the pleasure of the public.

Temple Of The Bearded Man

At the north end of the ballpark sits the handsome **Temple of the Bearded Man.** Two graceful columns frame the entrance into a smallish temple with the remains of decorations depicting birds, trees, flowers, and a grim "earth monster." It's doubtful whether anyone will ever know if the unusual acoustics here were used specifically for some unknown display of histrionics, or if it's accidental that standing in the temple one can speak in a low voice and be heard a good distance down the playing field, well beyond

what is normal (much like in the dome of St. Peter's Cathedral in Rome). Was this the "dugout" from which the coach whispered signals to his players down field? Some believe that only the upper class actually watched the game, and that the masses remained outside the walls and listened.

Great Ball Court

Of several ball courts at Chichen Itza (some archaeologists say nine), the most impressive is the **Great Ball Court,** the largest found yet in Mesoamerica. On this field, life and death games in the tradition of the Roman Colosseum were played with a 12-pound hard rubber ball. The playing field is 135 by 65 meters, with two eight-meter-high walls running parallel to each other on each side of the playing field. The players were obliged to hit the ball into carved stone circles imbedded in the vertical walls seven meters above the ground using only their elbow, wrist, or hip. The heavy padding they wore indicates the game was dangerous; it was also difficult and often lasted for hours. The winners were awarded jewelry and clothing from the audience. The losers lost more than jewelry and valuables, according to the carved panels on the site—they lost their *heads* to the winning

Temple of the Warriors

captain! There is a theory circulating that says the winners of the game were granted the "privilege" of losing their heads.

Temple Of The Jaguar

On the southeast corner of the ballpark, the upper **Temple of the Jaguar** was constructed between A.D. 800-1050. To get there you must climb a steep stairway at the south end of the platform. Two large serpent columns, with their rattlers high in the air, frame the opening into the temple. The inside of the room is decorated with a variety of carvings and almost visible remnants of what must have been colorful murals.

Sacred *Cenote*

Today's adventurer can sit in the shade of a *palapa* terrace and enjoy a cold drink near the sacred *cenote* (say-NO-tay). This natural well is 300 meters north of Kukulcan. The roadway to the sacred well, an ancient *sacbe,* was constructed during the Classic Period. The well is large, about 20 meters in diameter with walls 20 meters above the surface of the water (34 meters deep) where the rain god Chac supposedly lived; and to con him into producing rain, sacrifices of children and young adults were made here. Human bones have been found. On the edge of the *cenote* is a ruined sweat bath probably used for purification rituals before sacrificial ceremonies.

In 1885, Edward Thompson was appointed United States Consul in nearby Merida. A young writer greatly interested in the archaeological zones surrounding Merida, he eventually settled in Chichen Itza and acquired the entire area, including an old hacienda, for only US$75. For many years he had studied Diego de Landa's account of human sacrifice still going on at the time of the Spanish conquest. Stories of young virgins and valuable belongings thrown into the well at times of drought over hundreds of years convinced him there was treasure buried in the muddy *cenote* bottom. From 1903-07, with the help of Harvard's Peabody Museum, he supervised the first organized dive into the well. Fewer than 50 skeletons were found, mostly

those of children, male and female, smashing the virgin myth. Precious objects of jade, gold, copper, plus stone items with tremendous archaeological value were also dredged from the muddy water.

Thompson set off an international scandal when he shipped most of these important finds to the Peabody Museum by way of diplomatic pouch. He was asked to leave Yucatan and for years (1926-1944) a lawsuit continued over the booty. Ironically, the Mexican court ruled in favor of Peabody Museum claiming that the Mexican laws concerning archaeological material were inadequate. After the laws were toughened up, the Peabody Museum, in a gesture of friendliness returned many (but not all) of the artifacts from Chichen Itza's well of sacrifice.

The next large-scale exploration of the well was conducted in the 1960s, sponsored by the National Geographic Society with help from CEDAM (a Mexican organization of explorers and divers noted for having salvaged the Spanish ship *Mantanceros*) in the Caribbean. As Thompson suspected before his untimely departure, there was much more treasure in the *cenote* to be salvaged. Hundreds of pieces made of gold, silver, obsidian, copper, and carved bone, plus a few more skeletons were brought to the surface. In order to see in this well, thousands of gallons of chemicals (a unique experiment by the Purex Co.) were successfully used to temporarily clarify the water.

Observatory

One of the most graceful structures at Chichen Itza is the **Caracol,** a two-tiered observatory shaped like a snail, where advanced theories of the sun and moon were calculated by Maya astronomers. Part of the spiral stairway into the tower/observatory is closed to tourists in an effort to preserve the decaying building. The circular room is laid out with narrow window slits facing south, west, and the points where the sun sets at the summer solstice and equinoxes. The priests used these celestial sightings to keep accurate track of time in their elaborate calendrical system.

Kukulcan

The most breathtaking place to view all of Chichen Itza is from the top of **Kukulcan,** also called El Castillo. At 24 meters it's the tallest and most dramatic structure on the site. This imposing pyramid, built by the Maya on top of another smaller pyramid, was probably constructed at the end of a 52-year cycle in thanksgiving for allowing the world to survive the elements—maybe even Halley's Comet! Halley's swept by this part of the earth A.D. 837 (and most recently in 1986); the construction of the second temple was approximately A.D. 850.

Kukulcan was built according to strict astronomical guidelines. Giant serpent heads repose at the base of the stairs. There are four sides of 91 steps with the platform on the top for a total of 365　one step for each day of the year. On 21/22 March and September (days of equinox) between noon and 5 p.m., the sun casts an eerie shadow, darkening all but one bright zigzag strip on the outside wall of the north staircase. This gives the appearance of a serpent slithering down the steep north-facing steps of the pyramid, giving life to the giant heads at the base. It seems to begin at the bottom in the spring and at the top in the fall. This was first noticed only 20 years ago. In the days when there were only a few people on the grounds watching, you could observe not only the serpent slithering down the steps, but also watch the shadow on the ground move toward the road to the sacred well—maybe looking for a sacrifice? Today the ground is covered with people. A visit including the dates of the equinox is a good time to observe the astronomical talents of the Maya, but be prepared for literally thousands of fellow watchers.

Be sure to make the climb into the inner structure of Kukulcan, where you'll see a red-painted, jade-studded sculpture of a jaguar, just as it was left by the Maya builders over a thousand years ago. Check the visiting hours since the inner chamber is not always open.

Chichen Caracol

Others

The largest building on the grounds is the **Nunnery,** named by the Spaniards. From the looks of it and its many rooms, it was a palace of some sort built during the Classical Period. Meaning "Wall of Skulls," **Tzompantli** is a platform decorated on all sides with carvings of skulls, anatomically correct but with eyes staring out of large sockets. This rather ghoulish structure also depicts an eagle eating a human heart. It is presumed that ritualistic music and dancing on this platform culminated in a sacrificial death for the victim, his head then left on display, perhaps with others already in place in a gory lineup. It's estimated that the platform was built between A.D. 1050-1200 after the intrusion of the Toltecs.

A much-damaged pyramid, **Tomb of the High Priest** is intriguing because of its burial chamber found within. Sometimes referred to as the Osario (Spanish for "ossuary," a depository for bones of the dead), the pyramid at one time had four stairways on each side (like El Castillo) and a temple at the crest. From the top platform, a vertical passageway lined with rock leads to the base of this decayed mound. There, from a small opening, some stone steps lead into a cave about three meters deep. Seven tombs were discovered containing skeletons and the usual funeral trappings of important people, including copper and jade artifacts.

PRACTICALITIES

Accommodations

Only a few hotels are within walking distance of the ruins, all in the moderate price range. **Hotel Mayaland** is a lovely modernized colonial; it has 64 rooms, private baths, four dining rooms, pool, gardens, a/c, and satellite TV. A long winding staircase, leaded glass, tile floors, and slow-moving fans lend an exotic '30s ambience to the hotel. It's located in the heart of the Chichen Itza archaeological zone, declared a Heritage of Humanity by UNESCO in 1988. Rates are about US$108 d, less in the summer; tel. (800) 235-4079. **Hotel Hacienda Chichen Itza** contains original bungalows of the early archaeologists. The narrow-gauge railroad tracks used in the 1920s for transportation and hauling can still be seen. The hotel is open winter season only; rates are US$62 plus tax, call (800) 223-4084. **Villa Arquelogica**, owned by Club Med, is the newest hotel at Chichen Itza. "Almost" deluxe small rooms have private bath, and the hotel has a shallow swimming pool, bar, covered patio, dining room, and a unique library filled with books concerning the Maya and the pertinent area. Rates about US$40 d, reservations suggested; from U.S. tel. (800) 528-3100.

    Hotel Dolores Alba, 2.2 km east of the ruins, is rustic, clean, with swimming pool, private bath, and dining room; US$15 d. Free transport to the ruins available. Mailing address: Calle 63 #464, Merida 97000, Mexico, tel. 21-37-45. Be sure to designate that you want a room in the Chichen Dolores Alba, since this address also takes reservations for its sister hotel, the Merida Hotel Dolores Alba.

Hotel Mayaland

Piste

Piste, 2.5 km west of Chichen Itza, has a unique tradition of providing the work force for the archaeological digs at Chichen Itza. Originally the men were chosen because they were the closest; now it's a proud tradition of the people. Piste is growing up. The once-quiet village is becoming a viable addendum to Chichen's services. More hotels and restaurants are available each month as the number of tourists interested in Chichen Itza grows. Be sure to look around at the many cafes and gift shops as well.

Piste Accommodations

The **Hotel Mision Chichen,** just a few kilometers west of the ruins on Hwy. 180 and just outside Piste is rustic, has a pool, a/c, and dining room. Credit cards accepted; rates US$40 d. Reservations suggested; tel. from U.S. (800) 223-4084. Nearby you'll find the

Piramide Inn Hotel and Trailer Park. With cement pads, electrical and water hookups, the hotel area is peaceful, grassy, tree shaded, and has a swimming pool. The dining room is open to both hotel and trailer guests. Rates are moderate.

Food And Entertainment
The only restaurants within walking distance of the site are at the hotels. Check the hours since they're usually open for lunch only between 12:30-3 p.m. Bring your swimsuit—lunch guests are welcome to use the pool, a refreshing break in a day of climbing and exploring the ruins. Every evening a **Sound and Light Show** is presented in both the English and Spanish languages at the ruins. The English version is usually the second one of the evening and the fee is under US$3. Other than that there's no organized entertainment in Chichen Itza. However, the guests of the nearby hotels are generally well-traveled people, many with exciting tales to tell. Sitting under the stars on a warm night with a cold *cerveza* and swapping adventure yarns is a delightful way to spend many an evening.

TRANSPORT

Chichen Itza lies adjacent to Hwy. 180, 121 km east of Merida, 213 km west of Cancun, and 43 km west of Valladolid. If traveling by car you have many options. The roads to Chichen Itza are in good condition, as long as you slow down for the *topes* (traffic bumps) found before and after every village and school. Hitchhiking at the right time of day will put you in view of many autos on Hwy. 180, but be settled before dark or you may spend the night on the roadside; there's little traffic on this road after sunset.

By Public Bus
Local buses leave from Cancun and Puerto Juarez (a three-hour trip) to Piste; ask about the return schedule.

By Plane
Small planes offer commuter service to Piste from Cancun, Cozumel, and Chetumal. Check with Aerocaribe, in Cancun tel. 4-12-31, in Cozumel tel. 2-08-77, for information and reservations. A sample price is around US$60 OW from Chichen Itza to Cancun.

Escorted Tours
Escorted tours on modern a/c buses leave daily from Cozumel, Puerto Aventuras, and Cancun—day trips or overnighters. Check with your hotel or one of the many travel agencies in the city. They offer a variety of tours and prices; check around before you make a decision. The following tour is arranged by Yucatan Trails in downtown Merida (Calle 62, #482, tel. 21-55-52), where you can get price and time schedules. This is a creative way for a traveler touring more than just Quintana Roo to see more of the countryside and the Chichen Itza ruins. Fly to Merida first, spend a few days in the colonial city (it's rich with Spanish and Maya history), and then leave on the scheduled 9 a.m. bus which stops at Chichen Itza for a couple of hours and again in Valladolid for lunch, then drops you off in Cancun, arriving at approximately 6 p.m. Another reputable tour company located in Merida, **Mayaland Tours**, offers various trips including roundtrip daily tours to Chichen Itza and Uxmal as well as overnight private or shared tours. Day-trippers have limited time at the sites and take lunch lunch at one of the dining rooms at the charming Mayaland Hotel. For more information (from the States) call (800) 235-4079, Avenida Colon #502, Merida, Yucatan, Mexico 97000. Or check with your local travel agent.

The Balankanche Caves
Only six km east of Chichen Itza visitors will find the **Balankanche Caves.** Here you'll travel down under the earth and see many Maya ceremonial objects that appear to have just been left behind one day 800 years ago, when everyone left. Discovered in 1959 by a tour guide named Gomez, the caves were

*entrance to the
Balankanche Caves*

studied by prominent archaeologist Dr. E. Willys Andrews, commissioned by the National Geographic Society. What he saw, and what you can see today, was and is stirring: numerous stalactites and a giant stalagmite resembling the sacred "Ceiba Tree" surrounded by ceramic and carved ceremonial artifacts. This was obviously a very sacred site for the Maya, and it perpetuates the mystery of that ancient people: Why did they leave? Where did they go? Who were they? Where did they come from in the very beginning? And what is the secret of their complex hieroglyphics?

At the entrance you'll find a parking lot, a cool spot to relax, small cafe, museum, interesting photos of Maya rituals, and guides; a light and sound show is offered nightly. The entrance fee is under US$5, light and sound show under US$3; open 8 a.m.-5 p.m. Surrounding the site you'll find a botanical garden with a variety of identified plants native to the areas around the Yucatan Peninsula.

Travelers Note: Remember that on Sundays and holidays all museums and archaeological sites in Mexico are free and admission for children under 12 is free year-round.

Dzitnup

After leaving the Archaeological Zone of Chichen Itza on the road to Valladolid, travel a few km east and you'll see a small handmade sign that says Dzitnup. Follow the sign (about

one km off the main road) and you'll find a delightful underground *cenote*. Wear your tennis or comfortable walking shoes and your swimsuit in case you decide to take a swim. After a reasonably easy descent (in a few places you must bend over because of a low ceiling) underground you'll come to a beautiful circular pond of crystal clear water. It's really a breathtaking place, with a high dome ceiling that has one small opening at the top letting in a ray of sun and dangling green vines. You'll see dramatic stalactites and a large stalagmite; catfish and blindfish swim in the placid water. It's typical of the many underground caverns and grottos that are common around the peninsula, and well worth the small admission.

Uxmal

If staying in Merida for a few days, Uxmal is another Maya site that exhibits the advanced knowledge of architecture, imagination, science, and mystique of the ancient Maya. Located 80 km south of Merida (an hour's drive) in a range of low hills covered with brush, Uxmal is believed to have been the hub of a district of about 160 square km encompassing many sites, including Kabah, Sayil, Labna, and Xlapak. The Maya word Uxmal (oosh-MAHL) means "Thrice Built," referring to the number of times this ceremonial center was rebuilt—in fact, it's believed that Uxmal was built five times. In many instances structures were superimposed over existing buildings, built almost entirely in the Puuc style of pure Maya design (without outside influences such as the Toltecs at Chichen Itza). "Puuc" indicates the "hill" style of construction first observed at Uxmal in the Puuc hills. The work at Uxmal was begun in the 6th and 7th centuries, the Classic Period. It is characterized by delicately carved pieces of stone which were worked mosaic style into intricate designs and rich facades. After surviving a thousand years, some of the sapodilla-tree lintels—the cross pieces over doorways and windows—were removed by early American explorer John L. Stephens, taken to the U.S., and (tragically) destroyed in a fire along with many other priceless pieces. Many consider Uxmal to be the most ornate and complete complex yet found on the Peninsula.

History
Varied historical claims have been made about this Classic site. Some believe that it was founded by Maya from Guatemala Peten in the 6th century. Others contend that it dates back even further, perhaps to the Pre-Classic Period. By the time the Spaniards arrived it had been abandoned. An account of an early visit was given by Father Lopez de Cogulludo who explored the ruins in the 16th C., long after the Indians had abandoned the site. Without any facts to go on, he referred to the Quadrangle of the Nuns (Las Monjas) as the dwelling of the Maya "Vestal Virgins," who kept the "Sacred Fire." This comment demonstrates the beliefs the first Spaniards held about the evil of the Maya cult, based on some of the sacrificial rites they observed, no doubt. Cogulludo was followed by Jean-Fredric de Waldeck in 1836, who published a handsomely illustrated folio showing the structures of Uxmal peeking over thick brush. He compared them with the ruins of Pompeii. Only a few years later, the famous adventure duo, John L. Stephens and Frederick Catherwood, began their well-documented journey through the Peninsula in 1841. In the interim, the Indians must have cleared plots of land around Uxmal to plant corn, since Stephens comments that "emerging from the woods we came unexpectedly on a large open field strewn with mounds of ruins and vast buildings on terraces and pyramidal structures grand and in good preservation"—shown beautifully by Catherwood's sketches.

Frans Blom
The first real excavations began in 1929, led by the noted Danish archaeologist, Frans Blom. Blom was involved in many archaeological digs in the Maya hinterland, and his wife still lives among the Chiapas Indians today, carrying on her own work with the Indians she has come to love and crusade for—trying to save their Chiapas rainforest as well as their culture. Since Frans Blom, many other archaeologists have worked with the Mexican government at Uxmal; the result is a fine reconstructed site open for public enjoyment. Much more will one day be excavated, and who knows what exciting finds will be discovered! But for now the small area (700 by 800 meters) of Uxmal presents some of the finest examples of pure Maya design, without Toltec influence, to be seen.

Precious Water
Unlike most Maya centers in Yucatan, Uxmal was not built around a *cenote*, since there are none in this arid part of the Peninsula. Rainwater was collected by manmade *chaltunes* (cisterns) built into the ground, sometimes right inside a house or under a patio. Another method for saving water was the use of *aguadas* (holes in the ground lined with a watertight plaster substance). Because of the almost total absence of surface lakes or rivers on the Peninsula, the collection of water has been of prime importance for the survival of the Maya. Most of their religious ceremonies and idols were devoted to the worship of Chac, the rain god. The constant threat of drought inspired the people to build great centers of worship with hundreds of carvings and mosaics representing him and his prominent long hooked nose.

THE TEMPLES OF UXMAL

House Of The Magician

This "pyramid" is the tallest on the grounds, rising 38 meters and shaped in a distinctive elliptical form rather than a true pyramid. The west staircase, facing the nunnery and quad, is extremely steep (60-degree angle). Before you begin your climb do some leg stretches to loosen your muscles! Under this west stairway you can see parts of the first temple built on the site; a date on a door lintel is A.D. 569. On the east facade, the stairway has a broader slant and though still a steep incline, isn't nearly so hard on the legs. In the upper part of the east staircase you can enter an inner chamber which is **Temple Two. Temple Three** consists of nothing more than a small shrine at the rear of Temple Two. Climbing the west stairway brings you to **Temple Four** and an elaborate Chac mask with an open mouth large enough for a man to pass through. **Temple Five** dates back to the 9th C. and is reached by climbing the east stairway. From this viewpoint you'll be able to see the entire site of Uxmal and the surrounding brush-covered Puuc hills.

Nunnery

The Nunnery, northwest of the House of the Magician, is a courtyard covering an area of 60 by 45 meters, bounded on each side by a series of buildings constructed on platforms of varying heights during different periods of time. The buildings, which contain numerous small rooms, inspired the Spaniards to name it after the nunneries in Spain.

House Of The Turtles

A path leads south from the Nunnery to the **House of the Turtles.** This simple structure is 6.5 by 30 meters. The lower half is very plain but the upper part is decorated with a frieze of columns; a cornice above has a series of turtles along its facade. The turtle played an important part in Maya mythology.

Governor's Palace

Just south of the House of the Turtles is the **Governor's Palace,** considered by some to be the finest example of pre-Hispanic architecture in Mesoamerica. It sits on a large platform and measures almost 100 meters long, 12 meters across, and 8.5 meters high. With 11 entrances, the lower facade is plain, but the upper section is a continuous series of ornate carvings and mosaics of geometrical shapes and Chac masks. Two arrow-shaped corbel arches add to the delicate design of this extraordinary building. A double-headed jaguar in front of the palace (presumed to be a throne) was first found by John Stephens in 1841.

Uxmal—House
of the Magician

Locals sell souvenirs in kiosks outside the entrance to Uxmal.

The Great Pyramid

Another large structure is the **Great Pyramid** (30 meters high), originally terraced with nine levels and a temple on the top. According to early explorers, at one time four small structures sat on each of the four sides of the top platform described as "palace-like." The top story is decorated in typical Puuc fashion with ornate carvings and stonework depicting flowers, masks, and geometric patterns.

Others

Walking through the grounds you'll find many other structures and a ballpark. Visit the **Dovecote, Temple of the Old Woman, Phallic Collection, Temple of the Phallus,** other small structures, and as yet unexcavated mounds. You can pick up a guide (or he'll try to pick you up) at the entrance of the ruins. If you feel a need for this service (and they certainly can be informative), be sure you agree on the fee before you begin your tour. Something to remember: every guide will give you his own version of the history of the ruins, part family legend (if you're lucky) and part fairy tale. And let's face it, no one *really* knows the history of this obscure culture shrouded by the centuries. Many good books are available on the archaeological ruins of the larger sites (see "Booklist"). Grounds are open from 8 a.m.-5 p.m., admission charge is under US$1. A light and sound show is presented each evening in Spanish, 7 p.m., and English, 9 p.m.; admission is about US$2.

PRACTICALITIES

Uxmal is not a city; don't expect services of any kind. There are a few hotels with restaurants, but nothing else close by. To do justice to this fascinating antiquity, plan at least a full day to explore thoroughly. If coming from Cancun or any of the Caribbean coastal cities on a day trip, expect this to be a very long day! From Merida, only an hour away, it's easy to make this a day trip by bus or car.

Accommodations

You have your choice of three excellent hotels at Uxmal within walking distance of the ruins. All are in the same price category—US$40-50 d. For budget accommodations a little farther out, take a look at **Rancho Uxmal,** humble but clean and with a great restaurant. Other alternatives for budget accommodations are in Merida or in Ticul.

Villa Arqueologica is the newest of the three hotels, owned by a branch of Club Med. The rooms are small, attractive, and very functional, with twin beds, a/c, and private bathroom with shower. Both floors open onto a tropical courtyard. The flower-covered patio has a sparkling (shallow) pool, outside bar and table service, covered cabana area, and a complete library on the history and culture of the Maya. You'll find some French dishes along with local specialties in the large dining room. The rates are about US$48 d. Lunches and dinners average about US$11 pp. It offers an á la carte menu only. For more information and reservations, write to Club Med. Inc, P.O. Box 29805, Phoenix, AZ 85038, tel. (800) CLUB MED. **Hacienda Uxmal** is an older colonial-style hotel straight out of the 1920s. For years it's been a favorite of visitors, with beautiful tile walkways and comfortable spacious rooms with handcarved furniture and ceiling fans. A tropical garden cafe surrounds the pool; the indoor **Nicte Cafe** is open all day. Rates about: US$94 d. For information call owner/operators, **Mayaland Tours**, tel. (800) 235-4079, fax (99) 25-23-97.

A little farther down the road (1.5 km, walking distance for the hardy) is **Hotel Mision Uxmal.** Transport to the ruins is available. This has all the modern amenities including a pool, bar, dining room, and nice rooms with private bath and a/c. The dining room gives you a set menu including appetizer, entree, dessert, and beverage for about US$10.50, but if you only want a sandwich or soup or snack, just ask; it's available. Credit cards accepted, rates about US$50 d. Mailing address: 14 West 95th St., New York, NY 10025, tel. (in U.S.) (800) 223-4084.

Food

All three hotel dining rooms welcome visitors for lunch. Expect to pay about US$10.50 for a complete three-course lunch; ask what light meals are available. Bring your swimsuit for an after-lunch dip—great for cooling down before you return to the ruins for the next go-around. Although no other cafes are nearby, cold drinks are available at a kiosk just outside the entrance to the ruins and a small cafe serves light meals in the Visitors Center.

Entertainment

Every evening a **sound and light show** is presented in Spanish (first show, 7 p.m.) and English (second show, 9 p.m.) at the ruins overlooking the quad of the Nunnery. Escort-ed tours to the shows are available from Merida. If you've never seen one of these shows, check it out. It's mood-altering to sit under the stars surrounded by stark stone monuments in the warm darkness and listen to Latin-accented voices and a symphony orchestra echo in stereo from temple to temple, narrating the (so-called) history of the Maya while colored lights flash dramatically on first one and then another of these barren structures. Sometimes Mother Nature adds her own drama: the rumble of thunder from a distant storm, or jagged streaks of luminous light in a black sky. The already eerie temples reflect a supernatural glow, evoking the memory of the Maya, their mysterious beginnings, and still unsolved disappearance. Admission is under US$2; buy tickets either at hotels in Uxmal, in Merida at Government Tourist Centers, or any travel agency.

Shopping

The new **Visitor's Center** at the entrance to the Uxmal site is modern and beautiful. With the visitor in mind, the center offers clean restrooms, gift shops, a small museum, an auditorium where a short film promoting the Yucatan Peninsula is shown, a bookstore with a good supply of English-language books about the various ruins on the Peninsula, an ice cream shop, and a small cafeteria and cantina.

Outside the entrance are kiosks where local women sell the *huipil* (Yucatecan dress). Their prices can be much better than in gift shops; frequently they're made by the saleswoman or someone in her family. Some dresses are machine-embroidered or made of polyester, though many are still handmade on white cotton with bright embroidery thread. Be sure you get what you want. Ask if the colors are fast and how to care for it; you may or may not get the straight information. The *huipiles* worn by Maya women always look snow white with brilliant colors. Don't forget to bargain.

The only other shopping at Uxmal is at the small gift shops adjoining the hotels near the ruins. Most of them sell the usual curios, clothing, tobacco, postage stamps, and post cards. The exception is the **Villa Arqueologi-**

Ladies sell colorful huipils *at Uxmal.*

ca Hotel, where high-quality Maya reproductions depicting ancient idols are displayed. You can find reproductions in many places, but unlike these, most are not of the best quality and have very little detail. The prices also reflect the excellent workmanship, a little more costly than some.

Getting There
The best way is to plan a couple of days away from the Caribbean coastal area, making Merida your headquarters, either escorted or independently. If traveling on your own,

buses leave Merida's main station (Calle 69, #544) daily starting at 8 a.m. and continuing frequently throughout the day. Check at the bus station in advance since schedules are apt to change. Allow about 1¹/₂ hours for the trip (79 km)—be sure to check the return time to Merida.

If driving, the highway (261) from Merida to Campeche City passes close to the Uxmal ruins, and is a good road. From Merida the drive takes about one hour. Travel agencies in Merida have information about escorted tours to visit the ruins at Uxmal. Check with the government tourist office at Teatro Peones Contreras on Calle 61 in downtown Merida.

Yaxcopoil
If driving from Uxmal to Merida, save a little time to stop at a turn-of-the-century hacienda right off Hwy. 261 and clearly marked. A half-hour visit (about US$.45) gives a great insight into what life must have been like in the days when Mexican haciendas operated like small fiefdoms. Hundreds of Indians provided the labor necessary to grow and harvest the thorny henequen plant which, until after WW II, made the owners of these small kingdoms millionaires. At **Yaxcopoil** (yawsh-co-poe-EEL) there are remnants of the 1890s and 1900s furniture used in the drawing rooms and dining rooms, giving a hint of the gracious life the *patrones* enjoyed. Take a look into the kitchen with its unique wood stove made from white tile, pictures of the family, framed documents showing dates of events, even the old safe. This is a stroll into the past. With luck you may have as your guide Ernesto Cullum Yam. A Maya, he was born in Yaxpoil. His parents are still alive, ages 87 and 90, and tell of life on the hacienda when they worked—under much different conditions than now.

ISLA DE COZUMEL

INTRODUCTION

Cozumel ("Land of the Swallow") is a Caribbean island surrounded by water the color of imperial jade. Edged with stretches of white sand and craggy castles of black limestone and coral, its shoreline is continuously washed by an inquisitive, restless sea. The island rose from the sea in the Pliocene or Pleistocene epoch to its maximum height of 45 feet above sea level. At 47 km long and 15 km wide it's the largest of the three islands off the east coast of Quintana Roo—and the largest island in the Republic of Mexico. The other islands lying off the Quintana Roo coast are Isla Mujeres and Contoy. Cuba is 95 miles north and Cancun is 30 miles northwest. Across a 3,000-foot-deep channel that's 19 km offshore, Cozumel was a sacred mecca for Maya noblewomen who traveled in large dugout canoes to worship Ixchel, the goddess of fertility.

A calm sea on the lee (west) side of the island makes it ideal for swimming, diving, water-skiing, windsurfing, beachcombing, or relaxing in the sun. It's also the developed side, where clusters of buildings in the (only) town of San Miguel de Cozumel house 50,000 residents and visitors. Offices, shops, banks, markets, hotels, restaurants, and two docks are all concentrated in this small seaside town. The east coast is another world, with few people and little activity but dotted with isolated coves and bays, some with placid water, others with spectacular surf crashing on the beach and spraying mist on passing windshields. Clear water and the proximity of at least 20 live reefs make snorkeling a must, even for the neophyte. Exploring the Maya ruins in the overgrown interior of the island is an adventure by motorcycle, bike, car, or foot. The people of Cozumel, in their quiet way, are accepting and friendly to the growing number of visitors who come each year. Although Cozumel, with its lively discos and steady influx of divers and cruise ships, is more upbeat than Isla Mujeres, it still lacks the jet-set feeling of Cancun—perhaps because it's a real town where fishing and diving flourished long before outsiders arrived.

Climate

The climate is warm year-round (average 80° F). The heaviest rains begin in June and last through October. It's possible for rain to fall almost every day during that time, but the usual afternoon shower is brief and the ground absorbs moisture quickly, so any travel interruption is minimal. During wet months, expect high humidity. November through May is generally balmy, with lower humidity and an occasional cool evening (average 78° F).

FLORA AND FAUNA

Birds

In 1925, Ludlow Griscom from the American Museum of Natural History was one of the first ornithologists to discover Cozumel's varied and concentrated birdlife. Since then, Cozumel has been considered a prime birding site in the Western world; outside of town, civilization has not intruded into natural habitat. Except for the network of above-ground plastic water lines paralleling graded roads, the tangled brush, tall trees, and an occasional abandoned hut all ensure protected nesting grounds for these exotic winged creatures. If you enjoy watching birds, then getting up very early and trekking into one of several swampy areas on the island is worth the effort. One such place is located close to town behind the Sol Caribe Hotel. Here, at dawn, you're likely to see flocks of small multihued parrots, blue warblers, macaws, and spindly legged white egrets, while listening to a glee club of sounds echoing through the trees and across the murky water. Another marshy area that attracts fowl is just south of the junction where the cross-island road meets the east shore. A large swamp, accessible by car (a 4WD is best), parallels the coast behind the Punta Celerain Lighthouse.

Other Animals

Lizards and iguana skitter through the jungles; armadillos, deer, small foxes, and coati also call the Cozumel jungle their home. The iguana, more visible than the others because of its size and large population, is often seen sunning atop rocks along the east shore or even in the middle of the warm paved road that parallels the beach. Though the iguana is described as timid and said to move slowly, the traveler with a camera has to be lightning-fast to capture it on film. Once an outsider is spotted, it slips quickly into its underground burrow or up the nearest tree. The secret is not to be seen by the wary creature. (Photographers—keep trying, it can be done!) The iguana found in Cozumel commonly has

San Miguel is on the lee side of Cozumel with calm water and a tranquil bay.

shades of dark green, can grow up to two meters long, including its black-banded tail, and has a comb-like crest of scales down the middle of its back. Varicolored species are found on the Yucatan mainland.

Plantlife

Cozumel has never been known for its agriculture, partly because of the shortage of water. However, during the early 1900s chicle sap was gathered from numerous *zapote*

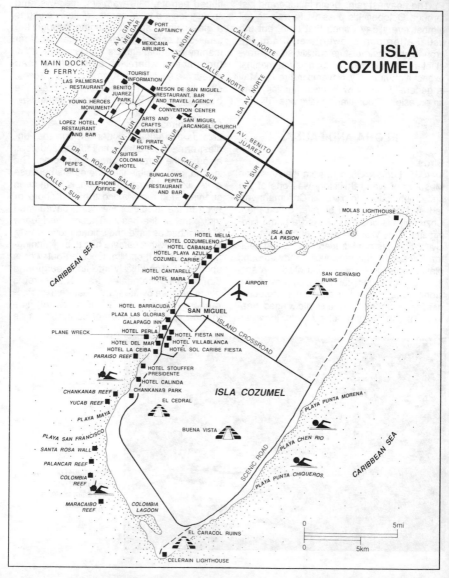

trees, which grow wild in the interior. Evidence of abandoned huts can be seen now and then where farmers once tried to eke a living from the thin, rocky soil. Coconut palms grew thick near the sea (before the devastating "yellowing" disease that has destroyed many trees) and it's still not unusual to see a sprouted coconut bobbing up and down in the surf. Many coconut trees take root that way, but if grown too close to the sea, they produce poor-tasting fruit. Take a stroll through the cool botanical garden at **Chankanab National Park,** where hundreds of tropical plants found on the island have been planted and labeled. A small entry fee (US$2) gives access for the day to the lagoon and beach.

Marinelife
Brilliantly colored fish, from tiny two-inch silver bait fish traveling in cloud-like schools to the grim thick-lipped grouper, lurk in and around graceful, asymmetrical formations of coral reminiscent of their names: cabbage, fan, and elk. You'll see rainbow-hued parrotfish, yellow- and black-striped sergeant majors, French angelfish, yellow-tailed damselfish, and shy silver-pink squirrel fish with their big sensitive-looking eyes. In shallow coves, daring Bermuda grubs come up out of the water to eat from your hand; watch the teeth!

HISTORY

Earliest Maya And Spanish
Cozumel's history consists of alternating bursts of unique activity and years of obscurity. During the Post-Classic Period, Cozumel was not only a sacred island but an important trading center. Artifacts, especially pottery remnants of the female figure made in distant parts of Mesoamerica, were left by women who traveled from all over Quintana Roo to worship Ixchel at shrines scattered throughout the jungle. After that era the island existed undisturbed until 1517, when it was briefly visited by Juan de Grijalva, who traveled from Cuba on a slave-hunting expedition.

He was soon followed by Spaniard Hernan Cortes, who embarked on his history-chang-

ing course in 1518. Cortes used Cozumel as a staging area for his ships when he launched his successful assault on mainland Indians. It was here that Cortes first heard of Geronimo de Aguilar, a Spanish shipwreck survivor of several years before. Aguilar had been living as a slave with his Indian captors. One story claims that when he heard of Cortes's arrival, he swam 19 km from the mainland to meet him. Because of Aguilar's fluency in the Maya tongue, he became a valuable accomplice in Cortes's takeover of the Indians. Francisco de Montejo also used Cozumel as a base in his war on the mainland. With the influx of Spaniards and accompanying diseases the Maya all but disappeared. By 1570 the population had dropped to less than 300.

Pirates And Chicle
The sparsely inhabited island led a placid existence until the late 1600s when it became a refuge for bandits of the sea. Pirates such as Jean Lafitte and Henry Morgan favored the safe harbors of Cozumel, especially during violent storms. The buccaneers frequently

JOHN L. STEPHENS AND FREDERIC CATHERWOOD

The literary names most associated with the Yucatan Peninsula are Stephens and Catherwood. Stephens was the writer and Catherwood, the artist. Stephens' books, *Incidents of Travel in the Yucatan* in two volumes, beautifully illustrated by Catherwood, are still used by archaeologists as references; anyone who hasn't already would enjoy reading these books as they travel through the Peninsula.

and created general havoc with their heavy drinking and violent fights, disrupting life within the small population of Indians and Spanish. In 1843 the island of Cozumel had been totally abandoned. Then refugees from the Caste War began to resettle it.

Cozumel again became a center of activity when the chewing gum industry began to grow in the U.S. For centuries, the Maya had been satisfying their thirst by chewing raw sap from the *zapote* tree which grows on Cozumel and throughout most of Central America. In the early 1900s, the developed world was introduced to this new sweet, bringing an economic boom to the Quintana Roo coast. New shipping routes included Cozumel, one of the best harbors along the coast suitable for large ships. Several big companies made fortunes on the nickel-pack of chewing gum, while the Indians who cut their way through the rugged jungle to tap the trees managed only subsistence. Because of these gum companies, however, obscure but magnificent jungle-covered ruins hidden deep in the forests were discovered, fascinating the urban explorers. This was the beginning of a large-scale interest in the Maya ruins by

outsiders that continues into the present. At one time the only route to Cozumel was by ship from the Gulf of Mexico port of Progreso. Cozumel's shipping income dwindled gradually as airstrips and air freight became common on the Peninsula. In addition, synthetics replaced Central America's hard-to-get chicle and is now used almost exclusively in the manufacture of chewing gum.

WW II And Cousteau

In 1942, as part of their defense network guarding the American continent, the U.S. government made an agreement to protect the coastline of Mexico. The American Army Corps of Engineers built an airstrip on Cozumel where the Allies also maintained a submarine base. After the war, the island returned to relative obscurity until 1961, when a TV documentary produced by oceanographer Jacques Cousteau introduced the magnificent underwater world that exists in and around its live reefs. Since 1974 statehood, Quintana Roo (including Cozumel) has enjoyed (or suffered) a rebirth into the world of tourism.

The Mexican government is making progress developing its beautiful Caribbean coast. For years it was believed that Cozumel itself would always maintain its pleasant small-town ambience, with just a smattering of tourism to add spice to the small island, and would never grow into a high-rise city; the water supply cannot support an enormous increase of people, plus everything needs to be shipped across the 19-km stretch that separates it from the mainland. But now the word is out, and the historical "Land of the Swallow" is about to see a new desalinization plant and the development of hotels on San Francisco Beach due to be open in 1991.

SAN MIGUEL DE COZUMEL

Cozumel has only one city: San Miguel. Though it's no longer a sleepy fishing village, it still has a relaxed, unhurried atmosphere, a good selection of restaurants from budget to gourmet, and hotels in every price range. Grocery stores, curio shops, banks, a post office, telegraph office, dive shops, and anything else you might need are available. The main street, known either as Malecon ("Seawall") or Av. Melgar, depending on which map you're studying, extends 14 blocks along the waterfront. The main dock is at the foot of Av. Juarez, in the center of town. Plaza del Sol, the large central plaza, boasts modern civic buildings and an imposing statue of the late Mexican president Benito Juarez. The surrounding streets are closed to vehicular traffic making it a pleasant place to stroll, shop, and enjoy the tranquility of Cozumel. In spring, masses of orange *flamboyane* (poinciana) flowers bloom on the surrounding shade trees under which local townspeople gather for festivals, religious celebrations, or friendly chats. Cafes and gift shops line the north side of the plaza.

ACCOMMODATIONS

Deluxe

The newer, more modern hotels located on or across the street from the water are north and south of town. Most of these fit the deluxe category. Sand hauled from the east side of the island covers razor-sharp coral and limestone, creating beautiful white beaches for their patrons (and the public). The hotels offer a variety of lures to get you out of town: spacious palm-shaded grounds, beach activities, diving equipment, charming outdoor patios and thatch-roofed bars, swimming pools, tennis courts, lively entertainment, and modern restaurants, with tour services and car rentals right on the premises. Taxis charge about US$2 from town to the hotel zones (one to four passengers).

Condominiums

Condos have not taken over the Cozumel shoreline—yet! A few are popping up here and there and one of the finest to rent is the small, intimate, well-laid-out **Condumel,** a 20-minute walk or a five-minute cab ride north of town. Condumel has its own beach and swimming dock where iguana sunbathe with the visitors. The condos each have one bedroom with a king-size bed, living room with sleeper sofa, roomy modern marble bathroom with tub and shower, and well-equipped kitchen ready for the cook. A few basic food items, including beer and purified water, are chilling in the fridge in case you don't want to go shopping right away. Fans and the offshore breezes usually keep your rooms cool, but there's also a/c if you want it cooler. Maid service is included in the price, and laundry service is available. Just ask, and you can borrow fins, mask, and snorkel to use while there. Rates for up to five people are US$88 per night Dec. 15 to June 1; US$65 per night June 1 to Dec. 15. The fifth person sleeps in a hammock. For reservations write to Condumel, attn. Ruth, P.O. Box 142, Cozumel, Quintana Roo, Mexico 77600; or call in Mexico (987) 2-08-92. Owner Bill Horn also manages Aqua Safari dive shop and will arrange diving trips and equipment.

a happy smile and fresh laundry at the Condumel

Hotels For Divers

Some hotels go out of their way to accommodate divers. One such hotel is the 12-room **Safari Inn** located above Aqua Safari Dive Shop downtown on Av. Melgar across from the Safari boat dock. The hotel is modern but simple, clean, a/c, and very convenient for diving expeditions. The rates are US$30 d, $35 t, $40 quad, and $45 for five. Write to

Condumel Condominium Hotel

Safari Inn, Box 142, Cozumel, Quintana Roo, Mexico 77600 for package information; tel. 2-01-01/2-06-61. Other hotels also offer dive packages, write for prices: **Casa Del Mar,** and **La Ceiba Hotel,** 8117 Preston Rd., Suite 170, Lockbox No. 4, Dallas, Texas 75225.

Budget

Hotels in the center of San Miguel are often less expensive and within walking distance of cafes, discos, shops, and the sea-front promenade. A wide variety of rooms is available: some small and sparsely furnished, others expansive with heavy colonial decor, central courtyards, restaurants, and comfortable gathering places to meet fellow travelers. Some hotels offer an economical junior suite with cooking facilities and private bath, a great bargain for families or small groups. Most have ceiling fans; some have a/c. With few exceptions, higher winter rates prevail from the middle of Dec. through Easter week, and reservations are recommended. Rates quoted in the hotel chart are for a double room during high season and can fluctuate; add 15% tax. Since the economy of Mexico changes almost daily, double-check prices on arrival if reservations aren't made in advance. There are no youth hostels on the island.

Camping

Cozumel has no campgrounds with facilities. However, hidden coves and isolated beaches on the east side of the island let the outdoorsperson enjoy roughing it. Bring everything needed to camp, including water. Don't expect even a tiny *tienda* to buy forgotten items. If you ask the tourism office about beach camping, they'll tell you to get permission from the navy, which occupies the large building south of town, on the ocean side across from the Costa Brava cafe and hotel.

FOOD

San Miguel has a variety of ways to spotlight mealtime. Fast-food stands and restaurants abound and fit all budgets. Seafood is exquisite and fresh. Yucatecan specialties simply must be tasted! *Camarrones con ajo* (shrimp

VICINITY OF SAN MIGUEL

1. Mayan Plaza Hotel
2. El Cozumeleno Hotel
3. Cabanas del Caribe Hotel
4. Playa Azul Hotel
5. Cozumel Caribe Hotel
6. Cantarel Hotel
7. Mara Hotel
8. Club Nautico de Cozumel
9. Condumel Condos
10. Los Portales Restaurant
11. Pizza Rolandi
12. Gonzalo de J. Rosado Library
13. El Hippopotamo Disco
14. post and telegraph office
15. Aqua Safari Diving
16. Maya Cozumel Hotel
17. Benito Juarez Municipal Market
18. Lions Club
19. Javier Rojo Gomez Baseball Park
20. Children's Park
21. health center (S.S.A.)

COZUMEL ACCOMMODATIONS

NAME	800 PHONE	LOCAL PHONE	FAX
FIVE STAR ★★★★★ US$80-220			
El Cozumeleño	(800) 437-3923	2-01-49	75-3269
Cozumel Caribe	(800) 327-2254	2-00-21	—
Fiesta Americana Sol Caribe	(800) FIESTA-1	2-03-88	—
Melia Mayan Cozumel	(800) 336-3542	2-04-11	—
Plaza Las Glorias	(800) 342-AMIGO	2-20-00	68-2769
Stouffer Presidente	(800) HOTELS-1	2-03-22	—
FOUR STAR ★★★★ US$80-160			
Best Western Playa Azul	(800) 528-1234	2-00-43	—
Cantarell	—	2--01-44	—
Coral Princess Club	(800) 253-2702	2-29-11	—
Fiesta Inn	(800) FIESTA-1	2-28-99	—
La Ceiba	(800) 777-5873	2-08-15	75-3265
Mara	—	2-03-00	75-3843
Sol Cabanas Del Caribe	(800) 336-3542	2-00-72	—
Suites Turquesa	—	2-14-21	—
Villa Del Rey	—	2-16-00	—
THREE STAR ★★★ US$40-115			
Bahia	(800) 446-2166	2-02-09	—
Barracuda	—	2-00-02	—
Casa Del Mar	(800) 777-5873	2-19-44	75-3265
Casitas La Plaza	—	2-08-78	—
Club Del Sol	—	—	—
Galapago Inn	—	2-06-63	—
La Perla	(800) 852-6404	2-01-88	—
Mary Carmen	—	2-05-81	—
Meson San Miguel	—	2-02-33	—
Paraiso Caribe	—	2-07-40	—
Soberanis	—	2-02-46	—
TWO STAR ★★ US$25 and up			
Aguilar	—	2-03-07	—
Almarestell	—	2-08-22	—
El Narquez	—	2-05-37	—
El Pirata	—	2-00-51	—
Kary	—	2-20-11	—
Maya Cozumel	—	2-00-11	—
Safari Inn	(800) 854-9334	2-06-61	—
Suites Elizabeth	—	2-03-30	—
ONE STAR ★ US$15 range			
Blanquita Hotel	—	—	—
Costa Brava	—	2-14-53	—
Flamingo	—	2-12-64	—

COZUMEL ACCOMMODATIONS, cont.

NAME	800 PHONE	LOCAL PHONE	FAX
ONE STAR ★ US$15 range, cont.			
Flores	—	2-01-64	—
Jose Leon	—	2-10-26	—
Lopez	—	2-01-08	—
Pepita	—	2-02-01	—
Posada Cozumel	—	2-03-14	—
Posada Edem	—	2-11-66	—
Posada Letty	—	2-02-57	—
Posada Yoli	—	2-00-24	—
Saolima	—	2-08-86	—
Vilchis	—	—	—
Villa Elizabeth	—	2-13-18	—

with garlic), *caracol* (conch), and tangy *ceviche* (fish or conch marinated in lime, vinegar, chopped onions, tomatoes, and cilantro) are all tasty treats. *Huachinango Veracruz* (red snapper cooked with tomatoes, green pepper, onions, and spices) is popular, and snapper is caught off the reef year-round; eating it a few hours after it's caught makes a good fish dinner perfect. Fresh seafood at its best is sold in most cafes.

Moderate Cafes

Budget-class **La Economica,** located two blocks from the plaza heading inland, gives ample servings of *pescado frito* (fried fish) and *carne asada* (grilled meat) for about US$2.50. Another budget-class cafe is **Los Morrnes**—great Mexican style hamburgers. Both of these cafes are off the main drag behind the plaza. **Las Tortugas,** Av. 10 between Av. Juarez and 2 Calle Norte, serves good tacos. **Pepe's,** one-half block south of the plaza on Av. 5 Sur, noted for its relaxed atmosphere and reasonable prices, has been popular for 20 years. **El Portal,** an open cafe facing the waterfront, serves tasty family-style food. A sturdy breakfast of bacon, eggs, beans, and toast costs about US$2.50. Open for breakfast, lunch, and dinner.

Las Palmeras, located at the foot of the pier in the center of town has been serving good food for many years and is always busy.

Italian

If you're ready for something different, try the Swiss-Italian specialties at **Pizza Rolandi** on Av. Melgar 22. Good pizza, lasagna, calzone, and salads, plus beer and great sangria. The outdoor patio/dining room is a pleasant place to be on a balmy Caribbean evening; indoor dining available in case of rain. **Karen's Pizza** is another place for fun and good food. Try the *taaaaallll* glass of beer, served in a wooden holder, in their large outdoor patio located on the closed-to-vehicles section of downtown.

Mexican Entrees

For the zany crowd, **Carlos and Charlie and Jimmy's Kitchen,** north of the plaza on Av. Melgar, tel. 2-01-91, is a lively restaurant that specializes in fun. Any respectable beer drinker owes it to himself to witness the beer-drinking contests held nightly. Sound like a place to drink and not eat? Surprisingly, the terrific food includes good Mexican entrees. Open nightly. For a leisurely lunch in a tropical atmosphere, **Las Gaviotas,** out of town past the Hotel Playa Azul, sits right over a blue silk sea. The view of clear water and bright-hued parrotfish waiting for a handout help make this a pleasant lunch spot. **El Capi,** located on Adolfo Rosado, tel. 2-03-86, serves great seafood. Yearning for an American hamburger and a football game? Go to the **Sports Page,** a video bar/ restaurant (usually a good money exchange also). Find it on the corner of 2nd and 5th avenidas.

More Expensive

The **Acuario Restaurant,** one-half km south of town on Av. Melgar south at Av. 11 (open noon-midnight), serves elegant fish and lobster dinners with cocktail service. Walls are uniquely lined with huge aquariums filled with tropical fish, including a few brightly colored eels. A new restaurant, **Donatello's,** serves delicious Italian specialities from seafood to pasta in a comfortable continental atmosphere. Try **Pancho's Backyard** for a patio ambience and tasty Mexican treats. Both on the seafront.

Morgan's, on the north side of the plaza, is an elegant/casual restaurant serving a Continental menu along with typical fish and Mexican entrees. You can spend a little or a lot. A special treat is crepe suzettes with a spectacular flaming show (and they taste terrific!). Music starts about 7 p.m.—it can be a rhythmic Argentinean group, including an expert on the exotic pan flute, or a mellow classical pianist—don't miss it! For two people expect to pay anywhere from US$15 to as much as US$40 for a good dinner including crepes, a drink, tax, tip, and entertainment—worth it.

Hotel Restaurants

On Wed. and Sat. at 8 p.m., the **Presidente** and **Sol Caribe** hotels present a Mexican buffet and folkloric entertainment (about US$25), offering literally dozens of tasty dishes, fun, and good music and dance. Reservations can be made through most hotels.

Street Vendors And Markets

During spring and summer, street vendors offer mangos on a stick, peeled and artistically carved to resemble flowers, about US$.50 each with your choice of lime or chili powder garnish, or both! A good selection of grocery stores, fruit vendors, and two bakeries make it easy to eat on the run. Nothing tastes better than a crusty hot *bolillo* (hard roll) fresh from the oven, a bargain at 25 cents each. The bakeries (one is a block north of the main plaza at 2 Calle Norte and the other on the corner of 3 Calle and 10 Av. Sur) sell a variety of pastries and cookies. The *tortilleria* makes corn tortillas all day; buy a kilo for only 50 cents hot off the *tomal* (griddle).

The **Centro Comercial** on Av. Juarez facing the plaza, and **Comercial Caribe** on Av. Juarez closer to the waterfront, are grocery stores stocking a wide variety of canned goods, fresh produce, notions, and alcoholic drinks. Expect American-made products to cost more. Looking for plain Mexican ground coffee in Cozumel markets is frustrating; instant coffee and coffee grounds with sugar added are all you can find. If you're desperate, American brands are available (at inflated prices) at **PAMA** on Av. Melgar.

WILD CANARIES

Early one morning while getting ready for thirsty sun worshipers in a still-deserted patio, a bartender was delighted to show two birdwatchers how a trickle of condensed milk or canned coconut cream in the bottom of an ashtray immediately attracted hundreds of wild brown and yellow *canarios*. With the first thick drops out of the can the tiny birds swooped in from every tree and bush in and around the patio until the bar was covered. It had taken on life with hundreds of happy, chortling creatures queueing up for a turn at the ash tray, obviously in milky heaven.

ENTERTAINMENT

Discos are popular in Cozumel. At night the town jumps with lively music, as energetic people meet and mingle. Dancing continues till morning at **Scaramouche** (Av. Melgar), **Grips** (Seafront/10 Norte), and **Neptuno** (Av. Melgar/11th). **Presidente, Mayan Plaza, Sol Caribe, La Ceiba,** and the **Mara** have music at cocktail hour and often during dinner. For a quiet evening of camaraderie and exercise for the brain, go to **El Encuentro,** a restaurant where San Miguel's chess and domino enthusiasts enjoy challenging visitors, open daily from 8 a.m.; Calle 1 Sur and Av. 10 Sur.

Special Events
The **Billfish Tournament** is held every year in May, bringing fishing enthusiasts from all over, especially boaters from the U.S. who cross the Gulf of Mexico to take part in the popular event. **Carnaval,** a movable fiesta usually held in Feb., is a great party with street parades, dancing, and costumes—all with a tropical flavor. Another popular event is the celebration of the patron saint of San Miguel, held the last week of September.

Cinemas
Cinema Cozumel is on Av. Melgar at 4 Calle Norte; **Cine Cecilio Borgues** is on Av. Juarez and Av. 35; showtime 9:15 p.m. at both. U.S. films are sometimes shown with original soundtrack and Spanish subtitles, but most are Spanish-language films.

The Museum
The **Museo de la Isla de Cozumel** is located on the waterfront north of the plaza in an old building that once housed a turn-of-the-century hotel. There are lovely informative exhibits of the wildlife, reefs, and corals surrounding the island, and artifacts of historic Cozumel. This small non-profit museum is definitely worth seeing (small admission) and

offers a bookstore, library, and meeting room; on the 2nd floor there's a pleasant outdoor cafe overlooking the sea.

The museum has begun a new evening program for visitors which is proving very popular. With reservations made early in the day at the museum, visitors (for a US$10 fee) are able to take part or just observe the turtles laying eggs and see the marine biologists and volunteers in action.

Everyone meets at the museum at about 9 p.m. A short slide presentation informs visitors about the plight of the sea turtles. After that, everyone is taken in buses to the beach and the fascinating evening begins. This is a wonderful family activity. If there has been hatching that day, the "turtlets" are gathered up and kept in buckets until dark when they are released, safer from predators. All guests take part in this, and children love observing and handling the tiny turtles and helping them safely to sea. Well worth the money!

The Turtle Program: During the summer months from June through Aug., giant sea turtles approach the east side beaches of the island to lay their eggs. For some years the eggs and turtles have been at risk because of those who raid the nests and kill the turtles. And though the government has made laws that should prevent this, there aren't enough funds to enforce the law. The people of Cozumel have begun a volunteer program to monitor the beaches late at night. Under the supervision of a marine biologist, the eggs are removed immediately after being laid and reburied at the fenced in hatchery beach and continually observed. This program has greatly increased the number of live hatchlings that make it into the sea. Anyone interested in joining the **Group of Friends of the Museum,** write to Av. Melgar and Calle 6 Norte, Cozumel, Quintana Roo, Mexico 77600; tel. 2-08-41 or 2-15-57.

Bullfights

For those into the traditional attractions of Mexico, a bullfight is scheduled on Wed. mornings at 9:30 during the high season. Check with your hotel for price and reservations.

COZUMEL SPECIALTY SHOPS

Orbi Cozumel	Av. Melgar, #27
Casa Ines	Av. 5 Norte, #3
Las Campana	Plaza Principal
Arte Y Diseno La Concha	Rosado Salas
Argentium	Rosado Salas and Melgar
Alexandra Jewelry	Av. Melgar
Animal Fiesta	Calle 4 Norte
Mi Casa	Av. Melgar, #261
ACA Joe	Av. Melgar and 4 Norte
Cinco Soles	Melgar and 8 Norte
Van Cleef Plaza	Av. Melgar, #54
Casa Blanca Santa Cruz	Av. Melgar, #33
Chachi Plaza	Av. Juarez, #5
Rincon Mexicano	5 Av. Norte, #48
Isla Mia	Avs. Juarez and Melgar
Roberto's Black Coral	Av. Melgar
Studio One Artists' Studio	Av. 25 Sur, #921
La Casita	Av. Melgar, #23 Norte
El Sombrero	Av. Melgar, #29

The Plaza

On Sunday evenings local citizens and tourists meet in the central plaza. Only a few women still wear the lovely white *huipiles*. Men in their best white hats look crisp and cool in the typical *guayabera* with its open collar and tailored pleats. Families (sometimes three generations) gather in the plaza to hear Latin rhythms and the tunes of the day presented by local musicians. The charming white gazebo takes on a modern look with the addition of powerful speakers placed around the park. Children, dressed as miniatures of their parents, run, play, and chatter in front of the live band. It's hard to say who does the best business—the balloon man or the cotton-candy vendor. This is a nice place to spend an evening under the stars, meeting the friendly folk of Cozumel.

SERVICES

The four banks in town—**Bancomer, Banpais, Banco del Atlantico,** and **Banco Serfin** are all on the main plaza: exchange dollars or travelers cheques between 10 a.m.-12:30 p.m. Since the advent of the cruise ships, almost everyone in town will accept dollars, but be sure you know the daily rate and check it out. There have been complaints that cruise-ship passengers often are taken advantage of with the exchange. The **long-distance phone office** is on Calle 1 on the south side of the plaza, open 8 a.m.-1 p.m. and 4-9 p.m. Long-distance calls can be made from many hotels as well. Calling collect will save a good part of the added tax. The **post office** is on Melgar close to Calle 7, open 9 a.m.-1 p.m. and 3-6 p.m., Mon. to Fri.; the **telegraph office** in the same building is open Mon. to Fri., 9 a.m.-8:30 p.m., Sat. and Sun., 9 a.m.-1 p.m., tel. 2-01-06/2-00-56. **Office of Tourism** (booth in plaza) is a font of information, usually manned by someone who speaks English. A complete list of hotels in every price bracket is available along with maps of the island and any general info you might need; tel. 2-14-98.

For **taxi** service it's usually a matter of standing on the sidewalk and waving your arm, or waiting on Av. Melgar at the foot of the downtown dock—taxis queue along the sidewalk on the waterfront. The taxi office is on Calle 2 Norte, tel. 2-02-36/2-00-41, and any hotel will call a taxi. The closest **U.S. Consular Office** is in Cancun, tel. 3-10-15. Cozumel has one **gas station,** five blocks from downtown at Av. Juarez and Av. 30, open 7 a.m.-midnight daily. Cozumel has

---

State Tourist Office of Quintana Roo

Alvaro Obregon 457
Chetumal, Quintana Roo

EMERGENCY PHONE NUMBERS

Police	2-00-92
Fire Department	2-08-00
Hospital	2-01-40
Red Cross	2-10-58
Ambulance	2-06-39
Clinic (24 hours)	2-10-81

government-sponsored **"Green Angel"** motorist assistance. If your car should break down on the coastal highway, stay with it until they come by to give you gas, parts, or what-

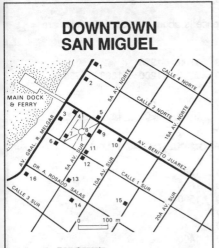

DOWNTOWN SAN MIGUEL

1. Port Captain
2. Mexicana Airlines
3. Las Palmeras restaurant
4. tourist information booth
5. Meson de San Miguel hotel
6. Lopez Hotel
7. Young Heros Monument
8. Benito Juarez Park
9. Convention Center
10. San Miguel Archangel Church
11. arts and crafts market
12. El Pirate Hotel
13. Suites Colonial hotel
14. telephone office
15. Bungalows Pepita
16. Pepe's Grill

ever help you need to get you on your way. The Green Angels cruise only on paved roads during daylight hours. Laundry can be left at **Lavanderia Manana,** Av. Circumvalacion #101. Charge is by the kilo, open 7 a.m.-8 p.m., Mon. to Sat., usually one-day service. Pickup service on request, tel. 2-06-30.

Camera Shops
Several camera stores in town sell film, rent underwater cameras, and have one-hour color-print processing service. **Aquascene,** tel. 2-03-79, ext. 102, is next to La Ceiba Hotel. **The Flash Camera Shop** is in Discover Cozumel Dive Shop (weather reports available here), tel. 2-02-80 or 2-03-97.

Medical Services And Pharmacies
In the event of a medical emergency, contact your hotel receptionist for an English-speaking doctor. **Hospital y Centro de Salud,** a small clinic with a doctor on duty, is open 24 hours a day, Av. Circumvalacion, tel. 2-10-81. One pharmacy, **Los Portales,** is located on Calle 11 Sur, tel. 2-07-41. Another is in Centro Comercial on the north side of the plaza. **Farmacia Joaquin** is on the plaza in front of the clock tower; open 9 a.m.-1 p.m. and 5-9 p.m., tel. 2-01-25. If still in need of help, call the American Consular Office in Cancun, tel. 3-10-15. Dr. Manuel Marin-Foucher Lewis is located on Adolfo Rosado Salas #260, tel. 2-09-12/2-09-49. Three dentists are listed in Cozumel's Blue Guide: Z. Mariles, tel. 2-05-07, T. Hernandez, tel. 2-06-56, and Escartin, tel. 2-03-85.

GETTING THERE

By Boat
Passenger ferries come and go from the downtown dock in San Miguel; car ferries use the **International Pier** across from the Sol Caribe Hotel where cruise ships dock. If crossing with a car, arrive 1 1/2 hours early and be prepared with exact change and your car license number when you approach the ticket window—or you may lose your place in line and possibly on the often-crowded ferry.

BY BOAT TO AND FROM COZUMEL

The new modern "waterjet" boat, the MV *Mexico* is quite comfortable and conveniently holds many passengers in airline-type seats, refreshments served. On the long ride to and from Cancun and Cozumel, a movie is shown (Mexican usually). Price around US$2.50 pp.

SCHEDULES TO AND FROM COZUMEL

From Playa del Carmen	0515	0645	1300	1500	1700
From Cozumel to Playa del Carmen	0430	0600	1200	1400	1600
From Cancun	0930	2030			
From Cozumel to Cancun	0715	1800			

The regular boats are still running; the price is about US$.50. Schedules are subject to change, so check it out.

From Playa del Carmen to Cozumel	0700	1100	1930		
Sundays only	0600	0900	1200	1600	1930
From Cozumel to Playa del Carmen	0500	0900	1800		
Sundays only	0400	0700	0900	1400	1800

AUTO FERRY SCHEDULES FROM PUERTO MORELOS

To Cozumel Sun., Mon., Tues.	0600	1200
To Puerto Morelos Sun., Mon., Tues.	1000	1600
To Cozumel Wed. and Fri.	0600	1500
To Puerto Morelos Wed. and Fri.	1100	
To Cozumel Thurs. and Sat.	1000	
To Puerto Morelos Thurs. and Sat.	0600	1400

By Air

Air travel from various points on the Yucatan Peninsula is becoming more common. There are flights from Merida to Cozumel (Aero Caribe), and from Playa del Carmen to Cozumel (Aero Caribe, runs hourly during most of the year, about US$10 pp OW); schedules change with the season. The airport is approximately three km from downtown San Miguel. Taxis and minibuses meet incoming planes. Taxi fare to town is about US$2 pp in a collective taxi (a van) that will take you to your hotel; it's more for the return trip in a private taxi. When departing, an airport-use tax (about US$10) is collected. This tax applies to all international Mexican airports, so hang

AIRLINES SERVING COZUMEL

United	2-04-68
Mexicana	2-02-63
Continental	2-05-76
Aero Cozumel	2-09-28
American	2-09-88

on to US$10 or $12 (price varies) for each international airport city where you plan to stay 24 hours or more. Change your money in town, as banks and some shops (when purchasing) give the best exchange rates, with hotels notoriously giving the worst. Cozumel has many small duty-free shops with a good selection of gifts. Sharp sport clothes and beautiful jewelry are available if you take the time to look around. Reading materials, especially English-language pictorial books about the area are found here and there. The airport has a dining room upstairs, and on the ground level a coffee bar opens for snacks.

GETTING AROUND

Getting around on the island is easy; it's flat and the roads are cared for. It's easiest in the city of San Miguel. The roads are laid out in a grid pattern with the even-numbered *calles* to the north of the town plaza, odd-numbered *calles* to the south; numbered *avenidas* run parallel to the coast.

Travelers, especially backpackers, should be aware that only escorted tourist buses make trips outside of the immediate area of San Miguel. To go to hotels north or south of town, you must take a taxi or go by car. Escorted tours around the island are available through any travel agency or your hotel.

Several transport options exist for exploring the outlying areas of the island on your own—which everyone should do! Avenida Juarez begins in downtown San Miguel at the dock and cuts across the middle of the island (16 km), then circles the south end. The road around the north end of the island isn't paved. Walking the flat terrain is easy, but distances are long. All of downtown San Miguel is easily reached on foot. The 70 km of paved island roads are flat and easily explored on bikes (rented at **Ruben's,** south side of the plaza, tel. 2-01-44, for about US$10 per day) and 125cc motorcycles (available to rent at several other shops in town; motorbikes and 125cc motorcycles rent for about US$30 daily).

Taxis will take you anywhere on the island and are available by the day; agree on price before your tour begins. Traveling with a local cabbie is often a real bonus since drivers know the island and its hidden corners better than most guidebooks (other than this one of course!). Remember: when the cruise ships arrive, all the taxis are at the International Pier, leaving the rest of the visitors rather high and dry. Ask at your hotel for ship times if possible and plan your movements around it. The same goes for the larger shopping centers: they are jammed when the ships are in port. A last option for seeing Cozumel is a car rental, which means total freedom to explore. Car rentals run approximately US $54 daily.

MOTOR BIKE RENTALS
Expect to pay about US$25-35 per day.
Aguilar, 3 Sur 98, tel. 2-11-90
El Dorado, Av. Juarez 10, tel. 2-23-83
Leo, la Sur No. 7, tel. 2-01-08
Santiagos, Hotel Cabanas del Caribe, tel. 2-00-17
Sol Y Mar, Hotel Presidente, tel. 2-03-22

CAR RENTALS
Arrendadora Peninsular, Av. Principal "Playa del Carmen," tel. 2-12-11
Autorent, Costera sur KM 4.5
Avis, 3 Sur 220, tel. 2-09-03
Budget, 5 Av. No. 0
Dollar, Costera Sur KM 3.5, tel. 2-20-25
Fiesta Cozumel, 11 Av. sur con Pedro Joaquin, tel. 2-07-25
Hertz, Av. Juarez, tel. 2-21-36
Rentadora Cozumel, 10a Sur 172, tel. 2-11-20
Thrifty, Av. Pedro Joaquin, tel. 2-17-69
Vista Del Mar Jeep Rental, Rafael Melgar 45, tel. 2-05-45 & 2-02-65

AROUND THE ISLAND

ARCHAEOLOGY

Nine Maya sites are scattered across the island. A few are difficult to reach, and only the hardy hiker will want to make the attempt. Most ruins on the island are of the "oratorio" type: small square buildings, low to the ground, with short doors that led early Spaniards to believe the places were once inhabited by dwarfs (a myth no longer believed). **El Cedral** is the exception; though a small temple, major ceremonies were probably held on this site. The story goes that a large Maya city was destroyed when the U.S. Army Corps of Engineers built an airstrip in dense jungle (now the location of the new Cozumel airport).

In ancient times gardens often were grown in this type of raised bed to protect the diminutive crop from jungle animals.

El Cedral

Several of the ruins are easily reached by car or motorbike. Just beyond San Francisco Beach on the main highway leaving town, a paved road takes off to the left and ends in 3.5 km at **El Cedral.** Small and not enormously impressive, this is the oldest Maya structure on the island. Amazingly, it still bears a few traces of the paint and stucco of the original Maya artist. But the deterioration indicates that hundreds of years have passed it by. A tree grows from the roof, with thick, exposed roots interminably tangled in and around stones of the ancient structure. Fat iguana with bold black stripes tracing their mid-sections guard the deserted, mold-covered rock structure; sounds of cows blend with the songs of countless birds and the resonant buzz of exotic unseen insects. Located in what is now a small farm settlement, El Cedral was once used as a jail in the 1800s. Right next to it is a rustic, modern-era stucco church painted vivid green. Go inside and take a look at two crosses draped with finely embroidered lace mantles—a typical mixture of Christianity and ancient cult, which some believe is associated with the "talking cross cult."

Aguada Grande

Aguada Grande is more difficult to reach. After crossing the island (via Av. Juarez) to the beach, turn left on the dirt road and travel 21 km to another dirt road going inland; it's about a 1.5 km hike to the site. This is .75 km from the northern tip of the island, the **Punta Molas** lighthouse, and **El Real** (30.5 km from San Miguel). If walking, the beach along here is difficult because of a rocky shoreline—you make better time on the dirt road. At about km 12, prepare for one of the most beautiful beaches on the island.

San Gervasio

San Gervasio is a well-preserved and recently reconstructed group of structures. Travel east on Av. Juarez, then left (north) on a dirt road (look for the San Gervasio sign) for approximately 10 km until it dead ends at the entrance to the site. The silence of these antiquities looming in the midst of dense brush, with only birds singing in the tall trees, overwhelms the visitor with an aura of what it was like centuries ago when only the Maya visited. San Gervasio has a snack bar for cold drinks and is open from 8 a.m. to 5 p.m., small entry fee.

WEST SHORE BEACHES

Chankanab Lagoon

Chankanab, located nine km south of San Miguel, is a national park. A small crystal-clear natural aquarium is surrounded by a botanical garden of 352 species of tropical and subtropical plants from 22 countries, as well as those endemic to Cozumel. The lagoon contains more than 60 species of fish, crustaceans, turtles, and intricately designed coral formations. This is a wonderful shady park to spend hours watching underwater activity. The lagoon is shallow, and until recently swimmers could go from the lagoon to Chankanab Bay (on the sea) through un-

derwater tunnels; the tunnels have collapsed and no longer assure safe passage. Now there's *no swimming.* Don't bring your crumbs and stale tortillas: caretakers frown on anyone feeding fish in Chankanab Lagoon. Without the tunnels opening to the sea, biologists must work at protecting life in the small area. Save food offerings for your short walk from the lagoon to the bay, where hundreds of fish will churn water along the shore to get a scrap of anything.

Chankanab Bay

This is a popular beach for sunbathers, swimmers, divers, and snorkelers to explore limestone shoreline caves. Showy sea creatures have no fear of humans invading their domain. For adventurous scuba divers, the coral reef which is close offshore is two- to 16-meters deep. A sunken boat, rusty anchors, coral-crusted cannons, and an antiquated religious statue all make for eerie sightseeing among the fish. A well-equipped dive shop is located here for rentals, air, sales, and certification instruction. Several gift shops, a snack stand, and a restaurant are all conveniently located near the beach where shade *pala-*

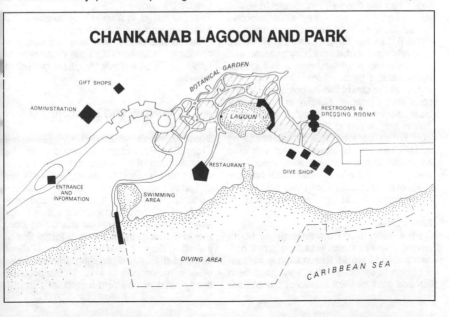

CHANKANAB LAGOON AND PARK

BOTANICAL GARDEN
GIFT SHOPS
ADMINISTRATION
LAGOON
RESTROOMS & DRESSING ROOMS
RESTAURANT
DIVE SHOP
ENTRANCE AND INFORMATION
SWIMMING AREA
DIVING AREA
CARIBBEAN SEA

Chankanab Bay

pas, freshwater showers, dressing rooms, and lockers are all included in the small entrance fee of US$2. This is a national park open from 9 a.m.-5 p.m. daily.

San Francisco Beach

Following the main road past Chankanab (14 km from town), you'll come to **Playa San Francisco** on the right. This 3.5 km of busy beach has two open-air restaurants, dressing rooms, bar, gift shops, volleyball net, wooden chaise lounges, and snorkeling equipment rental (US$5 per day). During the week, it's relatively quiet, but during busy seasons and on weekends it's inundated with tourists, many brought by bus from cruise ships that anchor in the downtown harbor. San Francisco is also a popular Sunday destination for local citizens. Fresh fish and Mexican specialties are served to the accompaniment of loud, live music, romping kids, and chattering adults. The bay is usually filled with dive boats attracted to nearby San Francisco Reef (see p. 156). No one knows exactly how the new hotel construction will affect future Sunday-afternoon fun at San Francisco Beach.

Beach Clubs

On the main road from town going south toward San Francisco Beach, a small *balneario* called **Paloma Beach Club** is a pleasant place to spend an afternoon: good fresh fish and cold *cerveza* served at the outdoor cafe, white-sand beach, and good swimming and snorkeling. More and more of these little beach clubs are popping up along this area. Another one, **Playa Maya,** four km south of Chankanab, offers a small, calm swimming area on a narrow strip of sand. A snack stand is open daily, and you'll find beach facilities, dressing rooms, and a bar.

Isla De Passion

This tiny island in **Abrigo Bay** has secluded beaches and a rocky shoreline good for underwater exploring (no cafes, restrooms, or any other facilities). Often the destination of Robinson Crusoe picnic trips, it is now a state reserve.

WINDWARD BEACHES

South To North

From **San Francisco Beach** around the southern end of the island are many beaches. Some are good for swimming; some are dangerous for swimming but great for beachcombing. Add sunning, camping, and birdwatching to provide more than enough reason to visit this shoreline stretching from **Punta Molas** at the north tip to **Punta Sur** at the south. To visit beaches on the east shore north of the island-crossing highway, take either a motorcycle or 4WD for the unpaved sandy road. If you rent a jeep for this trip, make sure that the 4WD hasn't been disengaged by the rental agency. Because of its condition, the 24.5-km road is seldom used, and few people see these beautiful beaches. If you decide to hike along this coast, you'll make better time in many areas on the road than on the rocky portions in between sandy beaches.

The first two beaches, **Santa Cecilia** and **Playa Bonita,** are good beachcombing spots, and **Playa Bonita** is a good camping beach (no facilities). For the real adventurer, the "Brown Map of Cozumel" shows trails from this dirt road to various little-known Maya ruins, abandoned *cenotes,* and caves. This kind of jungle trek requires carrying all essentials. From the Maya site at **Castillo Real** to the north, no more sandy beaches come before the lighthouse on Punta Molas. Many ships have sunk along this violent shore: cannons and anchors are occasionally found to prove the legends.

Chen Rio
At the end of the cross-island highway is tiny **Mescalitos Cafe.** Turn right (south) and the first beach is Chen Rio (km marker 42). Space for tent campers and a few camping vehicles is on a broad flat area next to the beach. Chen Rio is also the site of the only motel on the east side of Cozumel, **Punta Morena.** From here the beach becomes **Playa de San Martin** and after that, **Punta Chiquiero,** with a protected cove for swimming in crystalline water. A small restaurant, the **Naked Turtle,** sits on the edge of a lovely crescent bay with white sand. A bar serves *ceviche,* snacks, hard and soft drinks; next door is the dining room. You can camp on the beach—with a tent or a vehicle—but there are no facilities. If driving an RV, check with the restaurant owners before you park.

Isolated Beaches
Along the highway from here to Punta Celerain is access to many beaches and the remains of a few small ruins. A dirt road meandering parallel to the coast behind sand dunes leads to **Punta Celerain Lighthouse.** All along this road you'll find paths turning out to the left, all leading to beautiful isolated beaches. A small conch-shaped Maya structure is seen here. It was badly damaged during Hurricane Gilbert. One of the docents at the museum in town explains how the small openings at the top were used as a warning—the wind blowing through creates a foghorn effect. According to archaeologists it was built between A.D. 1200-1400 as a ceremonial center and navigational guide using smoke and flames tended by the Maya keeper. Behind this small building, a dirt path over a sand dune goes to another great beach for swimming, sunbathing, and beachcombing.

Punta Celerain Lighthouse

Punta Celerain

This lighthouse is four km from the main road. From a distance it appears white, tall, and regal; up close it needs a paint job. Next to the lighthouse is a small army base with soldiers on guard. An exciting spot, it's well worth the detour to wander around the point where a strong surf crashes over the irregular black limestone shore in great clouds of misty surf, spraying tall geysers through jagged blowholes. The family at the lighthouse is friendly, and usually you'll run into them on the grounds either doing their laundry or cooking. Ask to climb to the top for a spectacular 360-degree view of the island (a tip wouldn't hurt); don't forget your camera and wear comfortable walking shoes. The view one way is a long strip of white sand with a lacy scalloped edge of turquoise waves; in the opposite direction you'll see red marshy swamps in the middle of green scrub jungle; beyond it all—unending sea. On Sunday the lighthouse keeper sells cold drinks and fried fish. The soldiers nearby often hike back to the barracks carrying several iguana ready to be prepared for lunch, much like their ancient ancestors.

Back on the paved road just as it rounds the curve and turns north, a large sign warns of the consequences of taking turtle eggs. There's a stiff fine for this since the turtle is a protected species; they come to shore here in large numbers during the summer to lay their eggs. You'll often find a soldier (with tent) standing guard over the sign. This coastal watch keeps tabs on the boating activity between Cozumel and the Yucatan coast; boatloads of illegal drugs are frequently picked up along here. A return to the paved highway takes you through the hotel zone and on into downtown San Miguel.

WATER SPORTS

Cozumel is probably best known for its plethora of rich dive spots and reefs. The island and its resident divers are proud of its marinelife and welcome all who wish to share the diving experience. They also are dedicated to protecting the reef and reef dwellers. As guests, everyone is asked to consider this as they drift in this wonderful fragile underwater world.

Snorkeling

Snorkeling and diving are the most popular outdoor activities on Cozumel. If you can swim but haven't tried snorkeling, Cozumel is the finest place to begin. For those who don't know, snorkeling is floating along the surface of the water with your face (in a mask) underwater while you breath through a plastic tube called a snorkel. The little glass window on your mask gives you heady visions of the colorful underwater world found nowhere else. For beginners it's easy to find a fascinating marine environment close to shore without swimming or boating; in many cases you need only step from your hotel. Along the lee side of the island almost all beaches are ideal sites. If it's your first time, practice with a snorkel and mask while sitting in shallow, calm surf with your face under water and breath through the snorkel that protrudes above the surface. (Or use your bathtub to learn before leaving home.) Once accustomed to breathing with the tube, the rest is simple. Wear fins which make it easier to maneuver in the water. A few easy-to-reach snorkeling sites include: Chankanab Bay and San Francisco Beach, Presidente Hotel beach, Hotel Cozumel Caribe beach, and La Ceiba Beach (where there's an underwater plane wreck). Rental equipment is available at hotels and dive shops. For the pros, check with a dive shop and you'll find many trips that motor groups to a suitable reef daily.

Scuba Diving

If you've always wanted to learn to scuba dive, here's the place to do it. A multitude of dive shops and instructors offer certification, or instruction sufficient for one dive, but use a lot of common sense finding a *qualified* instructor. Look at his qualifications, ask if he's ever had an accident while in charge, ask about him around town (try the harbor master). It's your life you're placing in his hands. Thousands of people come to Cozumel because of the surrounding reefs, and there are occasional accidents! Fairly simple dives for the neophyte are on offshore fringing reefs. Caves and crevices line the shore, and coral heads rise to within three meters of the surface.

Cozumel Divers Community

Cozumel's diving community has created a new organization called **The Cozumel Association of Diving Operators** referred to as CADO. In their ongoing efforts to promote safe diving, CADO has initiated some new guidelines for divers who come to Cozumel. Neophytes as well as experienced divers must know the guidelines. Everyone should be aware that drinking alcoholic beverages within several hours of a dive or between dives is a risky practice. Alcohol may actually increase your susceptibility to such problems as nitrogen narcosis and decompression sickness. The same goes for ingesting certain prescription and non-prescription drugs; check with your doctor.

CADO encourages safe-diving practices for its members (which include most of the dive shops on the island) and an awareness of the physical condition of its divers. Listed below are a few of the guidelines you will encounter: 1. If a divemaster even thinks he smells alcohol on a would-be diver, he will not allow him/her on the dive; even if this means losing a reserved boatload of customers. 2. Experienced divers will be asked to prove their abilities if they haven't been diving for some time. A diary of dives should be kept and shown to the divemaster along with the diver's certification card. If no diary is available, do not be surprised if the divemaster insists on a trial dive of under 30 feet to check out the diver's capabilities. 3. With a resort course certification, dives will be no deeper than 30 feet. 4. Those who suffer from asthma or other breathing problems should not consider scuba diving. 5. Would-be divers who have had open-heart surgery should stick to snorkeling. All of these precautions are taken to protect the diver. For more information on alcohol consumption and diving ask for the PADI pamphlet titled *Deep Thoughts* provided by PADI and Anheuser-Busch at dive shops.

Some experienced divers prefer wall diving, while others find night diving more exciting. Certain reefs are for only the most expert diver. Boat reservations must be made in advance. Diving is an exciting sport, and the clear waters around Cozumel allow outstanding photographs; underwater camera rentals are available at some dive shops. **Note:** All divers should be aware that even touching the delicate coral reef kills it. Take care not to scrape your equipment or push off from the coral with your feet. These delicate creations of nature take millions of years to build.

Reefs are often close offshore giving easy access to snorkelers.

DIVE SPOTS

Plane Wreck

The average non-diver wouldn't think of a wrecked plane as a reef. However, if it sits on the bottom of the sea it serves as a reef by affording schools of fish shady hiding places on the white sandy bottom. A 40-passenger Convair airliner (engines removed) reposes upside down after being purposely sunk in 1977 for the Mexican movie production of *Survive II*. The water's clarity allows a clear view of the submerged wreck, located 100 meters off the La Ceiba Hotel pier. Beyond the wreck are huge coral heads in 14 meters of water. At the plane wreck, a 120-meter trail has been marked with underwater signs which point out the various types of marine-life on La Ceiba reef. The visibility is up to 30 meters, and the average depth is nine to 17 meters. A pillar of coral is an impressive sight and multicolored sponges are outstanding here.

Paraiso Reef

About 200 meters off the beach just south of the International Dock (between the Presidente and the dock), **North Paraiso Reef** can be reached either by boat or from the beach. It averages nine to 17 meters deep and is a site of impressive star and brain coral, and sea fans. The south end of the reef, farther offshore and located south of the International Dock, is alive with churning reef life. This is a good spot for night diving.

Chankanab Caves And Reef

For easy-access diving, go to **Chankanab Beach.** A series of three caves on the shoreline provides a unique experience. Along the shore, steps are carved from coral for easy entry into water that surges into large underground caverns. Within seconds, you're in the first cave filled with hundreds of fish of all varieties. Striped grunt, snapper, sergeant majors, and butterfly fish are found in all three caves. Dives average five to 12 meters.

A boat is needed to dive Chankanab Reef, several hundred meters offshore south of Chankanab Beach (sometimes referred to as Outer Chankanab Reef). There's good night diving here in depths of eight to 15 meters where basket starfish hang out with octopus and jail-striped morays. At the drop-off, stunning coral heads are at a maximum depth of 10 meters; in some spots coral is within three meters of the surface. Coral heads are covered with gorgonians and sea fans; striped grunt and mahogany snapper slowly cruise around the base. This is a good location for snorkelers and beginning divers.

Tormentos Reef

This is a medium-depth reef with innumerable coral heads in eight to 12 meters of water above a sandy bottom. The heads are decorated with fans, gorgonians, and sponges. With little current, you can get excellent photos. Along the sandy bottom are great numbers of invertebrates: flamingo tongue shell, arrow crab, black crinoid, coral shrimp, and sea cucumber. When the current is going north, the farthest section of the reef drops to 21.5 meters, where you'll see deep-sea fans, lobsters, and immense groupers.

Yocab Reef

One km south of Punta Tormentos, Yocab Reef is fairly close to shore, shallow (good for beginners), and alive with such beauties as queen angelfish, star and brain coral, sponge, and sea whip. The coral reef is about 120 meters long, with an average depth of nine meters, and coral heads from the floor about three meters. When there's current it can be two or three knots. (The local bus makes daily runs to this beach for about US$.25.)

Tunich Reef

A half-km south of Yocab—directly out from Punta Tunich—this deeper reef (15-24 meters) has about a 1½-knot current or more, and when it's stronger you could be swept right along to Cuba! It's loaded with intricately textured corals, and the water activity attracts manta rays, jewfish, and barracuda; a good reef to spot shy moray eels.

San Francisco Reef

Another popular reef is located one km off San Francisco Beach. The abbreviated (one-

Isolated pockets of Maya often live much like their ancient ancestors.

half km) coral runs parallel to shore; this is a boat dive into a site teeming with reef fish of many varieties and brilliant colors. Depths average 17-19 meters.

Santa Rosa Wall

This sensational drop-off, which begins at 22 meters and just keeps going to the black bottom of the Caribbean, really gives you a feeling for the ocean's depth. Strong currents make this a drift-dive, a site for experienced divers only (watch your depth gauge). You'll discover tunnels and caves, translucent sponge, stony overhangs, queen, French, and gray angelfish, white trigger fish, and many big groupers.

Paso Del Cedral

This flat reef with 22-meter garden-like valleys is a good wall dive. In some places the top of the reef begins 15.5 meters from the surface. Sealife includes angelfish, lobster, and the thick-lipped grouper.

Palancar Reef

The reef most associated with Cozumel Island is actually a five-km series of varying coral formations about 1.5 km offshore. Each of these formations offers a different thrill. Some slope, and some drop off dramatically into winding ravines, deep canyons, passageways, or archways and tunnels with for-mations 15 meters tall—all teeming with reef life. Startling coral pinnacles rise to 25 meters from the sloping wall. Much deeper at the south end, the top of the reef begins at 27 meters. **Horseshoe,** considered by some to be the best diving in the Caribbean, is a series of coral heads which form a horseshoe curve at the top of the drop-off. The visibility of 66-86 meters plus a solid bronze, four-meter-tall, submerged modernistic sculpture of Christ, make this a dramatic photo area. The statue, created especially for the sea, was sunk on May 3, 1985, with great pomp and ceremony and the presence of Ramon Bravo, well-known TV reporter and Mexican diver. The much-discussed reef lives up to its good press.

Colombia Reef

Several kilometers south of Palancar, Colombia Reef is a deep-dive area, with the top of the reef climbing from 25-30 meters. This is the same environment as Palancar, with canyons and ravines; here the diver may encounter giant turtles and huge groupers hiding beneath deep overhangs of coral. Seasonally, when the water cools down, you'll see spotted eagle rays (water temperature averages 74 degrees in winter and 82 degrees in summer). This reef is best for experienced divers, as there's usually a current; visibility 50-66 meters.

Maracaibo Reef

At the southern tip of the island, this reef is an exhilarating experience. For the experienced only, Maracaibo is considered by most to be the ultimate challenge of all the reefs mentioned. At the deepest section, the top of the wall begins at 37 meters; the shallow area, 23 meters. Unlike many other reefs, coral formations here are immense. Be prepared for strong currents and for who-knows-what pelagic species of marinelife, including shark. Dive boats do not stop here on their regular trips and advance reservations are required for this dive.

Other Good Diving Areas

Not shown on most maps are **Cardona Reef, La Francesa Reef, Barracuda Reef,** and parallel to Barracuda, **San Juan,** for *experienced divers only*—currents can be as much as six knots. In that kind of current a face mask could be ripped off with the wrong move. The faster the current, the clearer the water and the more oxygen, definitely a specialty dive (somewhat like a roller-coaster!). Check with Aqua Safari for more information, including length of time to reach these reefs; three hours in a slow boat, an hour in Aqua Safari's fast boats. Reservations necessary. A handy scaled map-guide with water depths around the island (and other reef information), "Chart of the Reefs of Cozumel Mexi-

co," is put out by Ric Hajovsky; it's available at most dive shops.

DIVE TRIPS

Note: Many package dive trips originate in the U.S., with airfare, hotel, and diving included. Unless you have your own boat, many of the reef dives mentioned may be arranged through one of the many dive shops in town, or by some of the hotels that have their own equipment and divemaster. All equipment is provided and sometimes lunch and drinks. Prices vary, so shop around. For beginners, scuba lessons for certification or a resort course for one-day dives are available at most of the same shops. Be sure to check the qualifications and track record of the dive shop and divemaster you choose. A few are outstanding, most are good.

Also, shop around for your needs and level of diving. **Aqua Safari** has an excellent reputation for safety, experience, good equipment, and happy divers who return year after year. Aqua owns two large fiberglass boats geared for 16-18 divers each, with platforms for easy entry and exit. A typical dive day consists of two dives on different reefs with a stop at the beach for a seafood lunch. The exact location is determined by the divemaster on each boat according to the weather conditions,

Cozumel dive boats

urrents, and divers' requests and experience. The fee is about US$40 plus 20% tax check; these prices change often). This ncludes two tanks, weights and belt, backpack, dive guide, lunch, and refreshments. Additional gear may be rented. They have a ew lights available for night diving but suggest that you bring your own.

Another dive shop that is highly recommended is **Caribbean Argonauts**, with divemaster German Mendez. German is knowledgeable and safety conscious. In the U.S. call (817) 261-8677, in Cozumel tel 2-12-32, or fax (987) 2-25-64. German, like so many local divers, is dedicated to preserving the reefs that surround Cozumel.

For a quickie morning dive **Blue Angel Divers**, with a six-diver capacity, is back by 1:30 p.m. The boat is fast and comfortable, with easy entrance and exit. Ricardo Madrigal, a divemaster who caters only to advanced divers, can be reached by phone, tel. 2-16-31; he supplies tanks, weights, and belts—*only*. All other scuba equipment must be supplied by the diver. Ricardo first checks your ability, and when satisfied you're in the expert class makes specialty trips to the mainland for diving and camping or trips to the Barracuda and San Juan reefs in his Bertrim twin-engine boat. All scuba divers must show a certification card before going on boats or renting tanks.

Notice To Divers

Since 1980, a refuge has protected marine flora and fauna on the west coast of Cozumel from the shore up to and including the Drop-

COZUMEL DIVE SHOPS

For information about the following dive shops write to Cozumel Association of Dive Operators CADO/Cozumel Hotel Association, Box 414236, Miami Beach, FL 33141-0236.

Aqua Safari	tel. 2-01-01
Caribbean Argonauts	tel. 2-12-32
Aqua Sports Maya	tel. 2-25-59
Blue Angel	tel. 2-16-31
Blue Bubble	tel. 2-18-65
Caribbean Divers	tel. 2-11-45
Cha Cha Cha	tel. 2-23-31
Cruiser's Divers	tel. 2-11-24
Del Mar Acuaticos	tel. 2-06-40
Dive House	tel. 2-19-53
Dive Paradise	tel. 2-10-07
Dzul Ha	tel. 2-11-49
El Clavado	tel. 2-04-82
Fantasia Divers	tel. 2-12-10
Fiesta Cozumel	tel. 2-09-74
Marine Sports	tel. 2-29-00
Nautilus Dive Center	tel. 2-00-02
Neptuno Divers	tel. 2-09-99
Paul Padilla Perez	tel. 2-02-21
Ramon Zapata Divers	tel. 2-05-02
Scuba Scuba	tel. 2-13-79
Snorkocozumel	tel. 2-06-51
Turismo Aviomar	tel. 2-04-77
Victor Brito	tel. 2-18-42
Victor Casanova	tel. 2-15-36
Yucab Reef	tel. 2-18-42

Off (El Cantil). It is illegal to fish or to remove any marine artifacts, including coral, from the area. So, scuba divers and snorkelers, take only pictures. No one wants this product of millions of years to be damaged; on the contrary it must be protected and saved for future generations of divers to enjoy.

DIVE SAFETY

Because of the growing influx of divers to Cozumel from all over the world, the small island continues to increase safety services. The newest is the **SSS** (Servicios de Seguridad Sub-Acuatica) available for US$1 per

AFFILIATED DIVE SHOPS

Adriana Boat	Dive Cozumel
Aqua Safari	Dive Paradise
Anita Boat	Dives Unlimited
Blue Angel	Diving World
Careyitos	Fantasia Divers
Clear Water Divers	Kaapalua
Cruisers Divers	Neptuno Divers
Del Mar Acuaticos	Palancar Divers
Deportes Acuaticos	Pro Dive
Discover Cozumel	Yucab Reef

dive day (at participating dive shops). This entitles the distressed diver to the use of Cozumel's hyperbaric chamber, marine ambulance, and fully trained round-the-clock personnel (each facility offers 24-hour service). All divers are welcome to use these services; however, non-participants pay regular commercial rates, so check with the dive shop before you choose.

OTHER WATER ACTIVITIES

Boat Tours

For the non-diver, glass-bottom boats provide a close-up view of Cozumel's flamboyant underwater society. Small boats cruise along the lee side of the coast, and bigger motorized launches travel farther out to the larger reefs. Prices vary accordingly. Ask at your hotel or one of the dive shops. From US$2-6 pp. Another popular cruise is the "Robinson Crusoe," which also varies in size and type. One boat is even designed to look like a pirate ship out of the 1600s. Destinations vary, though they're usually along the lee side, which guarantees a white beach for good swimming. The crew dives for and cooks lobster or fish over an open fire for your lunch. Depending on how extensive the lunch, prices start at about US$15.

Charter Boats

Customized boat trips can be arranged through Bill Horn at **Aqua Safari**, tel. 2-01-01, for crossing the channel to Tulum for a day of sightseeing at the Maya ruins; return trip at your leisure. Trips to Cancun and Isla Mujeres, or some other mainland destination can also be arranged.

Off-island Excursions

Trips to Cancun, Isla Mujeres, Playa del Carmen, or a number of other mainland destinations can be arranged. Boat/plane/bus excursions to the Maya ceremonial centers are offered through your hotel or travel agency. Tulum is close by boat or plane and too good to miss. Xelha, a natural aquarium harboring thousands of tropical fish is also a pleasant stopover when going to the ruins at Coba or Tulum.

Fishing

Cozumel boasts good deep-sea fishing year-round. Red snapper, tuna, barracuda, dolphin, wahoo, bonito, king mackerel, and tarpon are especially plentiful March through July, also the high season for marlin and sailfish. Hire a boat and guide for the day at the downtown dock or at **Club Nautico de Cozumel.** Small to large boats, including tackle, bait, and guide, cost from US$125 to US$825, half and full day, depending on size of boat, number of people, and season. Arrangements can be made at the boatmen's co-op, tel. 2-00-80, Pancho's, tel. 2-02-04, or call Club Nautico de Cozumel at Marina Puerto de Abrigo Banco Playa, mailing address Box 341, Cozumel, Quintana Roo, Mexico 77600; tel. 2-01-18. **Aquarius Travel** has 11 different boats for all types of fishing, including deep-sea fishing, on Calle 3 Sur No. 2, Box 105, Cozumel, Quintana Roo, Mexico. Sample of scheduled trip prices: Bonefishing, full day, US$180, two persons; deep-sea fishing, from US$200 and up. Bill Fish Release Tournament and Marlin Tournament take place in May each year.

Miscellaneous

Instruction and equipment for windsurfing and water-skiing can be rented at **Pancho's,** two blocks northeast of the plaza, corner of 2 Calle and 10 Av. Norte, tel. 2-02-04. At the Hotel Presidente south of town, **Viajes y Deportes del Caribe** offers boat rentals (small and large fishing boats, ski boats, sailboats, and motorboats). Windsurfing instruction and sail boards are also available. Hobie cats, jet skis, windsurfers, and sailboats can be rented at the Mayan Plaza Hotel beach.

Other Activities

Several hotels north and south of town have tennis courts and for a small fee non-guests can use them. **Sea Horse Ranch** offers horseback expeditions into the Cozumel bush, where you will see off-the-track Maya ruins and even the **Red Cenote.** English-speaking guides explain the flora and fauna of the island. Regular tours leave daily Mon. through Sat., reservations needed, tel. 2-19-58.

SS *Britanis;* **2.** Midnight buffet, SS *Britanis;* **3.** On the *Britanis* bridge with Captain Fokian Ardavanis and crew; **4.** Enjoying a breezy deck at sea; **5.** Showtime! SS *Britanis*

1. Cancun shoreline; **2.** Calinda Hotel, Cancun

1. Fiesta Americana Condessa, Cancun; **2.** Nichupte Lagoon, Cancun;
3. Cancun Palace Hotel, Cancun; **4.** Crowne Plaza Hotel, Cancun

1. Maya archaeological site, El Castillo, Tulum; **2.** Chichen Itza; **3.** Coba

1. Cancun parasailing; **2.** Snorkeling at Garrafon Beach, Isla Mujeres;
3. Pool games at the Hyatt Regency, Cancun; **4.** Enjoying the sun and the sea, Cancun

1. street snacks, Quintana Roo; **2.** Young Yucatecans vacationing at Don Armando's Bungalows close to Tulum; **3.** Fiesta dancers at the Hotel Sol Caribe, Isla Cozumel; **4.** German Mendez from Caribbean Argonauts Divers; **5.** Celebrating the first day of spring, Chetumal

ISLA MUJERES

Isla Mujeres is just eight miles across the bay from Cancun via several transportation options. Many visitors return year after year, hop the ferry, and spend a few hedonistic days relaxing or diving on the outlying reefs of Isla Mujeres. This finger-shaped island lying off the east coast of the Yucatan Peninsula is eight km long and 400 meters at its widest point. While exploring the small island, take a walk through Fortress Mundaca, snorkel along the coast, visit the lighthouse, and see the marine biology station—devoted to the study of the large turtle. Visitors are not encouraged, but if you're a science buff and can speak the language, give it a try.

Though the overflow of tourists from Cancun and Cozumel is very noticeable—the island is relatively quiet, especially if you choose to visit during the off season—June and Sept. are great! For some adventurers, Isla Mujeres is a favorite even though it's "growing up" with more visitors than ever. Everyone should snorkel at least once at teeming Garrafon Beach (it's teeming with fish *and* tourists!). The easygoing populace is getting used to all the people; the small town still smiles at backpackers. Travelers from budget to (almost) deluxe can easily find suitable lodgings though in the budget category it's getting harder.

Isla Mujeres has a large naval base, with many ships in its harbor. By the way—the Mexican Navy doesn't like people photographing the base, ships, or crewmen on duty. If you're struck with the urge to film *everything,* ask someone in charge first. Before tourism, fishing was the prime industry on the island, with turtle, lobster, and shark the local specialties. Today the turtle is protected; they may NOT be hunted during any time of the year. The eggs are *never* to be taken and stiff fines are given those who break this law.

History
One legend tells us that the name Isla Mujeres ("Island of Women") comes from the buccaneers who stowed their female captives

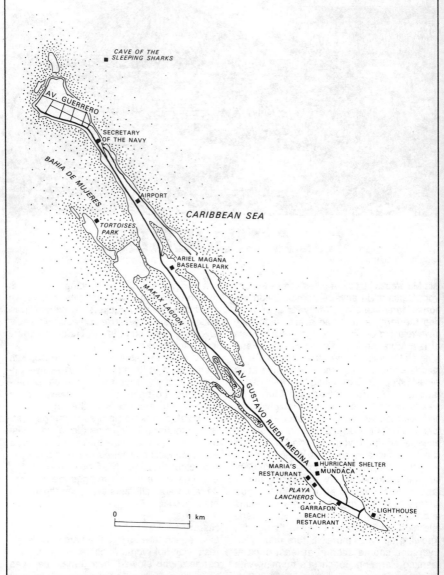

ISLA MUJERES

CAVE OF THE
SLEEPING SHARKS

AV. GUERRERO

SECRETARY
OF THE NAVY

BAHIA DE MUJERES

AIRPORT

CARIBBEAN SEA

TORTOISES
PARK

Ariel Magaña
BASEBALL PARK

MAKAX LAGOON

AV. GUSTAVO RUEDA MEDINA

HURRICANE SHELTER
MARIA'S
RESTAURANT   MUNDACA
PLAYA
LANCHEROS
GARRAFON
BEACH   LIGHTHOUSE
RESTAURANT

0   1 km

here while conducting their nefarious business on the high seas. Another more prosaic (and probably correct) version refers to the large number of female-shaped clay idols found on the island when the Spaniards arrived. Archaeologists presume the island was a stopover for the Maya Indians on their pilgrimages to Cozumel to worship Ixchel, female goddess of fertility and an important deity to Maya women.

SIGHTS

The city is 10 blocks long and five blocks wide. Avenuda Hidalgo, the main street, is where the central plaza, city hall, police station, cinema, *farmacia,* and large supermarket are located. Most streets are really only walkways, with no vehicles allowed (although they frequently squeeze by anyway). The ferry terminal is three blocks from the plaza; if you're traveling light, you can walk to most of the hotels when you get off the ferry. Otherwise, taxis queue up along Av. Hidalgo close to the ferry dock.

GARRAFON NATIONAL PARK

Snorkeling at Garrafon Beach has been heralded for years. However, so many day trippers come each day from Cancun that the beach is not only terribly crowded from 10 a.m.-2 p.m., but many of the fish seem to be hanging out someplace else. Get there early in the morning for the best snorkeling! Garrafon Beach is five km out of town with a close-in coral reef that's a great spot for beginners.

It has little swell and is only a meter deep for about five meters offshore, after which the bottom drops off abruptly to six meters. This is a good place to introduce children to the beauties of the ocean through a glass. The brazen fish—which aptly describes Bermuda grubs—gaze at you eye to eye through your mask; if you have food they'll follow you almost onto shore. Feeding the fish stale bread or tortillas makes for good pictures —the fish literally jump out of the water to grab the treat, so watch your fingers!

Swim past the reef and you'll see beautiful angelfish that seem to enjoy hanging around a coral-encrusted anchor and a couple of antiquated ship's cannons. For the non-snorkeler, there are *palapa* sun shelters and beach chairs on the sand—that is until the tourist boats from Cancun arrive. After that the beach gets crowded and loses its tranquility. Garrafon is a national park, open from 8 a.m.-5 p.m.; about US$1 pp admission. The ticket taker doesn't arrive until 8 a.m., but even earlier someone will usually let you in.

Garrafon Beach is popular with tourists and residents.

Amenities

Built into the steep cliff which backs the beach are a dive shop (snorkel, mask, and fins for about US$6 a day), a seafood cafe, lockers, showers, and changing rooms. Taxi fare (up to four passengers) from town to Garrafon is about US$2, from Hotel Del Prado at the northern tip of the island, US $2.50. Coral outcroppings along this beach add much to the beauty of Garrafon, but can be razor sharp and dangerous. Even the coral that isn't dangerous should be avoided —don't walk on it or scratch your initials into it. It took millions of years to establish and it's ridiculous to kill it in one thoughtless moment.

MAYA RUINS

A short distance past Garrafon, at the south tip of the island on a cliff overlooking the sea, is what's left of an ancient Maya temple used as a coastal observation post. It's little more than a pile of stones now after Hurricane Gilbert's devastation. To get there, continue on the main road from Garrafon until you can see the lighthouse road going off to the right, then take a well-traveled dirt path to your left. These ruins were first seen and described by Francisco Hernandez de Cordoba in 1517. In addition to being a temple of worship to Ixchel, goddess of fertility, the slits in the walls of the temple facing the four cardinal points were used for sophisticated astronomical observations—part of Maya daily life. Two of the walls of the Maya structure have slid into the sea along with the corroding cliff, and in September of 1988 Gilbert all but destroyed it. Today, the lighthouse keeper looks after what's left of the small temple, sells fresh fish *ceviche*, and makes colorful hammocks and black coral jewelry. A friendly guy, he's more than happy to let you try out the hammocks, will answer all questions (if asked in Spanish), and loves to pose for the camera (especially for a tip). This is a magnificent spot to see both the open sea on the windward side of the island and peaceful Mujeres Bay on the protected side. If traveling by taxi, ask the driver to wait while you look around. Or let him go—you can walk back to Garra-

lighthouse keeper preparing ceviche

fon Beach and catch a taxi to town (till 5 p.m.). The walk all the way to town is long and sweaty—figure about two hours.

FORT MUNDACA

To make a visit to Fort Mundaca meaningful, dwell on a touching local legend from the mid-1800s. It tells of a swashbuckling slave-trading pirate, Fermin Mundaca de Marehaja, who fell in love with a young woman on Isla Mujeres, Prisca Gomez, also called *Triguena* ("The Brunette"). In some versions she was a visitor from Spain, in others she was from the island. After 10 years of plying the seas and buying and selling slaves, he retired to the land to court her, unsuccessfully. Coincidentally, pirates were slowly being put out of business by the British Navy right about then. Mundaca built a lavish estate to woo her further, but to no avail. She married another

Mujeres man and ultimately moved to Merida and the high life, leaving the heartsick slave-trader behind to live alone in the big house with only his memories of the past. If you're a romantic, you'll feel a haunting melancholy while strolling in the once-gracious gardens of this deserted, almost destroyed estate. Mundaca lived the remainder of his lonely life on the island and left behind this inscription on his tombstone—*"como ere yo fui; como soy tu seras"* ("like you are I was; like I am you will be"). Fate can be fickle—and perhaps just.

Rumor has it that the government is going to restore Mundaca and make it into a park, which would be nice since it is literally rotting away now. To get to Fort Mundaca from downtown, follow the signs that say Hurricane Shelter, then take the dirt path going to the left 4.5 km from town.

Just before the Mundaca turnoff, there's a dirt road to the right (at four km) that takes you to the small center for marine biology studies. Again, this is not officially open to the public; however, visitors have been known to gain entrance simply by knocking on the door and asking.

BEACHES

The closest beach to downtown is **Playa Norte,** also called Coco Beach and Nauti-beach (perhaps because of the topless girls?), on the north edge of town, the lee side of the island. Here you can relax in the sun and swim in a blue sea as calm as a lake. In this shallow water you can wade for 35 meters and still be only waist deep. At the west end of the beach are *palapa* cafes, with both soft and hard beverages.

Four km south toward Garrafon on the main road out of town is **Playa Lancheros.** Several giant turtles swim around a large sea pen and submit to being ridden by small children—as long as they can stay seated on the slippery-backed animal. Clean white beaches attract sun-worshipers, and a large *palapa* cafe sells fried fish, snacks, drinks, and fresh fruit. Live music begins in the afternoon. Fishermen still bring in a good catch to this shore, and it's not unusual to see them cleaning nurse and tiger sharks caught close by. A bus from town travels as far as Playa Lancheros about every half hour; fare is about US$.30.

WATER SPORTS

Snorkeling And Scuba Diving

The snorkeler has many choice locations to choose from, and the common-sense approach is to snorkel with a companion. **Garrafon** is good, and the east end of **Playa Norte** has visibility up to 33 meters near the wooden pier, though on occasion the sea gets choppy here, clouding the water. The windward side of the island is good for snorkeling if the sea is calm; don't snorkel or even swim on the windward side on a rough day and risk being hurled against the sharp rocks. Besides cutting you up, an open wound caused by coral laceration often becomes infected in this humid tropical climate.

The dive shops on the island sponsor trips to nearby reefs for snorkeling and scuba diving. A lot of press has been devoted to Isla

Mujeres' **Sleeping Shark Caves.** Ask at the dive shop for detailed information. Although some divemasters will take you in among the sluggish though dangerous fish, others feel that it isn't a smart dive. Bill Horn, experienced diver/owner of Aqua Safari dive shop on Isla Cozumel, warns there's always danger when you put yourself into a small area with a wild creature. In a cave, even if a large fish isn't trying to attack, the swish of a powerful tail could easily send you crashing against a wall. Reasons given for the shark's somnambulant state vary with the teller: salinity content of the water, or low carbon dioxide. Between Cancun and Isla Mujeres, experienced divers will find excitement diving **Chital, Cuevones, La Bandera,** and **Manchones** reefs. Diving equipment can be rented at **Mexico Divers** at two locations—Av.

Rueda Medina and Garrafon Park, or at **El Canon,** Av. Rueda Medina, tel. 2-00-60.

Fishing

Deep-sea fishing trips can be arranged through any of the marinas. Spring is the best time to catch the big ones: marlin and sailfish. The rest of the year you can bring in good strings of grouper, barracuda, tuna, and red snapper. **Mexico Divers** (Av. Rueda Medina) just left of the boat dock offers a day-long deep-sea fishing trip which includes bait, tackle, and lunch. The **Boatmen's Cooperative** is helpful with questions about destinations, fishing trips, and boat rentals, tel. 2-00-86.

Robinson Crusoe Trip

If you enjoy group trips, the Robinson Crusoe boat trip includes snorkeling for a few hours at Garrafon Beach, a visit to the turtle pens, a cruise to Manchones Reef, and a *tikin chik* feed of fresh fish, caught by the crew and cooked over an open fire on a hidden beach somewhere along Isla Mujeres' coast. For more information ask at the Boatmen's Cooperative or your hotel.

Boat Regattas

Sailors from the southern U.S. have the opportunity to take part in sailing regattas each year. Organized by the Club de Yates of Isla Mujeres and started in 1968 from St. Petersburg, many participants come for this event scheduled for either the last week in April or the first week in May. Every two years in the spring groups sail to the island from Galveston, Texas, and from New Orleans. This is a challenging trip for the adventurous navigator.

This is also a great time for a party. The town opens its homes and hearts to people that have in many cases been returning for years and have become friends. The boaters reciprocate and open their vessels to the islanders. The kids of Isla Mujeres work all year long learning dances, and the women make the costumes for cultural entertainment. An annual basketball game takes place between the "Bad Boys" of the island and the boaters that visit, and no matter how they try, the boaters always lose. The name "Bad Boys" indicates these are the worst players on Isla Mujeres!

During Regatta Amigos, all the people take part, with boats head to head throwing— water balloons. Last year 182 children were on board one boat, attacking the adults. The town provides food, tequila, and bands; with music everywhere, there's dancing in the streets and a queen is chosen by the Commodore of the Regatta. This is good fun and it happens several times a year. During religious holidays visitors will find the same kind of good times. For more info and dates contact Club de Yates de Isla Mujeres, Av. Rueda Medina, tel. 2-02-11 or 2-00-86.

Dock Facilities

The marinas in Isla Mujeres are getting more sophisticated with many services available. **Pemex Marina** in the bay offers electricity, water, diesel, and gasoline, tel. 2-00-86. At the navy base dock you'll find a mechanic, tel. 2-01-96. **Laguna Makax** offers only docking facilities. For boating emergencies call either by radio, using the word *Neptuno* for the Coast Guard, or on VHF channel 16 or band 2182. Use channel 88 to get clearance to enter the country. Gasoline for cars and boats is at Av. Rueda Medina, tel. 2-02-11.

PRACTICALITIES

ACCOMMODATIONS

You'll find a surprising number of hotels on this miniscule island. Most of them are small, simple, family-run inns downtown near the oceanfront. None can really be considered luxury class, but some offer more services than others. Since most are clustered downtown, it's simple to shop (on foot) until you find the one that suits you.

First-class

Posada del Mar is an older multi-storied a/c hotel. Rooms overlook the waterfront with swimming either in the sea or the hotel's own lovely pool. A *palapa* dining room, bar, and snack pavilion adjoin the pool. From the boat dock turn left and walk four blocks. Rates about US$40 d; Av. Rueda Medina, #15-A, tel. 2-02-12.

Facing the windward side of the island, a fairly new hostelry called **Hotel Perla del Caribe** offers pleasant rooms with private bathrooms, a/c or fan (ask for your choice), snack bar, and pool; rooms have terraces and balconies—be sure to *ask* for one facing the sea (great view of the coast). The hotel's (rough-water) beach is good for sunbathing and walking; swimming only when the sea is calm. The staff is very friendly; we looked at four rooms before we found the one we wanted, and they were still smiling in the end when they brought our luggage. Credit cards okay, rates are about US$56 d during high season, but prices dropped to US$28 per night during the summer of 1989; three suites with kitchens are available. For reservations write to Av. Madero and Guerrero, North Point, Isla Mujeres, Quintana Roo, Mexico, tel. 2-04-44.

Another delightful small hotel is the **Na Balam** on Los Cocos beach just a short walk to the sea. All junior suites with cooking facilities, also patios and balconies; a *palapa* is open all day for drinks and food. Rates are about US$54 d. Located on Calle Zazil-Ha (the road to Hotel Del Prado), tel. 2-02-79. For something small and intimate and away from town, check out **Maria's Kan Kin Restaurant Francaise** near Garafon Beach. Just a few rooms available. For the visitor who plans on a longer stay, two-bedroom apartments are available on the beach at Chez Megaly, located at Av. Rueda Medina Playa Norte, tel. 2-02-59.

A Little Better Than Moderate

These hotels are clean, with pleasant staffs and charming surroundings that make them stand out from the others in this category. From the boat dock turn left for two blocks, then right for a half block to **Hotel Berney.** This three-story hotel is built around a patio and small pool, with restaurant and bar. The rooms are simple (though colorful), clean, and have purified tap water. About US$30 d, a/c rooms slightly higher, located on Av. Abasolo #3, tel. 2-00-26.

Close to the central plaza on the windward shore is **Hotel Rocamar,** a three-story hotel with balconies overlooking the often wild sea. From the boat dock it's one block to the right and two blocks inland. The hotel provides lounge chairs for sunning on the beach; remember swimming can be treacherous here. Clean rooms, hot and cold water, ceiling fans, bar, restaurant serving good food, and a friendly staff. Rates about US$26 d; Av. Nicolas Bravo, tel. 2-01-01.

Cabanas Maria del Mar blends the old and the new. Located on Nautibeach, one of the nicest on the island, the newer rooms offer a/c in a two-story building, about US$45 d. The old cabanas are thatched, comfortable in a laid-back tropical way, about US$35.

ISLA MUJERES ACCOMMODATIONS

NAME	ADDRESS	TELEPHONE
Belmar	Av. Hidalgo	2-04-30
Caribe Maya	Av. Madero	2-01-90
Carmelina	Av. Guerrero #9	2-00-66
Cielito Lindo	Av. Ruedo Medina #78	—
El Caracol	Av. Matamoras #5	2-01-50
El Marcianito	Av. Abasolo #10	2-01-11
El Zorro	Av. Guerrero #7	2-01-49
Hotel Berney	Calle Abasolo	2-00-25
Hotel Cabanas	Av. Carlas Lazo #1	2-01-79/2-02-13
Isla Mujeres	Av. Miguel Hidalgo #3	2-02-67
Isleno	Av. Guerrero & Madero	2-03-02
Las Palmas	Av. Guerrero #20	—
Margarita	Av. Rueda & Medina N. #9	2-01-46
Maria Jose	Av. Madero #27	2-01-30
Marie de los Angeles	Juarez #35	—
Na Balam Jr. Suites	Calle Zazil Ha #18	2-04-46
Osorio	Av. Madero & Juarez	2-00-18
Perla Del Caribe	Av. Madero & Guerrero	2-04-44/2-02-36
Poc-Na Youth Hostel	Matamaras #15	2-00-90/2-00-53
Posada Del Mar	Av. Rueda Medina #15	2-00-44/2-03-00
Posada San Jorge	Juarez #29–AN	2-01-54
Roca Mar	Av. Guerrero & Bravo	2-01-01
Rocas del Caribe	Av. Madero #2	2-00-11
Su Casa Sur	Ocean Front Houses	2-02-65
Vistalmar	Av. Rueda Medina	2-00-96

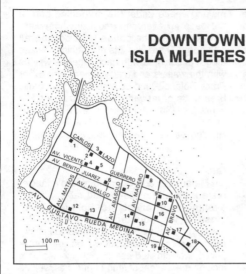

DOWNTOWN ISLA MUJERES

1. El Cabanas Hotel
2. Poc Na Hostel
3. Social Security Clinic (I.M.S.S.)
4. post and telegraph office
5. Javier Rojo Gomez Market
6. Ciro's Restaurant
7. Office of Tourism
8. Hotel Rocas del Caribe and Restaurant
9. Magana Movie
10. city hall, police, and traffic office
11. Immaculada Concepcion Church
12. Posada del Mar restaurant and bar
13. lighthouse
14. Osorio Hotel
15. Martinez Hotel
16. public library
17. telephone office
18. port captain
19. ferry terminal

Bucanero is a new hotel located above the Bucanero restaurant. Just a few rooms on the second and third floor, ask in the restaurant for prices of hotel rooms. Right across the street at **Pizza Rolandi,** ask to see their rooms over the restaurant.

Moderate

Osorio used to be considered a budget hotel, but price-wise it no longer fits the description. However, **Osorio** is a spotlessly clean hotel with large rooms, hot and cold water, twin or double beds, private bath, fans, and window screens. Right over the street, the rooms can be noisy. From the boat dock turn left and walk 1½ blocks, then turn right on to Madero; Osorio is across from **Hotel Martinez.** About US$30 d; Av. Madero #15, tel. 2-00-18.

Run by a long-time Isla Mujeres family, **Hotel Martinez** offers clean, quiet double rooms with good cross ventilation. **Note:** house rules require you to be in by 10 p.m. and no one can leave before 6:30 a.m. Follow directions to Osorio, then cross the street; Av. Madero #14, tel. 2-01-54.

Budget

As you will soon discover, budget-priced hotels are no longer as easy to find as they once were. Please look at budget hotel rooms carefully before paying your money; they change from day to day. What can be clean and friendly one day, can be dirty the next. Hot water can be an elusive, unreliable item. If these things are more important than your pocketbook, don't look at budget hotels.

The youth hostel **Poc Na** has reopened for business. For the backpacker this is really a terrific bargain. The hostel offers clean, dormitory-style rooms, communal baths and toilets, and rates less than US$5 per day (including a locker) plus a few returnable deposits, and extra charges if you choose to use the hostel's linens. The cafeteria is simple and though it was closed last June, it should be open now. Poc Na is located at 15 Matamoros Ave., tel. 2-00-90.

For another wallet-saver, take a look at the **Caribe Maya;** it's old but clean and has 20 rooms which rent for about US$13 d. Both the **Hotel Lopez** or the **Posada San Jorge** offer pleasant, *usually* clean, spartan rooms for about US$15 d, located on Av. Juarez #29-A North (We recently received a note describing Posada Jorge as "very dirty.") The rooms tend to be warm, with only a tired ceiling fan to circulate the air. Some very simple *palapa* bungalows across from Garrafon

Beach were under construction, and the owner promised they would be *muy barato* (very cheap); ask at Mexico Divers (also called Buzos de Mexico). As you get off the dock make a left-hand turn and you'll find the dive shop very close on the left side of the street (ocean side).

FOOD AND ENTERTAINMENT

As always, seafood is the highlight of most restaurant menus on Isla Mujeres; the fish is caught right in the front yard. Around town are dozens of indoor and outdoor cafes, simple and informal, plus a number of small fast-food places selling *tortas,* tacos, and fried fish.

Bucanero
On Hidalgo, this large outdoor cafe serves good seafood and Yucatecan specialties for breakfast, lunch, and dinner. Prices are reasonable—a breakfast of bacon, eggs, beans, and toast runs about US$3. Good fried fish and *chiliquiles.*

Sergios
On Guerrero, this is a combination cafe, bar, and art gallery with an open-air 2nd-story dining room. The food is tasty (though the servings are rather small); try the chicken tacos. The lobster is good—and no longer a bargain anywhere! At cocktail hour 6-8 p.m. drinks are two for one. The owner/artist Sergio is friendly and willing to answer questions about the island.

Pizza Rolandi
This small cafe will always rank high on our list not only for having good food, but for having a caring staff. One day in March of 1988, Isla Mujeres was caught in a tremendous tropical storm. It wasn't raining buckets—it was raining truckfuls. The early lunch crowd would ordinarily be emptying out and a new crowd coming in, but no one was moving. The water had risen knee deep in front of the cafe and various flotsam was floating by— along with a couple of kids paddleboarding up the street and enjoying every drop. Rolandis played host to the entire crowd for hours,

making space under the dry-roofed part of the patio for everyone (most of whom were already wet). The coffee kept coming all afternoon. There was lots of laughing, visitors all got acquainted with each other as well as with the waiters and management. Hurray for Pizza Rolandi—and be sure to try their garlic bread; it's great with beer. A pizza for two averages US$5. Ask about a few hotel rooms on the upper floors of Pizza Rolandi. On Av. Hidalgo between Madero and Absolo, tel. 2-04-30.

Ciro's
On Matamoros and Guerrero, this is a fancier restaurant with glass-topped tables; in the evening light reflects from old-fashioned glass lamps mounted on the walls. The clean, modern, fan-cooled, open-sided dining room serves all day. Good food, moderate prices, well-stocked bar, and choice seafood, including excellent shrimp-in-garlic as well as lobster. Good bargain breakfast: bacon and eggs with toast and black beans about US $2.50. Special omelettes with ham, bacon, and cheese are just a little more.

Maria's Kan Kin Restaurant Francaise
If your palate yearns for something Continental, get a taxi and have an elegant lunch at **Maria's** (close to Garrafon Beach). She serves in a *palapa* dining room overlooking the Caribbean. A small seawater tank holds live lobsters from which you can take your pick. The sophisticated menu offers curries, snails, and rabbit, and her prices are accordingly more expensive. Closed Sunday. A good meal for two with a cocktail can average US$15 to $20.

Chez Megaly
Go for the pink buildings on Nautibeach. Sit by the sea and enjoy Caribbean food with a European flavor. Good food with a great view and ambience of the sea; located at Av. Rueda Medina Playa Norte, tel. 2-02-59; closed Monday.

Other Cafes
Other food places offer poolside barbecues, including **Del Prado,** and **Gomar's** colorful

*Maria's Kan Kin
Restaurant*

Mexican patio (they advertise barbecue chicken and baked potatoes but don't have them; other than that the food is good though pricey). Be sure you try the *licuados* (liquified fruit in sweetened water and ice) at a small open stand across from the playground. The **Cafe Mirtita** on the main road across from the sea serves great (brewed) coffee and all-around good food. It's very clean and reasonable. A newish addition is a wild and crazy place called **Bad Bones,** serving *good* American specialties. From the dock turn left and head north, it's next to the north lighthouse and doesn't look like any other cafe on the island. Twice we went there for lunch and it was closed, but they seem to be open for dinner consistently.

Markets

If you prefer to cook your own, the *mercado municipal* opens every morning till around noon; it has a fair selection, considering everything must come from the mainland. There are two well-stocked supermarkets—including liquor and toiletries. **Mirtita** (Juarez #14, tel. 2-01-27) is open 6 a.m.-noon and 4-6 p.m. Larger **Super Bertino** (Morelos #5, tel. 2-01-57) is on the plaza, open 7 a.m.-9 p.m. **La Melosita** is a mini super open from 10 a.m. till midnight, with candies, piñatas, film, sundries, cigarettes, gifts, and snacks. Located on Av. Hidalgo 17 & Abasolo, tel. 2-04-45.

Panaderia La Reina makes great *pan blanco* and *pan dulce,* open 6 a.m.-noon and 5 -8 p.m.

Entertainment

Isla Mujeres has a few good nightspots. A new glitzy disco is the **Casa Blanca,** lots of locals as well as tourists report a good time; Av. Hidalgo #1, tel. 2-02-67. The **Calypso** (Rueda Medina Playa North, 2-01-57), the **Tequila Video Bar,** and **Broncos Video Bar** are all good, noisy fun for an evening.

Other evening activities: the movies (theater on Morelos near the plaza), ball games in the plaza, an occasional boxing match, dancing in the plaza during special fiestas, listening to the military band that comes to the navy base, or (the most common) visiting in the plaza or sitting by the sea and watching the stars reflect off the water.

Special Event

The **Isla Mujeres International Music Festival** takes place the second weekend in October. The island rocks with bands and dancers from everywhere. Room reservations are a must. For more information about the exact date of the festival and travel package details, contact Kerrville Festivals, Inc., Box 1466, Kernville TX 78629, tel. (512) 257-3600.

SERVICES

A well-stocked **drugstore** is at Av. Juarez #2. **Farmacia Lily** is on Av. Francisco Madero and Hidalgo. A limited selection of **newspapers** and **magazines** can be found on the corner of Juarez and Bravo. Check at the **photo studio** for film. Two banks in town will change money Mon.-Fri. between 10 a.m.-noon: **Bank Atlantico** (Av. Juarez #5) and **Banco Serfin** (Av. Juarez #3). The **post office** (Av. Guerrero 15) is open 8 a.m. to 8 p.m., Mon. through Fri., half-day Sat., and is closed Sun. and holidays. General delivery will accept your mail and hold it for 10 days before returning it. Addresses should read: your name, Lista de Correos, Isla Mujeres, Quintana Roo, Mexico. The **telegraph office** next to the post office (Av. Guerrero #13) is open from 9 a.m.-9 p.m. weekdays and on Sat., Sun., and holidays from 9 a.m.-noon. Money orders and telegrams will be held for 10 days only. Address to your name, Lista de

ISLA MUJERES EATERIES

NAME	ADDRESS	TELEPHONE
Abarrotes	Av. Hidalgo	2-01-75
Bad Bones	next to the North Lighthouse	—
Brisas Del Caribe	Rueda Medina	2-03-72
Bucanero	Juarez #13 and Hildago #11	2-02-36
Buho's Restaurant, Bar, & Disco	Carlos Lazo #1	2-02-11
Carnitas	Av. Hidalgo #4	—
Ciro's Lobster House	Matamoros #11	2-01-02
El Garrafon Restaurant	Garrafon Park km. 7	—
El Limbo Restaurant & Bar	Hotel Roca Mar	2-01-01
El Patio	Av. Guerrero #4	—
El Peregrino	Madero #8	2-01-90
Gomar	Av. Hilgado & Madero	2-01-42
Guillermos	Calle Benito Juarez	—
Hacienda Gomar	Beach Road to Garrafon	2-01-42
La Estrellita Marinera	Av. Hidalgo	—
La Melosita	Av. Hidalgo #17 and Abasolo	2-04-45
La Pena	Guerrero South	—
Las Palapas	Playa Cocos North Beach	—
Los Jardines	Calle Morelos	2-03-59
Malos Huesos Cafe	Rueda Medina & Lopez Mateos	—
Miramar	Av. Rueda Medina	2-03-63
Mirtita	Av. Rueda Medina	—
Pizza Rolandi	Hidalgo between Madero and Abasolo	2-04-30
Roberts	Calle Morelos	2-04-51
San Martin	Mercado Municipal	—
Sergio's Restaurant Gallery	Guerrero 3–A Sur	2-03-52
Taqueria Alex	Av. Hidalgo	—
Tequila Video Bar	Matamoros & Hidalgo	2-00-19
Tropicana	Nicolas Bravo & Rueda Medina	—
Villa Del Mar	Rueda Medina #1 Sur	2-00-31

Telegrafos, Isla Mujeres, Quintana Roo, Mexico. A **long-distance telephone** is located in the lobby of the Hotel Maria Jose at Av. Francisco Madero. Also, Club de Yates offers long-distance telephone service for a small service charge (on Av. Rueda Medina in front of the gas station). Some hotels offer long-distance phone service, but be sure to ask about the service charge on collect calls.

Travel Agencies
For all of your travel needs contact **Club de Yates de Isla Mujeres.** They can fix you up with side trips to the mainland or fishing trips from Isla Mujeres. Even if you don't want a ticket but have a problem while you're on the island, stop in and ask for help—they'll do their best to help you out. To get to Club de Yates coming off the dock, turn left and walk about 150 meters; their office is on the left.

Medical
In the event of a medical emergency there are several options on Isla Mujeres. Ask your hotel manager to recommend a doctor. If that's not possible the following medical contacts might be helpful. **Centro de Salud** (health center) is located at Av. Guerrero on the plaza. Emergency service 24 hours daily,

	IMPORTANT TELEPHONE NUMBERS
City Hall	2-00-98
Police station	2-00-82
Customs office	2-01-89
Chamber of Commerce . Av. Juarez	2-01-32
Office of Tourism Av. Guerrero	2-01-88

open for regular visits 8 a.m.-8 p.m.; tel. 2-01-17. An English-speaking doctor, Dr. Antonio Salas, is open daily, tel. 2-04-77, 11 a.m. to 2 p.m.; tel. 2-01-95 5 p.m. to 9 p.m. Doctor Antonio Torres Garcia is also available 24 hours, tel. 2-03-83.

GETTING THERE

Many hotels and travel agencies arrange escorted day tours to Isla Mujeres. But for the independent traveler who wishes to do it on his own it's quite easy. It can be confusing not knowing that there is more than one boat

ISLA MUJERES SHOPPING HINTS

NAME	ADDRESS	COMMENTS
Artesanias Prisma	Garrafon Park	souvenirs and crafts
Bazar Pepe's	Av. Hidalgo #4	clothing and souvenirs
Caribbean Queen Handicrafts	Madero Norte #25	wool rugs, Mexican curios, gifts
Caribbean Tropic Boutique	Av. Juarez #3	souvenirs and crafts
El Nopal	Guerrero & Av. Matamoros	authentic clothing and crafts
Gomer Restaurant and Boutique	Hidalgo & Av. Madero	clothing
Isleno T-shirt & Shell Shop	Calle Guerrero 3-A Norte	—
La Loma	Av. Guerrero #6	arts, crafts, collectors masks
La Melosita	Calle Hidalgo #17	piñatas, mini-super
Mariola Boutique	El Garrafon National Park	souvenirs
Mari-Tona	Garrafon Park	clothing and souvenirs
Paulita	Morelos & Av. Hidalgo	imports
Rachat & Rome	in front of main pier	fine jewelry
Vamily	Av. Hidalgo & Parque	clothing and souvenirs

going to the island from different departure points. One is called a ferry and the others are called boats. A passenger boat from the Puerto Juarez dock is located a few km north of Cancun and makes trips almost hourly throughout the day from 5 a.m.-6 p.m.; it takes just under hour, and costs about US $.50. Check the schedule since it changes often. At the foot of the dock in Puerto Juarez you'll find a Tourist Information Center sponsored by the municipal government, with bilingual employees; ask for a map of Isla Mujeres. There's a *usually* clean restroom (small fee).

A ferry leaves Punta Sam (five km south of Puerto Juarez) daily and carries passengers and cars. You really need a good reason to bring a car to this short island with narrow, one-way streets. RVs can travel on the ferry, but there are very few places to park (no hookups) on a sandy beach. The trip on the ferry from Punta Sam is slightly longer. If driving, arrive at the ferry dock an hour before departure time to secure a place in line; tickets go on sale 30 minutes in advance. For those traveling the Peninsula by bus, it's easier to make ongoing connections in Puerto Juarez than in Punta Sam. **Aerocaribe** flies from Cancun and Cozumel to Isla Mujeres three times a week. Fare is about US$35 OW, and the schedule changes constantly; be sure to check this out well in advance. For airport info on Isla Mujeres, call 2-01-96. From Cancun and Cozumel check with your hotel or travel agency.

Note: Be aware of the time that the last passenger boat leavs the island. If you haven't a hotel reservation you might have to sleep on the beach, and it can rain anytime of the year in the tropics.

GETTING AROUND

Mujeres is a small and mostly flat island, and in town you can walk everywhere. The eight-km length is a fairly easy trek for the experienced hiker. Other options include taxi, bicycle, motorcycle, or the municipal bus. A tour around the island in a taxi (three passengers) and back to your hotel should cost about US$8-9 and takes about an hour, including stops to watch the lighthouse keeper making hammocks, see the Maya temple on the south tip, and observe turtles at Playa Lancheros.

By Bicycle
Bicycle rentals are available at **Arrendadora Maria Jose** on Madero #16, tel. 2-01-30; **Arrendadora Carmelina** on Av. Guerrero #6; and **Arrendadora de Bicicletas Ernesto** on Av. Juarez #25. Rental fee is around US$10 per day.

ferry to Isla Mujeres

BOAT SCHEDULES TO AND FROM ISLA MUJERES

Please keep in mind that transportation on the water to and from Isla Mujeres is referred to either as a boat or a ferry. There is a difference. The ferry carries cars and passengers, the boat carries only passengers. The biggest difference however is that the ferry leaves from Punta Sam (much less frequently) and the boats leave from Puerto Juarez often, all day long. Know the schedule to save valuable vacation time, it can change anytime. If you're going to the island without reservations hoping to get a room; (and yes it can be done—*usually*), be sure to know when the last boat or ferry leaves the island—just in case. A recent traveler was having such a good time snorkeling that he neglected to look for a room till too late, slept on the beach—and it rained. Price for passengers is about US$.50 pp, and for cars about US$1.50. **Delicate stomachs note:** on a rough day, I prefer to take the car ferry for a smoother ride.

BY BOAT FROM PUERTO JUAREZ		FROM ISLA MUJERES TO PUERTO JUAREZ		BY CAR FERRY FROM PUNTA SAM TO ISLA MUJERES		FROM ISLA MUJERES TO PUNTA SAM	
A.M.	P.M.	A.M.	P.M.	A.M.	P.M.	A.M.	P.M.
5:30	1:30	4:30	1:30	7:15	12:00	6:00	1:15
8:30	3:30	6:30	3:30	9:45	2:30	8:30	4:00
10:30	4:30	7:30	5:30	10:00	5:15	11:00	6:30
11:30	5:30	8:30			7:45		9:00
	7:15	9:30					
		11:30					

By Motorcycle

Most of the bikes on the island are newish and come with standard or automatic shift for the same rate. Be sure to check the bike for damage before you take responsibility. Beware of narrow one-way streets and numerous children darting back and forth. Rates are fairly standardized in most of the *rentadoras*. **Pepe's Moto Rental** (Av. Hidalgo and Matamoros) charges about US$60 per day or US$10 hourly for a Honda 250. This is the best size for two people. The smaller bikes rent for US$20 daily, US$3.50 hourly— all require a deposit. It's quite simple to rent, no minimum age and no driver's license required at either of the following: **Gomez Castillo** (Av. Bravo and Hidalgo, tel. 2-01-42); **Moto Servicio Joaquin** (Av. Juarez #7B, tel. 2-00-68).

By Taxi

Taxis are many, easy to get, and the fares reasonable. To go anyplace downtown the fare is about US$1. At the taxi stand on Av. Rueda Medina all fares are posted; open 6 a.m.-11 p.m, tel. 2-00-66.

By Bus

The municipal bus operates 6 a.m.- 9 p.m. daily; about US$.25. It runs from Posada del Mar on Av. Rueda Medina to Colonia Salinas (a small suburb of homes facing the windward side of the island), departures every half hour.

VICINITY OF ISLA MUJERES

Contoy

From Isla Mujeres, take a one- or two-day trip to Contoy, an island 24 km north of Mujeres. The small bit of land (2.5 by .5 km) is a national bird sanctuary. Outside of wayward flamingos, heron, brown pelicans, the magnificent frigatebird, olivaceous cormorants, and a couple of humans at the biology station, you'll find only a lush isolated island—the kind of place around which fantasies are spun. From a tall viewing tower (about three stories of steps) open to the public, you can see most of the island. Under a shady arcade there's an information display with lighted photos of numerous birds, including full details of each specimen. A white beach close by provides a refreshing swim with delicate tropical fish. Often you'll swim amid large schools of young trumpetfish, almost transparent as they glide through the water sucking up small fish and shrimp. Tiny flying fish in groups of 10-30 or more skim the surface as they flee large predators. A day at Contoy is well worth the money. Check around for the best rate; about US$25 pp, depending on the type of boat.

Getting To Contoy

Among others, trips are provided by Richard Gaitan aboard his 10-meter sailboat, the *Providencia*. The two-day trip is well worth the time, which includes all meals (mostly fresh-caught fish, liquor extra), snorkeling equipment, a cruise around the island, and time for hiking and exploring. Bring your own sleeping bag for the beach, and don't forget sunscreen, bug repellent, and mosquito netting. The boat anchors close to shore near some excellent birdwatching sites (bring your camera and Fielding's *Mexico Bird Guide*). Rick can be contacted at the Boatmen's Cooperative in town.

Other boatmen offer one-day trips departing 8 a.m. and returning 7:30 p.m. These cruises typically include a stop at the reef to snorkel (equipment provided), fishing off the end of the boat en route (if you wish), a light breakfast snack of *pan dulce* and fresh fruit, and a delicious lunch of *tikin chik* (fresh fish caught along the way and barbecued at Contoy) along with Spanish rice and green salad. Soda and beer are extra. The captain often treats his passengers to a lime/salt/tequila drink on the return trip. Most of the boats are motor/sailers, usually motoring north to Contoy and raising the sail for the trip back to Isla Mujeres. Many of the boats are neither luxurious nor too comfortable (wooden benches), but look forward to meeting about 15 people from various parts of the world. Check at the marinas or at Dive Mexico for Contoy trips. Signs giving full information are seen literally all over town, or contact the Cooperativa, tel. 2-00-86.

NORTHERN
QUINTANA ROO COAST
FROM PUERTO MORELOS TO PAMUL

Anyone looking for isolation can find it on Quintana Roo's Caribbean coast between Cancun and Boca Paila. Along this 153-km stretch are dozens of fine beaches, some with facilities for camping, several with modest cabanas, and a few with more deluxe accommodations. Others offer nothing but nature's gifts: the sun, white sand, and blue sea—free! Often the only way to spot the entrance to these beaches is by noting the kilometer count on small highway signs that begin at Chetumal and end at Cancun (360 km). To get to some of them you must leave Hwy. 307 at the Tulum turnoff and continue on the uneven, potholed road that parallels the sea. This road ends at Punta Allen, an isolated bit of paradise with little more than a lobstering village, but what a place to forget about civilization for a while!

PUERTO MORELOS

Hurricane Gilbert hit this Quintana Roo coastal area in Sept. of 1988. This was one of the most devastated areas and Puerto Morelos suffered tremendous damage. It's a small town and it is taking much longer than other towns to put back together, mainly because of money. However, these people are survivors, and slowly docks, homes, hotels, and other structures are being rebuilt. We have attempted to mention those places (which may have been your favorites) and the status of their construction.

Port City

Puerto Morelos, on the northern Caribbean coast, is 17 km south of Cancun. It has limited accommodations and few attractions to detain ordinary tourists. At one time its only claim to fame was the one vehicle-ferry to Cozumel. But more and more people are beginning to notice Puerto Morelos' peaceful mood, lack of tourists, and easy access to the sea. As with some of the other towns on the Caribbean coast, divers are bringing low-key attention to this small town, using it as a base to explore the rich coastline. Until Hurricane Gilbert, Puerto Morelos had been the coastal headquarters of CIQR (Centro de Investigaciones de Quintana Roo), an ecological-study organization sponsored by the Mexican government, the UN, and other environmental groups dedicated to maintaining the ecosystem of the Quintana Roo coast. The building was thrashed and there was little sign of activity when last seen, but ask one of the locals for the most current information and CIQR'S present location.

Canoe Harbor

In pre-Hispanic times this was a departure point for Maya women making pilgrimages in large dugout canoes to the sacred island of Cozumel to worship Ixchel, goddess of fertility. Remnants of Maya structures are located near the coast and throughout the jungle. Though small, the ruins are not considered insignificant, but as usual there's a shortage of money to investigate and restore them. The descendants of Indians in these parts occasionally find artifacts dating to pre-Columbian times, which sadly are often sold

QUEEN CONCH

A popular easy-to-catch food beautifully packaged—that's the *problem* with the queen conch (conk). For generations inhabitants of the Caribbean nations have been capturing the conch for their sustenance. The land available for farming on some islands is scant, and the people (who are poor) have depended on the sea—especially the conch—to feed their families. Even Columbus was impressed with the beauty of the peach-colored shell, taking one back to Europe with him on his return voyage.

The locals discovered a new means of making cash in the 1970s—exporting conch meat to the U.S. The shell is also a cash byproduct sold to throngs of tourists looking for local souvenirs. An easy way to make money—except for one thing: soon there will be no more conch! In recent years the first signs of overfishing have become evident: smaller-sized conch are being taken, and fishermen are finding it necessary to go farther afield to get a profitable catch.

It takes three to five years for this sea snail to grow from larvae stage to market size. It also takes about that long for planktonic conch larvae carried into fished-out areas by the currents to replenish themselves. What's worse, the conch is easy to catch; large (shell lengths get up to 390 cm) and heavy (about three kg), the mollusk moves slowly and lives in shallow crystalline water where it's easy to spot. All of these attributes are contributing to its demise.

Biologists working with various governments are trying to impose new restrictions that include closed seasons, minimum size of capture, a limit on total numbers taken by the entire fishing industry each year, limited numbers per fisherman, restrictions on the types of gear that can be used, and most important—the cessation of exportation. Along with these legal limitations, technology is lending a hand. Research has begun, and several mariculture centers are now experimenting with the queen conch, raising animals in a protected environment until they're large enough for market or grown to juvenile size to be released into the wild.

A new research center at Puerto Morelos (on Yucatan's eastern coast, in Quintana Roo) is in operation and recently released its first group of juvenile conchs to supplement wild stock. This is not always successful. Sometimes one group of larvae will survive, and the next 10 will not—for no clear-cut reason. In the wild, not only does the conch have man to contend with, it also has underwater predators: lobsters, crabs, sharks, turtles, and the ray.

The conch is not an endangered species yet—but it must be protected for the people that depend on it for life.

to private collectors, and their archaeological value is never measured. If caught with the genuine article, whether a pottery shard you may have picked up at one of the ruins or a piece bought from a local, you will be fined and your treasure taken from you. Remember that old Latin saying, *Caveat emptor!*

SIGHTS AND SPORTS

A short walk through town reveals a central plaza, shops, a cantina, and nearby military base. Puerto Morelos' most spectacular attraction is its reef which begins 20 km north of town. Directly in front of Puerto Morelos, 550 meters offshore, the reef takes on gargantuan dimensions—between 20 and 30 meters wide. For the scuba diver and snorkeler this reef is a dream come true, with dozens of caverns alive with coral and fish of every description.

Snorkeling
Snorkeling is best done on the inland side of the reef where the depth is about three meters. Snorkelers can expect water clarity up to 25 meters along the reef.

Scuba Diving
The reef has been a menace to ships for centuries. Early records date losses from the 16th century. Many wrecks have become curiosities for today's divers, who come from great distances to explore the Quintana Roo coast. Puerto Morelos can provide the most experienced diver with exciting destinations, including a wrecked Spanish galleon with coral-crusted cannons—clearly visible from the surface five meters above. Looking for another kind of excitement? **Sleeping Sharks Caves** are eight km east of Puerto Morelos. Intriguing, yes, but the sharks still claim proprietorship.

Fishing
A never-ending variety of fish provides good hunting for sportsmen. Onshore fishing is only fair off the pier, but if you're interested in deep-sea fishing, ask around the plaza or make arrangements at the hotel **Posada Amor.**

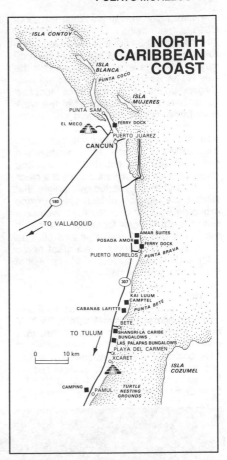

ACCOMMODATIONS

Budget
No one minds if campers spread their sleeping bags north and south of the lighthouse away from town, houses, and hotels. Choose a high spot (so you'll stay dry). It can get gritty if the wind freshens, and if it's very still be prepared for mosquitoes. Remember, the beach is free and this is a safe, peaceful town.

The **Posada Amor** is a simple, 19-room, friendly, family-run hotel with ceiling fans, shared baths (some private), and hot water; rates about US$20. They offer a good restaurant with a Continental breakfast for about US$3, a fresh salmon plate US$5.50, and fried chicken US$4.50. If you're adventurous ask about a tour that's a little out of the ordinary, offered by a veterinarian involved in the Sian Ka'an Reserve. Manuel picks up passengers around 2 p.m., then takes them to a boat where they become part of the work crew. Dinner is served on board while traveling. Ultimately the boat arrives at Manuel's work area and passengers will see crocodiles, turtles, and birds. The crocodiles are dealt with at night, counted, tagged, and cared for. This is a night trip since the crocs are out and easily spotted with a light that catches the red glow of their eyes. Anyone expecting a luxury boat shouldn't even consider this trip. It's only for those interested in the fauna of the Sian Ka'an and curious about crocs and turtles. It's a great photo safari and the cost is about US$45 pp. Ask at the Posada Amor for reservations.

Apartment Living

Going south on the same street as the Posada Amor, across the street from the school and the beach look for the **Reef Inn,** four comfortable, clean, efficiency apartments that have cooking facilities, washer, hot water, and small living room. The manager speaks English; rates are about US$20 d, US$25 for three or four persons, add US$5 if you plan to use the kitchen. At Av. Rafael & Melgar #4, Puerto Morelos, Quintana Roo, Mexico 77580. If you arrive when no one is home you'll see a perfect example of the casual environment in this little town. You will find a note that says:

1. Put your luggage inside.
2. Lock door and take key (it's in the doorknob).
3. See room rates on envelope.
4. Deposit money in envelope.
5. Turn this sign around (on the back it says occupied).
6. Put envelope in slot in Apt. 4 (manager).

I'll make change later if needed.
Be back soon, thanks, manager.

Almost Deluxe

Hotel Playa Ojo de Agua has been rebuilt with 12 modern rooms including kitchens, ceiling fans, dive shop, and pool. This beautiful beach just north of town center is as lovely as ever. Write for information: Ernesto Munoz, Colle 12 #96, Colonia Yucatan, Merida, Yucatan 97000, Mexico.

Bed And Breakfast

Before Gilbert, **Amar Suites** was a large stucco house on the beach. It was knocked down, but the owners have already construct-

This tranquil dock offers good fishing.

ed five small cabanas that sleep two to four people. Each has a loft bedroom, simple cooking facilities, toilet and shower, fan, TV (!), and a small sitting area. These are very spartan accommodations close to the sea. Summer (low) rates are US$20, and winter (high) are US$40. For more information write to Apto Postal 136 A, Cancun, Quintana Roo, Mexico.

FOOD AND SERVICES

Restaurants
Several small budget cafes serving typical Mexican food and good seafood circle the main plaza. The **Posada Amor Restaurant** can usually be depended on for outstanding *mole poblano* and other regional dishes at moderate prices. The **Maison del Tiburon** is a good vegetarian restaurant; **Dona Zenaidas Restaurant** offers a good selection of local fare. The **Pelican** and the **Palmeras** both serve fair pizza and hamburgers. On the way out of town south of the turnoff on Hwy. 307, check out the *palapa*-roofed **Oasis Carib,** a vegetarian cafe.

Markets
Local markets carry fresh fruit and vegetables plus a limited selection of sundries. Supplies of basic food items can be sketchy and intermittent. If camping or backpacking, it's advisable to stock up in Cancun. Two pharmacies in town appear well stocked with the usuals.

Services
Puerto Morelos has one of the few **gas stations** along this route (also at Tulum, Playa del Carmen, and Puerto Felipe Carrillo). If driving, be advised to top off your tank whenever you find a gas station. Besides being few and far between, it's not unusual for a station to run out of gas, so get it wherever and whenever possible. If you run out near the coast and can find a dive shop, they're usually willing to help out with a couple of gallons of outboard motor gasoline. Though laced with oil, it might get you to a gas station without doing irreversible damage to your car. Also, many rural towns have a supply of gas in five-gallon drums even though you don't see a sign or a gas pump. Ask at the local store. **Larga-distancia** telephone service is found just south of the military camp, open 8 a.m.-1 p.m. and 4-7:30 p.m. daily. The **bank** is open to cash travelers cheques from 9:30 a.m.-1 p.m., Mon. to Friday.

TRANSPORT

Getting There
Buses from north and south stop at Puerto Morelos frequently. From Cancun it's about a 40-minute drive, from Chetumal about five hours. Hitching is reasonably easy from the larger towns (Chetumal, Cancun, Puerto Felipe Carrillo, Playa del Carmen); try Hwy. 307 where the service roads enter the towns.

Vehicle Ferry
The vehicle ferry to Cozumel departs Puerto Morelos beginning at 6 a.m. It departs daily, (see "By Boat To And From Cozumel" p. 148). Check the schedule the night before in case it changes. Be at the dock two or three hours early to get in the passenger-car line. It also expedites things to have correct change and the car's license number. The ticket office is open 5-6 p.m. The trip takes two hours and can be a rough crossing so put on your elastic cuffs if you tend to get seasick (see "Health"). For those with sea legs (and stomachs), light snacks are sold on the passenger deck.

PUNTA BETE

Punta Bete, a four-km stretch of beach, is a complete tropical fantasy—swaying palms hover along the edge of pure white sand, with gentle blue crystal waves running across the shore. Swimming is perfect in the calm sea, and 10-20 meters offshore the rocky bottom makes a perfect snorkeling area. As recently as 1965 there were no tourists along this part of the coast. At that time Quintana Roo was only a federal territory. There wasn't even a road to this fine white-powdered beach. Family groups, mostly descendants of the Chan Santa Cruz Indians, tended their small, self-sufficient *cocals* (miniature coconut plantations). Together a family harvested enough coconuts each year to earn spending money from the resulting copra. The custom continues today (although a coconut blight begun in Miami in 1980 has spread south to the Quintana Roo coast, in some areas decimating the coconut palms). We saw one man wrestle two 70-kg bags of fresh coconuts (a harvest representing several months' labor) onto a bus to Merida (three hours each way), sell them in the public market, and come home with about US$50!

ACCOMMODATIONS AND FOOD

Along the four-km stretch are several places to stay in a variety of price ranges. Each of them (depending on your travel style) is ideal.

Budget
You have a choice of two campgrounds right next to each other—one also offers small cabanas. **Xcalacoco** (SHKAH-lah-co-co) **Beach** is a trailer park next to the sea with showers and toilets for campers and self-contained recreational vehicles, moderately priced. Next door, **Xcalacoco Campground** can be a social experience if you wish. However, it's still large enough to lose yourself in your own little coconut grove, hammock slung between palms (close enough to the sea that breezes blow the mosquitos away, but be prepared with bug repellent and mosquito netting anyway). On the grounds are clean bathrooms and showers, separate *palapas* for socializing—or for cover in case of an unexpected shower. The pure water supply comes from nearby wells (boil it anyway);

Xcalacoco—a simple campground

fires are not allowed, so if you want to cook, bring a backpacking stove. To camp on the beach the rate is about US$2 pp; a few cabanas rent for about US$10 d: individual bathrooms, no electricity, fairly clean. A small cafe/bar is open part of the day. For reservations write to: Familia Novelo Cardenas Attn.: Sr. Miguel, Av. Sur #548, Cozumel, Quintana Roo, Mexico; tel. 2-18-36.

El Marlin Azul Bungalows
Hurricane Gilbert destroyed this once-charming small resort. The word is they will start rebuilding soon. For information write to: El Marlin Azul, Calle 61 #477, Merida, Yucatan, Mexico.

Note!
Before shedding your shoes to stroll along the southern part of Punta Bete beach, look it over. Often sharp little bits of coral hide in the sand. When swimming beware of the sharp limestone in the shallow places; if you have diving booties they are ideal around here.

TURQUOISE REEF RESORTS

Luxury Campout Kai Luum Camptel
For the traveler who wants to avoid the glitz of the highrise but doesn't want the work of setting up a campsite, Kai Luum is the lazy man's campout. In the tradition of the British safari, it's camping with a touch of class. Though there's no electricity, Kai Luum offers modern tents on the beach with large comfortable beds, communal hot and cold showers, clean toilets very close by, and daily maid service. Each tent is shaded by a shaggy *palapa* roof and strung with two hammocks facing the sea for lazy afternoons.

The restaurant is one of the great attractions at Kai Luum—the food is outstanding. Prepared by Maya cooks, the menu is overseen by owner Arnold Bilgore, who happens to have a gourmet touch and plans something new and unusual (often Continental) every day. The dining room is a large *palapa* structure on the sand, where a sumptuous buffet breakfast always includes tropical fruits, fresh juice, sweet rolls, hot coffee, tea,

chocolate, and a different hot dish each day. Dinner is served under the sparkling light of hundreds of candles. Arnold jokes that next to the church, Kai Luum is the biggest buyer of candles in Mexico. The bar is at one end of the dining room: each person makes and keeps track of his own drinks with a numbered pegboard. The whole feeling of the resort is much like the honor system at the bar—relaxed, intimate, friendly. If you have a problem, see Mino, Arnold's son who grew up on the beach and is now the manager of the operation. The restaurant attracts travelers from other resorts in the area as well, and if you wish to be one of them, reservations are necessary. There are no telephones, so if you aren't staying at Kai Luum and would like to eat at the restaurant you must drop by and make arrangements in advance.

Everyone enjoys browsing in Kai Luum's boutique where the discerning shopper can purchase unique treasures from throughout Latin America, including hand-woven fabrics and colorful clothing from Guatemala. If you find something too big to carry home, the management will pack and ship it for you. You have a choice of water-sports at the new activity center near the Capitan Lafitte swimming pool next door (walking distance). Called **Buccaneer's Landing,** the activity center serves all three Turquoise Reef Resorts, **Kai Luum, Capitan Lafitte,** and **Shangri-La.** They've got a personable, highly skilled and trained staff, including a registered PADI dive instructor, and boats and "state-of-the-art" equipment are available. Other activities including snorkeling trips, beach picnics, and fishing trips are offered as well as scuba instruction, PADI certification, check-out dive, and a short "resort course" good only for the length of your holiday.

Buccaneer's Landing offers **Vagabonder** day-trip suggestions to various sights close by, including appropriate travel tips and maps. If you've always wanted to see Belize, ask about extended Vagabond trips that include both the Punta Bete coast and Belize. Rates at Kai Luum are US$40 pp, double occupancy (surcharge for holiday periods), and include breakfast, dinner, and 15% government tax. Three persons maximum in each tent, no children under 16. Economical three-day rates available during the summer. No credit cards, travelers cheques okay. For accommodation reservations write to Turquoise Reef Group, Box 2664, Evergreen, CO 80439, in Colorado tel. (303) 674-9615, from anywhere else, (800) 538-6802, fax (303) 674-8735.

Deluxe

Cabanas Lafitte has been around for many years, and it is as well known for its charming managers, Jorge Fuentes and family, as it is for its fine service, wonderful beach location, good food, swimming pool, and pleasant game room. All provide a serene backdrop for welcome camaraderie among the people who return year after year from distant parts of the globe. The stucco oceanfront cabanas have double and king-sized beds, hot water, ceiling fans, private bath, and along with daily maid service each room is provided with a handmade reed broom to help keep the sand out. Buccaneer's Landing (see "Kai Luum" above), a full dive shop on the premises, has a good selection of rental equipment including sailboards. The management provides transport by skiff to nearby Lafitte Reef, an exciting snorkeling destination. Here, a lazy day of floating on the clear sea will bring you face to face with blue chromis, angelfish, rock beauties, and often the ugly grouper—a great place to use your underwater camera. Fishing is another satisfying sport—you'll always come away with a tasty treat that the restaurant chef will be happy to prepare for your dinner. Hands off the large handsome turtles you may see and don't expect to find turtle soup or conch *ceviche* on the menu. The management makes it clear that they support the preservation of this endangered species. And speaking of species, every afternoon between 5-6 p.m. a flock of small colorful parrots flies over the swimming pool; unmistakable with their awkward wing movements and peculiar squawk.

During high season it's best to have reservations. Rates include breakfast and dinner,

US$60 pp double occupancy. Ask about the economical summer-season three-day package and El Cofre, a large two-story beachfront duplex for large families. No credit cards, cash and travelers cheques only. Car rentals are now available at Lafitte. For more information and reservations write to: Turquoise Reef Group, Box 2664, Evergreen, CO 80439; from Colorado tel. (303) 674-9615, from anyplace else, (800) 538-6802, fax (303) 674-8735.

A delightful addition to the coastline just beyond Punta Bete is **Shangri-La Caribe.** Exotic bungalows with private bath, fans, tile floors, hot water, beach bar, swimming pool, and pool bar; car rentals available on site. Rates include breakfast and dinner, about US$60 pp, oceanfront suites US$175 per day for one to four persons, children under six free in same room with parents, seven to 12 US$28.50, 13 and over full charge. No credit cards.

Just south of Shangri-La Caribe, the lovely new **Las Palapas Cabanas** is comfortable, clean, upscale, with a pool, dining room, and a great beach. Rates include breakfast and dinner, tax, and tip; US$114 s, US$136 d, US$188 t. For reservations, contact Turquoise Reef Group, tel. (800) 538-6802, fax (303) 674-8735, from Colorado tel. (303) 674-9615.

TRANSPORT

Getting There

If arriving by plane in Cancun, taxis are available; arrange your price before you get in the cab. Figure approximately US$45 (up to four passengers). From Playa del Carmen (a ferry arrival point from Cozumel), taxi fare is less. Car rentals are available at Cancun Airport, which is a straight shot north on Hwy. 307; look for the large sign on the left side of the road that says Capitan Lafitte; here you'll find both Lafitte and Kai Luum. From Capitan Lafitte it is approximately eight kilometers farther to Shangri-La.

PLAYA DEL CARMEN

For years there was but one reason to go to the small village of Playa del Carmen—the Cozumel Island ferry dock. And though thousands of people pass through here each year on their way to or from Cozumel (a popular island 19.2 km off the Quintana Roo coast), many come just to enjoy the laid-back pleasures of the small town. Playa offers the latest transportation to get to Cozumel—conventional boat, water jet, and flights from the airport near the center of town. But the town is taking on a personality of its own and adds to its modest beginnings each year. Nature did its part by endowing the small town with a broad beautiful beach, one of the finest in Quintana Roo. It's still uncluttered by high-rises—but maybe not for long! Condominiums have begun to spread along the beach south of the dock, with promises of more coming. The unfinished shell of a new hotel still stands where the old Playacar hotel used to be. But other new ones (such as the lovely **Las Palapas Hotel** with 50 oceanfront units) are showing up along the beach. Call Turquoise Reef Group at (800) 538-6802. If you haven't been there for awhile you'll be surprised at the many simple hotels that are popping up everywhere overnight. The same

two funky campgrounds still hold their space near the beachfront, but who knows for how long!

Visitors have a vast selection of restaurants to choose from, several dive shops, and a busy efficient bus terminal. This once slow-moving fishing village is becoming a "destination" to consider while traveling along the Caribbean coast. Swimming is a pleasure and Playa's proximity to attractions such as Tulum, Xelha, Cancun, and coastal Hwy. 307 makes it a convenient stopover. For lovers of early morning walks along the water, the village's long beach is perfect to stroll for hours, sometimes without seeing another soul—almost a thing of the past). If you enjoy watching crabs scurry about, wading in the surf, or catching fluttering sea birds in the eye of a camera lens—then early morning on the beach at Playa del Carmen is just the place for you.

Traffic Note

The road going to the dock is now a one-way street; watch the signs and follow the traffic flow which turns left just before the dock and takes you in front of the military base, through the parking lot, and then left along the plaza.

one of the new waterjet boats that travel between Playa del Carmen and Cozumel

There's a white-suited man that gives out traffic tickets quite regularly, then asks for payment right then—US$5. He may indeed be a policeman, but it's doubtful. However, to avoid the hassle, watch the signs.

SIGHTS

By far the nicest thing to do in Playa del Carmen is to enjoy the people and the sparkling Caribbean. Take a walk through the village.

Only two or three years ago you would've been escorted by children, dogs, little black pigs, and incredibly ugly turkeys. Nowadays mostly tourists crowd the streets—everywhere. Once off the main thoroughfare into town the streets are potholed and bumpy—Playa's lack of sophistication and Topsy-like growth is appealing. The milkman no longer delivers milk from large cans strapped to his donkey's back; now he travels the streets in a dilapidated unmarked station wagon. At the familiar honk the village ladies bring their jars

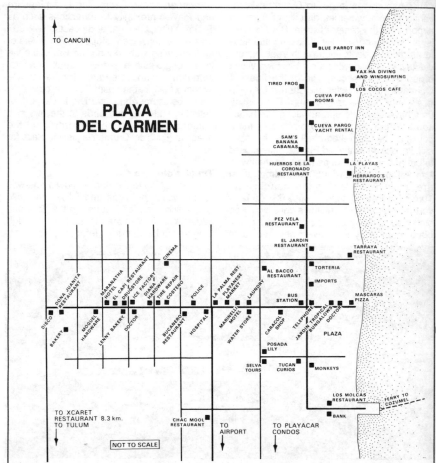

and pots to be filled. The number of small curio shops, cafes, and cantinas increases daily, and there's a movie theater. Yes, Playa del Carmen has become a "tourist resort"— and the increase in prices reflects this metamorphosis. However, it's still a bargain compared to Cancun or Cozumel.

The cool early hours are best for walking along the beach. Warm afternoons are perfect for swimming and snorkeling, snoozing on the sand, or watching the magnificent man-o-war frigate bird make silent circles above you, hoping to rob another bird of its catch. Ferries from Cozumel come and go all day; in addition, luxury cruise ships anchor close by in the bay, and tenders bring tourists to shore who crowd into all the gift shops. The ship's passengers have a choice of lounging on the beach, hosted by Los Molcas Hotel (for now), or being escorted immediately to large modern buses and whisked off to the more famous sights of Xelha and Tulum. You can count on Playa del Carmen's beach being filled with jet-setters when ships are in port; the rest of the time it plays host to a mixed conglomeration of young and old, archaeology buffs, students of the Maya culture, backpackers, adventure seekers, sunlovers who prefer the ambience of Playa del Carmen over Cancun, independent travelers from many parts of Europe, and just plain folks who enjoy the white sand and blue Caribbean wherever they find it.

Dive Adventure
For an unusual dive adventure, ask Huacho at Cuevo Pargo (Box 838, Playa del Carmen, Quintana Roo, Mexico 77710) about **Calypso Scuba Safari**. This involves a deluxe camp on wheels—a super-bus with toilets, showers, freezer, and kitchen, along with tents, good food (including fresh lobster and good tender steaks), beach equipment from windsurfers to parlor games, and stopovers in extraordinary camp and dive sites along the Caribbean to the sea.

ACCOMMODATIONS

You can still see remnants of damage wrought by Hurricane Gilbert, but the village has picked itself up, rebuilt where necessary, and continued to improve. Many new small hotels are available and others are better than ever.

Luxury
Until the new hotel by the dock is completed, the closest to luxury lodging is the **Villas and Condominiums Playacar** located on the beach on the south side of the boat dock. These are privately owned and rented when not in use by their owners. They are beautifully designed in a convenient location either right on the beach or a short walk away. A five-minute stroll from town, each has one to three bedrooms, a fully equipped kitchen, washer and dryer, and living room. Some have balconies, and there's a swimming pool. These are great for families or small groups, or for those who prefer to do their own cooking. Prices begin at US$80 for a one bedroom, depending on time of year. For more information write to Box 396, Cancun, Quintana Roo, Mexico 77500.

Almost Luxury Class
Los Molcas Hotel is very close to the foot of the ferry dock and the beach. It has nicely decorated, air-conditioned, spacious rooms with private bath, plus swimming pool, dining room, terrace dining, and three bars. The hotel offers tours to Chichen Itza, Tulum, and Coba, diving equipment, and laundry service. Rates start at about US$80 double. For reservations write to Turismo Aviomar, SA, Calle 60 #469, Merida, Yucatan, Mexico 77500.

Suites Quintas is a lovely place to stay; if it were on the beach it would be rated "luxury," but it's located on the main street into town about halfway to the highway. The suites are about US$75 double. The complex is clean, modern, nicely furnished, air-conditioned, and beautifully decorated—except for one thing; no toilet seats! I have a feeling that will change if many Americans stay there.

Moderate Hotels
A modern pleasant motel-style hostel, **Maya Bric** offers a swimming pool, cafe, and 18 clean rooms with fans, bathroom, and hot water—all just a few minutes' walk from downtown cafes, the dock, and the beach; about

Los Molcas Hotel

US$28 d, less in the summer. The **Hotel Costa del Mar** complex sits on the beachfront next to the Blue Parrot. Spacious rooms, tile bathrooms, hot water, and a small pool, plus an indoor and beach restaurant (prime rib advertised for US$18!). The **Maranatha Hotel** is on the north side of the main street coming into town. They offer a swimming pool, dining room, bar, tile floors, fans, private bathrooms, some with kitchenette, double beds, and they take MasterCard and Visa. **Jardin Tropical** is an unexpected surprise. Located between a dentist's office and a gift shop across from the park two doors up from Mascaras restaurant and the beach, once through the gates you'll find yourself in a small tropical garden complete with Tony the Parrot and three small *palapa* bungalows. Some rooms have private bathrooms; others share. One bungalow is large enough for a family. Mosquito netting furnished. Prices start at US$30 d, discounts for extended stays. You can always just show up and take your chances, but for reservations send a two-day deposit c/o Christine, Box 1434, Cancun, Quintana Roo, Mexico 77500. Allow a couple of months for roundtrip letters.

A Robinson Crusoe-type hotel is the **Blue Parrot Inn** on the beach north of town. It's a whimsical stucco tower structure with *palapa* roof, tile floors, spotlessly clean shared bathrooms, lots of hot water, one or two double beds in each room, and an ice chest with soda and beer (in the more expensive rooms) along with purified water. For a midnight swim you need only step out your front door. Each room has a view of the water, and just a short walk north on the white sand takes you where you can watch fishermen throw their nets or return in their open launches with the morning catch.

The Blue Parrot offers a large selection of rooms from simple thatched-roof rooms on the sand to spacious two-story stucco cabanas with fantastic views. A beachside deli serves up cold drinks and light snacks.

Room rates begin at US$40-140 during the high season and US$25-65 during the low season. For more information and reservations write to Box 652737, Miami, FL 33265, tel. (904) 775-6660, toll-free (800) 634-3547. Or directly to Mexico write to Box 64, Playa del Carmen, Quintana Roo, Mexico, 77710, fax (52) 988-44564 (address to "Caja 20," Cancun, Quintana Roo, Mexico 77500).

Cabanas Nuevo Amanecer offers private baths, double beds, and *palapa* roofs for US$20-25. Clean and pleasant. For reservations write to Arlene King, Apto Postal 1056, Cancun, Quintana Roo, Mexico, 77500.

Apartments

Quinta Mija offers three one-bedroom fully furnished apartments with living room, kitchen, bathroom, and a small pool for US$60 per night (located behind the Blue

Parrot Inn). For reservations contact, Turquoise Reef Resorts, Box 2664, Evergreen, CO 80439, from Colorado tel. (303) 674-9615, from anyplace else tel. (800) 538-6802, fax (303) 674-8735.

Budget Hotels

Playa del Carmen has a CREA youth hostel. You can't miss the sign as you come into town. Good value—too bad it's not closer to the beach. Follow the signs from the main street into town about one km. Fairly new, clean, single-sex dorms, dining room with reasonably priced food, basketball court, and auditorium; it's well worth the effort.

Faces Hotel sits on the side of a small hill a few minutes from the beach. The entrance is on Av. 5 Norte, and the hotel offers clean rooms with screens, hot water, shared and private bathrooms, and fans, plus a swimming pool in a small garden with lots of greenery. Managers Alba and Marcel take good care of their visitors. Depending on the season and which room, rates begin at US$10-30. The owner of Faces also owns the charming Hotel Trinidad in Merida.

The **Tucan** is a good buy for a simple hotel. Follow the signs, about two blocks beyond the Blue Parrot turnoff. The rooms have overhead fans, hot water, group refrigerator, mosquito netting, peace and quiet (usually), and friendly staff. It's one of the best structures on Av. 5 Norte; rates are about US$15 s or d. The old standby, **Posada Lily** has watched Carmen grow from a wide spot on the beach to a viable resort. One block west of the plaza, on the main road coming into town from Hwy. 307, it's the bright blue motel; clean, with a hot shower and good ceiling fans.

Another quaint place to stay is **Cuevo Pargo Hotel,** with nine rooms that share clean bathrooms and showers. Purified water, ceiling fans, simple, homey atmosphere. Before Gilbert there were a couple of houses with kitchenettes available that slept three to four. No information on these right now. Room rates start at US$20-30. We've heard of two new hotels, but have not seen them: **Casa de Gopal** has large rooms and a pool under consturction; the **House of Benji** and **Narayan Restaurant** are located on the beach north of the dock. To quote from a reader, this is "a little bit of India."

Camping

The two campgrounds in Playa del Carmen are dirty, noisy, and not recommendable, but if you're a masochist, check them out: **Las Ruinas** and **Brisa del Mar.**

FOOD

New restaurants are growing even faster than hotels in Playa del Carmen. Around the

the Blue Parrot palapa bungalows

central plaza several small cafes serve a variety of good inexpensive Mexican, Italian, and Chinese food. The **Molcas Hotel** serves good food, but it's hard to spend less than US$20 there for a meal. If you want to stick with the typical Yucatecan food at moderate prices or are looking for good fresh seafood, try **Dona Juanitas** on the main road close to Hwy. 307. Two fishermen's sons provide only the freshest catch, which is nicely prepared. The bakery called **Lennys** is a great afternoon snack stop—good lemon pie and other goodies.

Chac Mool restaurant is clean and serves great Yucatecan food and a hearty breakfast, moderately priced. A small cafe called **Comida Integral** serves great coffee, breakfast, and snacks. **Limones** is a popular dinner house serving excellent fish and shrimp. It's often crowded and you might have to wait. **Chicago** is an upscale open-air restaurant/bar/gathering place for visitors interested in getting the news (CNN) and sporting events on one of four TV sets. Good food, too. **Mascaras** is on the first block off the beach across from the plaza. Their pizza and pasta are excellent. Try the spinach canneloni—marvelous! Be sure to take a close look at the brick wood-burning oven where most everything is baked. Mascaras makes good fresh limeade, served in bulbous glasses with lots of purified ice. You can also get *big* margaritas and cold Yucatecan Leon Negra *cerveza*. Adding to the international variety of foods available, there is a Chinese restaurant called **Yut Kun** north of the square on the same street as Mascaras. For variety try the nachos at **La Caballa**, or lunch at **Ixchell**. **Flippers Cafe** is clean, and has good food and a lively clientele.

Groceries

Several small grocery stores around the plaza and on the main street coming into town have an ample supply of fruit, vegetables, and basics. A good variety of meat is available at the butcher shop, and there's a **rosticeria** that sells fresh roasted chicken. Nearby is the purified ice shop, a drugstore, and bakery. Liquor is sold across from the Molcas Hotel and several other locations in town.

ENTERTAINMENT AND SERVICES

The cinema is usually open on the weekends with Spanish-language films. Dona Juanitas cafe becomes a disco with videos later on in the evening. As usual, people gather at the plaza and poke around the gift shops. Sitting on the end of the pier and watching the stars is *muy bueno* on the Caribbean; when you tire of that, a before-dinner drink on the patio of one of the many outdoor cafes generally comes with lots of fellow travelers to swap travel stories with.

Services

If taking the ferry to Isla Cozumel for the day, park your car at the public parking lot just beyond the **military camp** right on the waterfront, a half block from the dock; fees are posted. Somehow, one feels secure leaving the car next to the army camp, but do lock up regardless. (Rumors are wonderful in the small villages of the Caribbean coast. The newest is that the car ferry will soon be moving from its home port at Puerto Morelos to a new dock just south of Playa del Carmen.) **Banco del Atlantico** located up the street from the ferry dock cashes travelers cheques (commission) between 10 a.m. and 12:30 p.m. Mon. to Friday. *Larga-distancia* phone service is located across from the plaza next to the vegetable stand, open daily from 8 a.m. to 1 p.m. and 3-8 p.m. There are now three phone lines into Playa del Carmen, easing the waiting time. Maybe by the time the new hotel is completed, Playa will have total telephone service. Two **hardware stores** will help you out with twine, a gas can, or a knife blade, and there's a **doctor** *and* a **dentist** in town (ask at your hotel). Playa del Carmen has postal service now, a small building between the police station and the mayor's office.

GETTING THERE

By Air

Playa del Carmen's small airstrip is five blocks south of the main plaza and is open from 7 a.m. to 5 p.m. daily. Most of the flights go to and from Isla Cozumel (about US$10 OW). Reservations are not necessary, but if it's convenient, drop by the airport and make them in advance to ensure a seat. Otherwise, arrive at the airport an hour before you wish to fly. The first flight leaves Playa del Carmen at 7:20 a.m., then every hour thereafter during the busy season. Check the schedule; it's always subject to change.

By Taxi

Taxis at Cancun International Airport will bring you to Playa del Carmen. If there are several passengers, you can make a good deal—bargain with the driver before you start your journey. Expect the trip from Cancun to Playa to cost about US$40-50. Nonmetered taxis meet the incoming ferry at Playa del Carmen and are available for long or short hauls; again, make your deal in advance. A trip from Carmen to Tulum (with three passengers) can be about US$25-30 RT, depending on supply and demand, and the time of year. If you're interested in a good diving spot, tell the cabbie. He may share with you his favorite cove that you'd never find on your own, and in fact he might join you for a swim.

By Ferry

Five RTs leave each day from Playa del Carmen to Cozumel, with a choice of the old ferry or the new modern jetboat. The ferry crossing is usually a breeze. However, the calm sea does flex its muscles once in awhile making it difficult to berth the boat snugly against the dock. When this happens, hefty crewmen literally swing each passenger over the side into the capable hands of two other strong-armed receivers on the dock—quickly followed by the individual's luggage. This adds a bit of adventure to the voyage. But if it isn't your forte, delay your departure till the next day—the sea seldom stays angry for long. Young boys with imaginative homemade pushcarts or three-wheel *triciclos* meet incoming ferries at the dock to carry luggage for a small fee. (See "To And From Cozumel By Boat" p. 148.)

By Bus

Three bus lines provide this small town with the best bus transportation on the coast. From Merida via Cancun (a five-hour trip), three 1st-class buses and seven 2nd-class buses arrive daily. Buses arrive frequently from Chetumal and other points south as well. Playa del Carmen is an ideal base for many attractions along the Quintana Roo coast. Buses going north to Cancun's bright life travel the 65 km in 50 minutes. If sightseeing on the bus south to Chetumal, just a word to the driver and he'll drop you off at the turnoff to Tulum, to Xelha Lagoon National Park entry road, or one of the small beaches south along the coast. Ask what time his schedule brings him back, since you must be on the highway waiting to return to Carmen.

Hitching

Because of the ferry traffic, this is a good place to try for a hitch going north or south.

XCARET

About an hour's drive south of Cancun and a half km off Hwy. 307 along a limestone dirt road, Xcaret is the site of a small group of pre-Columbian ruins. Recently **Xcaret Ecoarchaeological Park** has been developed around the ancient Maya structures. Here visitors spend the day wandering tree-lined paths, exploring the ruins and surrounding jungle, swimming, snorkeling, and picnicking. For years the ruins were hidden in the overgrown jungle next to a small inlet known mostly by divers and adventurers. Not spectacular in themselves, the ruins you see near the parking area are just the tip of the iceberg according to archaeologist Tony Andrews. He says many more structures are scattered throughout the bush; already 60 buildings and more than 500 platforms have been uncovered. Whether by accident or because their location near the sea required navigational lookouts, the Maya often placed their ceremonal structures in magnificent locales.

Within the park, a crystalline *cenote* (at the entrance to a cave with an underground river) used to be the beginning of an adventure for scuba divers who would dive into the water and proceed through a pitch black cave. Today, visitors to the park are given life vests and can float down the underground river with the benefit of light and fresh air via open-air skylights carved into the roof of the cave. It takes about 20-30 minutes to float atop the slow-moving water. Visitors rave about it. (There are exits along the way if you should feel the need to get out before you reach the end of the waterway.)

A powder-white beach with *palapa*-provided shade edges the warm blue sea. On site, would-be scuba divers can take a three-hour course that allows them to dive no deeper than 30 feet; it's deep enough to enjoy an excursion into the *cenotes,* the caverns, and the inlet filled with colorful darting fish.

When completed, the park will resemble an ecological Disneyland; a good place to spend the day (as long as it doesn't attract Disney-size crowds). Almost complete is a museum which will contain Maya artifacts found in the area, an aquarium, a botanical garden, a sanctuary for fish and corals, plus a sheltered area for dolphins. Local artisans create *tipico* arts and crafts.

At the park entrance you'll find a large parking lot, a gift shop, a dive shop offering renatl snorkeling gear, a bar, a snack bar, an open-air cafe which serves light meals, lockers, restrooms, picnic areas, an infirmary, and lifeguards. Admission, US$10 pp, good for the entire day. (Another cafe at the corner of the turnoff in Xcaret, called **Rancho Xcaret,** serves excellent fresh fish meals.)

Sacbes

Archaeologists will continue excavating this area rich with hidden history. They are convinced they'll eventually find traces of a

Maya site at Xcaret

dive boat, Isla Mujeres

1. Snorkeling off the tip of the Camino Real Hotel, Cancun; 2. Isla Mujeres harbor; 3. From Isla Mujeres you can see the tall towers of Cancun; 4. Isla Mujeres; 5. Isla Mujeres, north end

1. Isla Cozumel; **2.** Chankanab Bay, Isla Cozumel; **3.** San Gervasio, Isla Cozumel;
4. San Francisco Beach, Isla Cozumal; **5.** Isla Cozumel

1. Akumal Bay; **2.** Akumal Bay; **3.** Ancient cannons guard Akumal

1. Playa de Carmen Beach; **2.** Xelha Lagoon; **3.** Club de Maya, Puerto Aventuras;
4. Chemuyil; **5.** Kailuum Beach

1. Puerto Aventuras; **2.** Roy Blom enjoying a "long" beer; **3.** Carlos and Charlies Cafe, Puerto Aventuras

sacbe beginning at Coba and ending at Xcaret. The scientists conjecture that this small cove was used as a protected harbor and debarkation point for Maya sailors who traveled up and down the coast in dugout canoes.

Snorkeling

Xcaret is a marvelous spot for beginning snorkelers, especially children. The water is shallow and there's little current, though you must either climb over the rocks to enter the water, or jump off the small wooden platform. It's not necessary to go far beyond the limestone shoreline to discover colorful denizens of the sea; resident schools of parrotfish and blue and French angelfish almost always put in an appearance. One problem is fighting off the tourists that have discovered the lovely small *caleta*. Come early in the day and you might have the small bay almost to yourself. Although most folks make Xcaret a one-day trip, there are several simple rooms available for around US$25.

PAMUL

Another small beach that deserves exploring is Pamul. If you're a natural packrat, you'll like the beachcombing here: shells, coral, and sometimes interesting jetsam from ships far from Yucatan shores. This is not one of the wide white beaches so common along the coast; in some places Pamul is steep and rocky, in others narrow and flat. The water is crystal clear, allowing you to examine the fascinating life within the shallow tidepools cradled by rocks and limestone. Snorkeling is better the closer you get to the reef 120 meters offshore. On the way the sea bottom drops off to about eight meters and its colorful underwater life can absorb you for hours.

Diving Near Pamul

If you are self-contained with your own compressor and equipment, the Quintana Roo coast offers miles and miles of pristine dive spots, and the waters near Pamul are especially ideal for scuba diving. The south end of Pamul's beach is sandy, but the shallow water along here harbors the prickly sea urchin—look before you step, or wear shoes while you're wading. Fishermen and divers

GIANT TURTLES AND THE INDIANS

At one time the giant turtle was plentiful and an important addition to the Indian diet. The turtle was captured by turning it over (no easy matter at 90-100 kilos) when it came on shore to lay its eggs. Any eggs already deposited in a sandy nest on the beach were gathered, and then the entire family took part in processing this nourishing game. First, the parchment-like bag of unlaid eggs was removed from the body, then the undeveloped eggs (looking like small hard-boiled egg yolks). After that, the meat of the turtle was cut into strips to be dried in the sun. The orange-colored fat was put in calabash containers and saved for soups and stews, adding rich nutrients and considered an important medicine. They wasted nothing.

Today CIQR, a protective organization, along with the government keeps a sharp lookout along the coast for egg poachers during the laying season. Turtle-egg farms are being developed to ensure the survival of this ancient mariner. Sadly, the poacher of the '90s travels the entire coast, and each beach is hit night after night. The turtle can lay as many as 200 eggs in an individual nest or "clutch." One beach may be the instinctual home for hundreds of turtles (at one time thousands) that return to the site of their own hatching each year.

Turtles can live to be a hundred years old, which means they can lay a lot of eggs in their lifetime. But as the poachers steal the eggs on a wholesale basis, the species
continued on next page

continued from previous page
could eventually be wiped out entirely. If caught, poachers are fined, and can be jailed—though the damage has been done. When released they usually return to their lucrative habits. In most Mexican market-places a ready market for these eggs exists among superstitious men who believe the eggs are an aphrodisiac.

The survival of the giant sea turtle lies within the education of the people—locals and visitors alike. Shoppers will see many sea turtle products offered for sale: turtle oil, tortoise shell combs, bracelets, rings, buttons, carvings, and veneer inlaid on fur-niture and jewelry boxes, plus small stuffed, polished hatchling paper weights. **Note:** It is against the law to bring these products into the U.S. and other countries. If discovered they will be confiscated. Sad-ly, many travelers are not even aware of the law, and often the products get by the inspectors. If tourists refused to purchase these products, the market would dry up—a big step toward preserving these gentle lumbering beasts.

along this coast are a jovial group always ready for a beach party, potluck style, when fishing is good—especially during lobster season (July 15 through March 15).

Turtles

If it's a bright moonlit night in July or August, you may be treated to the unique sight of large lumbering turtles coming ashore and laying thousands of eggs in the sand. If you're there a few weeks later it's even more exciting to watch the tiny (about eight cm in diameter) hatchlings make their way down the beach to begin life in the sea. Much has been written about protecting the turtles of the Caribbean from man, but nature in the form of egg-eating animals provides its own threat to this endangered species. On the beach of Pamul, more than half the eggs are scratched up from the sand and eaten by a variety of small animals that live in the sur-rounding jungle.

Practicalities

You have a choice of two lodgings in the area, **Cabanas Pamul,** a small hotel on the beach, or the campsite at the south end of the hotel. The hotel would be considered spartan but it's usually clean and does have electricity between sunset and 10 p.m., hot and cold water, and shared bathrooms, about US$34 d for a cabana. The campsite has room for 15 RVs. All spots have electricity and water, eight are large pads with sewer-age hookups (US$8), seven will accommo-date small trailers (US$5), and you can use the showers and toilets in the hotel. Campers fee is about US$1 pp including bathroom privileges. The small cafe next to the hotel is run by the family that owns the hotel and usu-ally offers fresh-caught seafood plus other typical dishes at reasonable prices, open 8 a.m.-8 p.m. A small *cenote* nearby provides water for Pamul; do boil it for drinking. Other-wise, bottled water can be bought from the hotel manager. Mailing address is Apto, Postal 1681, Cancun, Quintana Roo, Mexico 77500.

CENTRAL
QUINTANA ROO COAST
FROM PUERTO AVENTURAS TO TULUM

PUERTO AVENTURAS

The corridor between Cancun and Chetumal is buzzing with the growth of new resorts, both large and small. One of the most ambitious developments is an enormous marina (advertised as the largest in the Caribbean) located just a few minutes south of Akumal. Some of these waterways are left from the days of the Maya, simply improved and opened to the sea. In other cases they are totally manmade and will soon be ready to moor almost 300 boats up to 120 feet in length with a draft of 10 feet.

The Marina
At the marina yachtsmen will find everything they need: gas and diesel, a spare-parts store, minor maintenance shop, purified water and ice, bait, 24-hour radio station and medical service, restrooms and showers, car rentals, travel agencies, shopping center, hotels, yacht club, and restaurants. Access into the marina is through a carefully planned channel, well marked for navigation and ready with an escort service 24 hours a day.

Golf, Tennis, And Diving
Construction has been in progress for almost two years, and while much has been completed, it will probably be another two years before the entire community will be finished. An 18-hole golf course is a big attraction at Puerto Aventuras and will be the scene of world-class golf tournaments. Nine holes were just about ready for playing when Hurricane Gilbert drove tons of salt water on the new grass. Nine holes should be ready for

play by the time you're reading this book. Condos will be spaced around the golf course with an upscale hotel in the center of the fairways. Golf carts will be available for rent.

One tennis court is completed and work is in progress on several more. Eventually there will be an international tennis club with 25 courts. But the big attraction is expected to be the University of the Sea, a five-star PADI institution for diving instruction where divers will not only learn about diving but can take continuing courses on the preservation of the Belizean reef which runs from the tip of Isla Mujeres to the Bay of Honduras in Belize.

A nautical shopping village meanders on and around the marina with a boutique, supermarket, Carlos 'N' Charlie's restaurant, and other small shops getting ready to open.

As you turn into Puerto Aventuras, ask for the **Papaya Republic Restaurant** for pricey gourmet food.

CEDAM Museum

Artifacts brought from the sunken ship *Mantanceros* are seen at the CEDAM Museum located along the waterfront. There's a small collection of belt buckles, cannons, coins, guns, tableware, and various clay relics from Maya ruins along the Quintana Roo coast. The *Mantanceros* ("Our Lady of the Miracles"), a Spanish merchant ship that left Cadiz, Spain, in 1741 headed for the New World loaded with trade goods, foundered and sank on the reef two km north of Akumal. No one knows for certain why the *Mantanceros* sank since there were no survivors. How-

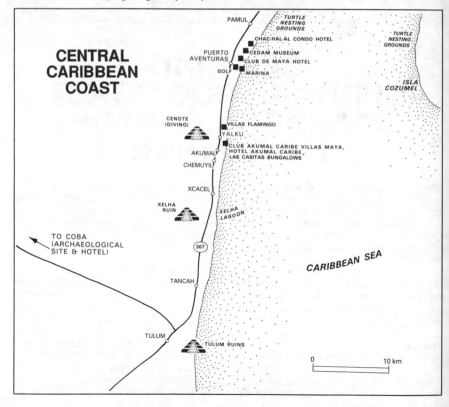

ever, the CEDAM organization spent several years salvaging it, beginning in 1958. Research suggests the ship probably engaged in a violent battle with a British vessel and then drifted onto the treacherous reef now known as Punta Mantanceros.

Hotels

In June 1989 the first hotel, the **Club de Maya,** celebrated its grand opening with the Miss Universe entrants as the first visitors. The Club de Maya is a small, intimate hotel with 30 rooms. It faces the marina on one side and a shimmering white beach and the translucent water of the Caribbean on the other. The hotel has a swimming pool, pool bar, lobby bar, dining room with a Swiss-trained chef, health spa called Body And Sol, and a juice bar. All water-sports equipment is available. The rooms are spacious, with views of the marina or the ocean, tile floors, king-size beds, game room, and 1st-class room amenities.

Two condo-hotels are ready for occupancy, each with complete kitchen facilities, living room, balconies, and access to slips for the boaters. Hotel manager Rene Hersberger tells us that every effort will be made to keep prices at a reasonable level. Rates through April 1990 are US$92 double, and the Chac-Hal-Al condos with kitchen average about US$139 per night. For reservations and more information tel. (800) 451-8891, or (305) 341-9173.

AKUMAL

About 100 km south of Cancun, Akumal Bay is a crescent of intensely white sand along the blue Caribbean. This quiet beach, edged with hundreds of wind-bent coconut trees, is home to an ever-growing resort that survives nicely without telephones, TVs (well, there are one or two showing up—with satellite dishes!), or bustling activity. The traveler desiring the tropical essence of Yucatan *and* a dash of the good life will appreciate Akumal. Compared to Cancun it could not be described as luxury class but is more luxurious than many of the small resorts along the coast. It offers a good range of hotel rooms, dining, and activities.

The barrier reef that runs parallel to the Quintana Roo coast protects Akumal Bay from the open sea and makes for great swimming and snorkeling. Proximity to the reef and easy access to the unspoiled treasures of the Caribbean make it a gathering place for divers from all over the world. For the archaeology buff, Akumal is 10 km north of Tulum, one of the few walled Maya sites located on the edge of the sea. From Tulum, it's five km north to Xelha, a natural saltwater aquarium where divers (even amateurs) snorkel or scuba among surrealistic limestone formations that give the eerie impression of an ancient sunken city. In Maya, Akumal means "Place of the Turtle," and from prehistoric times the giant green turtle has come ashore in summer to lay its eggs in the warm sands of the Caribbean.

Flora

Akumal is surrounded by jungle and coconut groves. In March, bright red bromeliads bloom high in the trees, reaching for a sun that's rapidly hidden by fast-growing vines and leaves. These "guest" plants that find homes in established trees are opiphytes rather than parasites: they don't drain the sap of the host tree but instead sustain themselves with rain, dew, and humidity; their leaves absorb moisture and organic requirements from air-born dust, insect matter, and visiting birds. The bromeliad family encompasses a wide variety of plants, including pineapple and Spanish moss. The genus seen close to Akumal is the tillandsia, and the flame-red flower that blooms on the tops of so many of the trees here is only one variety of this remarkable epiphyte. While searching out bromeliads, you undoubtedly will see another epiphyte, the orchid.

History

Akumal was a small part of a sprawling coconut plantation until 1925, when a *New York*

CEDAM AND THE BIRTH OF AKUMAL

In 1958 a small group of Mexican divers were salvaging the *Mantanceros,* a Spanish galleon that sunk off the Palencar reef in 1741. These men, originally Mexican frog men active during WW II, were first organized in 1948 and called themselves CEDAM (Club de Exploracion y Deporte Acuaticos de Mexico—a non-profit organization). This was not the typical fun-and-games type of dive club; its members were dedicated to the service of country, science, and humanity.

While diving the *Mantanceros* they camped on the beaches of Akumal, two km south of the dive site. This bay, part of an enormous copra plantation owned by Don Argimiro Arguelles, was (and still is) a deserted crescent beach of white sand edged by hundreds of coconut palms. Then the only way in and out of Akumal was by ship. As owner and captain of the ship which the divers leased for a work boat, Don Argimiro spent much time with the group. It was during one of those relaxed evenings around the campfire that Akumal's destiny was sealed. Arguelles sold Pablo Bush (organizer of the charter group of CEDAM) the bay and thousands of acres of coconut palms north and south of Akumal.

Pablo Bush's tropical lagoon had no airstrip nearby, and even if there had been one, there would have been no road to reach it. So for twelve years the creaky vessel, *SS Cozumel,* plied the waters between the Island of Cozumel and Akumal carrying divers, drinking water, and supplies. The only change to the environment was the addition of typical *palapa* huts built for the divers.

The CEDAM organization, in the meantime, was gaining fame and introducing Cozumel and the Yucatan to the diving world. Visiting snorkelers and scuba divers were entranced, and the word soon spread about the exotic Mexican Caribbean coast.

In 1960 the thought of promoting tourism began to circulate; but Quintana Roo was still a territory. Pablo Bush and other movers and shakers began talking road and airport. The government began listening. But governments move slowly, and it was three governors and two presidents later that the road was finally completed. In the meantime, Cancun was born, Quintana Roo became a state, and finally Akumal bloomed. The beautiful bay continues to grow. Today several hotels, restaurants, dive shops, and many other services make visitors (not only divers) welcome.

In 1966, CEDAM International was born and gave new meaning to the initials: Conservation, Ecology, Diving, Archaeology, and Museums. Akumal is the main headquarters for both CEDAM groups in the Caribbean and it's here that international symposiums and seminars are still held for the active divers of the world. CEDAM has had an active part in archaeological exploration in several *cenote* dives where artifacts from the early Maya were retrieved.

In 1968 (before Cancun), the owners of Akumal formed the Club de Yates Akumal Caribe, A.C. (A.C. means Civil Association, non-profit). They turned over 5,000 acres of land to the government and donated the Cove of Xelha for a National Park. The aim was to open the isolated area to tourists, and in so doing jobs were available to the local residents. CEDAM provided housing, food, electricity (added in 1982), running water, a school for the children, and a first-aid station with a trained nurse. Till this time, the sparse population lived in the shadow of their ancient ancestors, few ever exposed to modern civilization. Water had to be brought from deep wells eight miles inland until finally four generators and two desalinization plants (which went out of commission during each storm) were brought in.

In 1977 a fire destroyed one of the original large *palapa* structures built on the beach; the closest fire protection then was in Cancun. The only communication even today is by short wave radio. Although still rather primitive (who knows for how long), all who visit Akumal fall in love with its slow, rustic way of life and tropical beauty. Houses are springing up, and though many more visitors come today, the wide beaches are still never *too* crowded.

Times-sponsored expedition along the then-unknown Quintana Roo coast stumbled on this beautiful bay; it was another 33 years before the outside world intruded on its pristine beauty. In 1958, Pablo Bush formed the nucleus of CEDAM, a renowned diver's club, and introduced Akumal to world-class divers. Soon the word was out. The first visitors (divers) began making their way to the unknown wilderness. At that time, the only access to Akumal was by boat from Cozumel. A road was built in the 1960s. Since then, Akumal has continued to grow in fame and size each year, but it was Bush who introduced this part of Mexico as the "diving capital of the world." Though many people come here, it still remains beautiful, tranquil, a place to study the sea and stars.

The Beach

The porous sand of Quintana Roo never gets hot enough to burn. There are kilometers of white shore to beachcomb, with lots to investigate: conch shells, lacy red seaweed, an occasional coconut that has sprouted after soaking in the sea for months, and the ever-present crabs, all sizes and colors, popping in and out of their sandy holes. Take a walk at dawn. The sun bursts from the sea, spotlighting leaping fish as they jump at winged breakfast-bugs hovering just above the surface of the water. When the sun rises higher, late sleepers stake out spots on the beach and create a colorful patchwork of beach towels on the sand. Fortunately, the beach is so large that it never gets crowded—only coveted spots under shady palms become scarce. A *palapa* bar, open until 1800, serves beer, cocolocos, piña coladas, and more. This is a friendly place to meet other travelers and swap adventure stories.

WATER ACTIVITIES

Two dive shops on the beach rent equipment, including boats and motors, for scuba divers and snorkelers. The **Kapaalua Dive Shop** offers a three-day dive certification course. If you just want to make one dive on the reef, instructors give a four-hour "resort course,"

providing equipment, transportation, and one escorted dive. If you decide to take a resort course from any dive shop, check to make sure that you'll be making the dive with a divemaster on a one-on-one basis. Kapaalua is fully PADI certified. Many divers come for the excitement of exploring the wreck *Mantanceros,* sunk in 1741. Although it was completely salvaged, a job that took CEDAM several years, the sea still yields an occasional coin or bead from this ancient Spanish merchant ship. A good collection of memorabilia from the *Mantanceros* is on display at the CEDAM Museum at Puerto Aventuras (just a few km north) open from 8 a.m. to 5 p.m. daily, with a small entry fee charged. A multitude of dive spots are hidden in the reefs about 130 meters offshore.

Snorkeling

Akumal Reef not only protects the bay from the open sea but also provides calm swimming areas ideal for snorkeling. A good spot within wading distance is the rocky area on the north end of the bay. Floating along the surface of the water and looking through your private window into the unique world below can become habit-forming along this coast. Take it slow and easy, and you won't miss anything. Search the rocks and crevices that you'll drift over, even the sandy bottom—what may look like a rocky bulge on the floor of the sea may eventually twitch an eye and turn out to be a stonefish hiding in the sand: hands off, he's deadly! You'll even see a new crop of sea urchins growing once again. Most of the urchins disappeared after the **El Nino** current passed through several years ago.

Fishing

World-class fishing is done farther out to sea, where piscatorial game, including marlin, sailfish, and bonito, grow to enormous size. The **Kapaalua Dive Shop** will arrange outings including all gear, but make reservations in advance if possible.

Yalku Lagoon

Though within walking distance from Akumal, finding Yalku from the highway can be tricky—but not impossible. Driving south from Pamul,

Yalku Lagoon

the unmarked entrance is a dirt road across from a ranch house with a broad stone wall and a tall windmill. This secluded tiny replica of Xelha Lagoon is worth a snorkel for the many fish you'll see in a quiet hideaway. Parrotfish gather here in numbers and make a multi-colored glow just below the surface. A current of fresh water flows into this small lagoon which is at most three meters deep; the visibility is about five meters. This is just a stony little pond—no rooms, no cafes, no toilets, no tourists, just fish and you. On the ocean side of the Yalku, lovely villas are springing up on private property. From Akumal it's about a half-mile stroll, north on the road that runs past Half Moon Bay.

ACCOMMODATIONS

There are limited accommodations at Akumal. During the off season you'll have little difficulty finding a room. However, if traveling between 1 Dec. and 15 April, make reservations. No camping is permitted at Akumal, but just a few kilometers south good beaches

with camping facilities are available at Xcacel (sha-SELL) and Chemuyil (shem-oo-YEEL). The hotels at Akumal are all on the beach, close to the sea—perfect for a tropical vacation.

Hotels

While Akumal cannot be considered a budget resort area, the most economical choice is **Club Akumal Caribe Villas Maya,** the original cottages built for the CEDAM diving club. The owners replaced the elderly thatched roofs with Western-style coverings a few years ago. These roomy cabanas on the beach are clean, with private bath, tile floors, a/c, and cooking facilities in some; even the lighting has been improved for readers. There are plenty of water sports, but if you prefer to stay on land, check out their tennis and basketball courts. Bungalow rates start at about US$64 d, including tax; the oceanfront hotel is about US$92 d, including tax. **Villas Maya** also offers three lovely condos on a separate beach around the point north of Akumal Bay. Each has two bedrooms, two bathrooms, fully equipped kitchen, and living room with two sofa beds. These rent for US$115 per night for up to four adults; two children could also be squeezed in. For something special ask about the Cannon House Suite and Cannon House Studio.

One of the newest facilities on Akumal Bay is the beachfront hotel (still part of Villas Akumal) offering 21 rooms on three floors, with lovely views of the Caribbean and the garden area, which includes a swimming pool and a pool bar. The rooms each have full bath, compact refrigerator, and a small porch or balcony. Winter rates are US$92 d, including tax. These rooms are just a few steps from the sea, Lol Ha Restaurant, and all the other facilities of Akumal.

Villas Flamingo, four smashing new villas built on Half Moon Bay (the next bay north and close enough to Akumal for guests to enjoy its restaurants and other facilities) offers luxury living: an ocean view and tasteful furnishing lend a tropical ambience; each villa has an enormous living room, fully equipped kitchen, dining room, upstairs bedroom, large terrace with barbecue grill, daily maid service, laundry facilities, a/c, and a swimming pool shared by the four individual villas. Prices begin around US$105 up to US$300, depending on size of villa, number of people, and season. For reservations and information on all of Club Akumal's facilities, including dive packages with a room and some meals, contact Akutrame Inc., P.O. Box 13326, El Paso, TX 79913, tel. in Texas (915) 584-3552, outside of Texas toll-free (800) 351-1622; from Canada call toll-free (800) 343-1440.

Las Casitas Akumal, at the north end of the beach with the bay at your front door, has airy, furnished condominiums with two bedrooms, two baths, living room, kitchen, and patio; daily maid service included. Walking distance to restaurants, grocery store, snack stand, dive shop, sandy beach, and beach bar. Up to five persons, US$150 plus tax; for reservations and information write: 6900 Skillman #201, Dallas TX, 75231, tel. in Texas (214) 553-1552, in Mexico tel. 4-10-45/4-16-89. **Hotel Akumal Caribe** (also known as **Ina Yana Kin**), on the south end of the beach, is a two-story hotel. All rooms are simple but delightful, with private bath and terrace, plus bar, restaurant, swimming pool, fishing and diving arrangements, car rental office, disco, game room, and lounge with cable color TV. Rates are about US$80 d. Make reservations through your travel agent or write: Hotel Akumal Caribe, Av. Bonampak and Coba, suites Atlantis, local 10, Cancun, Quintana Roo, Mexico 77500.

Just around the bend from Half Moon Bay (going north) **Quinta del Mar,** another lovely villa, faces the sea and can accommodate over six people. Three bedrooms, $3^1/2$ baths, living room, dining room, fully equipped kitchen, red-tile floors, and lots of windows to bring in the luxuriant outdoors. Terraces on both floors have stunning views of the Caribbean. Though having transportation is much more convenient, Quinta del Mar is within walking distance (one km) from the dining rooms and activities of Akumal Beach. It's also a short walk to Yalku Lagoon and a swim in your own private aquarium. Weekly rates: summer US$1100, winter US$1400, holidays US$ 1600. For more information contact Arlene Pargot, 850 Washington Ave., Martensville, NJ 08836, tel. (908) 469-6932. This area is a residential park with building lots for sale.

OTHER PRACTICALITIES

Food

The largest of several restaurants in Akumal is **Zasil** open for breakfast, lunch, and dinner. On the north end of the beach next to Las Casitas, it's housed under an enormous traditional *palapa* roof with a garish obtrusive sign

*entrance to
Akumal resort*

that for a minute makes you forget you're in Paradise. Several times a week, a busload of tourists is brought in from cruise ships that anchor off Cozumel, Cancun, and Playa del Carmen—don't eat here then! Next to the dive shop on the beach **Lol Ha** serves the best food at Akumal. Open for breakfast and dinner, you can expect tasty food, especially wonderful fresh fish, and a friendly staff! Prices are not cheap (though much cheaper than Cancun), but the food is worth it. When you sit down for breakfast a basket of home-made sweet rolls is brought to your table immediately, and if you should happen to be here on Thanksgiving, the cook prepares a turkey dinner American-style (almost), and all gringos in the area come and party well into the night, using the pilgrims as a good excuse. Adjacent to Lol Ha is a snack bar serving lunch from noon to 5:30 p.m. and **Pizzas Lol Ha** serves from 1-9 p.m. The beach bar is open for drinks from 11 a.m. to 11 p.m.; between 4 and 5 p.m., happy hour means half-price drinks. A smaller open-air restaurant at the south end of the beach is part of the **Ina Yana Kin Hotel** complex. The food is generally good, specializing in Mexican rather than Yucatecan entrees. Their Continental breakfast is served with a large platter of fresh tropical fruit.

Akumal is a family vacation spot, and to prove it kids can discover great ice cream cones at **El Bucanero Ice Cream Parlor.** Just before the main entrance/arch to Akumal resort, a small general/grocery store called **Super Chomak** sells a limited selection of groceries, cold drinks, liquor, beer, ice, sundries, fresh fruit, and vegetables. If you plan on staying at Akumal for any length of time and you're cooking, the store takes orders for chicken and meat. Attached to the store is a small fast-food window selling tacos and *tortas;* open from 7 a.m. till 9 p.m.

Entertainment

Usually you can find one disco that's open. During high season or any time there's an appreciative audience, music continues into the wee hours. More and more nighttime entertainment is springing up along the coast between Chetumal and Cancun though as yet it's comparatively tame. Without the bright glare of city lights, however, Mother Nature provides her nightly spectacular of stars, moon, and rippling water—far better than any Hollywood screen.

Shopping

Two gift shops, one next to Zasil and a larger one called **Mariselva Boutique** farther down the beach, sell a little of everything: typical Maya clothing, leather sandals, shawls, postcards, pottery, original Maya art and reproductions, black coral and silver jewelry, and a good selection of informative books (in English, French, and German) about the Peninsula and the Maya. Stamps are sold at the Villas Maya lobby, and mail is taken from there to the post office every day except weekends and holidays.

Dive Shops

Akumal's dive shops have excellent equipment for rent, and they offer a good selection for sale. Rental fees vary slightly between both shops. Contact the **Kapaalua Dive Shop** for advance dive information: Akutrame Inc., P.O. Box 13326, El Paso, TX 79913, tel. in Texas (915) 584-3552, outside of Texas, (800) 351-1622; from Canada call (800) 343-1440. Kapaalua is a PADI training facility. Rentals include kayaks and sailboards.

Services

Laundry service is available around the corner from Chomak Super—leave clothes before 9 a.m. for next-day pickup. The closest **bank** is 36 km north at Playa del Carmen. A convenient **gas station** is at the junction of Hwy. 307 and the Tulum ruins road, 24 km south. Stations are located in Playa del Carmen and Puerto Morelos. Remember the gas stations are just that, with no mechanics. However, there's a good **mechanic** in the village of Tulum on Hwy. 307. He doesn't have a sign but is easy to find (on the left side of the road going south) by the many cars parked under a large metal awning; prices are reasonable.

TRANSPORT

By Taxi

Taxis will bring you to Akumal from Cancun or from the ferry docks at Playa del Carmen. Arrange the price before you start. The average fare from Cancun to Akumal is around US$45 (up to four passengers, this price is now controlled by a taxi driver's union); from Playa del Carmen it's approximately half that.

By Car

Traveling by car is the most convenient way to get up and down the coast. From Cancun, it's an 80-km, one-hour drive south on Hwy. 307 to Akumal. From Merida take Hwy. 180 east to Cancun and turn south on 307 (both good two-lane highways), which passes the entrance road to Akumal. Car rentals are available in Cancun and Merida, or if you're using public transportation but want to explore some of the dirt roads and off-the-track beaches south of Akumal for only a day, car rentals are available at **Capitan Lafitte,**

Shangri-La Resorts, and **Puerto Aventuras,** resorts all fairly close to Akumal. Check with the manager for all details (rentals priced just about the same as those in Cancun). Highway 307 is good, and the side roads (though rough and potholed) are driveable.

Bus

Local buses frequently pass the Akumal turn-off, going both north and south throughout the day. Ask the driver to drop you off (it's not a regular stop); from there walk about one km toward the sea. The bus from Playa del Carmen to Tulum makes the trip several times each day. Ask the driver what time you must be on the highway to be picked up.

Hitchhiking

There's not a lot of traffic on the highway. If hitchhiking, it's best to start from one of the larger cities, Cancun or Merida, or from a small town along the highway, either Playa del Carmen or Puerto Morelos. As anywhere else, women shouldn't hitchhike alone.

AVENTURAS

This little beach entertains private guests: government-sponsored families from diverse locations on the Yucatan Peninsula. Here in a hostel-like recreation area, children play on a small palm-shaded beach, swim in shallow water, or romp in a playground of simple equipment. Visitors are free to use the beach close by, but please check at the office for permission to use the restrooms. No camping permitted.

AVENTURAS AKUMAL

A breathtaking bay of turquoise water lapping still another white sandy beach is practically next door to Akumal. It's a great walking beach, and not too far away there's a small Maya structure mostly hidden by jungle growth. However, this beach isn't occupied only by gulls and crabs; modern comfortable condos and a hotel with pools and bars are

perched along the water's edge. The condos are privately owned but can be rented from absentee owners.

Club Aventuras

This upscale Club-Med-type resort offers beautiful beach, swimming pool, daily events, movies, satellite TV, organized activities, a CEDAM dive center, windsurfing and sailing, lighted tennis courts, dive instruction, watersports including snorkeling, pedal boats, canoes, and kayaks. The all-inclusive price includes round-trip non-stop airfare from Dallas/Fort Worth International Airport, transfers between airport and hotel, hotel accommodations, all meals, domestic drinks, watersports, daily and nightly entertainment, introductory scuba diving course, and all gratuities at the hotel. Packages vary—three-, four-, and seven-night trips. Prices fluctuate depending on the time of year and room location, starting at US$449 pp, to $779 pp. For reservations and information contact your travel agent and ask for **Adventure Tours USA, Inc.,** Club Akumal Aventuras.

Don't expect to be able to just drop in and have an enchilada and a *cerveza* at one of their lovely dining rooms—unless you want to buy a "package." These packages include lunch, dinner, and a specific number of drinks, and are rather pricey. But, if driving by, do stop and take a look. Private condos are for rent and your choice ranges from studios to two bedrooms to full-blown villas. Rates start from US$75 per day in off season to US$225 in high season and on up; includes maid service. For more information write to Mike Mulgrew, Aventuras Akumal, Apto Postal 1341, Cancun, Quintana Roo, Mexico 77500.

CHEMUYIL

The poor-man's Akumal, Chemuyil (shem-oo-YEEL) is a tranquil beach with natural attributes of powder-fine sand, turquoise sea, and crowds of shady coconut palms. More crowded each year, the water is calm, thanks to the reef, and snorkeling and fishing attract many day visitors for a fee of about US$1 pp. The Romano family who run this beach resort also make a home for various wildlife. The newest additions are a young puma and two unusual white giant sea turtles. Former border, a jaguar named Daktari, grew very large and though of his surrogate mother Judy Romano, for tourist-security reasons he now makes his home at the Chetumal zoo.

The entrance fee is paid at the front gate after you turn off Hwy. 307 at the sign directing you to Chemuyil. Feel free to camp here among the trees for about US$3 pp; public restrooms and showers available. Pay fees and get information at the circular *palapa* refreshment stand near the entrance of the parking lot.

The "Chemuyil Special", devised by an international clientele and Eduardo on a rainy day at the bar, is a refreshing drink served in a coconut-shell bowl with straws. It has strong overtones of Kahlua but slips down as easily as a chocolate ice cream soda. *Warning!* It tends to sneak up on the unwary. No wonder this bar becomes a fiesta every night, and you really can dance on the bar! If on the next day you suspect a hangover, Eduardo can fix you up with a Mexican Alka Seltzer. First he brings out a "mystical" slice of the *zapote* tree and sets it on the counter. Then he puts a jigger on top of the wooden round. He pours tequila almost to the top, and finishes filling it with Squirt. Placing the wood round on top of the jigger he gives it three sound taps on the counter, upside down, then the bedeviled one gulps it quickly. Actually, the ceremony is worth the time, as long as it's *someone else* taking the cure!

Eduardo bartending at the open bar on the beach of Chemuyil

Accommodations And Food

The stand serves small packaged sweets, donuts, coffee, juice, and bananas plus beer, tequila, and fresh seafood, including lobster if the traps have lured a captive. They serve a large seafood platter which includes a healthy serving of all seafood delicacies in season like fish, shrimp, lobster, and crab, enough for five to eight people, for about US$87. People come year after year for this blue-plate special.

Although the barkeep does his best to control the cannibal flies that hover around the refreshment stand, if you're going to eat, sit at one of the colorful umbrella tables on the beach; the breeze helps a little. For US$10 each, there are 12 screened *palapa* rooms. Hammocks rent for about US$2 and the huts are well supplied with hammock hooks; there doesn't seem to be a limit to the number of people you are permitted to squeeze in. The concierge claims a record of 15!

Chemuyil can get crowded during the busy winter season. Day trippers from Cancun drive their rental cars to this beach, but only occasionally does it appear to be overcrowded with overnighters. Camp on the south end of the beach to avoid the day trippers. Trailers can park in the parking lot for about US$7 per night—no hookups, but use of showers and bathrooms is included in parking fee.

Anyone can be a successful fisherman in this bay; it takes little more than throwing a baited hook into the surf five or six meters off the beach. If you want to fish for something special, make arrangements with Eduardo or his son Danny to take you in a launch farther out to sea—the hunting grounds of great red snapper. Other trips can be arranged, including snorkeling or a short jungle trek to a nearby site of Maya ruins.

XCACEL

The beaches just keep coming, one right after the other—and all beautiful! Though this coast really hasn't been discovered by most of the world, some have found it and keep returning year after year. You can count on meeting some fascinating people: day trippers from Cancun, people in camper vans, on cycles, and some on foot. A few pack everything they can in campers and RVs and spend an entire exotic winter among Xcacel's (sha-SELL) palms for very little a month. For one night, a fee of about US$2 pp provides a clean shower and toilet but no hookups or electricity and often the space gets crowded fast. For about US$1.50, day trippers can use the beach, showers, and restrooms. The small restaurant here has gotten pricey, and is open only from noon-4 p.m. A hamburger is about US$6; fish is less. On certain days groups from cruise ships anchored in Playa del Carmen or

beautiful Xcacel beach

Cancun are bused to Xcacel for lunch at this little restaurant and the whole place gets a bit congested. If you're cooking your own meals, bring plenty of food and water; it's a long trek to the local Safeway.

Surf And Sand

The sea directly in front of the campgrounds can be rough, but only a few hundred meters north the reef shields large waves, producing calm water again—great swimming, fishing, snorkeling, and scuba diving on the reef. When beachcombing, wear shoes along this strip of beach to protect your feet from sharp little bits of coral crunched up in the sand. This is a good place to find shells, especially in front of the campgrounds after a storm. All manner of treasure can be found, from masses of dead coral (all white, now) to sea urchin

shells, keyhole limpets, maybe even a hermit crab carrying an ungainly shell on his back.

Hiking

If you're a hiker or birdwatcher, take the old dirt road which runs parallel to the shoreline from Chemuyil to Xelha, about five km in all. The road edges an old coconut grove now thick with jungle vegetation. Just after dawn, early birds are out in force looking for the proverbial worm or anything else that looks tasty. If at first you don't see them, you'll surely hear them. Look for small colorful parrots or brilliant yellow orioles; you may even see a long-tailed motmot. If you decide to hike to the mouth of Xelha National Park, bring your snorkeling gear, especially if you get there early before all the tour buses. Don't forget sunscreen and bug repellent.

XELHA

Xelha (shell-HAAH), a national park on Yucatan's east coast, is just five km south of Akumal. Xelha's lagoon consists of fresh and saltwater inhabited by rare and colorful tropical fish. Through small openings from the sea, a multi-fingered aquarium has developed through the centuries, providing a safe harbor for such exotic underwater life as the brightly hued parrotfish. As a national park, the lagoon is protected from fishing, thereby preserving these beautiful creatures for all to see. Xelha gets unbelievably crowded at certain hours when tour buses bring passengers from cruise ships docked at Cancun, Cozumel, and Playa del Carmen. Come early to avoid the crowds; Xelha is open from 8 a.m. to 5 p.m. and admission is about US$1. **Note:** do not wear tanning lotions or oils before jumping into the lagoon. These potions are hard on fish and other marinelife.

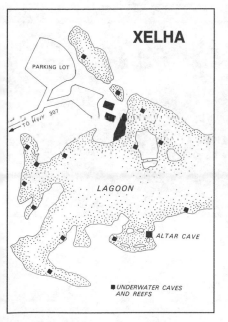

SIGHTS

Museum
The small maritime museum formerly at Xelha has moved to Puerto Aventuras north of Xelha and is open 8 a.m. to 5 p.m.

Snorkeling
You can stroll around the lagoon and see the bottom through incredibly clear water. Snorkeling is allowed in marked areas, and equipment is available to rent for about US$5 per day (and a wait in a long line after the tour buses arrive). In one of many underwater caverns that punctuate the lagoon's coast, you'll see the remains of a decaying Maya temple altar. There's little to authenticate its origins, but it is believed to have been located on the now-submerged shoreline. Little islands, narrow waterways, and underwater passages are marvelous to snorkel in amidst beautiful coral formations and a variety of warm-water fish.

Other Activities
The lagoon is surrounded by tropical vegetation and paths that wander around the ten square acres of water. Small platforms over the rocky limestone shore provide a perfect place for the non-swimmer to study the fish and sea creatures below. There are no shallow wading areas along the lagoon edge, but you'll find frequent platforms with steps to climb in and out of the marked areas where swimming and snorkeling are permitted. It's tempting and fun to feed the fish, which is okay as long as you give them the nutritious prepared food sold in plastic bags at the entrance under the large arch. Please do not throw your lunch leftovers into the water! The well-fed fish often ignore them and since the incoming and outgoing water moves slowly from the sea, the lagoon quickly becomes polluted.

Practicalities

Xelha has a cafe open during the day for lunch, snacks, and drinks. Lovers of coconut milk can buy the whole nut from a straw-hatted vendor who deftly swings his machete, preparing the fruit to order (straws included) under the cooling shadows of a palm tree. Not too many years ago, coconut milk was the only refreshment available. Outside the entrance to Xelha, large shops offer a variety of Yucatecan crafts, clothing, leather goods, locally carved black coral, postcards, and other arts and crafts.

Ruinas De La Xelha

Across the highway and about 200 meters south of Xelha lies a small group of ruins. Be prepared for a bit of a stroll from where you park your car. The structures are mostly unimpressive except for the **Templo de Pajaros** (Temple of the Birds). Protected under a *palapa* roof, one wall still shows remnants of paintings and it's possible to make out the tails and outlines of the original art depicting birds and Chac (the Maya rain god). To get up close you have to climb out onto a small platform, but from there you have an excellent view. Other buildings to see are the **Mercado** and **Temple of the Jaguar.** A young boy is always available to guide you around; certainly worth a dollar or so.

Along a dirt path farther into the jungle you'll find an enchanting *cenote* surrounded by trees covered with bromeliads, orchids, and ferns. Dozens of swallows put on a graceful ballet, swooping and gliding low over the water, stealing a small sip each time. Thick jungle and vines surround the crystal clear water and it's a perfect place for a swim. Do wear a swimsuit—it's offensive to the Mexicans to have you skinny-dipping in their country—in fact it's against the law; some Mexican police will throw you in the slammer if they catch you. And although nudity on the beach is more common now then ever before, you still run a risk of being penalized.

Xelha Lagoon

TULUM RUINS

Five km south of Akumal on Hwy. 307, a side road leads to Tulum, the largest fortified Maya site on the Quintana Roo coast. Tulum, meaning "Wall" in Maya, is quite small (the area enclosed by the wall measures 380 by 165 meters). It has 60 well-preserved structures that reveal the stylized Toltec influence and an impressive history. The sturdy stone wall was built three- to five-meters high, with an average thickness of seven meters. Originally this site was called Zama ("Sunrise"). Appropriately, the sun rises directly out of the ocean over Tulum, which is perched on a cliff 12 meters above the sea. The first view of this noble, then-brightly colored fortress impressed the Spaniards in Juan de Grijalva's expedition as they sailed past the Quintana Roo coast in 1518. This was their first encounter with the Indians on this new continent, and according to ships' logs, the image was awe-inspiring. One notable comment in the log of the Grijalva expedition mentions seeing "a village so large, that Seville would not have appeared larger or better."

HISTORY

Tulum was part of a series of coastal forts, towns, watchtowers, and shrines established along the coast as far south as Chetumal and north past Cancun. Archaeologists place the beginnings of Tulum in the Post Classic Period after the Maya civilization had already passed its peak, somewhere between A.D. 700-1000. Although a stela dated A.D. 564 was found at Tulum, investigators are certain it was moved there from some other place long after it had been carved and date figures cut into it then. The structures reveal a strong Toltec influence, such as flat roofs, plumed serpents, columns, and even pottery shapes that have definitely been established as Toltec.

Talking Cross

From 1850, Tulum was a part of the Chan Santa Cruz Indians' "talking cross cult." The Spanish had taught the Indians Catholic rituals, many reminiscent of Maya ceremonies; even the cross reminded them of their tree of life. In fact for centuries the gods had been speaking to their priests through idols. In order to manipulate the Indians, a clever revolutionary half-caste, Jose Maria Barrera, used an Indian ventriloquist, Manuel Nahuat, to speak through the cross. They began three years after the end of the Caste War at a cross in a forest shrine near what is now known as Felipe Carillo Puerto but was then

TULUM

1. building 34
2. *cenote* (well of sacrifice)
3. adoratorios (altars)
4. structure 45
5. building 24
6. platforms
7. building 20
8. inner courtyard
9. Temple of the Diving God
10. Temple of the Frescoes
11. building 13
12. Temple of the Initial Series
13. structure 54

called Chan. A voice from the cross urged the Indians to take up arms against the Mexicans once again. Bewildered, impressed, and never doubting, they accepted the curious occurrence almost immediately. The original cross was replaced with three crosses that continued to "instruct" the simple Indians from the holy, highly guarded site. This political-religious cult grew quickly and ruled Quintana Roo efficiently. The well-armed, jungle-wise Chan Santa Cruz Indians (also called Cruzob) successfully kept the Mexican government out of the territory for 50 years. Even the British government in British Honduras (now known as Belize) treated this cult with respect, more out of fear of their power than out of diplomacy, and because they needed the timber trade. Around 1895 the Indians requested that the Territory of Quintana Roo be annexed by British Honduras, but the Mexican government flatly refused and sent in a new expeditionary force to try once again to reclaim Quintana Roo.

The Mexican army was doomed from the outset. They fought not only armed and elusive Indians but constant attacks of malaria and the jungle itself. The small army managed to fight its way into the capital of Chan Santa Cruz, where they were virtually trapped for a year. The standoff continued until the Mexican Revolution in 1911, when President Porfirio Diaz resigned.

Four years later the Mexican army gave up, the capital was returned to the Indians, and they continued to rule as an independent state, an embarrassment and ever-present thorn in the side of the broadening Mexican Republic. This small, determined group of Indians from another time zone managed to keep their independence and culture intact while the rest of the world proceeded to the 20th century. But life in the jungle is tough on everyone. With famine, malaria, and 90 years of fighting (and beating) the Mexican army, the Chan Santa Cruz Indians' population was reduced to 10,000. Weary, in 1935 they decided to quit the fight and were accorded the recognition given to a respected adversary. When their elderly leaders signed a peace treaty, *most* of the Chan Santa Cruz Indians agreed to *allow* Mexico to rule them.

Into The Twentieth Century

One of the few pure Chan Indian villages left in 1935 was Tulum, and today many residents are descendants of these independent people. Even after signing the treaty, the Indians still maintained control of the area and outsiders were highly discouraged from traveling through. A skeleton imbedded in the cement at the base of one of the temples at Tulum is the remains of an uninvited archaeologist, as a warning to other would-be intruders.

All of this has changed. With foresight, the Mexican government in the '60s recognized the beautiful Quintana Roo coast as a potential tourist draw, and the new state entered the 20th century. The advent of roads and airports has paved the way for the rest of the world to visit the unique ruins of Tulum. Workmen have been modernizing and enlarging the Tulum airstrip and the *unverifiable* rumor is it will be a new international airport to relieve the pressure on Cancun. The indigenous people welcome the tourist and what he represents, at least for now.

The once-thick stands of coconut trees along this part of the coast were part of an immense coconut plantation that included Akumal and Xelha and was owned by a gentleman named Don Pablo Bush. Bush initiated the CEDAM organization made up of a group of daring archaeological divers. Bush and CEDAM donated Xelha Lagoon to the government for use as a national park. CEDAM stands for Conservation, Education, Diving, Archaeology, and Museums.

SIGHTS

Tulum Structures

Tulum is made up of mostly small ornate structures with stuccoed gargoyle faces carved onto the corners of buildings. In the **Temple of Frescoes,** looking through a metal grate you'll see a fresco that still bears a trace of color from the ancient artist. Archaeologically, this is the most interesting building on the site. The original parts of the building were constructed around 1450 during the late Post-Classic Period. And as is the case with so many of the Maya structures, it was added to over the years.

Diving God

Across the compound a small *palapa* roof protects a carved descending god. This winged creature is pictured upside down, and has been described as the God of the Setting Sun by some historians. Others interpret the carving as representing the bee; honey is a commodity almost as revered on the Peninsula as maize. Because so little is known about the glyphs of the Maya, it may be many years before this and other questions can be fully answered and understood, if ever.

El Castillo

The most impressive site is the large pyramid which stands on the edge of the cliff overlooking the sea. The building, in the center of the wall on the east side, was built in three different phases. A wide staircase leads to a two-chamber temple on the top. Two serpent columns divide the entrance and above the middle entrance is another carved figure of the Diving God. The climb to the top rewards

El Castillo sits just above the Caribbean coast.

Small stalls across from Tulum archaeological site sell souvenirs and snacks.

you with a breathtaking bird's-eye view of the ocean, the surrounding jungle with an occasional stone ruin poking through the tight brush, and scattered clearings where small farms are beginning to grow. Until the 1920s the followers of the "talking cross" cult kept three crosses in a shrine in this pyramid. It was only after the curious, as well as respectable archaeologists, showed an active interest in obtaining the crosses that the Maya priests moved the Tulum crosses to X-Cacal Guardia, where they supposedly remain today, still under the watchful protection of the Maya priesthood.

Tulum's archaeological zone is open daily from 8 a.m.-5 p.m. At 8 a.m. few tour buses have arrived yet, making the cooler early hours a desirable time to explore and climb the aged structures. Opposite the main entrance to the site are a number of open stalls with typical tourist curios along with a growing number of small cafes selling soda pop and snacks. A small fee is paid across the street from the entrance to the ruins. Parking is available directly outside the Tulum site (if not filled with tour buses). On a recent visit, 29 tour buses were counted in front of Tulum. The fumes alone will surely destroy this marvelous old site if this kind of abuse continues.

Village Of Tulum

A few kilometers past the road to the Tulum archaeological zone on Hwy. 307 is the *pueblo* of Tulum. This small village (not surprisingly) has had a delayed reaction to all the tourists that come to their famous ruins down the road. The town has little to offer except a few simple markets, fruit stands, a couple of *loncherias,* and maybe most importantly a couple of mechanics. You'll spot one on the highway on the left side of the street just as you drive into town. There's no sign, but the large number of cars on the property is a dead giveaway. The owner and his son are good, cheap, and willing to help if they can. **Note**: When buying gas at the Tulum station, get out ot the car, make sure the gas pump gage reads "0," keep careful track of the amount, and count your change.

ACCOMMODATIONS AND FOOD

Only a few places to overnight are available in the immediate area of Tulum. Following the paved road from the parking lot along the coast you'll come to a series of unspoiled beaches edged by what remains of once-thick stands of coconut trees. Between Tulum and Punta Allen there are only simple cabanas on the beach. Many don't have public power and depend on gas lanterns or small generators for part of the day; most have a good supply of cold water and some sell bottled water, but if not, boil your drinking supply. Expect spartan accommodations all in the budget class. Remember that when you choose budget lodgings what was funky but clean one month may be a dirty dive the next month. Look at the rooms carefully—do you see fleas on the floor? If linens are furnished, check them out to make sure they're clean as well, the bathrooms and shower rooms ditto. Is there electricity? gas lanterns? candles? Make sure that you get what you expect or are led to expect. If you require deluxe rooms, your best bet is to headquarter at Akumal, 25 km north. The beach camps along the coast are open to RV parking, though most don't have hookups; ask the manager if in doubt.

Camping

Two combination cabana/campgrounds side by side are on the beach immediately south of the Tulum ruins. Follow the paved road going from the parking lot (about a 12-minute walk). The cabins are tiny. Bring everything— hammock, drinking water, bug repellent, mosquito netting, food (Tulum village has a few markets and small cafes where you can find inexpensive meals). If you're camping it helps to have a tent; when the wind blows it gets mighty gritty on this beach. The fees are minimal, about US$2 pp.

Budget

El Crucero Motel is conveniently located at the crossroads of Hwy. 307 and the Tulum ruins entrance road. It's a 10-minute walk to the ruins, and several restaurants are close. The rooms are plain, *usually* clean, and rates are about US$10 d. A guest recently reported the rooms "dirty and with bugs," but one month before another reader reported the rooms *adequate. Caveat emptor!* A few kilometers south of the parking lot, Cabanas Don Armandos offers 30 very simple cabanas with one bed and room for a hammock (mosquito netting a must!), communal toilet and showers, cold water, candles, sheets, and bottled water supplied. A great restaurant bar, Zasil Kin, serves good food, open from 7 a.m. to 9:30 p.m. This is a family-run operation; ask for the special of the day, it's usually delicious. Cabanas rent for about US$11 for two, camping available on the beach for US$3 pp. A little difficult to find, look for the sign Zasil Kin a few kilometers past the ruins on the bumpy road, officially called Boca Paila Road.

Another small group of 15 cabanas built in the spring of 1989 and called **Nohoch Tunich** is very spartan, but on a beautiful piece of the Caribbean coast. Expect tiny rooms, simple communal toilets, cold-water showers, and a small cantina serving cold drinks and simple meals. Very pleasant managers/owners. Rates for two are US$11 year-round.

Osho (formerly Cabanas Chac Mool) is at the end of the paved road leading south from the Tulum parking lot. You'll find clean cabanas with hanging double beds and mosquito netting, screenless shutters that open up to the outdoors, community bathrooms and hot-water showers, a dining room that serves good all-you-can-eat vegetarian buffets at each meal (US$18 daily), and a meditation room overlooking a beautiful bay. About US$36. **Cabanas Arrecife** is reasonably modern, stucco built, very clean, with well-kept grounds and (usually) an abundant water supply (boil your drinking water or use bottled), about US$15. Another camp, **Cabanas Tulum,** includes small cabanas with beds, bathrooms, ceiling fans, and cold water. Rates US$22. Check it out for cleanliness! There's a restaurant on the premises and a white beach that now hosts topless visitors.

Ana y Jose is another beach resort built in the summer of 1989 and looks to be developing into a very nice group of cabanas, all with private tile bathrooms, hot water, and double beds. All-stone construction and red-tile roofs with pleasant little touches like hanging plants makes it a cut above many of the cabanas along here. A colorful *palapa* restaurant overlooking the sea serves three meals a day. Cabana rates during off-season are US$25 and during high season US$30-35. For more information contact Bill Kerns, tel. (702) 348-9368, fax (702) 348-0646. Located at Carr Boca Paila, km 7, Tulum.

Cafes

Several readers have sent us troubling reports of Tulum's **Restaurant El Faisan Y Venado**— overcharging and rudeness—so try it at your own risk. This is deer country, but don't be fooled by the name of the cafe: the government has cracked down on serving the over-hunted *venado* ("deer"). Across from the gas station is a restaurant called **Alexandros.**

Formerly vegetarian, the food is okay and fairly reasonable, and the place is *usually* clean. The **Crucero Motel Cafe** serves reasonably priced simple food. A few fast-food stands at the **bazaar** across from the entrance to the ruins serve tacos, *tortas,* combination plates, and cold beer and soda. For more deluxe meals try the restaurants at Akumal (**Lol Ha** is good) or Puerto Aventuras about 20 and 25 km north of Tulum.

TRANSPORT

Getting There

The best way to get around on Hwy. 307 is by car. However, public buses going north and south stop at El Crucero Motel about every one to two hours from 6:30 a.m.-8:30 p.m. From here you can also catch a bus to Valladolid which passes Coba at 6 a.m. and noon; the return bus leaves Coba at 6 a.m. and 4 p.m. Both 1st- and 2nd-class buses are usually crowded by the time they reach Tulum; 1st-class allows no standing. Be there in plenty of time, the buses don't wait. It's always a good idea to check with the bus driver about destination, times, and return trips.

This is a busy place, so it's not difficult to hitch a ride. Be practical and wait where a driver can pull off the road easily.

SOUTHERN QUINTANA ROO COAST
FROM MUYIL TO CHETUMAL

MUYIL: ANCIENT MAYA SEAPORT OF SIAN KA'AN

One of the larger Maya sites within the Sian Ka'an Reserve is Muyil, also known as Chunyaxche. Situated on the edge of the karstic limestone shelf about 25 km south of Tulum, it has been the recent subject of a study conducted by Tulane University and the Quintana Roo Regional Center of INAH. Along with mapping the site to determine its size and settlement pattern, graduate students from Tulane and men from the village of Chumpon have been excavating for ceramics in order to provide dates of occupation as well as learning the use of the seaport at Muyil.

The potsherds dug up at the area indicate that Muyil was settled about 1 A.D. and occupied continuously until the Spanish conquest began. The author of the report, Archaeolo-

gist Elia del Carmen Trejo, notes that since no Spanish ceramics have been identified and because there is no mention of a settlement at Muyil in books from the period, he suspects that the population of Muyil perished in the forty years following the conquest. Many fascinating tidbits of information have been discovered. A large *sacbe* (roadway) at Muyil runs at least .5 km from the site-center to near the edge of the Muyil Lagoon. The upper (western) half of the road runs through mangrove swamp. There are six structures spaced along the roadway approximately every 120 meters. They range in size from small two-meter-high platforms to the large *castillo,* one of the tallest structures on the east coast. All but the westernmost of the

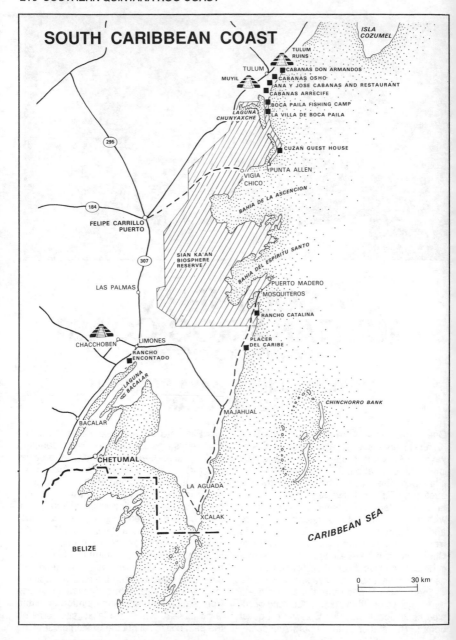

SOUTH CARIBBEAN COAST

ISLA COZUMEL

TULUM RUINS
TULUM
MUYIL
CABANAS DON ARMANDOS
CABANAS OSHO
ANA Y JOSE CABANAS AND RESTAURANT
CABANAS ARRECIFE
BOCA PAILA FISHING CAMP
LA VILLA DE BOCA PAILA
LAGUNA CHUNYAXCHE

CUZAN GUEST HOUSE

PUNTA ALLEN
VIGIA CHICO

BAHIA DE LA ASCENCION

FELIPE CARRILLO PUERTO

SIAN KA'AN BIOSPHERE RESERVE

BAHIA DEL ESPIRITU SANTO

PUERTO MADERO
MOSQUITEROS

LAS PALMAS

RANCHO CATALINA

CHACCHOBEN
LIMONES
RANCHO ENCONTADO

PLACER DEL CARIBE

CHINCHORRO BANK

LAGUNA BACALAR

BACALAR

MAJAHUAL

CHETUMAL

LA AGUADA

XCALAK

BELIZE

CARIBBEAN SEA

0   30 km

structures faces westward, away from the lagoon. They have center stairways facing westward to the roadway running to the west. The Maya always used directional precision that dealt with their beliefs involving the sun and Venus. The sections of roadway between each structure begin on center at the foot of each stairway, but when they arrive at the next structure to the west, they connect with it at the northeast corner, not on the centerline. It is as though one were always meant to pass these structures along their north side; as yet no one knows why.

The *castillo,* located in the midpoint of the *sacbe* stands 21 meters above the water levels of the lagoon. At the summit is a solid round masonry turret, which is up till now unique on ancient Maya structures. From the summit it's possible to see the Caribbean.

Locals report that Juan Vega (the alleged "white king of the Maya") operated a chicle business at Muyil in the early 1900s. During the height of the post-caste war conflict, Juan Vega was kidnapped by the Maya Indians as a young child. His entire family and young companions were put to death, but because he was carrying religious books and could read he was allowed to live. The Maya had a curious acceptance of the Christian religioun. Because of certain similarities they managed to weave it into their own beliefs and would often listen with conviction to the advice of Juan Vega given from hio books.

Although Vega was a captive of these people, he was given tremendous respect and spent his entire life in the village, marrying a Maya and raising a family of mestizos in the village of Chumpon. Chumpon is referred to by knowledgeable outsiders as the jungle vatican. Vega saved the lives of many Mexican soldiers that were captured and doomed by the Maya until he stepped in and read to them the laws of the Christian God from his worn books. In 1961, Quintana Roo was still a no man's land with no roads, and only through a fated fluke Vega was described to Paul Bush by a relative from the village of Chumpon who feared the man was dying of an illness.

Fortunately, Paul Bush, a compassionate man, acted quickly. With the help of the relative and the use of a small plane (to spot the hidden jungle village) and a helicopter (by foot it was a three-day expedition into the village) Juan Vega was rescued, but only after he asked the chief's permission to leave. The man was very ill, but after surgery and a long stay in a Mexico City hospital, he was once again fit. While in the hospital the newspapers gave an account of Vega and his past. This brought an old soldier to visit Juan Vega, one that lived because of the intervention of the "white Maya king." Vega had one request in Mexico, to visit *Abuelitos* (the virgin of Guadaloupe). When able, he made his pilgrimage to the shrine and then returned to his village and family in Chumpon.

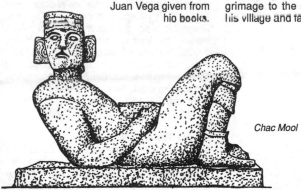

Chac Mool

ROAD TO PUNTA ALLEN

If you're driving south to Punta Allen on the Boca Paila Rd. (south from the Tulum parking lots and parallel to the coast), fill your gas tank at the Tulum crossroads gas station since there's not another on the coastal road to Punta Allen (57 km). (Traveling north on Hwy. 307, the next gas station is in Playa del Carmen. Traveling south to Chetumal on 307, there's one in Felipe Carillo Puerto). After leaving Hwy. 307 from Tulum on Boca Paila Rd., the road to Punta Allen appears to be paved and smooth—fooling the uninformed!

The road is only smooth for about six km beyond the ruins, and then it becomes potholed, ridged, and rugged. Though it's slow going, bumpy, and uncomfortable, all vehicles can handle this all-weather road.

TULUM TO PUNTA ALLEN

Boca Paila Fishing Lodge

This pricey small resort caters to fishermen looking for excellent saltwater fly-fishing for bone fish. It offers seven bungalows, food, and excellent service. In some cases clients are flown in from Cozumel or Cancun; weekly price includes six days of fishing, accommodations, food, boat, and shared guide. Prices begin at US$1825 double occupancy, less for non-fishing spouses. Daily price is about US$300 double occupancy. Call in the U.S. (800) 245-1950, (412) 935-1577, or write Frontiers, Box 161, Pearce Mill Rd., Wexford, PA 15090.

Casa Blanca Lodge

Another great fishing lodge is located on Ascension Bay. Again this is a small resort for the fisherman (and a non-fishing wife) with room for 14 guests. The attractive lodge is located on a palm-covered point just 100 feet from the edge of the blue Caribbean. The modern comfortable rooms are spacious and an open-air *palapa* is a bar/gathering spot where the evening is spent telling tall fishing stories. Weekly rates begin at US$2195 pp, double occupancy, accommodation, food, boat, fuel, shared guide, fishing license, and 15% government tax. For further information contact Frontiers, Box 959, Pearce Mill Rd., Wexford, PA 15090, tel. (800) 245-1950, (412) 935-1577, fax (412) 935-5388.

Across The Bridge

Another 10 km beyond La Villa de Boca Paila is the Boca Paila Bridge. The new wooden bridge crosses the canal connecting the lagoons with the Caribbean. This exotic spot, crowded with tropical vegetation and coconut trees, offers stretches of lonely beach north and south of the mouth of the lagoon. The water, though warm and inviting, is not clear enough for snorkeling or diving. The beach is open to campers. Be sure to bring all necessities, including food and water.

Continuing on the road, south of the bridge is **El Rancho Retiro,** a wonderful beach on a picturesque bay, it reminds one of a Tahitian island before the tourists discovered it. Behind the closed cabanas the explorer will find a lagoon called **Laguna Chunyaxe,** a stopover for migrant birds, including flamingos, herons, egrets, and many others. This area is all part of the **Sian Ka'an Reserve,** where there are over 300 species of birds living close by. **Bird Island,** a small island in the lagoon, hosts two species of crocodiles and is a great place to explore and observe wildlife. Ask at the restaurant (when open) if there's a guide available to take you to see a Maya ruin called **Chunyaxe.**

This is exciting country. Families of the area have lived here for many years. Most are fishermen and some will provide boat outings upon request. The setting is lovely, right on the edge of the bay where dolphins come to frolic every autumn. Visitors tell of petting the lovely creatures in the shallow water. It's necessary to travel about a km around the bay for the best swimming spot. You will see cabanas scattered about, but at last report they were closed. However, if you're interested, check at the restaurant.

Exploring Ancient Caves
If you're traveling with a small boat (rubber raft is best), narrow canals said to be built by the Maya curve inland to remnants of isolated ceremonial centers—all small and none restored or even excavated. This is a trip for intrepid adventurers with sturdy muscles; in some spots the channel narrows, and you have to carry your boat overland or wade through muddy swamps. Caves are scattered about—some you can swim into, others are hidden in the countryside; glyphs still intact on the inside walls suggest the Indians may have lived in them. A guide familiar with the area is suggested. Bring a flashlight, bug repellent, sunscreen, hat, and walking shoes that will survive in the water.

For the hardy type with lots of time, walking the 347 km from Puerto Morelos to Chetumal or Punta Allen can be high adventure. Taking at least three or four weeks (or longer if you take time to smell the flowers), this trip is only for the fit. While the main highway (307) is the most direct route to Chetumal, it often veers away from the beach and is oftentimes boring and flat with little to see except cars. Trekking to Punta Allen, Boca Paila Rd. sometimes disappears behind sand dunes, but it's never that long a trudge to dozens of fine beaches where you might be seduced into staying a day or a month—or forever.

In most cases there's no place to stay except the beach, where there are lots of coconut trees on which to sling your hammock—a tropical paradise. The Maya believe the hammock is a gift from the gods, but be sure to have mosquito netting with you for your

El Rancho Retiro has the look of early Tahiti.

nights under the stars. Simple cabana resorts are springing up as Cancun continues to spread southward down the Quintana Roo coast, but be prepared for long stretches on this dirt road with nothing but vacant beach and small ranchitos.

Restaurants are also sparse on this stretch of road until you reach Punta Allen; come prepared with your own victuals and water. Once you reach Punta Allen you either have to hoof it back or make arrangements with a villager for a ride.

PUNTA ALLEN

Punta Allen, part of the Sian Ka'an Reserve, is a small fishing village on a finger of land that overlooks a large bay called Bahia de la Ascencion. In the last century, ships would occasionally drift off course onto the dangerous reef that stands just off the coast. Maya boatmen, however, expertly navigate in and out of the submerged reefs and shallow spots that lie hidden across the mouth of the bay.

Considered the hottest lobster grounds in Mexico, wildlife groups in association with the local lobster cooperative and the Mexican equivalent of the National Science Foundation, are studying the way the Yucatecan fishermen handle the spiny crustaceans. The villagers don't use lobster traps as we know them but instead create artificial habitats. The lobsters grow within these habitats, and when they reach a predetermined size, the fishermen graff them by hand. For centuries the Maya built habitats from the spine of a particular palm tree which is becoming extinct from overuse. Fishermen within the Sian Ka'an reserve have been urged to use alternative materials. One style of habitat was built from a slab of concrete which is placed on wooden skis to lift it off the ground, giving space for the lobster to live in a shady environment. These were not as successful as was hoped and the search for alternate methods must continue.

Scientists (with manpower provided by organizations of volunteers such as Earth Watch) have been tagging and mapping the growth areas each summer since 1982 to decide if this concentration of lobsters leads to over-harvesting, or if protecting the habitat reduces the natural mortality rate of the open sea. Once they make their determinations perhaps they will be able to help preserve the lobster industry from being wiped out in

Punta Allen as it has been in other once-rich lobster-growing areas. Over-harvesting the lobster has depleted the spiny delicacy in several areas in the Gulf of Mexico and in Baja's Todos Los Santos Bay.

Sights

Along the way to Punta Allen you'll discover several beaches with white sand surrounded by thick jungle. The village itself is small and typical but not glamorous. Snorkeling, swimming, and fishing are good on some of the offshore islands. Walks will introduce you to unusual birds and maybe even a shy animal. Marshy areas close by are good for observing the nesting grounds and natural habitats of nearly 300 classes of birds identified by ornithologists.

Practicalities

All beaches are free to campers; certainly the polite way is to ask permission of the local villager whose house you'll be in front of before setting up camp. Dispose of your trash and leave the beach clean. RVs can park on the beach—there are no facilities. Swimming here is not the best, but the fishing is great!

Accommodations

Few accommodations are available at Punta Allen. For a long time the only place was **Cuzan Guest House,** a group of basic *palapa* cabanas, some shaped like tepees. Earth Watch Expeditions stay here. If you need all the modern conveniences of the States, *don't* come to Punta Allen. However, if you're interested in learning about the culture of a Maya fishing village, and your tastes run to low-key adventure, sleeping in primitive cabanas in hammocks (a few beds are available), community bathrooms (two only), simple food that is mostly from the sea—lobster is served frequently during the lobster season (15 July through 15 March)—then this is the place for you! Arrangements can be made with Armando—if he's not fishing—to take you motoring in his fishing launch to the reef, where snorkeling is outstanding. Another popular outing is a trip to **Cayo Colebre,** a small uninhabited island off the coast, where in spring you'll see hundreds of man-o-war frigates hanging like kites overhead, displaying the brilliant red mating pouches under their beaks to attract females. Fishing off Colebre, as well as several other uninhabited islands close by, is excellent. Ask about two-night Robinson Crusoe trips. Rooms at Cuzan Guest House begin at US$20. Breakfast and lunch are US$5 each, dinner US$12. Remember, this is a fisherman's house and not a resort! If you have any questions write to Sonia Lilvik, Apto Postal 703, Cancun, Quintana Roo, Mexico 77500. Allow a couple of months for return mail.

Another small resort, **Let It Be**, near the sea and **Lighthouse Yachtclub**, is under construction and slated to be open by the time you have this book in your hands. The owners are starting with eight to 12 cabanas with private bathrooms, shaded porch with hammocks, and a clubhouse that will include a restaurant and bar. A boat dock with gasoline and minimal boating supplies is also in the plans. At this stage of construction it looks as though rates will start at about US$30 d. Let It Be is located between the

town of Punta Allen and the lighthouse. All water sports are offered, including snorkeling, diving, and fishing. For reservations and information, write to **Let It Be**, Box 17, Felipe Carillo Puerto, Punta Allen, Quintana Roo 77200, Mexico.

Note: When going to Punta Allen, start out early in the morning to allow yourself enough time to get back in case it's not for you.

along the Placer coast

COBA

This early Maya site covers an immense area (50 square km) and hundreds of mounds are yet to be uncovered. Archaeologists are convinced that in time Coba will prove to be one of the largest Maya excavations on the Yucatan Peninsula. Only in recent years has the importance of Coba come to light. First explored in 1891 by Austrian archaeologist Teobert Maler, it was another 35 years before Coba was investigated by S. Morley, J. Eric Thompson, H. Pollock, and J. Charlot under the auspices of the Carnegie Institute. In 1972-75 the National Geographic Society in conjunction with the Mexican National Insti-

tute of Anthropology and History mapped and surveyed the entire area. A program funded by the Mexican government continues to explore and study Coba, but it is time-consuming, costly work, and it will be many years before completed.

Coba seems to be the favorite Maya ceremonial site of many independent travelers. The fact that the jungle hasn't been cleared away or all the mounds uncovered adds a feeling of discovery to the visit. For the visitor interested in exploring, it's important to know that the distances between groupings of structures are long (in some cases one to two km), and they're not located in a neatly kept park such as Chichen Itza. Each group of ruins is buried in the middle of thick jungle, so come prepared with comfortable shoes, bug repellent, sunscreen, and hat. A canteen of water never hurts.

Flora And Fauna

Coba in Maya means "Water Stirred by the Wind." Close to a group of shallow lakes (Coba, Macanxoc, Xkanha, and Zalcalpu), some very marshy areas attract a large variety of birds and butterflies. The jungle around Coba is perfect for viewing toucans, herons, egrets, and the motmot. Colorful butterflies are everywhere, including the large, deep-blue *morphidae* butterfly as well as the bright yellow-orange barred sulphur. If you look on the ground, you'll almost certainly see long lines of cutting ants. One double column carries freshly cut leaves to the burrow, and next

to that another double column marches in the opposite direction, empty jawed, returning for more. The columns can be longer than a kilometer, and usually the work party will all carry the same species of leaf or blossom until the plant is completely stripped. It's amazing how far they travel for food! The vegetation decays in their nests, and the mushrooms which grow on the compost are an important staple of the ants' diet. The determined creatures grow up to three cm long.

People

Thousands of people are believed to have lived here during the Classic Period. Though the numbers are drastically reduced, today pockets of people still maintain their archaic beliefs side by side with their Christian faith. They plant their corn with ceremony, conduct their family affairs in the same manner as their ancestors, and many villages still appoint a calendar-keeper to keep track of the auspicious days to direct them in their daily lives. This is most common in the Coba area because of its (up till now) isolation from outsiders, and because these people have maintained a very low profile when it comes to their ancient heritage.

THE RUINS

White Roads

The most important reason to visit Coba is to view the archaeological remains of a city begun in A.D. 600. These structures built near the lakes were scattered along a refined system of *sacbe* (roads). The remains of 40 *sacbe* have been found crisscrossing the entire Peninsula, but there are more here than in any other location. They pass through what were once outlying villages and converge at Coba, an indication it was the largest city of its era. One such *sacbe* is 100 km long and travels in an almost straight line from the base of Nohoch Mul (the great pyramid) to the town of Yaxuna. Each *sacbe* was built to stringent specifications: a base of stones one to two meters high, about 4.5 meters wide, and covered with white mortar. However, in Coba some ancient roads as wide as ten meters have been uncovered.

COBA
ARCHAEOLOGICAL
ZONE

TO NEVOXCAM
TO TULUM
CHACNE
PYRAMID   TO ZAC MUL
TO YAXUNA
TRAIL TO VALLADOLID
RUINS   NOHOCH MUL
HOTEL VILLA
ARQUEOLOGICA
PARKING & SHOPS
LAKE COBA
TO CHAN MUL
TICKET BOOTH
SWAMP
LAKE MACANXOC   STELA
MACANXOC
LAKE XKANHA   TEMPLE
UITZIL MUL   LAB MUL
GATEWAYS
ZACAKAL
KITAMNA   LAKE ZACALPUC
1 km
TO KUKIKAN
NUC MAL

a 12-story climb to the top of Coba's Nohoch Mul

of miles south in the Guatemalan lowlands) and the Classic Maya that lived in Coba. Both groups built lofty pyramids, much taller than those found in Chichen Itza, Uxmal, or elsewhere in the north part of the Peninsula.

Undiscovered

All along the paths are mounds overgrown with vines, trees, and flowers—many of these unexcavated ruins. More than 5,000 mounds wait for the money it takes to continue excavation. Thirty-two Classic-Period stelae (including 23 that are sculptured) have been found scattered throughout the Coba archaeological zone. For the most part they are displayed where they were discovered. One of the better preserved can be seen in front of the Nohoch Mul group. Still recognizable, it has a nobleman standing on the backs of two slaves and dated 780 in Maya glyphs.

PRACTICALITIES

Accommodations

There's one deluxe hotel in Coba, the **Villa Arqueologica,** part of a chain that has placed hotels at archaeological zones in several parts of Mexico, including Uxmal and Chichen Itza. Each hotel has a well-equipped library with many volumes containing histories of the area and the Maya people. Run by the owners of Club Med, it has *small* attractive rooms, a/c, shallow swimming pool, outdoor bar and dining, good *tipico* and French food, and a gift shop which carries quality reproductions of Maya art. Groups from Europe are bused in all year long; reservations could be important even though the hotel is often quiet. Rates are US$48, plus tax, meals extra; in the U.S. for reservations call (800) 528-3100.

A couple of other modest inns are located on what could be called the main street of Coba. **Restaurant Isabel** is no longer a restaurant, but you'll find a few simple *cabanitas* for under US$8 d; *very* spartan but clean, with electricity, two beds, and cold water only. **Bocadito's** cabins are a little more uptown—private bathroom, cold water, two beds, and a place for a hammock.

The Pyramids

While you wander through the grounds it helps to use the map. When you enter, follow the dirt road a few meters until you come to the sign that says Grupo Coba directing you to the right. A short distance on the path brings you to the second-highest pyramid at the site (22.5 meters), called **Iglesia.** After climbing many stone steps, from the top is a marvelous view of the surrounding jungle and Lake Macanxoc. Farther to the right (southeast on a jeep trail) is a smaller pyramid called **Conjunto Las Pinturas,** so named because of the stucco paintings that once lined the walls, minute traces of which can still be seen on the uppermost cornice of the temple. From the summit of this structure is a dizzying view of **Nohoch Mul,** tallest pyramid on the Peninsula (42 meters, a 12-story climb!). At the fork just beyond the Grupo Coba, a path to the left leads to that great temple. Watch for signs and stay on the trail.

Scientists conjecture there may be a connection between the Peten Maya (hundreds

Food And Gift Shops

Where three years ago there was nothing, tiny shops and outdoor cafes are springing up near the entrance to the Coba ruins. You'll find cool drinks and good snacks at **Restaurant Cinco Lagos** and **Restaurant Coba.** These are close to small gift shops that carry the *usual* and include black coral factories onsite. One gift shop advertises their available bathroom (there's a public restroom across the street from the ruins site). In Coba you'll find the cafes at the inns clean and pleasant. The food, though limited in choice, is *tipico* and can be quite good. **Bocadito** has pleasant surroundings and tasty, inex-

learning history from the master—a local guide

pensive food. Close by, a tiny bakery sells good *pan dulce,* and a small store sells cold soda pop. The food at **Villa Arqueologica** is fairly good though pricey, and if you bring your swimsuit you can take a dip after lunch and relax in their garden. The bar serves a terrific planter's punch, especially welcome when you come out of the jungle hot, sweaty and tired from hiking and climbing the pyramids. Sandwiches cost about US$4.50, full meals average US$8-10.

Getting There

Getting to Coba is easiest by car. The roads are good, and from Coba you can continue on to Valladolid, Chichen Itza, and Merida, or the coast highway (307) that goes south to Chetumal and north to Cancun. If traveling by local bus your schedule is limited to two buses a day. Northbound buses depart Tulum at 6 a.m. and noon, stopping at Coba town at 7:30 a.m. and 1:30 p.m. before continuing to Valladolid. Taxis at Coba are available to take you to Nuevo Xcan. From here you can catch a bus to Merida. Southbound buses leave Valladolid at 4 a.m. and 2 p.m., stopping at Coba at 6 a.m. and 6 p.m. on the way to Tulum and points north on Hwy. 307. When you get on and off the bus, ask the driver about the return trip and times. These schedules are frequently changed! Bus travelers tell of waiting in Coba for a bus that just skips it entirely at certain times of the year. It's a three-km walk to the highway, where other buses pass. (If you're planning to spend the night, make sure you have reservations or get there very early in the day.) You'll often run into travelers on the trail at the Coba ruins who are willing to give you a ride. Organized bus tours are available from hotels and travel agencies in Cancun, Playa del Carmen, and Cozumel.

FELIPE CARRILLO PUERTO

Anyone that has driven Hwy. 307 from Tulum to Felipe Carrillo Puerto in the past five years can't help but notice the varied changes taking place. Only a few years ago the main activity seen along this two-lane road was machete-swinging workmen battling to keep the jungle vines and ferns from overtaking the roadway. Today, trees have been removed and jungle has been cleared away to make room for small ranchitos. The people keep a few cattle and pigs, and grow corn, squash, and tomatoes. Also large areas have been planted with citrus trees, a government-backed experiment to help the farmers.

From Tulum to Chetumal it's an easy drive that takes you through Felipe Carrillo Puerto. For anyone curious about the past of the Chan Santa Cruz Indians (also called Cruzob) it's well worth a stopover to investigate this small colonial city with some of the richest history in Quintana Roo. It has yet to be discovered by tourists and remains a simple quiet town.

Around an unexciting central plaza several small hotels offer moderately priced rooms, not fancy, but clean. The **Esquivel Hotel** is owned and operated by a family that can trace its beginnings back as far as the Caste War in the 1800s. **Faison y Venado** is a newer hotel on Hwy. 307 which also houses a good cafe. Venado (deer) meat is on the restricted list and not on the menu; however, the waiter will quietly offer it to those customers he feels comfortable with. For anyone interested in preserving what's left of the deer population along this coast, don't order venado if it's offered. Another long-time stopover, the **24 Hour Cafe,** still serves reasonably priced, tasty food. The bus station is close by in case you choose to continue your journey by bus.

Felipe Carrillo Puerto is an eclectic mix of modern young folks shopping for the latest hit at **Videolandia** and some of the oldest Maya (descendants of the once-violent Cruzob) who

are still hoping for British help to conquer the Mexicans and get them out of their homeland.

Chan Santa Cruz History

When the Caste War was going badly for the Maya, smart leaders reintroduced the "talking cross." This unearthly oracle encouraged the Indians, dictating tactical orders, and predicting victory in their fight against the outsiders. The talking cross gave them strength, and told them they were the chosen race, true Christians, and children of God.

In a way, they *were* the victors; they managed to resist and hold off the Mexicans for more than 50 years. A few old-timers still cling to the belief that one day the Maya will once again control the Quintana Roo coast. These traditionalists still sanctify the cult of the "talking cross" more than ninety years after being conquered by the Mexican federal army. Their fathers and grandfathers rejected the peace treaty negotiated between their leaders and the Mexicans, took their families into the jungle, and began new villages where they continued their secretive lifestyle, calling themselves *separados.*

The talking cross has a long history. Early Spaniards in the 1700s reported seeing one at Cozumel. The cross itself had been an important symbol in the ancient Maya cult, representing the four cardinal points. Recent studies also indicate that the Maya knew full well that a human voice was responsible for the "talking," but they believed it was inspired by God. Who can prove otherwise?

Chan Santa Cruz Today

Chan Santa Cruz (meaning "small holy cross"), is now called Felipe Carrillo Puerto. Today's city folk refer to old-timers as *antiguos,* and while the younger generation has too many modern things to enjoy to actively take part in the ancient tradition, one gets the feeling that deep within themselves these youngsters admire the *antiguos'* tenacity and belief in the impossible dream.

IMPORTANT DATES IN THE HISTORY OF THE MAYA

1847: The beginning of the Caste War.

1849: The Caste War goes against the Maya and they retreat, getting lost in the thick jungles of Quintana Roo.

1850: The "talking cross" appears at the cenote and delivers commands for reviving the war against the white.

1850-58: The Maya warriors have their ups and downs, but life goes on for the Indians as they manage to hold off their adversaries.

1858: The Maya capture the fortress of Bacalar (just outside of Chetumal) and begin building a ceremonial city complete with church, palaces, barracks, and schools. This is the beginning of their total independence from the rest of Mexico.

1863: The British at Belize recognize the Indian state and engage in arms trade with them.

1863-1893: The Maya lose great numbers of people due to epidemics and internal conflicts.

1893: Mexico and Britain wrangle a peace treaty; the Indians no longer have their important source of arms.

1901: Under General Ignacio Bravo, the Mexican federal army takes over the stronghold city of Chan Santa Cruz and renames it Felipe Carrillo Puerto.

1901-15: While the Mexicans occupy the Maya city with brutality, the Maya in the jungle continue to raid and harrass the Mexicans, virtually isolating them from the rest of Mexico.

1915: The Mexicans give up and return Quintana Roo to the Maya.

1917-20: Influenza and smallpox epidemics decimate the Indians.

1920-29: Chicle boom. General May, the Indian leader, accepts a peace treaty with Mexico, distressing the more militant Indians.

1929: These militant traditional Maya disclaim May's "sell-out" and revive the cult of the Cross at X-Cacal Guardia.

PRACTICALITIES

Cycling
Since most of the Yucatan Peninsula is flat and the primary arteries are in good condition, the Caribbean coast appears to be the gathering place for cyclists. When exploring off the main roads, cyclists should be prepared for bumpy, irregular, and hard-packed dirt surfaces which become a muddy morass when it rains. Bring spare tires and a repair kit. Repairs are a big problem in most areas; few cycle shops exist. With a motorcycle you can travel almost any road on the Peninsula, but beware of the swampy shoulders near the sea.

Other Transport
There's frequent bus service between Chetumal and Cancun with stops in between. Buses travel from all over the Yucatan Peninsula to Hwy. 307 and up and down the Caribbean coast.

XCALAK PENINSULA

Xcalak Peninsula History

This low-lying limestone shelf bounded by the Quintana Roo mainland on the west, Espiritu Santo Bay on the north, Chetumal Bay on the south, and the Caribbean sea on the east is a mosaic of savannah, marsh, streams, and lagoons, dotted by islands of higher ground with dark soil and high forest, a rich refuge for Quintana Roo wildlife. The jungle has kept hidden for centuries the remainder of Maya life that once thrived on this narrow peninsula.

From a report of a survey made in Feb. of 1988 by archaeologists Anthony P. Andrews (University of South Florida), Tomas Gallareta Negron (Tulane University), and Rafael Coboa Palma (Tulane University), I learned of a reconnaissance of archaeological sites on the coast of the Xcalak Peninsula. This survey focused on the coastal strip between Punta Herrero on Espiritu Santo Bay and Boca Bacalar Chico, the canal that divides the Xcalak Peninsula from Ambergris Cay in Belize. Only sites on the shoreline and its immediate vicinity were visited; the interior areas were not surveyed. Money and time were devoted to the most threatened sites along the rapidly developing coast. Only in recent years a road has opened this once isolated area to home builders and a few (so far) small resorts, but many new developments are on the drawing boards.

Early explorers Sylvanus Morley and Thomas Gann sailed up the coast from Belize in 1918 visiting a number of sites along the east coast. Several years later, in 1926, Herbert Spinden and Gregory Mason passed by the area, and then in 1958 an amateur explorer, Michel Peissel, traveled down the coast, reporting new Maya sites at San Lorenzo, San Antonio, Rio Indio, and Guadalupe. Other reports were noted in 1973 and again in 1984. Although these were not in-depth studies, with each expedition more unknown archaeological structures were reported.

The coastline itself is a series of sandy beaches and dunes interrupted by rocky promontories that often connect with the off-shore Belizean reef that runs along the entire coast. This shore is dominated by still-healthy coconut plantations planted in the early 20th century. Andrews suggests that prehistoric sites located on the high ground behind mangrove-fringed estuaries are likely to have been the parent communities of the fishing villages and camps whose remains have been found along the shoreline. Very little is known about the pre-conquest history of the peninsula because it was already abandoned by the time the Spaniards attemped (unsuccessfully) to establish a village at Espiritu

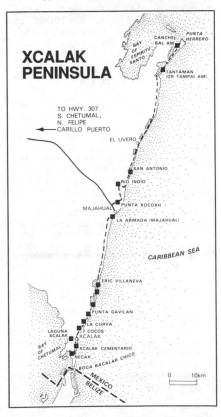

Santo Bay in 1621. However, it became a sanctuary for Maya refugees fleeing Spanish control in the interior as well as a haven for pirates, British logwood cutters, and Belizean fishermen.

Modern history of the area began with the founding of the port of Xcalak in 1900 as a military base for a project to dredge a canal across the southern end of the peninsula to connect it to Chetumal Bay. The project never got off the ground and instead a small rail line was laid between Xcalak and La Aguada on Chetumal Bay. In the following years, lighthouses were built at Xcalak and Punta Herrero. Large coconut plantations of several kilometers each were established at El Uvero and Xcalak. Smaller plantations and fishing camps were set up at Tantamam, Rio Indio, Benque Soya, Majahual, Rio Huach, and Punta Gavilan. In 1910 Xcalak's population numbered 544 with a few additional people scattered among the *cocales* (small coconut plantations) and ranchos along the coast. Many of the original colonizers were Yaqui Indians deported from their homeland in northwestern Mexico following their resistance to the Diaz regime. In the ensuing years, the population has fluctuated. The major industries—*cocales* and fishing—have been disrupted several times with the onslaught of major hurricanes.

Thick jungle hides many sites that will some day shed more light on the Maya past and their unique lifestyle. One local man tells of vine-shrouded structures where statues remain intact—the average person is not interested in fighting thick undergrowth with machete in hand and wading through muddy swamps to satisfy his or her curiosity. This is the realm of scientists—and (sadly) grave robbers. Hopefully the development and pillage of the Xcalak Peninsula will not move faster than scientific exploration.

Placer

For the explorer looking for virgin territory, a drive along the Xcalak Peninsula is an adventure—though long! A paved road breaks off the highway (307) just south of the Limones road and meanders toward the sea for 57 km through varied scenery. Much of this land has been cleared of jungle, and small ranchitos are scattered about. In some areas mangrove swamps line the highway and are home to a large variety of birds, including hundreds of egrets and the graceful white heron. However, sometimes the "rainy" season, has so little rain that many of the swamps dry out and the birds go elsewhere. Closer to Hwy. 307, the tall trees which have been left are covered with green and red bromeliads, orchids, and ferns. In spring colorful flowers brighten the landscape.

After about 55 km on this paved road, there's a turnoff to the left (north) going to Uvero and Placer. Many getaway houses are growing up along this part of the coast as well as the beginning of a few small diving destinations. You can count on this area being fairly deserted for a long time, at least until they pave the road! Right now, the dirt

MANATEE BREEDING PROGRAM

The state of Florida, under the auspices of the Miami Seaquarium and Dr. Jesse White, have begun a captive/breeding program hoping to learn more about the habits of the manatee and to try to increase the declining numbers. Several manatees have been born in captivity; they along with others that have recuperated from injury or illness will be or have been released into Florida's Crystal River where boat traffic is restricted. They are tagged and closely observed. Florida maintains a 24-hour hotline where people report manatees in need of help for any reason. Rescues can include removing an adult male from a cramped storm drain or rushing to the seaquarium newborns that somehow managed to get separated from their mothers and have washed ashore. These newborns are readily accepted by surrogate-mother manatees and are offered nourishment (by way of a thumb-sized teat under the front flipper) and lots of TLC. Medical aid is given to mammals that have been slashed by boat propellers as a result of cruising boats. The manatee has a playful curiosity and investigates anything found in its underwater environment, many times sustaining grave damage.

road has been improved. And though still not a paved road, it takes from 20 to 30 minutes to travel to a small resort called **Placer del Caribe** which caters especially to divers. This is a charming place, with four beautifully furnished spacious rooms, hot and cold water, tile bathrooms, comfortable beds, and a broad terrace with cushy chaise lounges to laze on while overlooking the beach and sea. A little farther down the beach Placer del Caribe has four *palapa* bungalows. This resort caters to divers interested in exploring **Chinchorro Bank,** and fishermen looking for bonefish. Chinchorro Bank is a virgin wonderland of crystalline water where lobster, conch, and sunken ships are just waiting for divers. Pilots are welcome to land their small planes on a private strip close by. Non-divers are welcome, though there's little else to do except relax and enjoy the sun, sea, and stars. There's no electricity at Placer, but the managers run a generator a good part of the evening. Guests enjoy meals family style in the main house. For all information and reservations (recommended) concerning Placer del Caribe, call in the U.S. (800) 237-7552 or (800) 960-6060. Drop-in rates in August of 1989 were US$75 per room (two persons), meals included. Dive packages for a five-night stay including lodging, meals, boat transportation to dive site, and guide run US$650 pp. **Note:** this is a long way from Cancun, so start out early if you don't have reservations—just in case a return trip becomes necessary.

Rancho Catalina

If you continue on the road past Placer del Caribe to km 42, you'll find a simple lodge devoted to fishermen and divers. This small retreat run by an American couple, Kathy and Steve (no language problem here!), is on a white-sand beach dotted with coconut palms. A reef close by makes it perfect for snorkelers as well as fishermen. Away from the busy world, they offer two basic, comfortable rooms with private tiled bathrooms, cold water (admittedly the water pressure is weak and the water merely dribbles out of the faucet), a simple wooden clubhouse, family-style dining, pleasant fellowship, and a boat to take you on fishing or diving expeditions. Prices are US$50 d, including room and all meals. Fishing and diving expeditions extra. For more information write: Kathy Lomax-Brisco, Apto Postal 77, Chetumal, Quintana Roo, Mexico 77500. Allow plenty of time for your mail to get there and be returned.

Overland To Xcalak

To go to Xcalak don't turn off to the left onto the unpaved road as you would to get to Placer; stay on the paved road until it dead ends at Majahual on the sea, a geographic point on the map but no town. A military camp guards the point, but they're just a bunch of friendly kids ready with smiles and information (unless, of course, you're a bad guy). Here turn right on the dirt road (south) to reach Xcalak, another 66 km. The jungle along this road hasn't been disturbed much and is teeming with animals and noisy birds. From Majahual, the road parallels the coast to Xcalak. This trip is especially conducive to travel in a small camper. Like an early explorer, you'll discover miles and miles of isolated beach—few facilities, just the turquoise sea, transparent white crabs, a variety of fish waiting to be caught for your dinner, and curious birds checking out the newest visitor to their deserted paradise. It's all free—so far.

Bring plenty of food, water, and especially gasoline since you'll not see another gas station until you're back on the highway. This isolation won't last too much longer, however, as several attempts are being made to open businesses. One, at km 52 is a little gem called **Costa de Cocos.** Eight delightful *palapa* bungalows with a modern Swiss Family Robinson ambience. Divers find a fully equipped dive shop and P.A.D.I. training facility with individual attention and a chance to dive Chinchorro Bank, wrecks, and caves. Reservations (tel. 800-443-1123) are an absolute must in this "desert island" spot, if just to make sure there's enough food. Drop-ins take the chance of finding "no room at the inn"; it's hours back to another hotel. All pretty primitive—for now. Even the turtles still come to lay their eggs during the summer.

Xcalak

Xcalak (schka-LAK), a tiny fishing village located across the bay from Chetumal, is the southernmost tip of Quintana Roo. Trekking there is an extraordinary expedition for those with a wellspring of energy and plenty of time. If you plan to stay for a few days, bring your camping gear even though Xcalak does have a small simple hotel (and a large new one is on the drawing board). A couple of *tiendas* sell simple food and supplies. Here is an ideal place to rent an outboard skiff and explore the coast's many coves and bays. It's easy to strike a deal with a local fisherman to take you across the reef to breathtaking **Chinchorro Bank,** 26 km off the coast, which covers a large area (43 km north to south, 17 km east to west). Scuba divers call this world-class diving, with crystal-clear water and a huge variety of colorful fish, delicate coral, and three sunken ships clearly visible from above. Xcalak is just a short distance from a channel that separates Mexico from Belize's Ambergris Cay. In days past, Mexican soldiers dug by hand the often-shallow channel to ensure border security between the two countries.

Another option for a shorter journey to Xcalak is a two-hour boat trip from Chetumal's downtown docks. And still a further possibility is to fly to Xcalak. Its airstrip can handle any twin-engine plane. If you're in your own plane, flying once over the village will bring someone to the airport to take you to town. Small planes with pilot are available to hire in Chetumal for a trip to Xcalak. You'll be dropped off, then picked up at an arranged time. If it's just a day trip and the pilot stays, the cost is less. For information to get to Xcalak either by outboard motorboat or plane, contact the Secretaria Estatal de Turismo, Palacio de Gobierno, Chetumal, Quintana Roo, Mexico 77500.

Back On The Road To Chetumal

On Hwy. 307 between Felipe Carrillo Puerto and Chetumal you'll see turnoff signs for several villages; some have small Maya sites, including **Chacchoben, Ichpaatun, Chichmoul, Tupak, Chacmool, Los Limones**—all minor archaeological sites off the main track but in the middle of the historical area where the Chan Santa Cruz Indians held court for so many years.

Bacalar

Thirty-eight km north of Chetumal (on 307) lies a beautiful multihued lagoon called **Las Lagunas de Siete Colores** (The "Lagoon of Seven Colors"). Bacalar, complete with 17th C. Fort San Felipe, is a small town founded by the Spanish to protect themselves from the bands of pirates and Maya that regularly raided the area. Today, part of the fort has a

along the coast of the Bacalar Lagoon

Hotel Laguna overlooks the "Sea of Seven Colors."

diminutive museum housing metal arms used in the 17th and 18th centuries. A token assortment of memorabilia recalls history of the area. The stone construction has been restored, and cannons are still posted along the balustrades overlooking beautiful Bacalar Lagoon. The museum is open daily except holidays, small entry fee charged.

Near the town plaza and across from the old fort is a small budget *casa de huespedes* —not fancy, a youth hostel and a trailer park. Close by, built into the side of a hill overlooking the colorful Bacalar Lagoon, is **Hotel Las Lagunas,** moderately priced, with clean rooms and private baths. Special touches make it an out-of-the-ordinary stopover: local shells decorate walls and ceilings, and ornate fences are neatly painted in white and green. The friendly owners, Señor Carlos R. Gutierrez and his wife, can usually be found in the outdoor dining room. A small pool (filled only during high season) and outdoor bar look out across the unusually hued Lagunas de Siete Colores. A diving board and ladder make swimming convenient in the lagoon's sometimes blue, sometimes purple, sometimes red water; fishing is permitted and you can barbecue your catch on the grounds. Rates are about US$25-30 d. Ask about a bungalow including kitchen facilities. Reserve in advance during tourist season and holidays; the rest of the year there are few people around. Write: Hotel Laguna, Bacalar, Quintana Roo,

Mexico. Send one night's fee and allow plenty of time for the mail to reach its destination.

Close by is the **Laguna Milagros Trailer Park** with tent camping also permitted, about US$2-3 pp. Restrooms, showers, sun shelters, narrow beach, small store, and open-air cafe combine to offer an exotic milieu on the edge of the lagoon.

Rancho Encantado

Thirty-five miles north of Chetumal (200 miles south of Cancun) an enchanting small resort lies on the edge of Bacalar Lagoon. Part of the **Turquoise Reef Group** that specializes in laid-back, relaxing resorts that excel in "doing nothing," this mini resort includes six *casitas* built with native hardwoods and Mexican tile and sits in a lush Eden of tropical shrubs, coco palms, and fruit trees—all just a few steps from the shore of Bacalar Lagoon. Each unit contains a small sitting room, convenience kitchen/dining room, bathroom, stove, refrigerator, and deck with a view of the garden or lagoon. A 40-foot *palapa*-roofed structure is the social center of the resort. Here visitors enjoy a tropical buffet breakfast and candlelit dinner (both included in the room rate; US$110 d including Mexico's 15% tax).

If you don't wish to "do nothing," you can be as vigorous as you desire with a variety of activities. The archaeology buff has the rarely visited **Kohunlich** Maya site with its giant masks close at hand, as well as several un-developed sites across the border in northern Belize. Take an excursion through the Quintana Roo savannah to tour Mexico's southern Caribbean coastline, or plan a scuba trip to the Caribbean's **Chinchorro Banks.** Rancho Encantado offers boat rides through the mangroves, a picnic on a deserted island, bird-watching, snorkeling, or windsurfing. Ask about the private villa with three bedrooms, 2½ baths, and private dock located on the waterfront a short distance from Rancho Encantado; price given on request. For more information and reservations contact the Turquoise Reef Group, Box 2664, Evergreen, CO 80439; in Colorado tel. (303) 674-9615, the rest of the U.S. tel. (800) 538-6802), fax (303) 674-8735.

PLACES TO VISIT

Cenote Azul

Thirty-four km north of Chetumal (on Hwy. 307) is a circular *cenote* 61.5 meters deep and 185 meters across filled with brilliant blue water. This is a spectacular place to stop for a swim, lunch at the outdoor restaurant, or just a cold drink.

Kohunlich

Sixty-seven km west of Chetumal on Hwy. 186, turn right and drive eight km on a good side road to this unique Maya site. The construction continued from late Pre-Classic (about A.D. 100-200) through Classic (A.D. 600-900). Though not totally restored nor nearly as grand as Chichen Itza or Uxmal, Kohunlich is worth the trip if only to visit the exotic **Temple of the Masks** dedicated to the Maya sun god. The stone pyramid is under an unlikely thatched roof (to prevent further deterioration from the weather), and unique gigantic stucco masks stand two to three meters tall. The temple, though not extremely tall as pyramids go, still presents a moderate climb. Wander through the jungle site and you can find 200 structures or uncovered mounds from the same era as Palenque. Many carved stelae are scattered throughout the surrounding forest.

Walking through luxuriant foliage, you'll discover a green world. Note orchids in the tops of trees plus small colorful wildflowers, lacy ferns, and lizards that share cracks and crevices in moldy stone walls covered with velvety moss. The relatively unknown site attracts few tourists. The absence of trinket sellers and soft-drink stands leaves a visitor feeling he or she is the first to stumble on the haunting masks with their star-incised eyes, mustaches (or are they serpents?), and nose plugs—features extremely different from carvings found at other Maya sites. Even the birds hoot and squawk at your intrusion as if you were the first. Like most archaeological zones, Kohunlich is fenced and opens from 8 a.m.-5 p.m.; small fee. Camping is not allowed within the grounds, but you may see a tent or two outside the entrance.

CHETUMAL

Chetumal, a good base for the many sights in the southern section of Quintana Roo, is also the gateway to Belize. The capital of this young state, Chetumal is without the bikini-clad, touristy crowds of the north and presents the businesslike atmosphere of a growing metropolis. A 10-minute walk takes you from the marketplace and most of the hotels to the waterfront. Modern sculpted monuments stand along a breezy promenade that skirts the broad crescent of bay. Also explore the back streets, where worn wooden buildings still have a Central American/Caribbean look. The largest building in town—white, three stories, close to the waterfront—houses most of the government offices.

Wide tree-lined avenues and clean sidewalks front dozens of small variety shops. The city has been a free port for many years and as a result has attracted a plethora of tiny shops selling a strange conglomeration of plastic toys, small appliances, exotic perfumes (maybe authentic?), famous-label clothes (ditto), and imported foodstuffs. Because the tax in Chetumal is only six percent instead of the usual 15, it's a popular place for Belizeans and Mexicans to shop. The population is a handsome mixture of many races, including Caribe, Spanish, Maya, and English. Schools are prominently scattered around the town.

Climate
Chetumal is hot and sticky. Though sea breezes help, humidity can make the air terribly uncomfortable. High temperatures in Aug. average 100° F, in Dec. 86° F. In the last 34 years, three destructive hurricanes have attacked the Mexican Caribbean coast, and Hurricane Janet all but destroyed Chetumal in 1955. Not something to be too concerned about though—these devastating blows are infrequent. The most comfortable time to visit is the dry season from Nov. to April.

Flora And Fauna
Chetumal is noted for its hardwood trees, such as mahogany and rosewood. (Abun-dance of wood explains the difference in rural housing between the north and south ends of the Peninsula. Small houses in the south are built mostly of milled board, some with thatched roofs; structures with circular walls of slender saplings set close together are still common in the north.) Copious rainfall in the Chetumal area creates dense jungle with vine-covered trees, broad-leafed plants, ferns, and colorful blossoms. Orchids grow liberally on the tallest trees. Deer and javelina roam the forests.

CHETUMAL

1. Xul-Ha bathing resort
2. hospital (I.S.S.S.T.E.)
3. Payo Obispo Zoo
4. airport
5. Javier Rojo Gomez Public Library
6. Conasuper market
7. health center (S.S.A.)
8. civil hospital
9. El Palmar bathing resort
10. La Laguna de las Milagros bathing resort
11. Paradise Restaurant, Bar & Nightclub
12. Han Dal Gas Station
13. Consulate of Guatemala
14. city hall
15. EXPOFER Fair Installation
16. House of Culture (C.R.E.A.)
17. Quintana Roo Social Club

SIGHTS

Calderitas Bay
On Av. Heroes eight km north of the city is **Calderitas Bay,** a breezy area for picnicking, camping, and RVing. The trailer park is one of the few in the state that provides complete hookups for RVs, including a dump station and clean showers, toilets, and washing facilities. Right on the water's edge, the spotless camp is in a park-like setting fringed with cooling palm trees. Amateur divers will find exotic shells, and the fishing is great. Nearby public beaches have *palapa* shelters which are normally tranquil, but on holidays they're crowded with sun- and fun-seekers.

Isla Tamalcas
Tiny **Isla Tamalcas,** two km off the shore of Calderitas, is the home of the primitive *capybara*. This largest of all rodents can reach a length of over a meter and weigh up to 50 kg; it's found in few other places in the world. The animal is covered with reddish-yellowish-brown coarse hair, resembles a small pig or large guinea pig, has partially webbed toes, and loves to swim. It's referred to by the locals as a water pig, and is a favorite food of the jaguar. Isla Tamalcas is easily accessible from Calderitas Beach.

ACCOMMODATIONS

Although Chetumal is not considered a tourist resort, its low taxes and location on the Belize border make it a desirable marketplace and busy stopover for both Mexicans and Belizeans. If traveling without reservations, arrive as early in the day as possible to have your choice of hotel rooms. During the holiday season it's wise to reserve in advance. Many of the hotels listed are within walking distance of the marketplace, downtown shops, and waterfront.

Higher Priced
Chetumal doesn't have a true luxury hotel. The **Del Prado** (formerly the El Presidente) comes closest with general cleanliness, a/c,

pretty garden, and large clean swimming pool, a bar with evening disco music, and a quiet dining room with a friendly staff that serves a varied menu; about US$80 d, Av. Heroes con Chapultepec, tel. 2-05-44. The **Hotel Continental-Caribe** *advertises* itself as luxury, has a/c, restaurant, pool, bar with evening entertainment, and though the rooms

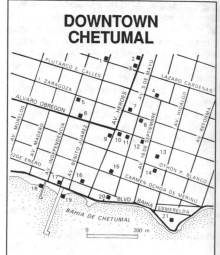

DOWNTOWN CHETUMAL

0   200 m

1. telephone office
2. Del Prado Restaurant
3. El Caracol Shopping Center and Fonagora (cultural center)
4. post and telegraph offices
5. Conasuper market
6. Leona Vicario Cinema
7. Arts and Crafts House
8. Superfama supermarket
9. Big Ben Hotel
10. Baroudi Hotel
11. Sergio's Pizza
12. Caribe Princess Hotel
13. Josefa Ortiz de Dominguez Gardens
14. Sagrado Corazon de Jesus Church
15. Aeromexico Airlines
16. state government office
17. Immigration Office
18. Fishing Club
19. El Mulle Amusement Park for Children
20. Sailor's Monument
21. state congress

are clean the overall appearance is not. Prices range from about US$65, Av. Heroes 171, tel. 2-04-41.

Moderate
The moderately priced hotels for the most part are friendly (some clean, some not, look before you pay), usually fan-cooled, and have hot water. Prices range from US$12 to US$35 d at: **San Jorge,** Av. Juarez 87, tel. 2-10-65; **Maria Dolores,** Av. Alvaro Obregon 206, tel. 2-05-08; and **Tulum,** Av. Heroes 2, tel. 2-05-18. The following hotels are small, modern, friendly, have a/c, restaurant, bar, and evening entertainment: **Hotel Real Azteca,** Av. Belize 186, tel. 2-07-20; **El Dorado Hotel,** Av. 5 de Mayo 21, tel. 2-03-15; and **Hotel Caribe Princess,** Av. Alvaro Obregon 180, tel. 2-09-00. Prices range from US$15.

Budget
The budget traveler has a choice of several hotels, a youth hostel at Bacalar, or camping at Calderitas Bay. Some of the *posadas* are spartan without hot water; a few have food available. At the following hotels, prices range from about US$10: **Colonial,** Benjamin Hill 135, tel. 2-15-20; **Tabasco,** Av. Zaragoza 206, tel. 2-20-45; **America,** Othon P. Blanco 11.

OTHER PRACTICALITIES

Food
It's easy to find a cafe to fit every budget in Chetumal. Walk down the street to Av. Alvaro Obregon for several fast-food cafes. On the same street, for seafood try **El Pez Vela;** for chicken go to **Pollos Sinaloa.** On the corner of Av. Efrain Aguilar and Revolucion is **Los Pozos,** a regional cafe serving typical Yucatecan dishes. If your taste buds yearn for good American red meat, try **Buffalo Steak,** Av. Alvaro Obregon 208. For *helado* and *postres* try **Carlena,** Av. A. Lopez Mateos 407, or **Fonagora,** on the corner of Av. Heroes con Lazaro Cardenas. The **public market** has just about everything you could need; three **Conasuper** markets can provide the rest.

Entertainment
For dancing, try one of these small discotheques: **El Elefante,** Blvd. Bahia; **Focus** at the Hotel Continental, Av. Heroes 171; **Huanos Astoria,** Av. Reforma 27; **Sarawak** at Hotel Del Prado, Av. Heroes con Chapultepec. Cinemas and theaters include: **Campestre,** Av. A. Lopez Mateos con Milan; **Avila Camacho,** Calle 22 de Enero; **Leona Vicario,** Av. Alvaro Obregon con Independencia; **Cine Juventino Rosas,** Av. Hidalgo. The larger hotels usually have a TV in the lobby; the Del Prado Hotel provides one for each room. **Javier Rojo Gomez Public Library** is on Av. Efrain Aguilar.

Sports
A yearly event in Chetumal is the auto road race. Open to drivers from all over the globe, it's gaining prominence in the racing world. This event takes place in December and hotel reservations should be made well in advance.

A popular sport in both Chetumal Bay and Bacalar Lagoon is windsurfing. State competitions are held in both areas yearly. What a great place to fly across the sea! Make reservations early since many others will have the same idea. For more information, write to the Secretaria de Turismo, Palacio de Gobierno 20. Piso, Chetumal, Quintana Roo, Mexico 77500.

Services
The **post office** is on Calle 2 A. You can send a telegram from **Telegrafos Nacionales,** Av. 5 de Mayo. **Long-distance** phone calls can be made from Tico-Tico, Av. Alvaro Obregon 7, or Novedades Caribe, Av. Heroes. For any **medical** emergency, there are several hospitals and clinics. Ask at your hotel for a doctor who speaks English. One **pharmacy** is on Carmen Ochoa de Merino y Heroes, tel. 2-01-62. Four **gasoline stations** and at least seven mechanics are in town. Several **banks** will cash travelers cheques Mon. to Sat. 9 a.m.-1 p.m. First- and 2nd-class buses use the new bus station on the outskirts of town. Ask about the Batty Bus to Belize that makes the trip daily. A visit to the **Tourism Office** is helpful; ask for their *Guia Turistica,* which lists

cultural activities, monuments, and murals open to the public along with addresses of all banks and other solid information about Chetumal.

TRANSPORT

By Air

Chetumal's modern airport still has only a few flights each day. An airport van provides transportation to hotels or downtown. Check with Aeromexico and Aerocaribe for possible flights in and out of Chetumal.

By Bus

Buses from points all over Mexico arrive throughout the day at the new modern Chetumal bus station located on the highway south of town. Taxis are available from the station into town. With the expanding road system, bus travel is becoming more versatile and is still the most inexpensive public transportation to the Quintana Roo coast. Buses to Chetumal arrive from Merida (5$^{1/2}$ hours), Mexico City (22 hours), plus frequent trips from Cancun and Campeche.

By Car

A good paved road connects Merida, Campeche, Villahermosa, and Francisco Escarcega to Chetumal; Hwy. 307 links all of the Quintana Roo coastal cities. There's little traffic, and gas stations are well spaced if you top off at each one. Car rentals are not yet available at the Chetumal airport; go to the Del Prado Hotel for Avis. Chetumal is a good place to rent your car since there's only a six percent tax instead of the usual fifteen.

Crossing Into Belize

Chetumal, Mexico, is a bridge away from the country of Belize. For the explorer, the archaeology buff, the diver, or the curious, it's easy to take a side trip into what was formerly British Honduras. The Rio Hondo River forms a natural border between Quintana Roo and Belize. Chetumal is the only land link between the two countries, from which Belize is easily reached by Batty bus or taxi. There's rarely a problem crossing the border as long as you show a valid passport. If you look poor you'll be asked to show money or proof of onward travel. If driving you must buy insurance with Belizean dollars; money-changers are waiting for you as you cross the border. The rates seem comparable to bank rates; however, you always take a slight risk when you buy local money from a street vendor. U.S. citizens and *most* others don't need visas, but a few countries do; check with your embassy before leaving home. Other than U.S. citizens that plan to travel on to Guatemala from Belize, check with the Guatemalan Embassy in Chetumal; Guatemala is not represented in Belize.

First timers interested in combining a trip to Mexico with a trip to Belize but don't know where to start, call **International Expeditions**; tel. (800) 633-4734. They provide good packages for a variety of interests whether they lean to natural history, archaeology, or diving and snorkeling.

CRUISES AND TOURS TO THE CARIBBEAN COAST

CRUISE SHIPS

One of the fastest growing industries in tourism is ocean cruising. What was once reserved for the idle rich is becoming commonplace for the ordinary vacationer—even the handicapped. Cruising is no longer a means of getting from point "A" across an ocean to point "B." Cruise ships are for fun! And the more luxurious the better—though for obvious financial reasons some ships cater more for fun and others more for luxury. But the passenger has many more options to choose from today, with ships that cater to all whims and all pocketbooks; daily pp prices can start as low as US$150 on up to $700.

Cruising is having an impact on most countries with seaports that cater to tourists. New cruise ships are under construction, and new docks, marinas, wharfs, and facilities that are being added to once-small port cities to accommodate day-long visitors are changing the makeup of these locations. Special-interest groups are finding a ship the perfect place to gather together, whether they are "Christian groups", families combining a cruise and a stop at Florida's Disney World, the Smithsonian Associates' naturalists and archaeologists, classical music fans with noted artists on board, the Theater Guild on their annual "Theater At Sea" cruise, or Alcoholics Anonymous. It's all for fun, and appropriate speakers and plans are coordinated with the ship's personnel.

The Money Factor

Shop carefully if price is the most important factor; prices are competitive. A variety of ships offer mass market Las Vegas-type cruises aimed at younger passengers interested in short three- to five-day trips. Upscale luxury boats reminiscent of 1st class on the "Queens"—Mary and Elizabeth—cruise for two weeks or longer and will cost the most. These are the ones with large cabins, restaurants where one orders from a complete menu, and passengers who are pampered outrageously—with a price tag to match. For the adventurer, small casual ships capable of traveling narrow river passages into often virgin territory where nature and people have not been exposed to the diluting effects of tourism—for awhile at least—run a gamut of prices from moderate to exhorbitant.

Ways To Cut The Cost
Go standby. Once you put your name on the list you'll have no choice of cabin location or size, and generally airfare is not included. Passengers are usually notified two weeks prior to departure. **Last-minute travel clubs** and **discount agencies** include cruises in their inventories available at the last minute. These clubs generally charge a yearly membership fee, around US$50. For that the member receives a newsletter with trips listed, phone numbers, and other pertinent information giving access to upcoming values. Those who are willing to pack up at a mo-

ment's notice (two weeks) can save from 10 - 50%.

By the same token, some cruise lines will give a substantial discount on those folks who will book and buy passage six months to a year in advance. **Cunard, Princess, Holland America,** and **Royal Cruise Line** are all willing to give from 10-50% discount. And of course, study the marketplace. Often ships offer specials for various reasons; study the travel sections of newspapers, and get to know your travel agent. Let him know what you would like and ask him to call you if and when the price is right.

Sharing a quad room generally gives you a good discount. If you don't have any roomies to bring along, some lines will sell you a same-sex quad for a set price; **Chandris Fantasy Cruises** offers a special **Single Saver** or guaranteed quad-share rate that includes airfare from your getaway city; they will give you that fare even if they are unable to find you a roommate.

Ask for **senior citizen discounts;** though not many ships give them there are a few— Chandris is one. The Chandris Fantasy Cruises give a 50% discount to the second passenger when the first passenger in the cabin pays full fare.

Chandris' SS Britanis *off the coast of Cozumel*

HISTORY OF THE *BRITANIS*

This dowager is one of the oldest passenger vessels in active service. Built in the U.S. by the Bethlehem-Quincy for Matson Line subsidiary Oceanic Steamship Co., the ship was completed in 1932, and began service as the *Monterey*. Along with two sister-ships, the *Mariposa* and the *Lurline*, it had a cruise range of 16,600 miles. The *Monterey's* normal route was from homeport San Francisco to Los Angeles, Honolulu, Pago Pago, Suva, Auckland, Sydney, Melbourne, and return. This charming service continued until Dec. 1, 1941, when the ship arrived home from a trip to Sydney. Two days later the *Monterey,* along with the *Matsonia* and *Lurline,* was chartered to the U.S. Maritime Commission for use as a troop transport.

The *Monterey* was ultimately outfitted with 4,150 berths from the original 728. The ship made a total of 27 voyages during her wartime career. She served in the Pacific until 1942, and from there went to the Atlantic until the end of 1943 where she took part in the North African Landings in November, 1942. Her prewar staff commanded by Captain Elis R. Johanson since 1934, stayed with her during the war.

Only once was the ship in immediate danger. On Nov. 6, 1943, in the Mediterranean enroute to Naples from New York and Liverpool, her convoy of 22 ships was attacked by German aircraft, one of which was hit by *Monterey's* guns. The ship escaped damage, but rescued 1,644 Canadian survivors from Grace Line's *Santa Elena.* The *Monterey* was a heroine and Captain Johanson received recognition from the Canadian government.

After the war, the *Monterey* was sent for refurbishing and renamed *Matsonia,* destined to be the Matson's flagship. After a multimillion-dollar job which transformed the ship into a tropically decorated luxury ship, the *Matsonia* made her first trip to Hawaii on June 6, 1957. With ups and downs in the passenger ship business over the years, she was again rechristened, the fourth *Lurline.* In 1970 she was sold to the Ajax Navigation Co. (Chandris Lines), reflagged Panamanian, and renamed the *Britanis.*

Modernization included adding a sparkling gambling casino in what was once the writing room, the library became the Gallery Bar, the ballroom was extended, and a cinema was added. Hail the modern passenger. The entire ship including the outside was modernized.

The *Britanis* is known as a happy ship. She is staffed by men and women from 30 countries with Greek officers and crew, and an international hotel staff. She offers excellent restaurant and room service, a good variety of onboard activities and entertainment, as well as interesting shore excursions. The old girl still has teak decks to walk on, plenty of brass to keep the seamen busy polishing, and though the rooms have the look of the past, they are spotlessly clean and all are carpeted.

Though new ships are being built every year to cater to the large demand for cruise vacations, the *Britanis,* built with super quality in 1932, fits well into the scheme of vacationers—some are repeaters who return year after year. They know what to expect on the happy ship.

CRUISING TO MEXICO'S CARIBBEAN COAST

To Quintana Roo

Several passenger ships include stops at Quintana Roo's islands and ports. **Cruise Line** offers its Fantasy Cruises, budget trips on well-equipped and well-appointed older vessels sailing out of Miami, stopping at Key West before continuing on to the Caribbean and Mexico's Playa del Carmen and Isla Cozumel. Tenders take passengers ashore, where they have the option of taking excursions to the Maya ruins of Tulum, Coba, or San Gervais, or a trip to Xelha, an inland lagoon described as a natural aquarium where you can swim, snorkel, or scuba dive among colorful tropical fish and even see an underground grotto with remnants of the ancient Mayan religion. Other passengers opt to lay around the white beach, enjoy the turquoise sea, or shop at the many *tiendas* for typical souvenirs.

Even the sundeck and pool are abandoned for a trip snorkeling off the coast of Cozumel.

Chandris has been named by *Cruise* magazine as giving the best dollar value in cruising for 1989. From around US$140 per day (depending on cabin choice) vacationers can fly from California and spend five nights aboard, enjoying the sea or engaging in activities designed for every taste: Las Vegas-type lounge shows, bingo, a great gambling casino, good food served from sunup to sunup, passenger talent show, costume party, or just a quiet corner where one can contemplate the sea or get lost in the adventure of a good book. There's even a special activity director for children. For complete information on the Chandris Fantasy Cruises call or write for a brochure and rates, 900 3rd Ave., New York, NY 10022, tel. (800) 621-3446.

Commodore Cruise Line's Caribe I offers a large ship which sails out of Miami, frequently with theme cruises. This is not a fancy ship, but passengers have fun. Prices average US$145 per day. For more information contact Commodore Cruise Lines, 1007 North American Way, Miami, FL 33132, tel. (800) 327-5617

Costa Cruises means cruising Italian style; everything is reminiscent of Italy including great pasta, pizza, and gelato. The shops offer trendy Italian-label clothing, there's at least one "toga night" each sailing, and strolling tenors capture the romantics on board with Italian love songs. Night is active in the casino and the disco. Rates start at about US$232 per day, including airfare. For more information contact Costa Cruises, World Trade Center, 80 S.W. 8th St., Miami, FL 33130, tel. (800) 462-6782.

Dolphin Cruises offers the *Sea Breeze,* a large ship that is often filled with young budget minded first-time cruisers to the Caribbean. The line specializes in seven-day cruises from Miami that average about US$225 per day. For a brochure and more information, write to Dolphin, 1007 North American Way, Miami, FL 33132, or tel. (800) 222-1003.

Holland America Line sails with a gracious Indonesian staff and Dutch officers. This is a traditional ship with excellent food and exceptional service, no tipping allowed. The mix of people is varied—older couples, families, and singles. Fare averages US$218 per day including airfare. For more information write to 300 Elliott Ave. W., Seattle, WA 98119, or tel. (800) 426-0327.

Norwegian Cruise Line offers the *Skyward* for short cruises to the western Caribbean. The mid-sized ship offers a variety of star-studded entertainment for all ages. Prices average US$230 per day, including airfare. For more information contact Norwegian Cruise Line, Kloster Cruise Ltd., 2 Alhambra Plaza, Coral Gables, FL 33134, tel. (800) 327-7030.

The **Royal Caribbean Line** offers clean, bright, and well-run ships. The cabins are small but functional. A good sports program is available, plus great entertainment and programs for all ages. Dress is casual. For more information contact Royal Caribbean Cruise Line, 903 South American Way, Miami, FL 33132, tel. (800) 327-6700.

The **Ocean Quest Line** offers a slightly different type of cruise. The line's 457-foot, 300-passenger ship, *Ocean Spirit,* sails from New Orleans and caters to the diving crowd. The seven-day voyage carries doctors, a four-man decompression chamber for treating aeroembolism (bends), and an air system encompassing two tank centers with 150,000 cubic feet of air, plus fast-filling, built-in tank systems on each of its eight dive boats. Divers can either bring their own equipment or rent on board. A US$200 certification course in scuba diving is offered as well as a multitude of water-sports equipment and events. Dress is casual and fine entertainment onboard can be had at the disco, pool, bars, or cinema. A small fitness center, shop, and film processing center make ship life convenient and pleasant. The *Ocean Spirit* combines the intimate qualities of a private yacht with the facilities of a modern cruise ship. Fare averages US$207 per day. For more information contact Ocean Quest, 512 S. Peters St., New Orleans, LA 70130, tel. (800) 338-3483.

The **Bermuda Star Line** offers the *Bermuda Queen,* which departs from New Orleans to the Caribbean coast on a seven-day cruise, US$895 to $1895 per person. Passengers will find roomy cabins and a friendly staff. This is not a regular schedule, so check with the company for more information, 1086 Teaneck Rd, Teaneck, N.J. 07666, tel. (800) 237-5361.

PACKAGE TOURS TO MEXICO'S CARIBBEAN COAST

Travelers come with many mind frames. Some want to be pampered and enjoy glitz; others like the sun and enjoy being lazy; still others wish to acquaint themselves with the Maya culture, while many wish to dive and explore the sea. There are special trips for all of the above.

A Potpourri Of Trips

A unique bus company, **The Green Tortoise,** takes travelers of a special ilk all over the U.S. in buses that have rebuilt interiors to accommodate sleeping and seating. And though the Green Tortoise goes to many places, we'll give you the specifics for trips to the Yucatan Peninsula with other like-minded folks who enjoy "doing" things in Mexico during the day and traveling at night while one of two drivers (always two drivers on trips to Mexico) takes the wheel. Travelers bring sleeping bags and sleep on foam-covered platforms and bunks in the bus; meals are cookout affairs where everyone helps. This is much like a camping trip and if you need a regular shower more than two-three times a week, better not come. There are no toilet facilities on the bus, but stops are planned to meet passengers' needs. The itineraries are decided beforehand and once in a region, a day is loosely planned with as much free time as desired by passengers. Food is not included in the fare; meals in a city are the responsibility of the passenger, for cookouts everyone chips in US$3 per meal. Trips planned include the **Jungle-Yucatan-Highlands Loop,** 3 1/2 weeks, US$699 plus food and one-way airfare from Mexico City to home; **Golden Coast-Jungle Loop,** combining San Francisco and Mexico City-Yucatan, 5 1/2 weeks, US$699 plus food plus one-way airfare from Mexico City to home; **Yucatan-Belize Loop,** RT from Merida, 3 1/2 weeks, US$329 plus food plus RT airfare to Mexico City. For more information contact Green Tortoise Adventure Travel, Box 24459, San Francisco, CA 94124, tel. (415) 821-0803.

Vagabonders is the travel division of the **Turquoise Reef Group.** The Vagabonders' **Dive Bundle** includes seven nights and eight days. A diver's surf-and-turf splurge on the

Calypso Scuba Safari bus

Turquoise Reef includes lodging, meals, four two-tank dive days, and more. Another special trip is called the **Vagabonder's Whole Enchilada,** 14 nights and 15 days spent making a circle of the Maya world of three countries (Belize, Mexico, and Guatemala) with relaxing intervals on the beaches of the Caribbean. Includes lodging, meals, guides, transportation and more. Some of these trips are offered to guests already at a Turquoise Reef Resort in the state of Quintana Roo and originate from one of three locations along Mexico's Caribbean coast: Kai Luum, Capitan Lafitte, or Shangri-La Caribe. The **Vagabonder's Potpourri** is a five-night/six-day trip that gives the traveler an intimate look at the Yucatan Peninsula, with its Maya treasures, and a taste of village and city life. This journey includes Merida, Uxmal, Labna, Sayil, Kabah, Chichen Itza, Valladolid, Coba, Tulum, and Xelha. For more information contact the Vagabonders, Box 2664, Evergreen CO, 80439, tel. (303) 674-9615 or (800) 538-6802.

Far Horizons: Cultural Discovery Trips originate in Miami, Dallas, or Los Angeles. First stop is the **Museum of Anthropology** in Mexico City where an overview of Maya prehistoric culture will be explained; from there a visit to Teotihuacan will illustrate how that ancient city heavily influenced Maya art and architecture. Other areas of Maya culture

visited include Palenque, Tulum, Coba, Edzna, Labna, Sayil, Kabah, Uxmal, Rio Bec, and Chichen Itza. For more information write or call Far Horizons, Box 1529, San Anselmo, CA 94960, tel. (415) 457-4575.

Barbachano Tours offers a central reservation office/number for almost all of the hotels in Cozumel. Various packages are available from numerous cities in the U.S.; some include dive packages for experienced divers or beginners. Prices are cheaper midweek. In conjunction with **Continental Airlines** Barbachano has initiated the **Cozumel Saturday Express** which departs Houston, Texas every Saturday at 1:39 p.m. and returns at 7:46 p.m. For more information call (800) 327-2254, or write to 1570 Madruga Ave., Penthouse One, Coral Gables, FL 33146.

For the explorer interested in seeing the colonial as well as the low-key part of Mexico's Caribbean, **Mex Treks** offers a 10-day adventure excursion which combines the vibrant and colorful city of Merida (and its many nearby Maya archaeological sites) with the private **Jungle Island Hideaway** on the Caribbean Sea. In Merida accommodations are at an intimate old colonial home with terraces, pool, art, and tropical foliage. At the Habitat, the primitive diving and fishing camp is on the wild south coast of Quintana Roo in the middle of a working coconut plantation within Sian Ka'an, the national ecological reserve comprising more than 1.3 million acres. The Habitat fronts the beach, where on one side guests will find sand dunes, sea, and the offshore barrier reef (fifth largest in the world) and on the other side a huge inland estuary bordered by mangrove swamps, coconut forests, and nesting islands for many varieties of tropical birds. The jungle stands on the opposite shore of the estuary. Time is spent snorkeling or scuba diving, fishing, exploring the jungle, or lying in the sun. For more information write to Mex Treks, Calle 68 #495, Merida, Yucatan, Mexico 97000, tel. 21-40-32/21-46-55. Allow plenty of time for round-trip mail to Yucatan.

Honeymoon time is anytime and the **Honeymoon Of Your Dreams Plus** is waiting at the Cancun Sheraton Resort and Towers. This special package includes a luxury suite with terrace and private jacuzzi, daily breakfast in your room or in the restaurant, domestic champagne, welcome drink, free day or night tennis and free use of the fitness center. Three nights and four days, US$539 per cou-

---

THINKING OF TAKING A TOUR?

Are you thinking of going on a package tour? The United States Tour Operators Association recommends you shop carefully before committing. Consider the price, itinerary, pace, and quality of hotels you'll be staying in. For a free pamphlet on choosing a tour, write: USTOA, 211 E. 51st St., Suite 12B, New York, NY 10022.

---

ple. Or another choice at the same hotel is the **Honeymoon Down Mexico Way** in the new deluxe **Towers,** where guests will enjoy a Caribbean view, welcome drink, daily Continental breakfast in the lounge, bottle of domestic champagne, free day and night tennis and complimentary use of the fitness center along with very special butler service; three nights, four days, US$369 per couple.

Underwater Adventure Tours offers seven-night trips to Cozumel. Accommodations are at all major hotels and include daily dive/boat trips to Palancar Reef and vicinity, unlimited air for offshore diving, tanks, backpacks, and weights. A five-night trip is also available which includes daily breakfast, standard accommodations, four boat trips to Palancar Reef and vicinity, air, equipment, and 15% tax. For more information call or write Underwater Adventure Tours, 732 W. Fullerton, Chicago, IL 60614, tel. (800) 621-1274.

Bargain Hunting?

Accommodations run the gamut from a little cabaña on the beach to a grand villa with servants; from a secluded inn to a first-class resort hotel. **Cancun/Yucatan Adventures** offers privately owned villas and condominiums and small hotels. Affordable family and group packages available. For information call (707) 765-1000, or write 122 American Alley, Suite C, Petaluma, CA 94952.

This local travel agency in Merida, **Mayaland Tours,** is really helpful and offers outstanding packages; contact them from the states at (800) 235-4079 or in Merida (ask for Linda) at Avenida Colon #502, Merida, Yucatan, Mexico 97000.

PHYSICALLY CHALLENGED TRAVELERS

More and more businesses dealing with tourism are making it easier for the handicapped to explore the world, thanks to people like Pat Gustke. This great lady knows firsthand what it takes to be a "physically challenged" traveler, and she has taken the world by the horns and is enjoying it all—at least most of it. Although the following refers to ship travel, much of what she says is excellent information for any traveler in the same predicament. Read on.

THE ABC'S OF PLANNING A WHEELCHAIR CRUISE
by Patricia P. Gustke

A cruise can be a relaxing experience in a wheelchair, with advance planning. But it can be a frustrating daily "obstacle course" if you leave it to chance and pick the wrong ship.

Selecting The Ship
Accessibility for "physically challenged" travelers—there are more than 35 million of us in America alone—varies widely from ship to ship. Of course, elevators are a necessity, but many things on board can cause problems—a raised edge at stateroom doors, narrow cabin doors, a step up to the bathroom, lack of grab bars, heavy doors and steps between inner and outer decks.

The best reading resources are Berlitz *Complete Handbook to Cruising* and Douglas Ward's *On Deck*. Then contact the "Organization for Promotion of Access and Travel," P.O. Box 15777, Tampa, Florida 33684. President Tom Gilbert will send a list of ships which have accessible cabins, including even the cabin numbers. Send a self-addressed stamped envelope, and I always include a donation, for his persistence is helping to change attitudes. More and more lines are converting a few cabins, but there are still precious few.

Planning Ahead
In wheelchair travel, it's best to accept the fact that there will be problems, but advance planning can minimize them. Our travel agent contacts the line to explain my medical problems (muscular dystrophy) and that I must use a wheelchair full-time. I also always call the cruise line myself to point out that I cannot climb stairs (an important point to make clear, since buses are the normal mode of transport—fine for those with lesser mobility problems but not for "permanent occupants").

If you are fortunate enough to sign up for a handicapped cabin, insist on knowing exactly what it includes. We sometimes use a regular cabin because of better location (many adapted cabins are in the bowels of the ship!). But we take special equipment and know in detail what problems we'll find.

In selecting a cabin, remember to choose the best cabin you can afford. It means more space, a larger bath, wider hallways. I cut on my grocery budget to splurge on the Promenade Deck, for I love the scenic view from the big windows and the constant procession of walkers and joggers.

Try for a mid-ship location, close to an elevator. Make your dining room selection well in advance. They want to place wheelchairs close to a door or the busy aisle, so we try to beguile the maitre d' for a quiet window table for two.

Arm yourself with what reading material you can find. Most lines provide excellent shore excursion descriptions ahead of time as well as on-board. Try to learn the words in local languages for "wheelchair," "elevator," "help," and "steps." I find "thank-you" in the local vernacular makes the difficult job of lifting a happier experience. (I've also found that it's almost always my responsibility to put others at ease. Somehow coping with a wheelchair leaves onlookers tongue-tied, and I must initiate conversations to let them know that my disability does not extend to my brain, thankfully.)

Airline reservations should be made early. The comfort of business or first class can be invaluable on a long flight. If you fly tourist class, request bulkhead seating. You'll be first to board and last to deplane. And the wonderful passenger agents become instant friends—they know all of the elevator secrets and usually whip you through customs so fast that agile passengers enviously eye your wheelchair.

If you can arrive a day or two early, all the better; or try to plan an overnight enroute so you don't start your cruise exhausted. Also, remember that you're often dealing with U.S. airports and jetways, and loading and unloading can vary from traumatic to harrowing, especially in a strange language. We always ask for the special narrow chair that airlines are supposed to have, but it's seldom available on foreign airlines, so I've learned to close my eyes, pray, and hope the men who carry me are sure-footed and strong. (I once was onloaded to a 747 in Aruba on a fork lift truck with no sides, and unloaded one time in Rio in a kitchen chair with no arms. So it's best to be adventurous!)

Toilet use is always a problem, for my husband Bob has to lift me. Anywhere in the world, we blithely enter the ladies' room (occasionally even the men's room)— a procedure no one seems to mind. But since the dimensions of airplane toilets were designed for anorexics, we try not to do our lifting routine there, for it leaves us face-to-face with barely room to move. So I limit liquid intake for 24 hours before a trip and drink sparingly enroute. I've also used atropine, which absorbs liquids in the body, but it should only be used under a doctor's supervision. It allows me to manage eight- to 10-hour trips with no comfort stops, but it's necessary to drink large amounts of water at destination. I always try to use the terminal restrooms before we board, or sometimes onboard before the plane takes off or after it lands (an easier feat than when the plane is in flight).

No matter where we travel, we must take along my special "accessories": they include my "limousine" (a junior-width wheelchair); crutches for the occasional step; my Roho cushion; a slide board; Ermintrude (my folding junior walker fitted with a toilet seat which doubles as a shower chair and folds neatly into a case. There's nothing like it on the market—we just improvised); my soccer shin guards (to protect my legs which bruise easily); and a handicapped license plate (even in Bangkok or Buenos Aires, we've found that everyone recognizes the international symbol, and it produces effects even in taxis or rental cars). This year we added a folding bed tray and folding mirror, which made eating, doing make-up, and washing up much simpler.

We make sure my medications are in our carry-on luggage, and pack all my clothes on metal hangers in plastic bags, which fold into my 30-inch suitcase and make Bob's job unpacking easier. And I find room for my best-looking clothes. Somehow people connect wheelchair users with hospital gowns, and I take great delight in donning chiffon, sequins, paisley shawls, gold lame—whatever makes me feel and look stylish.

continued

Of course, we arrange for visas, shots, passports, and a small amount of foreign currency for each country we will visit. And we always take a large supply of dollar bills; a trip through an airport or lobby with me and my "accessories" is quite a lesson in foreign aid!

In the future, there are other things we'll plan in advance. On our last cruise, I needed an extra mattress to ease Bob's job of lifting, and a grab bar by my bunk. I learned too late that housekeeping could have arranged for both. And there were other things on my wish list that couldn't be arranged: a stewardess bell within reach of my bunk, at least one ramped entry to the Promenade Deck without a heavy door, and elimination of that dreadful step up into the bathroom.

Once Aboard

Cruising is far less wearing than land travel, but there's no guarantee of perfect access. Chairs usually have to be junior width, so count calories and keep counting them aboard, or you may pop a rivet. The crew that has to carry you up and down the gangplank certainly appreciates it if you're a little less than five by five.

Our first chore aboard is often to remove the bathroom door so the chair fits. If there's a step or even a difficult lip, that, too, presents a problem. I've always had ample grab bars by the toilet and tub. Each wheelchair user basically has to figure out his own system: one man uses a slide board to transfer from his chair to a rolling stool in the bathroom, thence to the commode. Where there's a will, there's a way.

Our next step is to visit with our stewardess. I ask for extra pillows for propping me up in bed, for one chair to be removed for more space, and for early coffee and a late breakfast in the cabin each day. We often have afternoon tea or after-dinner coffee in our cabin too. (Do remember that extra service should earn an extra tip.)

Then we study the floor plan of the ship, for with its blueprint in mind, we can reach virtually anyplace on board. If there's a step or heavy door, crew will assist. Bob, in his usual efficient way, finds the special toggle switch on the elevator panel to hold open the door for safe loading. Even the beauty shops are usually designed so I can stay seated. If you're headed in for a floor show, arrive early for there's no such thing as an unnoticed entry by a wheelchair.

Shore Excursions

Shore excursions can be difficult if you can't handle bus steps. We confer immediately with the shore excursion director to see what's possible for me and usually use a private car and guide at each stop. The added expense of a few dollars a day is well worth it.

But you must be flexible. Debarking at a wharf is relatively simple, but at anchor is difficult. On a Cape Horn cruise last year, my greatest desire was a catamaran trip on the Beagle Channel, and somehow I was loaded—while at anchor! But it was a last-minute decision, dependent on wave conditions. And it must have looked exciting, for when the crew finally deposited me and chair inside, I was greeted by a round of applause.

If you plan pre- or post-trip excursions, let those in charge know a long time before you arrive that you'll need a taxi rather than the bus. And arrange for your own car and guide. Again, it may cost more but you learn more. I always let hotels know my special needs in advance, too.

The Personal Touch

The last cruise requirement is a physically able traveling companion. That's in the ship's rules, and I'm lucky that mine is trained as an engineer, a gentleman, and a banker. He also encourages me to be adventurous and treats me as if I'm completely healthy.

As for me, I've learned to smile no matter what and to develop an absolute will of steel, for often it's a fight every inch of the way to get where I'm going. So cultivate a "politely aggressive" attitude, never be afraid to ask others for help and above all, retain your sense of humor. I put that on every day, long before I dress, and it solves most of the problems of being "physically challenged."

BOOKLIST

The following titles provide insight into the Yucatan Peninsula and the Maya people. A few of these books are easier obtained in Mexico, most are non-fiction, several fiction that are great to pop into your carry bag for a good read on the plane, or any time you want to get into the Yucatecan mood. All of them will cost less bought in the U.S. Happy reading.

Coe, Michael D. *The Maya*. New York: Thames and Hudson, 1980. A well-illustrated, quick and easy-to-read volume on the Maya people.

Cortes, Hernan. *Five Letters*. Gordon Press, 1977. Cortes wrote long letters to the King of Spain telling of his accomplishments, trying to justify his action in the new world.

De Landa, Bishop Diego. *Yucatan Before and After the Conquest*. New York: Dover Publications, 1978. This book translated by William Gates from the original 1566 volume has served as the base of all research that has taken place since. De Landa, though the man that destroyed countless books of the Maya people, has given the world an insight into their culture before the conquest.

Diaz del Castillo, Bernal. *The Conquest of New Spain*. New York: Penguin Books, 1963. History straight from the adventurer's reminiscences translated by J. M. Cohen.

Fehrenbach, T.R. *Fire and Blood: A History of Mexico*. New York: Collier Books, 1973. 3,500 years of Mexico's history told in a way to keep you reading.

Ferguson, William M. *Maya Ruins of Mexico in Color*. Norman: University of Oklahoma Press, 1977. Good reading before you go, too bulky to carry along. Oversized with excellent drawings and illustrations of the archaeological structures of the Maya Indians.

Franz, Carl. *The People's Guide to Mexico*. New Mexico: John Muir Publications, 1972. A humorous guide filled with witty anecdotes

and helpful general information for visitors to Mexico. Don't expect any specific city information, just nuts and bolts hints for traveling south of the border.

Davies, Nigel. *The Ancient Kingdoms Of Mexico*. New York: Penguin Books. An excellent study of pre-conquest (1519) indigenous people of Mexico.

Greene, Graham. *The Power and the Glory*. New York: Penguin Books, 1977. A novel that takes place in the twenties about a priest and the anti-church movement that gripped the country at the time.

Heffern, Richard. *Secrets of the Mind-Altering Plants of Mexico*. New York: Pyramid Books. A fascinating study of many subtances used from the ancients in ritual hallucinogens to today's medicines.

Lawrence, D.H. *The Plumed Serpent*. New York: Random House, 1955. The legend of Quetzalcoatl presented in a sensual novel.

Lewbel, George S. *Diving and Snorkeling Guide to Cozumel*. New York: Pisces Books, 1984. A well-illustrated volume for divers and snorkelers going to Cozumel. The small, easily carried volume is packed with hints about Cozumel's dive sites, reefs, and marinelife.

Meyer, Michael and William Sherman. *The Course Of Mexican History*. This is a great one-volume history of Mexico. Oxford University Press.

Nelson, Ralph. *Popul Vuh: The Great Mythological Book of the Ancient Maya*. Boston:

Houghton Mifflin, 1974. An easy-to-read translation of myths handed down orally by the Quiche Maya, family to family, until written down after the Spanish conquest.

Riding, Alan. *Distant Neighbors: A Portrait Of The Mexicans*. Vintage Books. A different way of scrutinizing the neighbor so close to the borders of the U.S.A.

Sodi, Demetrio M. in colaboration with Adela Fernandez. *The Mayas*. Mexico: Panama Editorial, S.A. This small pocket book presents a fictionalized account of life among the Maya before the conquest. Easy reading for anyone that enjoys fantasizing about what life *might* have been like before recorded history in the Yucatan. This book is available in the Yucatecan states of Mexico.

Stephens, John L. *Incidents of Travel in Central America, Chiapas, and Yucatan*, two vols. New York: Dover Publications, 1969. Good companions to refer to when traveling across the area. Stephens and illustrator Cather-

wood rediscovered many of the Maya ruins on their treks that took place in the mid-1800s. Easy reading.

Thompson, J. Eric. *Maya Archaeologist*. Norman: University of Oklahoma Press, 1963. Thompson, a noted Maya scholar, traveled and worked at most of the Maya ruins in the 1930s.

————. *The Rise and Fall of the Maya Civilization*. Norman: University of Oklahoma Press, 1954. One man's story of the Maya Indian. Excellent reading.

Werner, David. *Where There is No Doctor*. California: The Hesperian Foundation. This is an invaluable aid to anyone traveling not only to isolated parts of Mexico, but to anyplace in the world where there's not a doctor.

Wolf, Eric. *Sons of the Shaking Earth*. University of Chicago Press. A fascinating anthropological study of Indian and Mestizo people of Mexico and Guatemala.

SPANISH VOCABULARY

While on the Yucatan Peninsula you'll find many people in the larger cities who speak English. However, once you're in rural villages and on isolated beaches, speaking Spanish becomes a necessity. Most Mexican people appreciate the effort you make, even if it's not perfect. On the peninsula don't be surprised to find some people who speak neither English or Spanish, only a Mayan dialect. This group grows smaller every year.

The ideal way to prepare for your trip is to begin practicing Spanish before you leave. Most bookstores in the States sell simple Spanish-language tapes that are accompanied by a book. These tapes are great to listen to in the car on the way to work, while shaving, gardening, doing the dishes, etc. Repetition succeeds.

Berlitz's *Spanish For Travelers* is a great help used along with a pocket dictionary. It is quite common in Mexico's hotel gift shops, but small English-Spanish dictionaries are not as common. Buy them before you leave home. Mayan-language dictionaries are not as easy to find, though limited grammar books are available on the peninsula.

Spanish is not difficult to speak if you learn a few simple grammatical rules:

Vowels:
   a: pronounced as in father
   e: as in ray
   i: as in gasoline
   o: as in stole
   u: as in crude

Consonants are similar to those in English. A few exceptions:
   g: before a, o, or u pronounced hard as in go; before e or i pronounced like an *h*
   h: silent
   j: pronounced like an English *h* (with air)
   ll: like *y* in you
   ñ: pronounced ny as in Spanish señor
   q: pronounced as *k*
   r: rolled with the tongue (takes a little practice)

   x: between vowels it's pronounced like a gutteral *h* as in Spanish Oaxaca
   y: pronounced ee

GREETINGS

Hello. Hi.	*Hola!* or *Bueno!*
Good day.	*Buenas dias* (in the morning). *Buenas tardes* (in the afternoon).
Good night.	*Buenas noches.*
How are you?	*Como esta usted?*
Very well.	*Muy bien.*
How goes it?	*Que tal?*
Goodbye.	*Adios* or *Hasta la vista.*
So long.	*Hasta luego.*
Please.	*Por favor.*
Thank you.	*Muchas gracias.*
You're welcome.	*De nada.*

COMMON EXPRESSIONS

Just a moment, please.	*Un momento, por favor. Momentito.*
Excuse me.	*Perdoneme. Disculpeme.*
I am sorry.	*Lo siento.*
Do you speak English?	*Habla ingles?*
Do you understand me?	*Me comprende? Me entiende?*
I don't understand.	*No entiendo.*
I don't know.	*No se.*
How do you say ... in Spanish?	*Come se dice ... en espanol?*
What?	*Como?*
Please repeat.	*Mande?*
Show me.	*Enseneme.*
This is good.	*Esta bueno.*
This is bad.	*Esta malo.*
Yes.	*Si.*
No.	*No.*
What time is it?	*Que hora es?*
What's going on?	*Que pasa?*
How much is it?	*Cuanto cuesta?*

GETTING AROUND

Take me to	Lleveme a ....
Where is ...?	Donde esta ...?
the road to ...	el camino a ...
Follow this street.	Siga esta calle.
Which way?	Por donde?
near	cerca
far	lejos
to the right,	a la derecha,
...left	...izquierda
straight ahead	derecho
open, closed	abierto, cerrado
How far?	Hasta donde?
entrance, exit	la entrada, la salida
airplane	avion
airport	el aeropuerto
airline office	la oficina de aviones
train station	la estacion de tren,
	...del ferrocarril
taxi stand	el sitio
taxi	el taxi
Please call me a taxi.	Pidame un taxi, por favor.
How long does it take to go there?	Cuanto se tarda en llegar?
What will you charge me to take me to ...?	Cuanto me covra para llevarme a ...?
bus	autobus or camion
bus stop	la parada
How much is a ticket to ...?	Cuanto cuesta un boleto a ...?
When are there buses to ...?	A que hora hay camiones a ...?
I want a ticket to	Quiero un boleto a ....
Is there a toilet on the bus?	Hay baño en el camion?
Where does this bus go?	Donde va este autobus?
When does one (it) leave?	Cuando sale? (...llega?)
Down! (To tell the bus driver you want to get off the bus.)	Bajan!
I'm going to	Me voy a ....
reserved seat	asiento reservado
reservation	reservacion
first class	primera clase
second class	segunda clase

CAR AND MAINTENANCE

gas station	una gasolinera
gas	gasolina
regular (gas)	nova
Fill it up, please.	Lleno, por favor.
Please check the oil.	Vea el aceite, por favor.
brakes	los frenos
map	el mapa
air	aire
radiator	el radiador
battery	la bateria
repair garage	un taller mecanico
mechanic	un mecanico
jack	un gato
towtruck	un grua
tire	una llanta
hole	bache
speed	velocidad
stop	alto
traffic bumps	topes

SERVICES

telegraph office	la oficina de telegrafos
public telephone	el telefono publica
post office	el correo
How much is it?	Cuanto cuesta?
postage stamp	estampilla
post card	tarjeta ostal
bank	el banco
Where is the ladies' room?	Donde esta el baño de damas?
...the men's room?	...de señores?

ACCOMMODATIONS

hotel	un hotel
a room	un cuarto
single	sencillo
double	doble
triple	para tres
with a ceiling fan	con ventilador
with air conditioning	con aire acondicionado
without air conditioning	sin aire acondicionado
bed	la cama

hammock	*la hamaca*	hot water	*agua caliente*
pillow	*la almohada*	purified	*purificada*
blanket	*la cobija*	soft drink	*un refresco*
towel	*la toalla*	beverages	*las bebidas*
bathroom	*el baño*	liquified fruit drink	*liquado*
shower	*la regadera*	ice	*hielo*
soap	*jabon*	the bill	*la cuenta*
toilet paper	*papel sanitario*	tax	*impuesto*
hot water	*agua caliente*	tip	*propina*
cold water	*agua fria*	waiter	*el mesero,* or more
quiet	*tranquilo*		commonly: *joven*
bigger	*mas grande*	to get a waiter's	*Oiga!*
smaller	*mas pequeno*	attention	
with a view	*con vista*	Bring me	*Traigame ....*
		beer	*cerveza*
		a table	*una mesa*

DINING

restaurant	*un restaurante*	*calabash*	small tree native to the
breakfast	*desayuno*		Caribbean whose fruit, a gourd,
lunch	*almuerzo*		is dried and used as a container
lunch special	*la comida corrida*		on the peninsula
supper	*cena*	*calesa*	horse-drawn buggy seen in
dinner	*comida*		some cities on the peninsula
menu	*la carta*	*chiliquiles*	corn chips and bits of chicken
house specialty	*especialidad de la casa*	*cochinita* or	chicken baked with spices in
knife	*un cuchillo*	*pollo pibil*	banana leaves
fork	*un tenedor*	conch	large edible mollusk common to
spoon	*una cuchara*		the Caribbean; often eaten as
napkin	*una servilleta*		*ceviche* or pounded and fried
plate	*platillo*	*escabeche*	spicy Spanish style of cooking
salt	*sal*		meat and game
pepper	*pimienta*	*naranja*	a sour orange used extensively
butter	*mantequilla*		in cooking
bread	*pan*	*panuchos*	small fried tortillas topped with
French (style) bread	*pan blanco*		blackbeans, lettuce, meat or
sweet roll	*pan dulce*		poultry, and spices
pastries	*postres*	*pok chuc*	broiled meat, tomato, onion,
roll	*bolillo*		and sour orange
sandwich on a roll	*torta*	*sopa de lima*	chicken broth, lime juice,
toast	*tostada*		tomato, onion
coffee	*cafe*		
cold water	*agua helada*		

INDEX

Page numbers in **boldface** indicate the primary reference; page numbers in
italics indicate information found in maps, charts, photos, etc.

ABOUT THE AUTHOR

Chicki Mallan

As a child Chicki Mallan caught the travel bug from her dad. The family would leave their Catalina Island home yearly, hit the road and explore the small towns and big cities of the U.S.A. This urge didn't go away even with a good-sized family to tote around. At various times Chicki and kids have lived in the Orient and in Europe. Traveling with kids opened doors at the family level all over the world. Even when people don't speak the same language, they relate to other parents—since kids are the same everywhere. When not traveling, lecturing, or giving slide presentations, Chicki, husband Oz, and twins Patti and Bryant live in Paradise, a small community in the foothills of the Sierra Nevada mountains. She does what she enjoys most, writing magazine and newspaper articles in between travel books. She has been associated with Moon Publications since 1983, and is the author of *Guide to Catalina Island*. In 1987, Chicki was presented the *Pluma de Plata* award from the Mexican Government Ministry of Tourism for an article she wrote about the Yucatan Caribbean which was published in the L.A. Times. Chicki is a member of the SATW, Society of American Travel Writers.

ABOUT THE PHOTOGRAPHER

Oz Mallan has been a professional photographer for the past 36 years. Much of that time was spent as chief cameraman for the *Chico Enterprise-Record*. Oz graduated from Brooks Institute of Santa Barbara in 1950. His work has often appeared in newspapers across the country via UPI and AP. He travels the world with wife, Chicki, handling the photo end of their literary projects which include travel books, newspaper and magazine articles, as well as lectures and slide presentations. The photos in *Cancun Handbook* were taken during several visits and many months of travel on the Peninsula.

The Thatch Is Just ONE Difference

THE TURQUOISE REEF RESORTS

a Posada del
apitan Lafitte

KaiLuum)⟩⟨⟩⟨ The Camptel

Shangri-La Cariba

1-800-538-6802

Turquoise Reef Group

MEXICAN GOVERNMENT TOURISM OFFICES

IN THE UNITED STATES
405 Park Ave., Suite 1002
New York, NY, 10022
tel. (212) 755-7261

70 East Lake Street, Suite 1413
Chicago, IL 60601
tel. (312) 565-2778

2707 N. Loop West, Suite 450
Houston, TX 77008
tel. (713) 880-5153

10100 Santa Monica Blvd., Suite 224
Los Angeles, CA 90067
tel. (213) 203-8191

1911 Pennsylvania Ave. N.W.
Washington, D.C. 20006
tel. (202) 728-1750

1522 S.W. 81st Rd.
Miami, FL 33156
tel. (305) 252-1440

CANADA
2 Bloor Street West Ste 1801
Toronto, Ontario M4W 3E2
Canada
tel. (416) 925-0704

1 Place Ville Marie, Ste. 2409
Montreal, Quebec H3B 3M9
Canada

EUROPE
60-61 Trafalgar Square
London WC2N 5DS
England
tel. 71-734-1058

4 Rue Notre Dame des Victoires
75002 Paris
France
tel. 331-4020-0734

Moon Handbooks—The Ideal Traveling Companions

Open a Moon Handbook and you're opening your eyes and heart to the world. Thoughtful, sensitive, and provocative, Moon Handbooks encourage an intimate understanding of a region, from its culture and history to essential practicalities. Fun to read and packed with valuable information on accommodations, dining, recreation, plus indispensable travel tips, detailed maps, charts, illustrations, photos, glossaries, and indexes, Moon Handbooks are ideal traveling companions: informative, entertaining, and highly practical.

To locate the bookstore nearest you that carries Moon Travel Handbooks or to order directly from Moon Publications, call: (800) 345-5473 • Monday-Friday • 9 a.m.-5 p.m. PST

The Pacific/Asia Series

BALI HANDBOOK by Bill Dalton
Detailed travel information on the most famous island in the world. 12 color pages, 29 b/w photos, 68 illustrations, 42 maps, 7 charts, glossary, booklist, index. 428 pages.   **$12.95**

INDONESIA HANDBOOK by Bill Dalton
This one-volume encyclopedia explores island by island the many facets of this sprawling, kaleidoscopic island nation. 30 b/w photos, 143 illustrations, 250 maps, 17 charts, booklist, extensive Indonesian vocabulary, index. 1,000 pages.   **$19.95**

SOUTH KOREA HANDBOOK by Robert Nilsen
Whether you're visiting on business or searching for adventure, *South Korea Handbook* is an invaluable companion. 8 color pages, 78 b/w photos, 93 illustrations, 109 maps, 10 charts, Korean glossary with useful notes on speaking and reading the language, booklist, index. 548 pages.   **$14.95**

SOUTHEAST ASIA HANDBOOK by Carl Parkes
Helps the enlightened traveler discover the real Southeast Asia. 16 color pages, 75 b/w photos, 11 illustrations, 169 maps, 140 charts, vocabulary and suggested reading, index. 873 pages. **$16.95**

BANGKOK HANDBOOK by Michael Buckley
Your tour guide through this exotic and dynamic city reveals the affordable and accessible possibilities. Thai phrasebook, color and b/w photos, maps, illustrations, charts, booklist, index. 214 pages. **$10.95**

PHILIPPINES HANDBOOK by Peter Harper and Evelyn Peplow
Crammed with detailed information, *Philippines Handbook* equips the escapist, hedonist, or business traveler with thorough coverage of the Philippines's colorful history, landscapes, and culture. Color and b/w photos, illustrations, maps, charts, index. 587 pages. **$12.95**

HAWAII HANDBOOK by J.D. Bisignani
Winner of the 1989 Hawaii Visitors Bureau's Best Guide Book Award and the Grand Award for Excellence in Travel Journalism, this guide takes you beyond the glitz and high-priced hype and leads you to a genuine Hawaiian experience. 12 color pages, 86 b/w photos, 132 illustrations, 86 maps, 44 graphs and charts, Hawaiian and pidgin glossaries, appendix, booklist, index. 879 pages. **$15.95**

KAUAI HANDBOOK by J.D. Bisignani
Kauai Handbook is the perfect antidote to the workaday world. 8 color pages, 36 b/w photos, 48 illustrations, 19 maps, 10 tables and charts, Hawaiian and pidgin glossaries, booklist, index. 236 pages. **$9.95**

MAUI HANDBOOK: Including Molokai and Lanai by J.D. Bisignani
"No fool-'round" advice on accommodations, eateries, and recreation, plus a comprehensive introduction to island ways, geography, and history. 8 color pages, 60 b/w photos, 72 illustrations, 34 maps, 19 charts, booklist, glossary, index. 350 pages. **$11.95**

OAHU HANDBOOK by J.D. Bisignani
A handy guide to Honolulu, renowned surfing beaches, and Oahu's countless other diversions. Color and b/w photos, illustrations, 18 maps, charts, booklist, glossary, index. 354 pages. **$11.95**

BIG ISLAND OF HAWAII HANDBOOK by J.D. Bisignani
An entertaining yet informative text packed with insider tips on accommodations, dining, sports and outdoor activities, natural attractions, and must-see sights. Color and b/w photos, illustrations, 20 maps, charts, booklist, glossary, index. 347 pages. **$11.95**

SOUTH PACIFIC HANDBOOK by David Stanley
The original comprehensive guide to the 16 territories in the South Pacific. 20 color pages, 195 b/w photos, 121 illustrations, 35 charts, 138 maps, booklist, glossary, index. 740 pages. **$15.95**

MICRONESIA HANDBOOK:
Guide to the Caroline, Gilbert, Mariana, and Marshall Islands by David Stanley
Micronesia Handbook guides you on a real Pacific adventure all your own. 8 color pages, 77 b/w photos, 68 illustrations, 69 maps, 18 tables and charts, index. 287 pages. **$9.95**

FIJI ISLANDS HANDBOOK by David Stanley
The first and still the best source of information on travel around this 322-island archipelago. 8 color pages, 35 b/w photos, 78 illustrations, 26 maps, 3 charts, Fijian glossary, booklist, index. 198 pages. **$8.95**

TAHITI-POLYNESIA HANDBOOK by David Stanley
All five French-Polynesian archipelagoes are covered in this comprehensive guide by Oceania's best-known travel writer. 12 color pages, 45 b/w photos, 64 illustrations, 33 maps, 7 charts, booklist, glossary, index. 225 pages. **$9.95**

NEW ZEALAND HANDBOOK by Jane King
Introduces you to the people, places, history, and culture of this extraordinary land. 8 color pages, 99 b/w photos, 146 illustrations, 82 maps, booklist, index. 546 pages. **$14.95**

OUTBACK HANDBOOK by Marael Johnson
Australia is an endlessly fascinating, vast land, and *Outback Handbook* explores the cities and towns, sheep stations and wilderness areas of the Northern Territory, Western, and South Australia. Full of travel tips and cultural information for adventuring, relaxing, or just getting away from it all. Color and b/w photos, illustrations, maps, charts, booklist, index. 450 pages. **$14.95**

BLUEPRINT FOR PARADISE: How to Live on a Tropic Island by Ross Norgrove
This one-of-a-kind guide has everything you need to know about moving to and living comfortably on a tropical island. 8 color pages, 40 b/w photos, 3 maps, 14 charts, appendices, index. 212 pages. **$14.95**

The Americas Series

NORTHERN CALIFORNIA HANDBOOK by Kim Weir
An outstanding companion for imaginative travel in the territory north of the Tehachapis. 12 color pages, b/w photos, 69 maps, illustrations, booklist, index. 759 pages. **$16.95**

NEVADA HANDBOOK by Deke Castleman
Nevada Handbook puts the Silver State into perspective and makes it manageable and affordable. 34 b/w photos, 43 illustrations, 37 maps, 17 charts, booklist, index. 400 pages. **$12.95**

NEW MEXICO HANDBOOK by Stephen Metzger
A close-up and complete look at every aspect of this wondrous state. 8 color pages, 85 b/w photos, 63 illustrations, 50 maps, 10 charts, booklist, index. 375 pages. **$13.95**

TEXAS HANDBOOK by Joe Cummings
Seasoned travel writer Joe Cummings brings an insider's perspective to his home state. 12 color pages, b/w photos, maps, illustrations, charts, booklist, index. 483 pages. **$11.95**

ARIZONA TRAVELER'S HANDBOOK by Bill Weir
This meticulously researched guide contains everything necessary to make Arizona accessible and enjoyable. 8 color pages, 194 b/w photos, 74 illustrations, 53 maps, 6 charts, booklist, index. 505 pages. **$13.95**

UTAH HANDBOOK by Bill Weir
Weir gives you all the carefully researched facts and background to make your visit a success. 8 color pages, 102 b/w photos, 61 illustrations, 30 maps, 9 charts, booklist, index. 452 pages. **$12.95**

ALASKA-YUKON HANDBOOK by Deke Castleman and Don Pitcher
Get the inside story, with plenty of well-seasoned advice to help you cover more miles on less money. 8 color pages, 26 b/w photos, 95 illustrations, 92 maps, 10 charts, booklist, glossary, index. 400 pages. **$13.95**

WASHINGTON HANDBOOK by Dianne J. Boulerice Lyons and Archie Satterfield
Covers sights, shopping, services, transportation, and outdoor recreation, with complete listings for restaurants and accommodations. 8 color pages, 92 b/w photos, 24 illustrations, 81 maps, 8 charts, booklist, index. 400 pages. **$13.95**

OREGON HANDBOOK by Stuart Warren and Ted Long Ishikawa
Brimming with travel practicalities and insider views on Oregon's history, culture, arts, and activities. Color and b/w photos, illustrations, 28 maps, charts, booklist, index. 422 pages. **$12.95**

IDAHO HANDBOOK by Bill Loftus
A year-round guide to everything in this outdoor wonderland, from whitewater adventures to rural hideaways. Color and b/w photos, illustrations, maps, charts, booklist, index. 275 pages. **$12.95**

WYOMING HANDBOOK by Don Pitcher
All you need to know to open the doors to this wide and wild state. Color and b/w photos, illustrations, over 60 maps, charts, booklist, index. 427 pages. **$12.95**

MONTANA HANDBOOK by W.C. McRae and Judy Jewell
The wild West is yours with this extensive guide to the Treasure State, complete with travel practicalities, history, and lively essays on Montana life. Color and b/w photos, illustrations, maps, charts, booklist, index. 450 pages. **$13.95**

COLORADO HANDBOOK by Stephen Metzger
Essential details to the all-season possibilities in Colorado fill this guide. Practical travel tips combine with recreation—skiing, nightlife, and wilderness exploration—plus entertaining essays. Color and b/w photos, illustrations, maps, charts, booklist, index. 550 pages. **$15.95**

BRITISH COLUMBIA HANDBOOK by Jane King
With an emphasis on outdoor adventures, this guide covers mainland British Columbia, Vancouver Island, the Queen Charlotte Islands, and the Canadian Rockies. 8 color pages, 56 b/w photos, 45 illustrations, 66 maps, 4 charts, booklist, index. 381 pages. **$11.95**

CATALINA HANDBOOK: A Guide to California's Channel Islands by Chicki Mallan
A complete guide to these remarkable islands, from the windy solitude of the Channel Islands National Marine Sanctuary to bustling Avalon. 8 color pages, 105 b/w photos, 65 illustrations, 40 maps, 32 charts, booklist, index. 262 pages. **$10.95**

BAJA HANDBOOK by Joe Cummings
A comprehensive guide with all the travel information and background on the land, history, and culture of this untamed thousand-mile-long peninsula. Color and b/w photos, illustrations, maps, charts, booklist, index. 400 pages. **$13.95**

YUCATAN HANDBOOK by Chicki Mallan
All the information you'll need to guide you into every corner of this exotic land. 8 color pages, 154 b/w photos, 55 illustrations, 57 maps, 70 charts, appendix, booklist, Mayan and Spanish glossaries, index. 391 pages. **$12.95**

CANCUN HANDBOOK and Mexico's Caribbean Coast by Chicki Mallan
Covers the city's luxury scene as well as more modest attractions, plus many side trips to unspoiled beaches and Mayan ruins. Color and b/w photos, illustrations, over 30 maps, Spanish glossary, booklist, index. 257 pages. **$10.95**

BELIZE HANDBOOK by Chicki Mallan
Complete with detailed maps, practical information, and an overview of the area's flamboyant history, culture, and geographical features, *Belize Handbook* is the only comprehensive guide of its kind to this spectacular region. Color and b/w photos, illustrations, maps, booklist, index. 212 pages. **$11.95**

JAMAICA HANDBOOK by Karl Luntta
From the sun and surf of Montego Bay and Ocho Rios to the cool slopes of the Blue Mountains, author Karl Luntta offers island-seekers a perceptive, personal view of Jamaica. Color and b/w photos, illustrations, maps, charts, index. 350 pages. **$12.95**

The International Series

EGYPT HANDBOOK by Kathy Hansen
An invaluable resource for intelligent travel in Egypt. 8 color pages, 20 b/w photos, 150 illustrations, 80 detailed maps and plans to museums and archaeological sites, Arabic glossary, booklist, index. 510 pages. **$14.95**

PAKISTAN HANDBOOK by Isobel Shaw
For armchair travelers and trekkers alike, the most detailed and authoritative guide to Pakistan ever published. 28 color pages, 86 maps, appendices, Urdu glossary, booklist, index. 478 pages. **$15.95**

MOSCOW-LENINGRAD HANDBOOK by Masha Nordbye
Provides the visitor with an extensive introduction to the history, culture, and people of these two great cities, as well as practical information on where to stay, eat, and shop. 8 color pages, 36 b/w photos, 20 illustrations, 16 maps, 9 charts, booklist, index. 205 pages. **$12.95**

NEPAL HANDBOOK by Kerry Moran
Whether you're planning a week in Kathmandu or months out on the trail, *Nepal Handbook* will take you into the heart of this Himalayan jewel. Color and b/w pages, illustrations, 50 maps, 6 charts, glossary, index. 450 pages. **$12.95**

NEPALI AAMA by Broughton Coburn
A delightful photo-journey into the life of a Gurung tribeswoman of Central Nepal. Having lived with Aama (translated, "mother") for two years, first as an outsider and later as an adopted member of the family, Coburn presents an intimate glimpse into a culture alive with humor, folklore, religion, and ancient rituals. B/w photos. 165 pages. **$13.95**

New travel handbooks may be available that are not on this list.
To find out more about current or upcoming titles,
call us toll-free at (800) 345-5473.

IMPORTANT ORDERING INFORMATION

FOR FASTER SERVICE: Call to locate the bookstore nearest you that carries Moon Travel Handbooks or order directly from Moon Publications:
(800) 345-5473 · Monday-Friday · 9 a.m.-5 p.m. PST · fax (916) 345-6791

PRICES: All prices are subject to change. We always ship the most current edition. We will let you know if there is a price increase on the book you ordered.

SHIPPING & HANDLING OPTIONS:
1) Domestic UPS or USPS first class (allow 10 working days for delivery):
$3.50 for the first item, 50 cents for each additional item.

Exceptions:
· **Moonbelt** shipping is $1.50 for one, 50 cents for each additional belt.
· Add $2.00 for same-day handling.
2) UPS 2nd Day Air or Printed Airmail requires a special quote.
3) International Surface Bookrate (8-12 weeks delivery):
$3.00 for the first item, $1.00 for each additional item. Note: Moon Publications cannot guarantee international surface bookrate shipping.

FOREIGN ORDERS: All orders which originate outside the U.S.A. must be paid for with either an International Money Order or a check in U.S. currency drawn on a major U.S. bank based in the U.S.A.

TELEPHONE ORDERS: We accept Visa or MasterCard payments. Minimum order is US $15.00. Call in your order: 1 (800) 345-5473. 9 a.m.-5 p.m. Pacific Standard Time.

MOONBELTS: A new concept in moneybelts. Made of heavy-duty Cordura nylon, the Moonbelt offers maximum protection for your money and important papers. This pouch, designed for all-weather comfort, slips under your shirt or waistband, rendering it virtually undetectable and inaccessible to pickpockets. Many thoughtful features: 1-inch-wide nylon webbing, heavy-duty zipper, and a 1-inch high-test quick-release buckle. No more fumbling around for the strap or repeated adjustments, this handy plastic buckle opens and closes with a touch, but won't come undone until you want it to. Accommodates traveler's checks, passport, cash, photos. Size 5 x 9 inches. Available in black only.   **$8.95**

ORDER FORM

**Be sure to call (800) 345-5473 for current prices and editions or for the name of the
bookstore nearest you that carries Moon Travel Handbooks · 9 a.m.-5 p.m. PST
(See important ordering information on preceding page)**

Name:_____Date:_____

Street:_____

City:_____Daytime Phone_____

State or Country:_____Zip Code:_____

Quantity	Title	Price

Taxable Total

Sales Tax (7.25%) for California Residents

Shipping & Handling

TOTAL

Ship: ☐ 1st class   ☐ UPS (no P.O. Boxes)   ☐ International Surface

Ship to: ☐ address above   ☐ other_____

_____

_____

Make checks payable to:
Moon Publications Inc., 722 Wall Street, Chico, California 95928 U.S.A.
We Accept Visa and MasterCard
To Order: Call in your Visa or MasterCard number, or send a written order with your Visa or
MasterCard number and expiration date clearly written.

Card Number: ☐ **Visa**   ☐ **MasterCard**

☐☐☐☐   ☐☐☐☐   ☐☐☐☐   ☐☐☐☐

Exact Name on Card: ☐ same as above   expiration date:_____

☐ other_____

signature_____

WHERE TO BUY THIS BOOK

Bookstores and Libraries:
Moon Publications Handbooks are sold worldwide. Please write our sales manager for a list of wholesalers and distributors in your area that stock our travel handbooks.

Travelers:
We would like to have Moon Publications Handbooks available throughout the world. Please ask your bookstore to write or call us for ordering information. If your bookstore will not order our guides for you, please write or call for a free catalog.

MOON PUBLICATIONS INC.
722 WALL STREET
CHICO, CA 95928 U.S.A.
tel: (800) 345-5473
fax: (916) 345-6751